# Film as ethnography

Similarities between ethnographic fieldwork, the classic research technique of social anthropologists, and the methods of 'observational' documentary cinema have stimulated a growing interest among anthropologists in the uses of film and video for research, teaching and communication with non-specialist audiences. These essays make up the most comprehensive appraisal yet published of the relationship between filmed and written representations of other ways of life. Topics dealt with include the validity of claims made for visual representation in anthropology, the implications of the 'constructed' nature of both written ethnography and documentary film and the communication of anthropological knowledge through the medium of television. The book is aimed at professional anthropologists and film-makers as well as students of film, visual communication and media studies. It should be especially welcomed by all those involved in the growing sub-discipline of visual anthropology.

The essays were originally prepared for a conference held in Manchester in 1990 as part of the Royal Anthropological Institute's IInd International Festival of Ethnographic Film. The conference was organised by the Granada Centre for Visual Anthropology, University of Manchester, with the help of the Centre for Visual Anthropology, University of Southern California. Funding for the Festival and Conference was provided by Granada Television.

# Film as ethnography

*edited by*
Peter Ian Crawford *and* David Turton

Manchester University Press  1992
In association with the Granada Centre for Visual Anthropology

Manchester and New York
*Distributed exclusively in the USA and Canada by St. Martin's Press*

*Published by* Manchester University Press
Oxford Road, Manchester M13 9PL, UK
*and* Room 400, 175 Fifth Avenue,
New York, NY 10010, USA

*Distributed exclusively in the USA and Canada*
*by* St. Martin's Press, Inc.,
175 Fifth Avenue, New York, NY 10010, USA

*British Library Cataloguing-in-Publication Data*
A catalogue record for this book is available from the British Library

*Library of Congress Cataloging in Publication Data applied for*

ISBN 0 7190 3682 8 *hardback*
    0 7190 3683 6 *paperback*

Reprinted in paperback 1993

Photoset in Linotron Ehrhardt
by Northern Phototypesetting Co Ltd, Bolton

Printed in Great Britain
by Biddles Ltd, Guildford and King's Lynn

# Contents

# List of illustrations

# Contributors

*Timothy Asch*, Department of Anthropology, SOS 154, University of Southern California, University Park, Los Angeles, CA 90089–0032 USA

*Marcus Banks*, Institute of Social and Cultural Anthropology, University of Oxford, 51 Banbury Road, Oxford, OX2 6PE

*Richard Chalfen*, Department of Anthropology, Temple University, Philadelphia, Pennsylvania 19122, USA

*Peter Ian Crawford*, Third World Information, Skt. Marcus Kirkeplads 24, 8000 Aarhus C, Denmark

*James C. Faris*, Department of Anthropology, University of Connecticut, Manchester Hall, 344 Mansfield Road, Storrs, Connecticut 06269-2158, USA

*Kirsten Hastrup*, Institute of Anthropology, University of Copenhagen, Frederiksholms Kanal 4, DK–1220 Kobenhaven, Denmark

*Felicia Hughes-Freeland*, Department of Sociology and Anthropology, University College of Swansea, Singleton Park, Swansea, SA2 8PP

*Kathleen Kuehnast*, Department of Anthropology, University of Minnesota, 215 Ford Hall, 224 Church Street S.E., Minneapolis, Minnesota 55455, USA

*Peter Loizos*, Department of Anthropology, London School of Economics, University of London, Houghton Street, London, WC2A 2AE

*David MacDougall*, 12 Meehan Gardens, Griffith, ACT 2603 Canberra, Australia

*Alan Macfarlane*, Department of Social Anthropology, University of Cambridge, Free School Lane, Cambridge CB2 3RF

*Wilton Martinez*, Department of Anthropology, SOS 154, University of Southern California, University Park, Los Angeles, California 90089-0032, USA

*Christopher Pinney*, Department of Anthropology and Sociology, School of Oriental and African Studies, University of London, Thornhaugh Street, Russell Square, London, WC1H 0XG

*Gary Seaman*, Department of Anthropology, SOS 154, University of Southern California, University Park, Los Angeles, California 90089–0032, USA

*André Singer*, British Broadcasting Corporation, Kensington House, Richmond Way, London, W14 0AX

*Keyan G. Tomaselli*, Centre for Cultural and Media Studies, University of Natal, King George V Avenue, Durban 4001, South Africa

*David Turton*, Granada Centre for Visual Anthropology, University of Manchester, Manchester, M13 9PL

*Dai Vaughan*, 86B Mill Lane, London, NW6 1NL

*Homer F. Williams*, Department of Anthropology, SOS 154, University of Southern California, University Park, Los Angeles, California 90089-0032, USA

*Terence Wright*, Department of Media Studies, Luton College of Higher Education, Park Square, Luton, LU1 3JU, UK

# Preface

This book is the outcome of a conference held at the University of Manchester in 1990 as part of the Royal Anthropological Institute's IInd International Festival of Ethnographic Film. In choosing the title 'Film as Ethnography' for the conference, our intention was to encourage the participants, who included both professional anthropologists and documentary film-makers, to think about the relationship between film and the written word as ways of producing ethnographic texts. Such a contrastive approach would, we hoped, produce insights into the nature, potential and limitations of both media and encourage anthropologists to take film more seriously as a way of communicating ethnographic knowledge.

We also had in mind that, over the past decade, anthropologists have become increasingly preoccupied with the nature of enthnographic knowledge itself, raising questions about its 'constructed' and subjective nature of a kind which film theorists and critics have long been asking about documentary film. This questioning of ethnographic objectivity – the so-called 'crisis of representation' in anthropology – has occurred at the same time as 'ethnography' has been gaining wider acceptance in the social sciences generally. In its non-anthropological usage, 'ethnography' is a synonym for the ethnographic method or 'participant observation', but in its anthropological usage – as in the title of this book – it refers to the text or description which is the end *product* of the ethnographic method. It is undoubtedly the similarity between the methods of ethnographic fieldwork and those of the 'observational' and 'cinema verité' styles of documentary film-making which lies behind the sharp growth of interest shown by anthropologists in film over the past twenty years and of which this book is but one illustration.

Over forty papers were read at the conference and we had space to include less than half of them. In making the selection we tried to represent the breadth and scope of the event while focusing on certain themes which most closely reflected the aims just outlined. The book is not, therefore, an objective record of the conference but a 'construction' of the editors. We recognise that others might have made a different, equally valid, selection and thereby have included several excellent papers for which we felt unable to find room. The internal division of the book also reflects our interpretations and interests: we could, for example, have easily allocated some of the papers to different sections. But despite a good deal of inevitable (and desirable) overlap between the four parts, each has a distinctive character which is why we have provided each with a separate introduction. Nor is the order in which one part succeeds another without its rationale: the general idea is that topics and issues discussed in later parts should presuppose, and be informed by, those discussed earlier.

The most fundamental or 'elementary' issue is the difference between pictures (both still and moving) and words as conveyers of information and meaning (Part One). The discussion of meaning is taken further by the examination of films as texts and therefore as susceptible to a literary style of analysis (Part Two). A further level of complexity is reached by the introduction of political and ethical considerations: the textual 'packaging', 'encompassing' and 'objectifying' of other people's lives and cultures which anthropologists are now trying to confront in their writing (Part Three). All these issues reach their most extreme development and are seen in their most stark light in the process of collaboration between anthropologists and television programme-makers, television being still the most important medium for bringing ethnographic films to the attention of the public (Part Four).

If we had to pick out one theme with which to characterise the book as a whole and upon which to rest our hopes that it will advance the debate about ethnographic film, it would be the concern to be found in virtually every chapter with the way 'audiences interact with films to produce meanings' (MacDougall, p. 90). A key chapter here is that by Martinez (the longest in the book), which provides both the theoretical background, from various 'reader-oriented' approaches in literary studies, as well as experimental evidence from a study of student responses to ethnographic films. The audience is seen in this book as, ideally, 'making sense' of films as equal partners with the film-maker rather than as mere de-coders or 'excavators' of pre-existent meanings.

The conference and film festival were the result of collaboration between various individuals and institutions. The Royal Anthropological Institute has, through its Film Committee, been responsible for a number of important developments in the field of ethnographic film in Britain during the past few years. These include the setting up of the biennial RAI Film Prize in 1980 and the organisation of the 1st International Festival of Ethnographic Film, held in London in 1985. The Director of the Institute, Jonathan Benthall, has played an indispensable part in promoting these activities and his energetic involvement in the 1990 Festival, as Chairman of the Festival Planning Committee, was essential to its success.

Local organisation was the responsibility of the Granada Centre for Visual

Anthropology at the University of Manchester. Paul Henley, Director of the Centre, carried the major organisational and planning burden, Naomi Vera-Sanso and Peter Crawford took on the tasks of Festival Co-ordinator and Conference Convenor respectively and Lynn Dignan provided vital administrative assistance. Albert Curtis, then head of the Audio Visual Technical Services Department at the University, and his staff ensured maximum technical efficiency with minimum fuss. The Faculty of Economic and Social Studies contributed to the costs of the conference with a grant from the University of Manchester's Research Support Fund. Daniel Marks, then of the Center for Visual Anthropology at the University of Southern California, played an important part in the planning of the conference (amongst other things, suggesting its title) and it was largely due to his enthusiastic involvement that North American anthropologists were well represented amongst the participants.

The Granada Centre for Visual Anthropology covered the costs of preparing the book for publication, a process that was complicated by the fact that we, the editors, were based in different countries. This made us heavily reliant on the institutional support both of the Granada Centre and Third World Information, Aarhus, Denmark. We should particularly like to thank Henrik Overballe, of Third World Information, for his help in solving various word processing problems and Paul Henley who was, as ever, a constant source of encouragement and perceptive advice.

Finally, neither the festival nor the conference would have been possible without the generous financial support of Granada Television. This was a further indication (following the establishment of the Granada Centre for Visual Anthropology and the sponsoring of the annual Forman Lecture in Visual Anthropology) of Granada's commitment to collaboration with professional anthropologists in making programmes for its *Disappearing World* series. We thank Granada not only for its support of the 1990 Festival and Conference but also for the contribution it has made, through *Disappearing World*, to the development of ethnographic film in Britain. The importance of that contribution is clear from the many references made to the series in the pages which follow.

Peter Ian Crawford, Aarhus
David Turton, Manchester
May 1992

**Part One**

# Authority, representation and anthropological knowledge

# Introduction

In her Introduction to *Principles of Visual Anthropology* (Hockings 1975), Margaret Mead lamented the 'criminal neglect' of the use of film in anthropological research.

All over the world, on every continent and island, in the hidden recesses of every industrial city as well as in the hidden valleys that can be reached only by helicopter, precious, totally irreplaceable, and forever irreproducible behaviors are disappearing, while departments of anthropology continue to send fieldworkers out with no equipment beyond a pencil and a notebook . . . . (p. 4)

She put this situation down to the 'gross and dreadful negligence' of a profession which had become wedded to 'outmoded methods' (pp. 5–6). It is possible, however, to think of other, more convincing reasons.

One of these she mentions herself, only to dismiss it: the realisation that film, even uncut footage, cannot be a record of 'objective reality'. Another might be that the recording and documenting of 'forever irreproducible behaviors' before they 'disappear' would be regarded by most anthropologists as, at best, a useful by-product of their discipline rather than its *raison d'être*. They would surely agree with Hastrup when she writes 'In anthropology (in contrast to folklore research) I would have thought that we had actually come to terms with the fact that the world changes all the time and what was, yesterday, is not necessarily more interesting than what will be, tomorrow' (p. 15 below). But Hastrup takes us much further than this into the possible reasons why anthropologists have not taken more readily to the camera as a research instrument and to film as a means of communicating ethnographic knowledge.

She does this by working out in detail the difference between pictorial images and words as ways of transmitting ethnographic knowledge. The essence of her position is that the difference is one of kind, not degree. The two 'modes of expression' are related neither by conflict nor complementarity because 'they do not operate on the same logical level. Rather, they are hierarchically related. Writings may encompass the images produced by films, but not the other way round (p. 21).

She argues for this position by setting up a number of oppositions between visual and written records. The visual is to the written mode as 'thin description' (giving us a record of the form of behaviour) is to 'thick description' (giving us an account of its meaning) and as map (giving us an overall view of a landscape) is to itinerary (giving us one route through a network of possible routes). The result is that the visual mode, on its own, has difficulty distinguishing behaviour from action, mere 'happenings' from socially significant 'events'. Apart from helping to explain why anthropologists have not embraced film and photography with more enthusiasm as an aid to research, Hastrup lays down a powerful and uncompromising challenge to those who believe that pictures can speak louder than words for the anthropologist. This is why we have placed her chapter first in the book.

If anthropologists in general have been relatively unenthusiastic about film, visual anthropologists, it seems, have been relatively unenthusiastic about still photography. This is born out not only by the contents of this book (which is hardly surprising, given its title) but also by *Principles of Visual Anthropology*, which contains only three (out of thirty-one) chapters on still photography. Hastrup offers, in passing, an explanation for this.

Film, she writes, occupies an intermediary position between the photograph and the written text in terms of 'flexibility'. The photograph not only limits the spectator to one 'central perspective' but is fixed in itself. With film, 'the pictures move but the spectator remains fixed'. Writing is the most flexible of the three modes because 'both the content and the reader are movable . . . the reader herself may stop, return and flick through the pages, creating her own images as she goes along' (p. 20).

Pinney (Chapter 2) offers not only a different but an opposite explanation: visual anthropologists have avoided the photograph because it offers too much, not too little meaning. Film uses movement and sequence to limit and direct the viewer's search for meaning (a point ignored by Hastrup), whereas the still image, especially if not 'authorised by its explanatory caption' (p. 38), offers the viewer almost total freedom to follow up or, perhaps better, 'construct' any number of meanings from those potentially contained within it. Rather than shying away from this 'natural ambiguity' of the photograph, visual anthropologists should exploit it. This would enable them, for example, to 'incorporate and emulate systems of image making from the very societies . . . (they) . . . are engaging with' (p. 38).

If Hastrup is arguing against the 'absurd' claims (p. 14) of visual anthropologists about the power of the pictorial image to convey ethnographic knowledge, Pinney is arguing against their prevailing obsession with ethnographic film. And if Hastrup is attempting to provide a basis for the fruitful integration of visual and written modes of expression in anthropology, Pinney is attempting to provide a basis for the fruitful integration of film and still photography within visual anthropology. The importance of both contributions is not that they present definitive accounts of these issues but that they formulate them with unusual precision, clarity and forcefulness. They thus offer the prospect of a more thoughtful and constructive debate in the future.

One possible criticism of Hastrup's approach (which she implicitly recognises in her opening paragraph) is that, by treating pictures (both still and moving) and words as logically opposed categories, she is able to ignore (or at least conveniently side-step) certain characteristics of film that, if taken seriously, could raise difficulties for her argument.

Firstly, there is the capacity of film, noted by Pinney, to lead the viewer, merely by the (not necessarily chronological) succession of images, along one particular narrative and explanatory path. Secondly, there is the fact that words, whether in the form of commentary, interviews or 'overheard' conversation, are normally a key ingredient of an ethnographic film. Although she acknowledges this characteristic of film, Hastrup does not pursue it, apparently because to do so would be to blur the contrast between the 'purely visual and the purely textual' (p 8) upon which her argument is based. 'With film, we normally do get a dose of words in addition to the visual record . . . but then we have a text' (p. 18), she writes, and again, '. . . seeing a group of Icelandic men in a sheep house does not tell where the women are at the same time or whether it is a coincidence that none are to be seen in the pictures. One can add that in words – but then we have a text, of course' (p. 16). She would obviously use the same argument to dispose of the objection that anthropologists and film-makers have long insisted on the importance of providing ethnographic films with explanatory texts or study-guides.

The vital role of 'a dose of words', whether spoken or written, in enabling films to communicate ethnographic knowledge is the subject of Loizos's chapter, in which he asks us to regard films as 'texts gaining depth from their connectedness to other texts' (p. 64). Both Hastrup and Loizos appear to have roughly similar objectives (to 'integrate visual anthropology in the larger field of anthropology' (p. 8) and to encourage anthropologists to think of films as 'contributions to mainstream anthropology' respectively), but their approaches are strikingly different. Whereas Hastrup relentlessly pursues, for the sake of argument (p. 8), what she admits is an exaggerated separation of pictures and words, Loizos examines 'a number of modalities with which documentary films communicate to us' (p. 50), all of which depend upon the close integration of pictures and words.

The 'documentation modality', for example, is 'that aspect of film which works to record or document what happens in front of lens *and microphone*' (p. 51, emphasis added). To illustrate this he chooses an extract from Brian Moser's *The Meo* (1972) which includes a sequence shot at Ban Xon Airport in North-East Laos. As body bags are unloaded from military transports we see, and hear in translation, a weeping soldier delivering a lament over the body of his dead brother. The first point of interest here is that words – the soldier's lament – play an integral part in this example of 'film as record'.

Secondly, the viewer is led, simply by the way the sequence is edited, to derive from the material a particular meaning, deliberately chosen by the film-maker. In his discussion of this extract, Loizos shows how the film-maker, by intercutting the lamentation sequence with shots of young soldiers in the mountains, invites us to think of the impact of the war on the Meo in general, rather than on the immediate group of mourners. This is an example of how film, even in its 'documentation modality' and even without resort to words, can take on the character of an itinerary, which Hastrup suggests is the exclusive preserve of the written text. For, as one image follows another, we are led along one route among many possible routes. As Pinney puts it 'Two still images which might be considered co-equal, assume the roles of before and after and become sites to be adjudicated upon when situated within filmic narrative' (Chapter Two, p. 27).

In one sense, of course, Loizos is helping to make Hastrup's point, namely that the pictorial image on its own has a limited capacity to convey ethnographic knowledge. But whereas Hastrup concentrates on the useful task of showing us clearly why this is logically so, Loizos takes it for granted and proceeds to examine how, in practice, films *do* succeed in communicating ethnographic knowledge, sometimes even more effectively than written ethnography. Here, for example, are some of his comments on the modality he calls 'context-enrichment', which he describes as 'one of the great strengths of ethnographic film' (p. 61) and to illustrate which he uses a sequence from *Waiting for Harry* (Kim McKenzie and Les Hiatt, 1980).

The film as research method, recording, probing, and sometimes being an agent or actor in an event allows us, through the addition of subtitles, to form a better understanding of the nature of the inquiry, and therefore of the quality of the material obtained. It makes field enquiries more accessible, and 'thicker' in Geertz's sense. We have words, plus intonations, plus pauses, plus facial expressions, and even a suggestion of the elusive quality of the relationship between anthropologists and informants, matters which an anthropologist alone might have difficulty writing about. (p. 60–61)

If Loizos makes a case for the anthropological significance of ethnographic films by showing how they work in practice, Crawford (Chapter Four) does so by setting out an ambitious analytical scheme which allows words and images to be treated as 'constituent elements of both visual and verbal processes of representation' (p. 71). His approach, from communication theory, is to identify the fundamental conditions of 'the anthropological process', seen as one of communication, and then to work out how filming and writing relate to each other within this process. Both, he argues, have to cope with the paradox that anthropological communication depends on presence and absence, or perhaps one might say, intimacy and distance. Thus films may use words for distancing, while written texts use images, both pictorial and verbal, to achieve a sensation of intimacy.

In order to be intelligible and explanatory (or articulate) film has to distance itself from its intrinsic 'presence' established by the image's insistence on 'being there'. Writing, on the other hand, wrestles with its intrinsic 'absence' in attempts to diminish the imposed distance between itself and the 'Other' and hence convey a sensuous understanding of what 'being there' is like. (p. 70)

A striking and welcome feature of this chapter (which is much too complex and wide-ranging to be encapsulated in two or three paragraphs) is that it seeks to establish an overall theoretical framework for thinking not only about film in anthropology but also about anthropology in its present 'representational crisis' – and about the future of both.

## References

*Book*
Hockings, P. (1975) *Principles of Visual Anthropology*, Mouton, The Hague.

*Films*
McKenzie, K. and L. Hiatt (1980), *Waiting for Harry*, Australian Institute of Aboriginal Studies, Canberra. Colour, 57 mins.
Moser, B. (1972), *The Meo, Disappearing World* series, Granada Television, Manchester. Colour, 53 mins. (Anthropologist: J. Lemoine).

*Kirsten Hastrup*

# Anthropological visions: some notes on visual and textual authority

In this chapter I seek to qualify the difference between visual and textual authority in anthropology. The method is one of contrasting pictures and words as two separate modes of creating and conveying ethnographic images. The procedure is not unlike the implicitly comparative identification of cultures, consisting in an exaggeration of difference (Boon 1982; Hastrup 1985a). In this case the exaggeration consists in separating completely the visual and the textual modes of representation, as if films had no subtexts and books never had pictures.

Having given this note of warning about my strategic use of the contrastive method, I shall stress also my conviction that there are very real differences between visual and textual authority *vis-à-vis* the ethnographic object. Ethnographic films may be constructed narratively in a way that may blur or diminish this difference, but in order to perceive its substance and to integrate visual anthropology[1] in the larger field of anthropology I have chosen the contrast between the purely visual and the purely textual representation as my point of departure. Thus I make no distinction between photos and films in the first place.

By way of opening, let me tell an anecdote from my own fieldwork in Iceland.[2] When working on a farm, I once attended a remarkable cultural event, namely a ram exhibition. This is a recurrent autumn ritual that takes place in many rural tracts when the collective task of collecting the sheep from the mountain pastures has been completed. The ram exhibition is a feast celebrating the successful recovery of the sheep and, as a matter of consequence, celebrating maleness (cf. Hastrup 1985b). The air was loaded with excitement for several weeks before the feast and, at the farm where I lived, it had been endlessly discussed which rams to select. I became caught up in the excitement myself and was immensely curious about the actual event.

As it happened I was not invited to participate. It was not a 'family event' but an exclusively male feast. However, the young farmer's wife at my farm eventually sensed my wish to go, and took me to the site of the exhibition which was the largest sheep-house of the tract. While she herself had no wish to enter, she reassured me that I was welcome to do so. I went in, dutifully equipped with notebook and camera – the material expressions of the anthropologist's second thought and third eye.

There were no women present but plenty of men and a mass of huge rams. The smell was intense, the light somewhat dim and the room full of indiscernible sounds from some 120 rams and about 40 men. A committee went from one ram to the next noting their impressions of the animal, in terms of its general beauty, the size of the horns and so forth. Measurements were made all over but the decisive measure (made by hand) was the size and weight of the ram's testicles. The air was loaded with sex and I realized that the exhibition was literally and metaphorically a competition of sexual potence. The men competed in the name of their rams but the meta-message was perfectly clear. As the sounds became clearer to my inhibited hearing, I heard endless sexual jokes and very private remarks. The bursts of laughter followed by side-glances at me conveyed an implicit question of whether I understood what was going on. I did.

From the periphery of the event, where I moved about in order to be inconspicuous, I took pictures and made notes, trying hard to look like an honorary male. It was impossible and, eventually, I had to leave out of sheer embarrassment. The men did not prevent me from staying but decency finally made me evade the thick and almost tangible maleness in the room. I was satisfied, however, to have been there and to have been able to document this remarkable event, of which I had never read anything in the literature. I even had photos from the sacred grove of a male secret society.

When, later, I saw the pictures, they were hopeless. Ill-focused, badly lit, lopsided and showing nothing but the completely uninteresting backs of men and rams. While I was taking them I had the impression that I was making an almost pornographic record of a secret ritual. They showed nothing of the sort but bore the marks of my own inhibition, resulting from my transgression of the boundary between gender categories.

This is the point: the nature of the event could not be recorded in photography. The texture of maleness and sex which filled the room had been an intense sensory experience, but it was invisible. The reality of the total social event had been transformed into a two-dimensional image, a souvenir (cf. Sontag 1979, p. 9). For me it invokes a particular memory, for others the information is very limited.

Probably better photographers, or just male ethnographers, could have made a finer photographic record of the ram exhibition. They would still have to realise, however, that pictures have a limited value as ethnographic 'evidence'. While one can take pictures of ritual groves and of the participants in the ritual, one cannot capture their secret on celluloid. This has to be told.

The difference between the printer's ink and the photographer's developing tank, however, is not the only explanation for the different potentials of textual and visual representations. They must be further qualified and positioned in relation to the reality of anthropology, which is remarkable mainly because of the fundamental continuity between the definers and the defined (Hastrup 1987a). Anthropologists – as people – belong to the class of things that are subject to their understanding (cf. Vendler 1984, p. 202). Whether equipped with notebooks or cameras, ethnographers always define reality at the moment they discover it. It is this continuity between subject and object which marks the construction of ethnographic knowledge and which must be taken into consideration when assessing the difference between visual and textual forms of authority.

## Place and space

A comparison between my grey pictures of horned rams and Icelandic men in rubber boots and the story about my experience immediately suggests that the difference between a photographic and a written record is analogous to the difference between 'thin' and 'thick' descriptions (Geertz 1973, pp. 6ff). While a thin description may capture *forms* – also of behaviour – it cannot of itself convey implicit *meanings*. Forms are culturally meaningless when studied independently of local meaning relations and contemporary conventions of representation (Boon 1982, p. 118). One culture's gesture of 'come' is another culture's 'go away'. As items of behaviour – and as images – they are similar, but as social actions they are worlds apart.

In the picture, the emphasis is necessarily on form, to which we then add meaning. By contrast, writing is essentially formless in itself, and meaning is created *through* the text, not by the textual substance.

Within one culture time may also redefine the meaning of forms. Icelandic rams may look the same all year round, but on the day of the ram feast they represent something special, namely their owners' sexual potence. Such are the local conventions of representation – but the photo never tells. In other words, while images show *part* of reality, the text invokes a particular *kind* of reality. Both modes of representation work through images, but the visual mode is related metonymically to reality, while the text rests on metaphor or allegory.

The camera is an extension of the ethnographic gaze. It aims specifically, and quite respectably, of course, at seeing, while ethnographic fieldwork in general aims at sensing the context of the seen – like the sexual texture of a ram exhibition in rural Iceland. The photograph remains a thin description of the happening, while the text allows for a thick description of the event.

The photograph evidently is a magnificent medium of recording, and in particular areas of research photography may be an invaluable means of measuring, counting and comparing, to paraphrase Collier (1975, p.213). Although the making of inventories or catalogues – of objects or items of human behaviour – is not the sole function of photography in ethnographic research (e.g., see Harper 1987), we can still identify the general potential of photographs as one of recording particular *forms* and visible patterns of organisation. The form conveys its own meaning.

This may be further qualified by reference to the distinction between place and space, introduced by Michel de Certeau. A *place* is the order of distribution and of relations between elements of whatever kind; it is an instantaneous configuration of positions (de Certeau 1988, p. 117). By contrast, *space* is composed of intersections between mobile elements, and is actuated by the ensemble of movements deployed within it (*ibid.*). 'Space occurs as the effect produced by the operations that orient it, situate it, temporalize it, and make it function in a polyvalent unity of conflictual programs or contractual proximities' (*ibid.*). A space is constantly transformed by successive contexts and has nothing of the stability that characterises a place. 'Space is practiced place' (*ibid.*).

As I see it, the photographs from the sheep-house show the *place* of the ram exhibition. We see men and rams in varying degrees of proximity and we get a feeling of the enclosure that contains only men and rams – no women and ewes, for instance. In that sense the record is true enough. It nowhere catches, however, the *space* created by the event, the existential space of cultural experience which made the air thicken with invisible knowledge.

While words or stories may transform places into spaces or vice versa, the picture remains a motionless image of a place. It is reality imprisoned (Sontag 1979, p.163). The picture may invoke the memory of the space for the person who experienced it, but it cannot reveal its texture or essence to outsiders. One could argue that film, in contrast to photography, does contain a record of movement and of spatial instability. Certainly, films in many ways mediate between images and texts, but they remain focused on place, as understood here.

Visual records thus have their own logic. In some cases they may yield unanticipated information. One case is that of the *blow-up effect*. My colleague Niels Fock relates, for instance, how it was only after seeing his own photograph from an Andean ritual that he realised how some men had actually been flinging the forbidden bolas during a cock-fight, only it had happened so quickly that the ethnographer had not actually *seen* it, while it lasted.[3] The blow-up effect is related to the implicit acknowledgement that photography generally provides a unique system of disclosures: 'that it shows us reality as we had *not* seen it before' (Sontag 1979, p.119). Even if actually *unseen* by the ethnographer, the photograph still only captures features of social life that are visible. And certainly many things happen in a society which the ethnographer never sees, and many more which cannot be seen at all. The blow-up potential of ethnographic pictures is fortunate but not essential to ethnographic authority.

Apart from the blow-up effect I should like to draw attention to what could be called the *show-up effect*. Again, my colleague Niels Fock provides the example. After reviewing his photographs from his fieldwork among the Waiwai, he realized that there were dogs in virtually all the pictures. They were all over the place wherever there were people. The ethnographer had noticed the dogs in the beginning of fieldwork and not without irritation, but after a while they had become unnoticeable.[4] They had become so much part of the landscape that only the pictures made the ethnographer recall their presence. I suppose that similar occurrences are part of other ethnographers' experience; forgotten facts that never went into the notebooks may be recalled – 'commonplaces' restored.

The show-up effect, as I see it, is related to a particular question that has arisen in visual anthropology: whether the camera can 'correct the possible bias of the reflective eye in the human observer' (Collier 1988, p. 76). It does take a keen eye to make ethnographic observations, but whenever 'correction' is called for it presupposes some shared standard of truth.

Until recently, the clinical gaze (Foucault 1973) was the sole guarantee asked for, but the visualist paradigm is certainly on the wane, in anthropology as elsewhere (Fabian 1983; Hastrup 1986). We have come to terms with the fact that a 'bias' is not necessarily an evil. It may even be important in directing the gaze towards particular spots, because it is informed by intuition and implicit knowledge. As such, the bias, which is no more and no less than a subjective view, may indicate that the ethnographer is on the track of socially significant relationships, that are themselves invisible. Both the blow-up and the show-up effects have potential value as means of disclosure, of course, but on the whole, it seems to me that to fetishize this potential and criminalise ethnographers who fail to exploit this medium is going too far.[5]

It fails to recognise the possible *make-up effect* of pictures, that is their potential for reconstruction, faking and pretending. (Lies may also be spoken in language, of course.) I need only recall my own experience of looking into Icelandic family albums of reconstructed family events to illustrate this (Hastrup 1986). Stressing the absolute truth value of pictures is logically consistent with a particular empiricist notion of anthropology, where everything depends on correct observation. Even if named 'participant observation', only observation bears the marks of science in this notion (cf. Holy 1983, p. 24). Margaret Mead, who was the one to speak of the criminal neglect of film in anthropology, is one distinguished exponent of the positivist era of anthropology, in which participation was only a means to observation at closest possible distance. She says, for instance: 'As the inclusion of the observer within the observed scene becomes more intense, the observation becomes unique' (Mead 1977, p. 6). This is fieldwork as a telescope.

Certainly, it is still important to go and see for oneself, but fieldwork as such is differently conceived in the post-positivist era. Participation is no longer seen as just a technique that yields objective data (Holy 1983, pp. 26ff); it is also a distinctive mode of creating 'data'. To a large extent it is fieldwork itself which generates the events, that are then portrayed as facts. Fieldwork is confrontation and dialogue between two parties involved in a joint creation of otherness and selfness (Dwyer 1977, p. 147). It is the interpersonal, cross-cultural encounter that produces ethnography (Clifford 1982, p. 144). Comprehending others leaves no one untouched (Ardener 1989b).

From this point of view the authority of ethnography is not located in the dictum that 'I saw it myself', but in the fact that the ethnographer shared time and experience with 'her people', in a process during which she gradually became her own informant on their reality (Hastrup 1986; 1987a; 1987b; 1990; 1992).

Even though veracity and visibility are no longer coterminous, the photographic record of social events is still an important supplement to the notes, possibly capturing features of behaviour that otherwise would have remained unseen. This also holds for ethnographic films, which may or may not be seen as extensions of photography. Echoing the stress on the blow-up effect of photographs, it has been claimed that ethnographic film records 'enable us to become better informed about ourselves and our organizational and adaptive possibilities . . .' (Sorenson 1975, p. 466). This is related also to the fact that with film, one can see everything over and over again.

Going back to old images is potentially revealing, of course, but I fail to understand how one can determine which kind of information is 'better' suited for the purpose of establishing ethnographic knowledge for the future. It seems, again, that the author of that statement is caught in the view that visibility is the main criterion of reality. Possibly this is a reminiscence of the so-called film perception of the world. As described by Chiozzi, this perception implies that the film eye is more perfect than the human eye, and that, therefore, it provides a more precise record of the happenings (1989a, p.8). In relation to our dear old discipline of words, so pitied by Margaret Mead (1975), this implicit evaluation is expressed in terms of a higher degree of recording *accuracy* in film (Balikci 1988, p. 32).

Accuracy is one thing, access to information, which has been discussed in a similar vein, is another. Thus, for some ethnographers, the camera has made the observer's task easier (Chiozzi 1989b, p. 44). For others it has allegedly brought them into areas where they might not have had access without a camera (Arson 1988, p. 431). Possibly the opposite experience is a more common one. The interesting question is not 'who' or 'when', however, but why this should be important at all. Evidently, I am not denying that access to information is important in ethnographic fieldwork, but I am objecting to the implication that we should ideally record 'everything' if we are to give a true portrait of the culture in question. That is impossible and, over the past decade, this has been an implicit target of the debate on representation and representativity in anthropology. It seems a waste of time if visual anthropologists ignore this debate and start it all over again. After all, visual anthropology must be a kind of anthropology to deserve its name (Rollwagen, 1988).

It is also *visual*, of course, which is why the problem of representation has taken a different course of discussion. Even if, therefore, the mode of representation seems to be given, films are not above questions of genre. We need only recall the long debates on the relative virtues of observational, participant, documentary and other kinds of film to hear the echoes of the discussion of genre in anthropology. The interesting point, in anthropology at least, is not genre in itself but how genre relates to life (Ardener 1985).

Whatever the genre of particular films, I contend that they generally focus on the forms and places of life. Due to the apparent materiality of these features they have been perceived as accurate records of the ethnographic reality. Pictures are taken as proof that something really happened; as Susan Sontag has noted for photographs, it is generally assumed 'that something exists, or did exist, which is like what's in the picture' (Sontag 1979, p. 5). Film is even more convincing; here the distance between reality and representation is almost entirely neutralised. The visual documentation has an immense power of seduction, which can hardly be discussed at all, precisely because the distance between reality and representation has been negated. This is the powerful *trompe-l'oeil* of ethnographic images (Ruby 1982).

To my mind it is impossible to rank visual and textual representations of ethnography in terms of different degrees of accuracy. Rather, they display different *kinds* of accuracy, related to the different anchorages of their authority: in place or space.

## Record and recollection

We have noted that ethnographic films are visual records. They are records of places, souvenirs of realities that were. It is in their nature to record only visible things; while we can take a close-up of the ram's private parts we cannot see its metaphorical expression of the owner's sexual abilities. We can tell that in words, however, and that is where it becomes absurd to claim that our celebrated field-notes are wholly anachronistic and inadequate (Chiozzi 1989a, p. 3). Truly, 'visual notes' – such as those made already by Boas – may complement the written ones, but they cannot replace them. Witnessing the slaughtering of a chicken is no portrayal of the chicken oracle, and we would not have wished to miss out on that piece of ethnography from the Azande (Evans-Pritchard 1937). This appears self-evident, but the battle over the relative strength of visual and textual modes of description is still fought in terms of which is the better, the more accurate or the more authentic, as if it were a matter of degree and not of kind.

It is my conviction that the sterile battle over degrees of authenticity may resolve into a fertile dialogue about kinds of authority if we allow the difference between the two forms of representation to be seen. To deny that there is any difference at all, as was done recently by O'Rourke, for instance (cited in Lutkehaus 1989, p. 432), is to blur the contours of ethnographic knowledge. Let us, therefore, take another close-up of the distinction between visual and textual modes of authority.

It seems to be the only unquestioned feature of photographs and films that they are *records* and, as such, they allow an invaluable documentation of cultural variety to be made for the future (Balikci 1988, pp. 40–41; Sorenson 1975, pp. 464–66; Hockings 1975, p. 40). The purpose of gathering visual data has often been described as bringing the exotic home (Balikci 1988, p. 41) and preserving and communicating alien realities (Chiozzi 1989, p. 13ff). With the exhortation to provide such records there usually goes a stress on urgency. From Margaret Mead (1975) onwards, most, if not all, visual anthropologists have emphasized the necessity of providing visual records before it is too late. 'We need to act quickly if we are not to lose for all time information . . .' (Sorenson 1975, p. 464). It is the idea of the vanishing world that haunts visual anthropology. Along with this idea comes a wish to establish visual archives, so as not to forget the variety of human behaviour. I think, however, that we should be careful not to allow the 'human zoo' attitude to dominate visual anthropology.[6]

Furthermore, I do not subscribe to the folklorist tradition of haste: those who really know are always at the point of dying out in the vision of the disappearing world, and scholarship is a constant battle with time. In anthropology (in contrast to folklore research) I would have thought that we had actually come to terms with the fact that the world changes all the time and what was, yesterday, is not necessarily more interesting than what will be, tomorrow. It will never be possible for anthropologists to document all histories serially; at best we can record particular conjunctures in the continuous development of societies.[7]

When we are conducting fieldwork, however extensively and meticulously, our records can never be exhaustive. They remain selective accounts of what actually happened. They are frozen images of particular stretches of life. This is not only a feature of visual records. Most anthropological analyses are done upon dead stretches of experience; upon data as recorded (Ardener 1978, p. 111). We never possess the successive instants of life, 'only our records of some of them, and from instant to instant we select aspects only' (*ibid.*). These are our data. The inherent problem for the recorder is to separate the programmatic from the accidental, to determine the meaning of social 'signs', and their potential for future events. This is the well-known problem of cultural ambiguity and the mis-match of categories.

Visual and written records part company from each other at this point. The concreteness of visual records (which is a corollary to their metonymical relationship to reality) tends to obscure the ambiguity inherent in any instance. The visual record remains 'thin', while the written record allows for 'thick' description by the method of 'language–shadows' (Ardener 1978, p. 112). This method implies an awareness of the lack of fit between native and observer's categories, and of the possibilities for misunderstanding; in anthropology there must be a presumed ignorance about the other culture (Ardener 1971, p. xvii; 1987, p. 39). With films this ignorance dissolves, because one cannot 'circumscribe' the observation with ambiguous categories, or words with multiple reference. Pictures are by their nature taken at face-value.

This is related to a feature of time, which presents itself differently in visual and textual records. It is often stressed that in order to be truly ethnographic, films must present a real-time sequence (e.g. Sorenson 1988, p. 468); to break up time would be a distortion of the truth (Balikci 1988, pp. 33–4). Going back and forth in time, however, is an all-important parameter in establishing the *context* of particular events – whatever they are – and the 'truth' must always be relative to context. Time-leaps are part of the language-shadows by which we encircle local signs that have no equivalents in our own language. The stretches of life that we analyse may be 'dead', in the sense that they do not exist any more, but their social significance must be established by reference to past and future events. Again, visual and textual authority part company from each other, the first one emphasizing instantaneousness and sequence, the second implying 'mean-whileness' and conjunction (Paine 1989).

What we have here is also a problem of statistics, as it were. Eyewitnesses' records – photographic or otherwise – never tell, by themselves, whether what they record is a unique event, a frequent feature or perhaps even a routine event in the society in question. Thus, seeing a group of Icelandic men in a sheep-house does not tell where the women are at the same time or whether it is a coincidence that none are to be seen in the pictures. One can add that in words – but then we have a text, of course. Film does not show the 'statistics' of social life, if you wish, which is a very real – even material – part of the context.

This is not just another way of saying that films can never be exhaustive, or that we are only interested in the typical, the routine or the frequent. Nothing ever exhausts reality, and the non-routine may provide important clues to the social space under investigation (Paine 1989). It is rather a way of stressing that whatever the virtues of visual records, they cannot sort out 'densities', whether semantic, historical or of events (Ardener 1982, p. 12; 1989a, p. 27). They produce 'flatlands' in which reference and meaning are potentially conflated.

Perhaps I should state, once again, that we may learn a lot from travelling in flatlands, also about hills. So I am not passing judgement on ethnographic film but attempting to mark out the distinction between pictures and words in relation to the transmission of ethnographic knowledge. This is also a way of directing attention to the problem inherent in the recurrent statement made by film-makers, that films are the best medium for dispersing the message of anthropology (Chiozzi 1989; Balikci 1988, pp. 41–42; Sorensen 1988). The implicit notion is that the purpose of anthropology is to convey to a general audience what actually happened at some place in the world at some point in time, because this is what film records establish. This is clearly a very modest perception of the scientific value of anthropology, which in my view is not only concerned with what happens but also with what must always happen (Fock 1989). In the identification of social spaces the context of singular events dissolves the simple logic of chronological time. The logic of culture, with which we are concerned, explodes the concept of history (Sahlins 1985) and conse-quently undermines the nature of ethnographic 'records' as generally perceived. 'The step from experiencing society to analyzing a record of the experience is thus a crucial one. Unlike the historian the social anthropologist does both the living and the recording' (Ardener 1978, p. 111). Living in a space which is partially filled with ram metaphors always implies much more than documenting the presence of 120 rams at one particular place. The step from experience to analysis here rests on an awareness that metaphors in their turn may induce particular local actions by men who take them literally (Fernandez 1986).

Many film-makers agree that there is a distinction between documentaries and ethnographic films proper, the latter demanding much more in terms of truly anthropological understanding (Balikci 1988, p. 33). Relatively harsh statements have been made about when we may speak of 'anthropological' or 'ethnographic' films at all (e.g. Rollwagen 1989). There is certainly a problem here, because for the non-anthropologist, all films dealing with exotic cultures may look equally anthropological, while to professional anthropologists it is much more a question of method and theory than of subject-matter. Within the genre of anthropological films, distinctions have been made between observational and the participatory films (MacDougall 1975, pp. 118–19), and between scientific, reflexive and narrative films (Harper 1987). This is a debate on genre between experts on the film medium and I shall abstain from venturing any opinion on the relative ethnographic truth value. I shall merely note that such debates and distinctions may serve the purpose of situating ethnographic films in relation to fieldwork and anthropology in general, which is a pertinent problem. It is also a point where the experience of visual anthropology may provide an important clue to the general debate on anthropological representation: in film it is obvious that the 'record' is at the mercy of local dramas and that, therefore, the choice of genre is not free but inherent in the material.

What has set visual records apart is the concreteness of their images. This is related to the incontrovertible power of fixation inherent in film. With films we can *see* at least part of the world for ourselves. Few film-makers would maintain that the pictures are independent of their own perceptions, but amongst the general public it is still widely claimed that pictures never cheat. One reason why visual records have been perceived as more accurate than writings is that films of necessity use images that are drawn from the 'other culture' itself; this makes 'it seem as if the away culture were speaking for itself' (Schechner 1985, p. 109). However, the assumption 'that film can be an unmediated record of the real world is based on the idea that cameras, not people, take pictures and the naive empiricist notion that the world is what it appears to be' (Ruby 1982, p. 125). In anthropology, we have had to come to terms with the fact that the ethnographer is part of the plot.

The result is not only one of 'blurred genres', to paraphrase Geertz (1983), but also a general abandoning of the idea of ethnographic records as an objective data-base of anthropology. Due to the continuity between subject and object, or between definition and discovery in anthropology, ethnographies are never unmediated records. The art of memory is a culture and timebound effort (Yates 1966). In the Western apprehension of 'history', this particular art of memory has been labeled science; in turn this has led to a confusion of history and pure memory (Wachtel 1986, p. 217; Hastrup 1987b, p. 262), whence also the confusion of records and realities.

There are no pure memories, however, only recollection (Wachtel 1986, p. 210). In contrast to arbitrary records, recollections are structured memories. The point is that the structuring of memory is not accidental. Recollections are structured according to contemporary significance; densities in the diachronic dimension reflect the event-densities of the synchronic (Ardener 1989a, p. 27).

While we may record huge masses of behavioural units and take pictures of hundreds of happenings, it is only through ethnographic fieldwork that we can identify which among them are socially significant. We are not ethologists – studying *behaviour* – but anthropologists concerned with *action*.[8]

In the visual records it is difficult to distinguish behaviour from action. Of course, the informed anthropological film-maker will know what is significant and what is not, but pictures cannot by themselves tell the difference. In other words, there is a latent risk of confusing mere happenings with socially significant events. Events are happenings of significance, as identified according to a particular cultural order (which contains its own chaos) (Sahlins 1985, p. 153). As happenings, they obviously have some objective properties but it is not these properties as such that define the event, rather it is the relation between the event and a given cultural system. This relation is invisible and cannot be recorded on film.

The cultural order is virtual; it exists only *in potentia*. But meanings are realised, *in presentia*, as events of speech and action (Sahlins, 1985). To convey the potential, words are needed. With film, we normally do get a dose of words in addition to the visual record that may fulfill this requirement, but then we have a text. I am overemphasizing the difference here for the sake of argument, because obviously films may be construed so as to be much more than sequences of happenings, also without adding a subtext. The visual mode of representation may be used narratively in a fashion which transcends the narrow vision of record and becomes structured recollections (MacDougall 1975).

Nevertheless, because of its focus on *place* and on *records*, film has been seen as a means of data-gathering rather than a medium of ideas. In the words of MacDougall, 'Because film deals so overwhelmingly with the specific rather than the abstract, it is often considered incapable of serious intellectual articulation' (MacDougall 1975, p. 116). This need not be the case, however, if the visual mode of representation is not reduced to a means of accurate, concrete and objective recording of cultures that are vanishing almost by definition. This 'insubstantial illusion of reality' (MacDougall 1975, p. 115) should be replaced by a more adequate anthropological vision in which the distinction between reality and representation is not blurred.

## Map and itinerary

We can proceed now to a final set of contrastive metaphors which will lead us even further into the problem of ethnographic authority. The picture makes us experience reality from, as it were, outside in. Our insight goes from the whole to the detail through a process of focusing within a set frame (Lévi-Strauss 1962). The text, by contrast, directs our attention from the detail to the whole in a process of framing and reframing.

This leads to the idea that the picture is related to the text as a total landscape to a chosen route in a network of roads. Returning to the conceptual world of de

Certeau, this amounts to two distinct modes of representation – a map and an itinerary. For the sake of my contrastive argument I suggest that the ethnographic film represents reality in a *map*, while the text represents it in the form of an *itinerary*. The first gives us a cultural tableau, while the second helps us to a guided tour around the social space (de Certeau 1988, p. 119). Both are accurate, but where one relies on a projection that totalises observations, the other points to a discursive series of operations.

The notion of map has been of current use in anthropology both in an iconic and a figurative sense (Crick 1976, p. 129–3). The extensive figurative use of spatial terms (like 'social landscape' and 'cognitive map') is a reminiscence of the Enlightenment charts of the world (Boon 1982, pp. 39ff). In the Age of Discovery the map gained pre-eminence over the itinerary, which before that had been the most reliable guide to the world. While the itinerary reflected a human-centred cosmology, relating the actual movements of people in space, the map bore the stamps of objectivity and of a new scientific view of the universe, where people were no longer at the centre. In this universe, the discoverers of new worlds became heroes and when anthropologists entered the scene, they aspired to a similar status. The ethnographic discoveries were presented in tableaux and the authority was located in the fact that 'I saw it myself'. The scientific value of ethnographic knowledge was a corollary of having actually observed particular phenomena and subsequently mapped them on to the chart of cultural differences. This notion of anthropology is on the wane, as previously noted: the itinerary has come back as a precise guide to the world. We have realized that we write cultures, we do not depict them (Clifford and Marcus 1986; Hastrup 1992).

Paradoxically, there is at the same time a burst of interest in visual anthropology. It is as if this sub-field is moving into the scientific space that is being vacated by anthropology in general. Such paradoxes cannot be solved, but they can be entered (Boon 1982, p. 46). One way of entry is to realise that the two forms of representation draw on distinct poles of human experience. One experience is that of belonging to a specific place, another of moving in a particular space. This is correlated with a sense of boundaries and difference on the one hand, with centres and transcendence on the other.

What gets onto the map is difference (Bateson 1972, p. 451); the map is not the territory, however, only a representation of the idea of the territory that was held by the maker of the map (*ibid.* p. 454). What is immediately conveyed by ethnographic films is cultural difference; that is what gets on the map. The inherent anthropological problem is that it creates a gulf between 'us' and 'them', and thus in spite of itself may be implicitly racist (Preloran 1975, p. 105). Despite the concreteness of the images, however, difference is in itself an abstract relation. The inherent problem in visual representation is precisely this: that it reifies and freezes cultural difference.

If the purpose of ethnography is to posit difference *and* to transcend it, texts are a necessary means (Clifford 1986, p. 99). Not any kind text of course, but ethnographic texts as conceived in the postmodern era (if this word is not outdated already) when the attempt has been made to reclaim life from frozen genres (Ardener 1985). This implies also a rigorously empirical approach – a concern with densities, silences and invisibilities among other things – which cannot be recorded in visual notes but can be recollected in language.

Surprisingly, the advocates of visual anthropology seem to devote a considerable part of their energy to refuting implicit allegations of subjectivity. While I would agree that we do have a problem of objectivity in anthropology, its roots are not to be found in the subjectivity shared by film-makers and other ethnographers alike. There are no entries into social spaces apart from living them. That means experiencing their differences, and recalling them afterwards. The ethnographer is irrevocably part of the plot. Subjectivity and objectivity are not mutually exclusive. We have realised that relativisation is our only mode of objectivity (Ardener 1987, p. 40).

Relativisation, or the recording of difference, must, however, be followed by a subsequent attempt at transcendence, or of objectivity, if you wish. This consists in contextualising, a process in which visual records leave something wanting with their stress on serial histories. In the context of recollections and ethnographies the time-consciousness is largely non-linear (Friedrich 1986, p. 128).

Before concluding this section I should like to stress that the film in many ways poses itself as an intermediary between the photograph and the text, also with respect to fixation and movement. With the photo, both the picture and the spectator are fixed; one can take a close-up, but cannot transcend the central perspective. The film permits changes of perspective; the picture moves but the spectator remains fixed. The text is the most flexible of the three forms in that both the content and the reader are movable; through the constant change of perspective in the textual route in context the reader herself may stop, return and flick through the pages, creating her own images as she goes along.

To sum up on maps and itineraries: the map – and the film – separates words and things, a sin that postmodern anthropology seeks to atone for (Tyler 1987, p. 172); the itinerary – and the ethnographic text – closes the disjunction by means of a (return to) the lived experience. This is in the ideal world – which may still not have occurred – but where 'the text is not to be seen as a depiction or a revelation within itself in what it says, but is to be 'seen through' by what it cannot say, to show what it cannot say and say what it cannot show' (*ibid.*, p. 197). It is this transparency which is the most powerful feature of the ethnographic text by comparison with the ethnographic film, which cannot be seen through, because it is already visual.

### Ethnographic authority

In the course of this discussion I have argued that visual and textual ethnographies are contrasted in a number of ways. The visual mode has been qualified with reference to place, thin description, record, behaviour, happening, frame and map. The textual mode has been classified with reference to space, thick description, recollection, action, event, reframing and itinerary. As an example of an analogical classification, these relations of opposition do not subsist independently but are actually determined by the contextual contrast itself (Needham 1980, p. 54).

My implicit point in this sketch of differences between the visual and textual modes of recording and representing ethnographic knowledge is that the authority is located in the relationship between the ethnographer and her narrative, whether visual or textual. Due to the peculiar continuity between subject and object in the anthropological discourse, there can be no claims to authenticity that are external to the process of understanding the world. This process links discovery and definition. The world expands when categories are established (Hastrup 1989). Anthropology is a means to this end.

Visual and textual forms of representation are not equally powerful means, however. While ethnographic films have plenty of virtues – and may satisfy part of our thirst for knowledge – this knowledge remains iconographic. Ethnographic writing, on the other hand, may invoke a degree of reflexivity which enables us to turn knowledge into consciousness, without which we cannot transcend the limitations of established forms, also of difference. With films, differences must be taken at face-value; in writings the context-values that are embodied in the visible differences can be assessed.

Because of their different ways of coping with the time parameter, films and writings also have different potentialities for conveying the timelessness that is part of human experience. Through the concreteness of the images, films depict instances that once were. In writings we may convey a more comprehensive truth of the ethnographic present, and thus transcend the instance of fieldwork (Hastrup 1990).

Ethnographic films are extremely powerful in conveying the plurality of the world; they may fulfill an important function as an historical resource for Third World peoples (MacDougall 1987, p. 58; Hammond 1988, p. 398), and as a means of advocacy (Elsass 1990). Their pertinence may differ, but their general value is indisputable.

As for their anthropological value, however, films are not on equal terms with ethnographic writing. They are not in conflict, nor are they just complementary modes of expression, because they do not operate on the same logical level. Rather, they are hierarchically related. Writings may encompass the images produced by films, but not the other way round, just as anthropological writings about the 'Other', by logical necessity, are hierarchically related to the voices of this stylized 'Other' (Dumont 1986, p. 266; Hastrup 1991).

There are logically two ways of recognising *alter*: hierarchy and conflict (Dumont 1986, p. 266). To the extent that films and writings are seen as alternative ethnographies, this is their choice. With all the differences listed above, I contend that the logical relationship must be one of hierarchy.[9] As 'encompassed' by the general anthropological context, ethnographic films share some of the virtues – and some of the vices – inherent in this context, to which they contribute their own.

I believe that an acknowledgement of the hierarchical relationship between writings and films in the construction of ethnographic knowledge is a necessary precondition for the development of a fertile exchange of authority between them.

## Notes

I wish to thank Peter Elsass (who made the film *The Earth is our Mother* on the Arhuacos and the Motilon-Bari of Colombia) for a valuable discussion of the first draft of this paper. Niels Fock also supplied pertinent comments, which helped me clarify some points.

1  For a recent review of the state of the art in visual anthropology, I refer to Chiozzi (1989).
2  Fieldwork in Iceland was conducted in 1982–83, supported by the Danish Research Council for the Humanities and the Icelandic Ministry of Education.
3  Personal communication from Niels Fock. The actual picture and a description of the ritual is found in Krener and Fock (1977–78).
4  Personal communication from Niels Fock. The ethnography of the Waiwai has been published in Fock (1963).
5  Margaret Mead is the one who actually uses the word 'criminal' in relation to the apparent neglect of film in anthropology (Mead 1975, p. 6).
6  The problem of the 'human zoo' attitude does not relate exclusively to film. On the contrary, it has been widely discussed as a general feature of anthropology's wish to preserve 'other cultures'. See for instance Bodley (1977).
7  For a discussion of serial and conjunctural history, I refer to Braudel (1980).
8  The distinction between behaviour and action may have different connotations in other contexts. Here I stick to the analytical distinction suggested by Ardener (1973).
9  Skinningsrud (1987, pp. 50–1) also discusses this relationship, but suggests that the two modes are complementary. Where 'ethnographic authority' is concerned, I think that the idea of complementarity is impossible to sustain.

## References

Ardener, E. (1971), 'Introduction', *Social Anthropology and Language*, Tavistock (ASA 22), London.
Ardener, E. (1973), 'Behaviour: a social anthropological criticism', *Journal of the Anthropological Society of Oxford*, 4, pp. 152–4.
Ardener, E. (1978), 'Some outstanding problems in the analysis of events', *Yearbook of Symbolic Anthropology*, I, pp. 103–21.
Ardener, E. (1982), 'Social anthropology, language and reality', D. Parkin (ed.), *Semantic Anthropology*, Academic Press (ASA 22), London.
Ardener, E. (1985), 'Social anthropology and the decline of modernism', J. Overing (ed.), *Reason and Morality*, Tavistock (ASA 24), London.
Ardener, E. (1989a), 'The construction of history: "vestiges of creation" ', M. Chapman, M. McDonald and E. Tonkin (eds.), *History and Ethnicity*, Tavistock (ASA 27), London.

Ardener, E. (1989b), *The Voice of Prophecy. Collected Essays*, (ed. Malcolm Chapman), Blackwell, Oxford.

Arson, H.J. (1988), 'Photography that Listens', *Visual Anthropology*, 1, pp. 415–32.

Balikci, A. (1988), 'Anthropologists and ethnographic filmmaking' in Rollwagen (1988).

Bateson, G. (1972), *Steps to an Ecology of Mind*, Ballantine, New York.

Bodley, J. H. (1977), 'Alternatives to ethnocide: human zoos, living museums and real people', E.Sevilla-Casas (ed.), *Western Expansion and Indigenous Peoples*, Mouton, Paris.

Boon, J. A. (1982), *Other Tribes, Other Scribes*, Cambridge University Press, Cambridge.

Braudel, F. (1980), *On History*, Chicago University Press, Chicago.

Certeau, M. de (1988), *The Practice of Everyday Life*, University of California Press, Berkeley.

Chiozzi, P. (1989a), 'Reflections on ethnographic film with a general bibliography', *Visual Anthropology*, 2, pp. 1–84.

Chiozzi, P. (1989b), 'Photography and anthropological research: three case studies', R. M. Boonzajer Flaes (ed.), *Eyes Across the Water*, Het Spinhuis, Amsterdam.

Clifford, J. (1982), *Person and Myth. Maurice Leenhardt in the Melanesian World*, University of California Press, Berkeley.

Clifford, J. (1986), 'On ethnographic allegory', in Clifford and Marcus (1986).

Clifford, J. and G. E. Marcus (eds.) (1986), *Writing Culture*, University of California Press, Berkeley.

Crick, M. (1976), *Explorations in Language and Meaning*, Malaby Press, London.

Crick, M. (1982), 'Anthropological field research, meaning creation and knowledge construction', D. Parkin (ed.) *Semantic Anthropology*, Academic Press (ASA 22), London.

Collier, J. (1975), 'Photography and visual anthropology', in Hockings (1975).

Collier, J. (1988), 'Visual anthropology and the future of ethnographic film', in Rollwagen (1988).

Dwyer, K. (1977), 'On the dialogic of field work', *Dialectical Anthropology*, 2, pp. 143–151.

Elsass, P. (1990), 'Self-presentation or self-reflection? Advocacy and anthropological filmmaking', *Visual Anthropology*, 4, pp. 161–173.

Evans-Pritchard, E.E. (1937), *Witchcraft Oracles and Magic among the Azande*, Oxford University Press, Oxford.

Fabian, J. (1983), *Time and The Other. How Anthropology Makes its Object*, University of Columbia Press, New York.

Fernandez, J. W. (1986), *Persuasions and Performances. The Play of Tropes in Culture*, Indiana University Press, Bloomington.

Fock, N. (1963), *Waiwai. Religion and Society of an Amazonian Tribe*, The National Museum, Copenhagen.

Fock, N. (1989), 'Den tjenstvillige kammertjeners dilemma. Kulturel tilpasning i Ecuador' in K. Hastrup and K. Ramløv (eds.), *Kulturanalyse. Fortolkningens forløb i antropologien*, Akademisk Forlag, København.

Foucault, M. (1973), *The Birth of the Clinic*, Tavistock, London.

Friedrich, P. (1986), *The Language Parallax. Linguistic Relativism and Poetic Indeterminacy*, University of Texas Press, Austin.

Geertz, C. (1973), 'Thick description: toward an interpretive theory of culture', in *id. The Interpretation of Cultures*, Basic Books, New York.

Geertz, C. (1983), 'Blurred genres: the refiguration of social thought', in *id.*, *Local Knowledge*, Basic Books, New York.

Hammond, J. D. (1988), 'Visualizing themselves: Tongan videography in Utah', *Visual Anthropology*, 1, pp. 379–400.

Harper, D. (1987), 'The visual ethnographic narrative', *Visual Anthropology*, 1, pp. 1–19.

Hastrup, K. (1985a), 'Anthropology and the exaggeration of culture', *Ethnos*, 52, pp. 311–324.

Hastrup, K. (1985b), 'Male and female in Icelandic culture', *Folk*, 27, pp. 49–64.

Hastrup, K. (1986), 'Veracity and visibility: the problem of authenticity in anthropology', *Folk*, 28, pp. 5–17.

Hastrup, K. (1987a), 'The reality of anthropology', *Ethnos*, 52, pp. 287–300.

Hastrup, K. (1987b), 'Presenting the past. Reflections on myth and history', *Folk*, 29, pp. 257–69.

Hastrup, K. (1989), 'The prophetic condition', in E. Ardener, *The Voice of Prophecy. Collected Essays*, (ed. Malcolm Chapman), Blackwell, Oxford.

Hastrup, K. (1990), 'The ethnographic present: a reinvention', *Cultural Anthropology*, vi, 1, pp. 45–61.

Hastrup, K. (1992), 'Writing ethnography: state of the art', H. Callaway and J. Okely (eds.), *Anthropology and Autobiography*, Tavistock, London.

Hockings, P. (ed.) (1975), *Principles of Visual Anthropology*, Mouton, The Hague.

Holy, L. (1984), 'Theory, methodology and the research process', R. Ellen (ed.), *Ethnographic Research*, Academic Press, London.

Krener, Eva and N.Fock (1977–78), 'Good luck and Taita Carnaval', *Folk*, 19–20, pp. 151–70.

Lévi-Strauss, C. (1962), *La Pensée Sauvage*, Plon, Paris.

Lutkehaus, N. C. (1989), ' "Excuse me, everything is not all right": on ethnography, film, and representation. An interview with film-maker Dennis O'Rourke', *Cultural Anthropology*, 4, pp. 422–37.

MacDougall, D. (1975), 'Beyond observational cinema' in Hockings (ed.) 1975.

MacDougall, D. (1987), 'Media friend or media foe', *Visual Anthropology*, 1, pp. 54–58.

Mead, M. (1975), 'Visual anthropology in a discipline of words' in Hockings (ed.) 1975.

Mead, M. (1977), *Letters from the Field 1925–1975*, Harper, New York.

Needham, R. (1980), 'Analogical classification' in *id. Reconnaissances*, University of Toronto Press, Toronto.

Paine, R. (1989), 'Beyond routine'. Ms.

Preloran, J. (1975), 'Documenting the human condition' in Hockings (ed.) 1975.

Rollwagen, J. R. (1988), *Anthropological Filmmaking*, Harwood Academic Press, Chur.

Ruby, Jay (1982), 'Ethnography as trompe l'oeil: film and anthropology', in J.Ruby (ed.), *A Crack in the Mirror. Reflexive Perspectives in Anthropology*, University of Pennsylvania Press, Philadelphia.

Sahlins, M. D. (1985), *Islands of History*, University of Chicago Press, Chicago.

Schechner, R. (1985), *Between Theatre and Anthropology*, University of Pennsylvania Press, Philadelphia.

Skinningsrud, T. (1987), 'Anthropological films and the myth of scientific truths', *Visual Anthropology*, 1, pp. 47–53.

Sontag, S. (1979), *On Photography*, Penguin, Harmondsworth.

Sorenson, E. R. (1975), 'Visual records, human knowledge and the future', in P. Hockings (ed.).

Tyler, S. A. (1987), *The Unspeakable. Discourse, Dialogue, and Rhetoric in the Postmodern World*, University of Wisconsin Press, Madison.

Vendler, Z. (1984), 'Understanding people' in R. A. Shweder and R. A. LeVine (eds.), *Culture Theory. Essays on Mind, Self, and Emotion*, Cambridge University Press, Cambridge.
Wachtel, N. (1986), 'On memory and history', *History and Anthropology*, 2, pp.207–24.
Yates, F. (1966), *The Art of Memory*, London.

# The lexical spaces of eye-spy

I want to make an argument about the desirability of not comprehending every-thing, of not being able to show through the narrative coherence of film our complete *mastery*. Specifically, I want to make an argument about the use of still images in visual anthropology and to argue against moving film, or at least a certain type of moving film. But in opposing film and photography as mani-festations of two different lexical spaces, I also want to argue that, under certain conditions, they are capable of imitating each other – that is, a certain practice of photography can come to look very much like film and a certain type of film to resemble still photography. The terms 'film' and 'photography', as well as denoting specific technical phenomena, also represent ideal types of *stillness* and *movement*. I will also deconstruct the polarity which the argument supposes and dispute the possibility of a 'context' which moving film appears to offer, and the self-presence embodied in the truncated stillness of the photograph.

## Ineluctable narratives

Jean-François Lyotard observes that in film 'all endings are happy endings' (1989, p. 173) even if this involves a murder, for this serves 'as a final resolution of dissonance' (*ibid.*). Lyotard here isolates the attraction of film for those who desire, through their emplotments, to demonstrate their professional capabilities; for those who, having set their ineluctable narratives in motion, demand the 'closure' and 'suture' of the proceedings. But there is paradox here in which *more* is desired precisely because it results in *less*. Moving film seems to be about more. As Metz (1985) notes, it disposes of the orders of sound and motion whereas still photography commands only vision. Photographs, by contrast, seem to offer less – they are the mere building blocks from which cinema is con-structed; the raw commodities on which film, as Lyotard argues, 'makes a return'. As even John Collier (primarily a still photographer) argues '*only* film or video can record the realism of time and motion or the psychological reality of varieties of interpersonal relations' (1986, p. 144). Just to scrutinize the assumptions in this one sentence would require a whole paper. Film is where the big money is and it is increasingly determining the definition of 'visual anthropology'. But it is equally possible to argue that visual anthropologists are worried by still photography because it offers too much and are attracted by moving film because it offers so much less. Still images contain *too many meanings* whereas the desirability of film lies precisely in its ability to constrain meaning through narrative chains of signification – what Eco terms 'syntagmatic concatenations imbued with argumentative capacity' (1982, p. 38).

In a strategy beloved of Malinowskian anthropologists, film situates otherwise undecidable images within sequences that produce argument and express intention. They close off plural readings in the temporal flow of succession and destruction. Two still images which might be considered co-equal, assume the roles of before and after and become sites to be adjudicated upon when situated within filmic narrative. Because film inhabits a larger lexis – it has movement, sound and so on – it challenges what appears to be the silence and immobility of the photograph. The nature of the moving film immerses the image in what Christian Metz describes as 'a stream of temporality where nothing can be kept, nothing stopped' (1985, p. 83).

## The lexical spaces of film and still photography

Metz contrasts the different spatio-temporal sizes of the *lexis* – the units of reading – of film and photography. 'Lexical' as used in the title of this paper is not quite the precise adjective, since with its specific connotation of the 'word', it stands opposed to Metz's earlier arguments that the photographic image comes as it were fully formed, as a sentence rather than a mere word. Following Hjelmslev, Metz talks only of the *lexis*, a unit of reading which in the case of sculpture would be a 'statue' and in the case of music would be 'the piece'(Metz 1985, p. 81). For Metz the lexis of film and photography are radically different, both formally and socially. Formally the photograph is 'a silent rectangle of paper' whereas film, even if only a few moments in duration, assumes a much larger lexis constituted through the size of the screen and the presence of sounds and movements. The social contexts within which films and photographs are read also differ, with the reading of film being normally a collective pursuit and that of photography, by and large, a solitary procedure.

More significantly, the temporal lexis of the film is *relatively fixed* whilst that of photography on the other hand is *completely free*. In the absence of a fast-forward button, the film spectator is trapped within a temporal regime, a *context* in which s/he is completely unable to intervene. By contrast, the viewer of the still photograph has a total temporal control over the image and decides for herself or himself how long she or he will gaze at it. Metz concludes 'where film lets us believe in more things, photography lets us believe more in one thing'. The suddenness and fixity which characterize photography parallel, for Metz, the childhood glance which fixes forever the fetish: 'photography is a cut inside the referent, it cuts off a piece of it, a fragment, a part object, for a long immobile travel of no return' (1985, p. 84).

Metz argues, then, that photographs embody a dangerous ambivalence, a truncation which threatens the context-seeking anthropologist who yearns for an explanatory 'mesh' in which to entrap his intentions. It will be clear by now that the opposition between photography and film appears to embody exactly the contest between fragmentation and context which Marilyn Strathern locates in the popular perception of Frazer as opposed to Malinowski and which can also be discussed within the idiom of 'art' versus 'artefact' (Faris 1988). Film hence embodies a certainty produced by 'context' although (I shall later argue) this 'finally' always plunges into a further *mise en abîme*, a further unstoppable regress. It is the ability of the film to represent a presumed ordered reality and its propaganda function (in which sequence and concatenation provides a forti- fication against undesirable and 'unwarranted' readings) which make it the preferred medium among anthropologists who practice what is called visual anthropology.

## Visual pleasure and motionless others

This contrast between the still and the moving forms the subject of Laura Mulvey's influential critique of the place of 'visual pleasure' in Hollywood narrative film. Mulvey shares Metz's Lacanian predilection and she suggests that narrative film fiction invokes an opposition between a roving male ideal ego (with whom, as Metz suggested, the camera and the audience identifies) and a static female site of visual pleasure. Women, signifying the possibility of castration, appear only as flat icons onto which the gaze of the ideal ego and the audience comes to fall in moments of scopophilic fetishism. (Scopophilia is used here, following Freud to denote the pleasure of looking which causes libidinal excita- tion.)

Let us be clear of the contrast which is being described here. On the one hand we have a male principle of movement. The male hero moves the action of the film ever onwards; his actions unfold in the depth of space and are followed by the camera and through this the audience come to identify with him. Women, by contrast, exist outside of this movement and function as passive sites of the ideal ego's (hence audience's) gaze. Thus, as Mary Anne Doane notes, the stereo- typical image of the woman on film is 'the woman gazing out of a window streaked by a persistent rain' (1987, p. 2). The figure of woman she claims 'is aligned with spectacle, space, or the image, often in opposition to the linear flow of the plot . . . there is something about women which is resistant to narrative or narrativization.' (1987, p. 5). Thus Sternberg claimed he would welcome his films being pro- jected upside down so that the audience would be able to appreciate the beauty of the still images (of women) in his films; images, Mulvey suggests, such as that of

Dietrich. Linda Williams has also identified a similar pattern in Muybridge's sequences of 'chronophotographs' – men lend themselves easily to 'doing' whereas women seem more suited to being 'seen'(cited in Doane, *ibid.*).

Mulvey makes an argument about the political functions of these 'visual pleasures' and advocates their destruction (1989, p. 26), but we should be clear that she is not suggesting a simple opposition between narrative (good) and visual (bad) pleasure, which would, of course, have implications for the argument which I am making. Rather she is arguing that it is the congruence of stillness and motion in such a genderized incarnation that is so problematic. Still images on their own can, of course, be the focus for a scopophilic fetishism, but when such images are located within narrative constructions they enter greatly more elaborate systems of *looking*. Mulvey argues that it is not simply looked-at-ness (the woman as two-dimensional icon) which cinema emphasizes, rather the camera constructs *looking* as the spectacle itself:

Playing on the tension between film as controlling the dimension of time (editing, narrative) and film as controlling the dimension of space (changes in distance, editing), cinematic codes create a gaze, a world and an object, thereby producing an object cut to the measure of desire. (1989, p. 25)

This is not peculiar to Hollywood narrative cinema. Mulvey's model is useful for understanding the construction of central Indian wedding videos, the production of which in many areas has taken over from portraiture as the main work of local photographic studios. These have a loose narrative thrust contingent on the absence of any editing which interferes with the sequence of events as they occurred in real time. They are chiefly concerned with showing the arrival of the *barāt* (the groom's bridal party, usually arriving from another town or village), what can only be described as a *surveillance* of the bride to be, long sequences of feasting, the *barāt*'s procession around the town, the marriage itself and the post-wedding celebrations. Sequences in which the bride becomes the focus of the camera (Figure 1) stand out as spaces of visual pleasure removed from the ordinary flow of events as the video constructs an inventory of what makes this bride so special. The narrative of film here grinds to a halt as motion metamorphoses to the cut-off-ness and fetishism of the still photograph, the site of female spectacle:

The beauty of the woman as object and the screen space coalesce; she is no longer the bearer of guilt but a perfect product whose body stylized and fragmented by close ups, is the content of the film and the direct recipient of the spectator's looks. (Mulvey 1985, p. 22)

It would also be interesting to analyse whether ethnographic film has recourse to the same strategy. Does the authoritative, usually male, voice-over assume the role of the ideal-ego, the traveller through space and depth (from Manchester to the ends of the earth) with whom the spectator identifies? His voice is the accompaniment to the movements of the camera, speaking as it were for the lens,

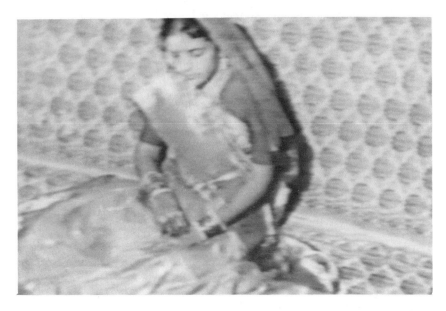

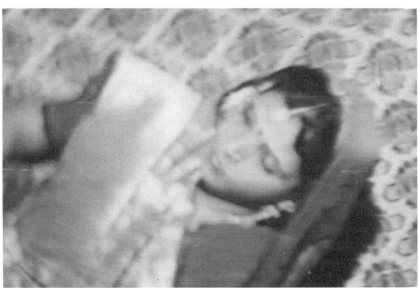

1  Stills from Venus Studio wedding video filmed in Nagda, central India, 1989. Courtesy of Venus Studios

as it comes to rest on the visual pleasures offered by a particular piece of ritual, before then moving off to rest on a time-worn peasant face or the patterning on a water pot, fulfilling the conditions specified by Mulvey in which 'the spectator (is) fascinated with the image of his like set in an illusion of natural space, and through him gaining control and possession of the woman [read the 'other'] within the diegesis' (1985, p. 21).

## Space/Time

I suggested earlier that film and photography were best understood as distinct technical procedures and also as ideal types. Between these two poles of stillness and flatness and motion and depth we can trace many intermediate forms such as that of the stereoscope in which, as is the case with film, depth is made possible through a multiplication of images. In the case of the stereoscope, a device which became phenomenally popular from the 1860s onwards, only two images – photographed from slightly different angles – are required to produce a three-dimensional effect when viewed through a hand-held viewer which unites the images in the field of vision. Whereas ordinary flat *carte-de-visites* were mere 'sun-pictures' for Oliver Wendell Holmes in a series of celebrated early essays, the stereoscope was a 'sun-sculpture', a process which, when applied to himself, enabled the representation 'not as a surface only, but in all our dimensions as an undisputed *solid* man of Boston' (1864, p. 146). In the stereoscope 'the mind feels its way into the very depths of the picture'(1864, p. 148) and although there is, of course, no literal motion possible, 'it is wonderful to see how nearly the effect of motion is produced by the slight difference of light on the water or on the leaves of trees as seen by the two eyes in the double-picture' (1864, p. 173). The stereograph moves further away from photography, which he notes is easily falsifiable, through 'the impossibility of [it] perjuring itself'. The stereograph, by virtue of its plurality of images, its distant imagining of a syntagmatic concatenation, creates something which in full-blown film we call *context*:

'At the mouth of *two witnesses*, or of three, shall he that is worthy of death be put to death; but at the mouth of one he shall not be put to death'. No woman may be declared youthful on the strength of a single photograph; but if the stereoscopic twins say she is young, let her be so acknowledged . . . . (Holmes 1864, p. 175)

The possibility of movement, articulated as a visual penetration through spatial depth, is stressed by Rosalind Krauss in an influential article on the contexts in which American landscape photography of the 1870s should be properly viewed. Her argument mobilizes the opposition between flat sites of visual pleasure and narrative depth, a polarity which mirrors that suggested by Mulvey.

Krauss contrasts two images titled *Tufa Domes, Pyramid Lake, Nevada* and suggests that each operates, today, within two different discursive fields. The first of these is Timothy O'Sullivan's original photograph dating from 1868, in which the rocks 'seem unreal and the space dreamlike . . . unbounded and directionless'

(1985, p. 131). A later lithographic copy (published in Clarence King's *Systematic Geography* in 1878) restores 'gravity and direction . . . to this space' (1985, p. 132). The O'Sullivan photograph is prized today as an aesthetic object – precisely for its distance from the quantitative idiom of the King lithograph – and yet, Krauss suggests, it is precisely within such a system of mapping and spatial penetration that we must understand O'Sullivan's work.

For Krauss the original 'context' in which O'Sullivan's image (and those produced by other Western landscape photographers) of the period should be viewed is a three-dimensional one which looks at them in their original stereoscopic form. In their currently popular form as large graphic flat prints they are part of a 'retrospective construction designed to secure it as art' (1985, p. 134). The 'aesthetic significations: sublimity, transcendence' they evoke suggest the images of visual pleasure in Mulvey's analysis which stand outside of narrative. Indeed, Krauss argues that to value O'Sullivan aesthetically is to compose a 'false history' (1985, p. 134), one that stands outside of its proper time.

Viewed in their original context, however, as stereoscopes, they take on depth and, more importantly for our present purposes, a temporal dimension is added and they assume a narrative structure. Krauss notes how nineteenth-century writing on the way stereoscopes should be viewed, particularly Oliver Wendell Holmes' series of essays, 'all dilate on the length of time spent examining the contents of the image' (1985, p. 138) and evoke metaphors of a 'dream-like exaltation' (1985, p. 138) which suggest the later writings of Christian Metz on the cinema.

Holmes, in fact, in one of his early essays (1858, reprinted 1864) uses his narrative of viewing stereoscopes to construct a narrative of travel from Niagara to the Holy Land in which the fall of his gaze over successive images constructs a filmic narrative of travel. By the time he gets to London the landscape of the metropolis has become a store of symbols in which narrative and depth is marked by masculine phallic masonry and women exist only as invisible absences, in dark recesses or in drops of blood:

London Bridge! less imposing than Westminster Bridge; but a massive pile of masonry . . . the parapet is breast high; – a woman can climb over it, and drop or leap into the dark stream lying in deep shadow under the arches. Women take this leap often. The angels hear them like the splash of drops of blood out of the heart of our humanity.

Holmes's stereoscopic London landscape also features the Monument (which 'looks like an inverted wineglass with a shaving-brush standing on it') from which women also jump off (1864, p. 189).

## The context of context

Mulvey's model of 'male' narration and 'female' visual pleasure has, I hope, been shown to be of some use for the understanding of subjects as diverse as Indian wedding videos, ethnographic film, current arguments about the role of

American landscape photography and Oliver Wendell Holmes's comments on the stereographic panorama of London.

It might appear that all this serves to undermine my original proposal, since what I appear to be arguing for is the visual pleasure without the narrative – for the still, flat icon. It might be objected that it is precisely this site of fetishistic scopophilia which is so problematic. It might seem that what I am arguing for here is an intellectual 'coffee-table' book, an anthropologically acceptable version of the work of Malcolm Kirk who eschews contextualisation in favour of cropped surface patterns of textures of light and colour; or Irving Penn, the itinerant *Vogue* photographer, who has provided a surprisingly germane justification for photographing people within the studio, at least away from *their* habitual context. Some of Penn's images, particularly those of veiled Moroccan women depicted as wrapped bundles of mystery suggest parallels with the bound Zande hunting net (collected by Herbert Lang from Zaire, Uele River region) displayed in the New York Center for African Arts *ART/artifact* exhibition (Vogel 1988, pp. 174–175; Faris 1988).

Both these images suggest the striptease – they engage with a narrative inevitability. To be made invisible in a system that demands narrative resolution is to mark the ineluctability of being made visible. One of the captions to the Zande net exhibit suggests that it should be opened so the materials and techniques used in its manufacture could be studied (Vogel 1988, p. 174).

The Zande net represents a failure in terms of the inspectional and explanatory framework of anthropological observation and collection. But it is not exactly this which I am suggesting we emulate. To do so would seem to present two possibilities. Firstly, a very knowing kind of commoditisation, in which we deny that what looks like 'lack of context' is in fact *our* context of a three-minute culture grounded in pastiche and montage (unintelligibility is the most quickly intelligible feature of any object); secondly, a Heideggerean poetic relation with art objects as 'things in themselves', something akin to Sontag's 'erotics', rather than hermeneutics of the object (Sontag 1964).

The first possibility would never transcend the cultural logic of late capitalism and the second possibility suggests that images and objects can assume an absolute self-presence, a complete and self-sufficient in-itself-ness. That this is not possible is suggested by the motion inherent in any still image.[1] It has been argued that it was the adoption of monocular perspective more than the invention of the movie camera that permitted moving images. For, from this event onwards, can be seen the operation of lines of vision – beams, angles, shafts – which Barthes calls the 'off-screen' space, 'as if the image launched desire beyond what it permits us to see . . .' (cited by Brunette and Wills 1989, p. 111). Brunette and Wills argue that 'the photographic still implicitly figures the historical shift and so has the idea of movement within it, before it, in turn, is redeployed within the series of stills that constitutes the cinema' (1989, p. 109).

Something akin to Barthes's idea of the *punctum* is taken up by John Berger in an important work which resolves some of the problems I've been raising here. In contrast to the *studium*, the *punctum* 'endows the photograph with the structure of the moving image' (Brunette and Wills 1989, p. 111). It is, in Barthes's words 'this element which rises from the scene, shoots out of it like an arrow, and pierces me'. Depending on one's reading, one can see Barthes's *punctum* either as something that aspires towards a transcendence, something akin to the ontology of the index in Peircean semiotics or as a *disseminatory* source of fragmentation. Following from this one can see film either as something which compounds these indexical truths, builds them, rather in the manner of Oliver Wendell Holmes's testifying voices, into something incontrovertible or as somehow attempting to contain and suppress all these diverse disseminations. Metz alludes to this when he argues that film is concerned with the *destruction* of the power of the photographic image.

It might be useful if I gave an example here of a use of stills which I am *not* proposing. There is a sequence of five photographs (Figure 2) in the Haddon Collection (Cambridge University) of the last surviving 'Bushman' in Natal, a man called Punch, who was reputed to be 100 years' old. Taken by W. F. Bushell in 1926, they show him smoking and talking and then standing to attention with his hat in his hands. Bushell explains:

I gave him a few cigarettes which made him very friendly. I wanted to see the top of his head, so we decided, mutually, to give three cheers for the King. Hence the picture where we are without our hats. (unnumbered ms., Haddon Collection)

Visual pleasure here is Punch's head and, in Lyotardian terms, all the narrative investment of the earlier frames produces this final return of the striptease of the hats. This might serve as a metaphor for all filmic knowledge which seeks resolution and revelation, an 'explanation' grounded in visibility. This is an extreme example but many arguments for the 'photo-essay' (cf. Harper 1987) suggest some attenuated form of this – a narrative involving documentation, revelation and the authority of the written caption.

## Acinema/aphotography

But this is only one possibility and still images need not conform so closely to such a filmic model. For a very different practice one need only look to Walker Evans's uncaptioned photographs in his collaboration with James Agee *Let Us Now Praise Famous Men* (1941), or Jean Mohr's uncaptioned images in his collaboration with John Berger *Another Way of Telling* (1982). Whilst the innovation of the former is clouded by Agee's excessive realism, Mohr's work is printed together with Berger's perceptive thoughts on the mechanics of what I'm arguing for here – 'another way of telling' – a form which certainly acknowledges narrative, but a narrative which is different from that of film. Briefly stated, this involves the exploitation of the natural ambiguity of the photographic message (Berger and Mohr 1982, p. 133) and does not attempt to constrain it with language. Its inherent movement is acknowledged but rather than disciplining these to the

2  'Punch' the Natal 'Bushman', photographed by W. F. Bushell, 1926. Courtesy of University Museum of Archaeology and Anthropology, Cambridge

forward flow of time and the exigencies of 'syntagmatic concatenation', the multiple meanings of images are encouraged to flow in more than one direction.[2] Berger and Mohr are not proposing the production of movement and meaning through the rapid displacement of relatively similar images (the minutely changing frames in film), but the much slower transposition of larger, *more different* images whose syntagmatic concatenation would be of an altogether different order. 'Meaning' here would be more 'mythic' and atemporal rather than narrational and temporally destructive.[3]

Escaping both the narrative and explanatory disciplines of documentary and the still image authorised by its explanatory caption would also enable us to incorporate and emulate systems of image-making from the very societies we are engaging with. In India, for example, one encounters radically different forms of photographic images which play elaborate games with both time and space, and the study of whose principles might provide models and inspirations which anthropologists could work with in the images which they make of India. One might, in this short space, briefly oppose two distinct patterns which suggest new configurations of the matrix formed by time, space, movement and stillness in the conventional practices of anthropological image-making. The first of these was common at the turn of the century in the documentation of court procedures and is illustrated by an album of the installation of the Raja of Bansda State in 1911 (Centre of South Asian Studies, University of Cambridge) in which differences over time are marked without any spatial variation (Figure 3). Conversely, much contemporary popular wedding and other photography utilises trick techniques which do exactly the reverse and record spatial displacement without any temporal distance (Figure 4). The trick photographic techniques mobilised here demonstrate the power – the magic – of the medium to transcend time and space. It is perhaps the many intermediate forms that lie between still photography and filmic narrative in the societies we study that we should be attempting to incorporate into our representations.

To follow this path, and the work of the Southampton-based Mount Pleasant Photography Workshop provides some useful models and offers many more possibilities than other modes of 'experimentation', which are usually conceptualised as some form or other of 'reflexivity'. Indeed one might go further and suggest that the current vogue for 'reflexivity', far from generating any 'new' forms of anthropological texts is, as the history of both anthropology and film suggests, a profound atavism of the most regressive type.

## The surface of the image

It can be argued that 'reflexivity' is as likely to *enforce* traditional sources of authority as subvert them (Pinney 1990). Likewise, 'textuality' can express just as much the authority of the *book* as the *inscription* of the letter (Derrida 1976). Both reflexivity and textuality attempt to invert the familiar system of looking. Just as Clifford (1988) notes that there is a growing process within written texts of 'writing back' by those who were previously merely *written about*, so within visual texts there is a great enthusiasm for the *returned look*. This ranges from those that consciously aim to question anthropology's inspectional regimes (as in, for instance, the use of Paul Hyman's photograph of an angry, gesticulating Moroccan shopkeeper refusing the gaze of the camera which is used on the cover of Paul Rabinow's *Reflections on Fieldwork in Morocco*), to those for whom it has become a popular slogan about the transnationality of looking, to those who argue that being looked at is good for you and that in this great mutual gaze all the peoples of the world should get to play with the technical toys.

The reasonable hope lying behind many of these attempts to scratch the surface of the negative is to subvert a naturalism on which the power of photography and other representations as *transcriptions* is thought to depend. This can seem to work so as to question either the truth value of a particular image or the neutrality of photography as a practice. An example of this was the pairing of photographs of Kenyah trophy skulls and a Josiah Martin composite photograph of his studio's *cartes-de-visite* in the *Lost Magic Kingdoms* exhibition (Museum of Mankind, London 1986) which draws our attention to the fact that photographs are *objects* imbued with great mystery which we collect and store in specially guarded places and that it is as objects with particular qualities that their power lies. The lower half of this pairing was made to serve a contemporary, modern purpose, it is made to demonstrate its materiality, to reveal the transparency of the image to be a surface effect of a particular class of *objects*. But curiously, this also seems to have been its *original* function as well since this is a cabinet card which reproduces a clutter of *cartes-de-visite* produced by this important Pacific studio.

The problem can be approached through another (anecdotal) route, although this is one which lies much nearer to the event of the conference at which this paper was presented. The poster used to advertise the conference (Figure 5) took as its basis a black and white still of Ongka from *The Kawelka: Ongka's Big Moka* (1974) and overlaid this with translucent colours in the manner of Warhol's *Marilyn Monroe*. Juxtaposing the iconic with the indexical, the *tran*scribed with the *in*scribed and monochrome with colour was intended to reveal the 'constructed nature' of film. This was the source of some objections from various patriarchs in the anthropological film-world, one of whom suggested that it would have been much better replaced by an image which demonstrated the possibility of 'authenticity' which anthropological films offered. When pressed as to how this might be accomplished visually it was suggested that something akin to a 'hallmark' be represented.

With remarkable felicity this proposal helps complete my argument by bringing us full circle from 'surface' to 'depth' to 'surface'. For what is a 'hallmark' but a proof of constructedness, a surface mark which guarantees the truth of all that lies within the object? Our critic's solution presents the appealing paradox that perhaps all attempts to 'authenticate' film and photography through 'hallmarking' would in practice only serve to destroy them,[4] but conversely it also

3 Installation of the Maharaul Shri Pratapsinhji, Bansda State, 1911. Courtesy of Centre of South Asian Studies, University of Cambridge

4  Pukhraj Jain and the India Gate. Wedding montage photograph by Suhag Studios, Nagda, 1983. Courtesy of Pukhraj Jain and Suhag Studios

5   Photograph of Ongka from *The Kawelka – Ongka's Big Moka* (Nairn, 1974), used as the basis for a poster advertising the Royal Anthropological Institute's IInd International Festival of Ethnographic Film, Manchester, 1990. (The poster was designed by James Straffon from an idea by Marcus Banks.)

suggests that the painted image of Ongka is the perfect hallmark. Space permits me only to assert, rather than demonstrate, that this can serve as a metaphor for all forms of reflexivity, which rather than being 'subversive' of creational authority merely re-energizes a powerful and dormant feature of all strategies of bringing into being. And all *transcriptions* ultimately assert their status as *inscriptions*.

## What the butler saw

The delineation of such cyclical strategies of truth and deception can help us to understand why it is that when we 'deconstruct' transparency (to use this perpetually misconstructed term) we find that the image has been doing this itself all along. As Jean-Louis Comolli argues, to point to the fact that films are 'made' rather than transcribed in heaven and to assume that this is in any way significant is to presuppose that film audiences are 'total imbeciles, completely alienated social beings' (1985 p. 759) not to have been aware of this from the outset. As Comolli argues, the spectator is 'never "passive" ', but always works (*ibid.*) and, although his comments are directed chiefly at the consumers of avowedly fictional films, the same argument applies to 'non-fictional' genres.

Several possible explanations suggest themselves. One might see this as the residue of an ideology of truth which took Plinian theories of painting as its central metaphor, this continually recurs in early photographic imagery, for instance, on the reverse of many *carte-de-visite* photographs from the 1870s onwards in which the truth of photography is approximated to the truth of painting. Alternatively, it might, like Velásquez's *Las Meninas*, be concerned with showing the representation of representation. This depiction of Velásquez in the act of creating the portrait of Philip IV and his second wife María Anna places the viewer in the position which they would have assumed had they been present (and they are shown only reflected in a distant mirror at the back of the painting). The painting has been the subject of much critical debate since Foucault used it as the frontispiece of *The Order of Things* to serve as an emblem of the Classical episteme. Many commentators have read reflexive intentions into it but we can, again, as easily reverse it and agree with David Carroll's reading of (one of) Foucault's own interpretations of it:

To represent the process of representation ... would be ... to contain within it a metarepresentation that is the ultimate word or the ultimate context or scene of representation, its end. Nothing seems to escape representation when representation itself is represented. (1987, p. 55)

## Signs of excess

Feminist writing on film also suggests that returning the gaze might not always be a confrontation with the viewing subject so much as a further variation within a system of looking in which, as Mulvey argues, objects are 'cut to the measure of

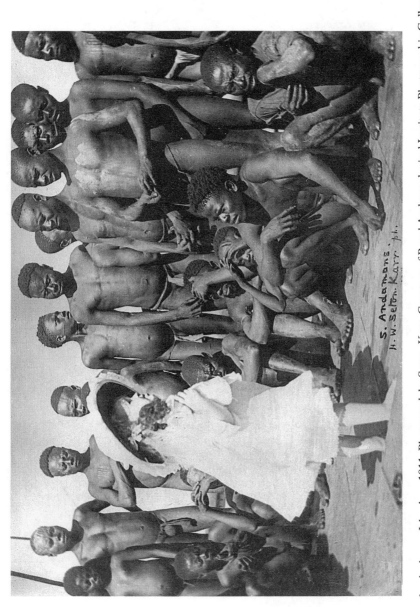

6   Andaman Islanders, 1911. Photograph by Seton-Karr. Courtesy of Royal Anthropological Institute Photographic Collection (acc. no. 33079)

**7**   Mursi watching a *Disappearing World* film. Courtesy of Granada Television and Leslie Woodhead

desire'. Following this, one might start by drawing a parallel between images of the 'other' *looking*, which are frequently endowed with a reflexive interpretation, such as Seton-Karr's Andaman image (Figure 6), and woman in Hollywood as a sign of 'excess', of what Doane describes as 'the peculiar susceptibility to the image – to cinematic spectacle in general – attributed to woman in our culture' (1987, p. 1). She gives the example of Mia Farrow in 'spectatorial ecstasy enraptured by the image' of a movie screen in *The Purple Rose of Cairo* (1984). The simple substitution of 'other' for 'woman' which I have proposed throughout this paper doesn't account for the complexity of Figures 6 and 7 but it gives at least some purchase on the nature of their extraordinary power.

There are transpositions and inversions of great subtlety here, but it does suggest that *looking* of a different kind is unable to transcend that wider system of looking which I have called here, metaphorically, film. The role of Mia Farrow is here assumed by twenty Andamanese men, and a small girl in white plays the role of staged spectacle, drawing their looks.

Figure 7, the frontispiece to André Singer's and Leslie Woodhead's survey of the *Disappearing World* series, suggests further complexities. We believe that the Mursi are watching 'themselves', they think of it as 'a box full of spirits' (Woodhead 1987); for Leslie Woodhead, who made this photograph, it was a transcendent visitation on an altar in a huge green cathedral. The moving image reverts to the still, the image which for Woodhead has become the film and an image which is interpreted in terms of a painting (Woodhead 1987, p. 7).

Our conclusion need only reiterate Mary Anne Doane's observation that,

The major breakthrough in feminist film theory has been the displacement of its critical focus from the issue of the positive or negative representations of images of women, to the question of *the very organization of vision and its effects*. (1987, p. 176, emphasis added)

It is now time that those who write and think about ethnographic film made a similar decisive break.

### Notes

1 One might make the argument that the possibility of the Zande net being 'art' depends on the fiction of the separability of such objects from the utilitarian world – it is the very boundedness of the net which removes it from the world of tools. However, this fiction cannot be perpetually maintained since there is always the possibility of 'opening', always the potential reversion to the world of tools indicated by Vogel. It is thus appropriate that within Danto's culturally contextualised Hegelian argument it is the prime example of an object which 'looks like' (has a perceptual contiguity with) 'Art' but is not: 'This net is included in this exhibition as an artefact that bears a completely spurious resemblance to a work of modern art. No one concerned – least of all the Zande – would have mistaken this tool for an art object.' (Danto 1988, p. 174). In other words, objects, like images and books, always speak of others of their class and can never be endowed with an entirely sufficient self-presence.

2 In a series of simple diagrams, Berger attempts to show that meaning can be extended

not simply along a narrative line but in all directions, as though the instantaneous image were an expanding circle. Events can be extended beyond themselves (1982, p. 121):

> The appearances of the event photographed implicate other events. It is the energy of these simultaneous connections and cross-references which enlarge the circle beyond the dimension of instantaneous information...the discontinuity which is the result of the photographic cut is no longer destructive, for on the photograph of the long quotation another kind of meaning has become possible. (*ibid.*)

3   I mean here 'mythic' specifically in Lévi-Strauss's sense of myths as 'machines for the obliteration of time' (1970, p. 16), but there are parallels with the dichotomy, established by commentators as diverse as Forge (1979) and Lyotard (1971), of art versus propositional language and *figure* versus *discourse*.

4   Constance Penley asks whether:

> presenting an image of a filmic process, even the process of the 'coming into presence' of the very film we are watching, is a way of making that process, the image of that process, more 'there', less imaginary (because truly 'present'), more directly apprehendable by perception. If the cinematic signifier shares the characteristic structuration of the Imaginary, then to insist on the *presence*, the 'materiality' of the image, would that not be to simultaneously (if unconsciously) insist on its *absence*? Indeed, would it not risk moving the imaginary quotient up another notch? To show the film in its materiality – for example to film a strip of film, or to emphasize the screen as surface through projecting not images, but clear light onto the screen – is to show the film in its 'materiality' at the very moment that it is no longer film. (1989, pp. 11–12)

## References

*Books and articles*

Berger, J. and Mohr, J. (1982), *Another Way of Telling*, Readers and Writers, London.

Brunette, P. and Wills, D. (1989), *Screen Play: Derrida and Film Theory*, Princeton University Press, Princeton.

Carroll, D. (1987), *Paraesthetics: Foucault. Lyotard. Derrida.* Methuen, London.

Clifford, J. (1988), 'On Orientalism', J. Clifford, *The Predicament of Culture. Twentieth-Century Ethnography, Literature, and Art*, Harvard University Press, Cambridge, Mass.

Comolli, J.-L. (1985), 'Machines of the visible', in G. Mast and M. Cohen (eds.) *Film Theory and Criticism*, Oxford University Press, New York.

Collier, J. (1986), *Visual Anthropology* revised edn., University of New Mexico Press, Albuquerque.

Danto, A. C. (1988), 'Artifact and art', S. Vogel (ed.), *ART/Artifact: African Art in Anthropology Collections*, Center for African Art, New York, pp. 18–32.

Derrida, J. (1976), *Of Grammatology*, Johns Hopkins Press, Baltimore.

Doane, M. A. (1987), *The Desire to Desire: The Woman's Film of the 1940s*, Macmillan, Basingstoke.

Eco, U. (1982), 'Critique of the image' in Victor Burgin (ed.), *Thinking Photography*, Macmillan, Basingstoke.

Faris, James C. (1988), 'ART/artifact: On the museum and anthropology', *Current Anthropology*, 29, pp. 775–9.

Forge, A. (1979), 'The problem of meaning in art' in S. M. Mead (ed.) *Exploring the Visual Art of Oceania*, University of Hawaii Press.

Foucault, M. (1970), *The Order of Things*, Tavistock, London.

Harper, D. (1987), 'The visual anthropological narrative', *Visual Anthropology*, I, 1, pp.

1–21.

Holmes, O. W. (1864), *Soundings from the Atlantic*, Sampson Low, Son and Marston, London.

Krauss, R. (1985), 'Photography's discursive spaces' in R. Krauss (ed.), *Originality of the Avant-Garde and Other Modernist Myths*, MIT Press, Cambridge, Mass.

Lyotard, J.-F. (1971), *Discours, figure*, Klincksieck, Paris.

Lyotard, J.-F. (1989), 'Acinema' in A. Benjamin (ed.), *The Lyotard Reader*, Basil Blackwell, Oxford.

Metz, C. (1985), 'Photography and fetish', *October* (Fall), 34.

Mulvey, L. (1989), 'Visual pleasure and narrative cinema' in Mulvey (ed.), *Visual and Other Pleasures*, Macmillan, Basingstoke.

Penley, C. (1989), 'The avant-garde and its imaginary' in C. Penley, *The Future of an Illusion: Film, Feminism and Psychoanalysis*, Routledge, London, pp. 3–28.

Pinney, C. (1990), 'The quick and the dead', *Society for Visual Anthropology Review*, VI, 2, pp. 42–54.

Rabinow, P. (1977), *Reflections on Fieldwork in Morocco*, University of California Press, Berkeley.

Sontag, S. (1964), 'Against Interpretation', *Evergreen Review*.

Vogel, S. (ed.), (1988), *Art/Artifact: African Art in Anthropology Collections*, Center for African Art, New York.

*Films*

Allen, W. (1984), *The Purple Rose of Cairo*, Orion (USA). Colour, 82 mins.

Nairn, C. (1974) *The Kawelka – Ongka's Big Moka*, Granada Television, 'Disappearing World' series. Colour, 52 minutes (Anthropologist: Andrew Strathern).

# Admissible evidence? Film in anthropology

I shall argue against the observational film-makers who treat films as free-standing creations, that as anthropologists we most fruitfully admit films in evidence when we can relate them most effectively to sources outside the film itself. Many films have been preceded by ethnography, or give rise to additional ethnography as a by-product of the filming process, so films do not need to be thought of as 'stand-alone' texts.[1] Secondly, I shall argue that the anthropological academy should drop its defensiveness about film as a learning and knowledge channel, and start to see those films which are thoughtfully made, as valuable repositories of cultural knowledge.

In the 1980s more anthropologists came to see the 'ethnographic record' in written anthropology as something more open-ended and provisional than we once supposed. This meant seeing our informants as more rounded than they had been as producers of kinship systems, economic data, myths and cosmo-logies. It became easier to value them for their songs, poems, laments, and worldviews, and to learn from their ways of thought. For some of us, films played an important part in this opening up of the things we felt able to treat as the proper subject matters for anthropology.

I wish to discuss a number of modalities with which documentary films communicate to us. I am not describing 'five types of films', since the modalities simply characterise passages in a film. Any given film can employ several of them, one after another. The modalities are abstractions, derived partly from a reading of the film-makers' intentions, partly from the ways the films are likely to be perceived and used by us.

The ground chosen to illustrate my view is representations of death in film, since although death is notoriously our universal fate, it is also, paradoxically, as subject to cultural elaborations as most other things which affect us.

## Documentation modality

First, I would like to discuss that aspect of a film which works to record or document what happens in front of lens and microphone. In the modern world we can point to ciné film records of vegetation growth, metal stress, bank robberies and, recently, children's court testimony where the child's identity needs to be protected, but the nuances of its evidence need to be available for court scrutiny.

Certain uses of film produce documents, in the historian's sense. They do not suggest that any document is to be taken at face value, or presents the whole truth and nothing but the truth about the events it depicts. Documents are routinely assumed to be interested, not impartial or disinterested; incomplete, and sometimes misleadingly unrepresentative. And at least one eminent historian, Marc Bloch, has written at length on the problem of forgery in historical sources.

Properly used and properly qualified, a film which documents the way something happened can offer academic anthropology records of lasting value. The still camera and the tape recorder were granted rapid, and virtually unquestioned acceptance by most anthropologists, for their basic 'recording' capacities. Malinowski's brilliant photographs, which adorned *Argonauts of the Western Pacific,* and *Crime and Custom in Savage Society* have never to my knowledge been subject to destructive criticism; and the collection of sound tapes with versions of myths, rituals, life-histories, music and song is an unremarkable matter in modern fieldwork. But film has had much slower and more cautious acceptance.

I wish to describe an extract from an early Disappearing World film, called *The Meo,* transmitted in 1972. The director was Brian Moser, the anthropologist, Jaques Lemoine, who had by then been working with Meo-speakers for eight years, and the film editor was Dai Vaughan. The filming was in North-East Laos, and the theme of the film was how the hill tribes of the region were trying to avoid being drawn into the war which was dominating their lives. The film starts with the sound of bombing in a valley, a sound which jars with our normal expectations of rural peace. Army units from both sides are reportedly pressing the villagers to join their forces.

We witness an exorcism to drive out the evil spirits who have fastened on a family due to an involuntary fratricide. Villagers declare 'The country is troubled and rotten'.

Then the film moves to a refugee settlement, where half the women are widows. We hear stories of people who have moved home a dozen times in as many years and see apathetic men smoking opium and incapacitated by injuries. A funeral takes place, which the film simply records without comment. We hardly need to be told that it is a funeral, but although we do not learn whose funeral it is, and the cause of the person's death, we are given a sense of how the mourners lament in this society, and how they group themselves around the corpse and the most closely bereaved. It is an enigmatic, lowering sequence. The earlier sequences of the film have been rich with explanatory commentary, conveying essential features of Meo culture, and the particularities of life in the village Lemoine has studied. The silence of the commentary during the funeral works to create a sense of tension and foreboding. In the extract shown during the public lecture, there are shots of Ban Xon airport, with military airplanes arriving, and the commentator explains that there are 900 military flights a day, moving troops in and out of the war zone. We then see body bags being unloaded from a plane, and carried across the tarmac. The camera then finds a small group of Meo, one a soldier, clustered around a corpse, and we hear a translation of a lament from the weeping soldier:

My little brother, what can I do? I will never be able to forget you. Where are you, my little brother, my little orphan? Ah, my little brother . . . if only I had foreseen your death, I would never have allowed you to go away – I would have forced you to stay with me, always. You are dead, my little brother. How will I ever be able to forget you? Ah, my little brother, why were you not born a girl? Then you could not have gone away to war. You would have stayed with me and you would not now be dead. Ah, my little brother, there were many soldiers in your band, but luck was not with you, my little brother. Little orphan we cannot stay brothers together for ever. My poor little brother could not remain with me all of my life. You are dead. Your body decays and melts for ever into the earth. Even if we could not have made a living together we could have lived on distant mountains and received news of each other. Now I am lone like an orphan. We were poor. There was no way for us to make a living. We have no land any more. I am left an orphan on this painful earth. I have no younger brother to come and help me when I am in need. Our soldiers are only a barrier. We are a fence to protect people of other races. Fighting has overrun our country. We have no homes left and my little brother is dead – he is no longer with me. We have entered the age of misery.

The camera follows one of the body bags and finally comes to rest among a small group of people grouped around one bag. The camera is filming at a distance, with the telephoto perspective of a zoom lens. As the lens brings us closer to the group, we hear the sound of lamentation, and can see that the people are weeping over a corpse which has been returned to them.

We are allowed to see the face of the corpse, although filmed from perhaps twenty feet away, and to see the grief-stricken, tear-drenched faces of several relatives, including a man in uniform, and a woman. As the lament is translated, the images take us away from the group and the corpse and we see shots of young soldiers in the mountains, some in groups, some alone, some smiling, some looking more serious. From time to time we return to the group. Towards the end of the lament, we leave the group and see another body bag being collected at another part of Ban Xon airport. The last images of the film are of a body bag on tarmac, alone.

That extract was chosen for several reasons. First, the film as a whole is a notable document, a film of record from a war zone, and it was doing and saying things which at that time mainstream anthropology had scarcely touched. Soon after the film was released, I had reason to look for writings by anthropologists which came to grips with war. Between 1945 and 1975, there were roughly fifty civil wars in the world, or one for every three members of the United Nations. The anthropological literature did not, with a few honourable exceptions, have much to say about this. In *The Meo* a documentary film-maker and an anthropologist collaborated to convey the impact of a distant war on a small tribal group, a notable expansion of our field of vision. *The Meo* was a historical document with both outreach and staying power.[2]

Another reason to draw attention to this particular sequence is to make plain the sense in which the dramatic narrative logic of the film would not permit the sort of 'additional information' which so many anthropologists have so often called for, when reviewing television documentaries. The lament for the dead brother is, for most of us, so moving we forget to ask clever ethnographic questions about brother relations in Meo culture, but simply imagine losing 'a dead loved person, a close relative' – one level of abstraction above the particularities of two brothers.

But once our empathic responses have had full expression, perhaps as anthropologists (whose professional deformation is sometimes to ask disquieting questions) we might start to think about that testimony of bereavement, a lament, and to want to understand it more fully, to know more about either this lament, or other laments among Meo people. The ethnographic questions could then be imagined, easily enough: Did we hear the whole lament? Was it largely spontaneous? (It certainly appeared to be). Was it unique, or part of a wider body of similar laments, thrown up by the war? Did it draw much from older traditions? Would it normally have been a public act, or a more private one?

To raise these questions so soon after the material has been at work on us has an alienated and distanced aspect, but it is also exactly what we do whenever we struggle to put into formal terms 'information from the field'. Death and a lamentation are specially sensitive, but the principle is the same for almost all cultural information.

However, to have attempted to answer such technical questions within that film, and at that point in the film would have been tastelessly inappropriate, in human and aesthetic terms. Earlier in the film there was a good deal of serviceable information about Meo culture, framing and framed by the dilemmas of peasants trying to avoid being dragooned into the war, but the film-makers definitely knew when to stop giving us conceptual information.

To suggest the film was a film of record is not to suggest a simple record, or the lack of a position taken towards the material. The editing of the lamentation sequence deliberately moved from the grief of the small group to raise questions about all the other Meo already drawn into the war, by moving away from the bereaved group to scenes of other soldiers, and wider contexts. It would have had a quite different effect if the images had remained those of the particular group of mourners. We would have been invited to think of the particular family and its loss, rather than to consider the impact of war on all the Meo, and other equally vulnerable peoples.

We can easily imagine another film, intended for students of anthropology rather than a more general audience, on a vertical axis to the horizontal line of this one, about how the Meo cope with death more generally, and the forms of lamentation in Meo culture. In such a film the same material could appear in a different 'position', and could be given a greater degree of supporting information, and it would not need to seem alienated or distanced; indeed, it could seem exactly what was needed.

## The explanatory mode

In the early days of cinéma vérité, and its lineal descendant, observational cinema, there was some fairly heavy propaganda from the film-makers and film teachers on commentary. It was allegedly authoritarian (the 'voice of God'), obstructive, and at worst, could make untruthful arguments which were unsupported by the film-as-evidence.

Observational doctrine held that the uncut shot, the long camera take, supported by the actual location sound and little more than a few times and dates, could allow events to speak for themselves, and to yield up their significance. The cinematographer Richard Leacock put it all very succinctly when he remarked that he hated to be told what to see, as opposed to 'seeing it for himself'.

This doctrine seems to have been conceived for situations where people were watching films about their own cultures, in their own languages. It is not at all clear how observational filming of an unfamiliar ritual in an unfamiliar culture could possibly yield up its meaning, as Parry (1989) has been at pains to point out. In an art gallery, I cannot unpack the symbolism of Botticelli's painting 'Primavera' by staring at it. To see is not to perceive, still less, to comprehend. There is a lot I need to know about the symbolism of the period, its ways of thought. So with film: if you bring enough experience or knowledge to the text, you need no help. But all of us need help with most other cultures much of the time. Commentary of some kind, whether in words, or in inter-titles, is often essential if we are to avoid bewilderment and misapprehension.

For anthropologists, the basic point of friction with observationalism's anti-exegetic stance was in the difficulty of a culture translating itself through action. The observational doctrine would have been acceptable to academic anthropology if it had gone on to say that the documentary film was not[3] *intended* to stand alone, but positively required a supporting written text. However, this was not the way observational cinema dealt with the issue, for the doctrine came from working cinematographers and film-teachers, and it sometimes appeared to be an attempt to make ethnographic films without either ethnographers or ethnography! Ethnography as a discipline was marginalised, and tainted with implied elitism – for wasn't everyone with eyes and ears 'doing ethnography' more or less all the time? The anthropologist was gently exhorted to suspend the right to conceptual comment, and to disappear up the observational rope, as silently as possible.

My next example is a film by Ian Dunlop, Howard Morphy and Dundiwuy

Wanabi, called *Madarrpa Funeral at Gurka'wuy*. The subtitle is 'a way of coping with death, in north-east Arnhem Land through ties of clan, religion and land'. The title accurately signals both the documentation and explanatory intentions.

The film deals with the cycle of rituals carried out when a young child died. It is 87 minutes long, and early on, there is a 2-minute sequence using animation of a map to show how the funeral affects a number of different local groups over a large area, and how the clan ancestors, in the Dreamtime, relate to the named areas. This is explained by Dunlop, in a measured and deliberate manner:

Today, the body of the Madarrpa child will be buried at Gurka'wuy on Marrakulu clan land of the Dhuwa moiety. But at the same time the child's spirit will be symbolically taken through Yirritja moiety's sacred places to its own clan land on Blue Mud Bay. Each phase of the funeral ceremony will embrace different clan land, and the journeys of different clan ancestral beings.

Gangan is about 60 km inland from Gurka'wuy. It is one of the most sacred areas for the Dhalwangu clan, the important mother's mother's clan to the dead child. This morning the men will continue singing of the ancestral beings at Gangan, while they continue painting sacred emblems from this country on the child's coffin. Then, in a Gumartj clan ceremony from Biranybirany in Caledon Bay, the child's body will be made ritually free to be placed in the coffin.

The singing will then return to Gangan. The men will dance the rushing waters of the wet season, sweeping down into the Gangan River, as they bear the painted coffin to the child. Next the child's spirit will be symbolically taken down the flooding rivers by Dhalwangu and Madarrpa Water Snake, to its own clan land at Djarrakpi. The child will be placed in its coffin and taken towards the grave. Finally, the ancestral crocodile spirit will take the child's spirit from Djarrakpi to Gunmurrutjpi to the sacred waters of the Madarrpa clan. Here Baru will make its nest. The child will be laid in the grave.

Dunlop's commentary continues to give context to the pictures: 'The shade for the baby's body, and beyond, the camp of Marrira, father of the dead child. The men are singing outside one of Marrira's huts. Inside the hut, the coffin is being painted.'

The camera now moves closer to a group of men with clapsticks, who are singing, and Dunlop continues: 'Nepaynga leads a Dhalwangu song about Wurrany the long-necked diving duck. It is on a log in the Gangan river, looking down into the water for fish'. The seated men chant, and click their clapsticks. They sing:

Diver bird in the paper bark swamp
Diving for fish . . .
Diver bird, sitting on a log
Shaking his feathers,
Diver bird, shaking his feathers,
Drying himself in the sun . . .

For the rest of the extract, the camera follows groups of men, and of women, who variously sing and dance, and in each case Dunlop identifies them for us by name, and states their kinship and clanship relation to the dead child.

In order to make the best, the wisest use of any film document which comes our way, we can ask, as a historian would do, for the fullest contextualisation of the information the document purports to present. *Madarrpa Funeral* has a good deal of very thoughtful explanatory narrative from Ian Dunlop to help us through what would otherwise be largely inaccessible material. We are able to follow the child's body through to the final interment, which is powerful, and involving. Without explanatory help, commentary or intertitles, we would literally not know what was going on, or who was who. Dunlop was concerned not to intrude upon grief, so a filming style in which the film-makers keep asking the subjects to identify themselves, and explain what they are doing was not an attractive option.

However, in this case, the film is only half the story. The other half is provided by a monograph by Howard Morphy (1984), the subtitle of which describes itself as an accompanying monograph to the film, and gives us a sustained interpretation of the complex symbolism of the clan laments, songs, and dances which we have seen on film, as well as an account of the filming. And because of the richness of the material, and the subtlety of interpretation, there would have been no way that the film could have simultaneously moved forward with the mourners, while standing still to unpack the exegetic burden, a point Morphy himself makes eloquently (p. viii). Indeed, his preface in a few hundred words gives a lucid contrast between the capacities and disabilities of the two media, film, and ethnographic writing.

This is the point to note that 'contextualisation', a modish word in anthropology, has two senses. Contextualisation internal to the text, implies how an event, custom, opinion are made comprehensible within the film, or article. But the other sense, equally important, refers to what other information resources exist external to the film or article, which will help situate it more completely.[4] The normal scholarly references to the work of other scholars, and the listing of sources are a conventional part of such contextualisation when we are writing but documentary films have not routinely taken on any functionally similar methods. Pure film-makers will shudder at the thought of being asked to think about the absence of footnotes, appendices, and cross-references in their films, but I am not suggesting any literal transfer of functions! Rather, that the absence of explicit contextualising conventions makes us have to think more about what we are looking at, than when we read a scholarly paper.

The epistemological implications of this point have yet to reach the film schools, although they are built into the examination regulations for the Manchester University MA in Visual Anthropology, and Robert Boonzajer's Amsterdam University course, where for their final projects, students are required not only to submit a finished film, but to submit a complementary essay which gives the film the intellectual background which will make it more richly informative. The film is thus 'freed' from the burden of too much exegesis, but the task of explanation is not allowed to go by default – on the contrary.[5]

## Explanation rejected

I wish to move to a very different film modality, one which rejects conceptual explanation root and branch. It is also time to remind readers that the modalities discussed may either characterise a whole film, or, more probably, a passage in a particular film. It is a well-accepted feature of documentary film-making that if a strongly explanatory passage has been constructed, it is aesthetically desirable to allow the film to 'breathe' for a while without further commentary, while the audience takes on board the information just offered, and is allowed the pleasure of watching images and hearing sounds without the intervening distraction of conceptual statements. Thus, films move from modality to modality, like passages at different tempi in musical composition.

But if a whole film rejects explanation, this is rather different from merely having the occasional passage free from commentary. A controversy about the value of such film within anthropology recently enlivened the pages of the Society for Visual Anthropology's *Review* and the issue has been the film-maker's deliberate refusal to explain. The film-maker in question is Robert Gardner, and the film, *Forest of Bliss* uses no commentary, no translations of speech, and hardly any intertitles. The film is a radical challenge to see what can we learn from looking, and listening. I shall discuss only the issues raised by Jonathan Parry (1989), partly for reasons of space, and partly because he alone of the film's rejectionists has spent any time in Benares, speaks the local language and writes authoritatively about the city.

Parry complains, firstly, that he cannot understand Gardner's intentions. If *Forest of Bliss* is a film about death in Benares, it can only be described as a determinedly lopsided one. It overstates the dark side, and understates the light. Secondly, the film is either unintelligible, or misleading about the ethnography of Benares. Thirdly, Parry suspects that the film will suggest to many Western audiences that Benares and Hinduism are an ineffable world apart which must elude our comprehension; that 'No explanation is possible'. Finally, he expresses deep unease about the commentary-free film as a vehicle for anthropological knowledge (I shall not deal specifically with this last point because the whole chapter is an attempt to address it).

Do Parry's criticisms do the film justice? First, Gardner's intentions: he signals to us the conventions by which we might best approach his film in perfectly intelligible ways. The information is offered us up-front, quite literally, in the opening film title, and what goes with it, the 'setting-up' of the film, and our expectations. The film is *not* called 'The sacred geography and ritual practices of a Hindu city' but something allusive, that we cannot yet react to, unless we happen to know certain Sanskritic texts and how they refer to Benares. Then, there is an authorial signature which takes full personal responsibility for the film, after the main title, 'a film by Robert Gardner'. There is also the epigraph from the poet W. B. Yeats, which gives us the leitmotif for the film:

Everything in this world is eater or eaten,
the seed is food and the fire is eater.

The fact that the film does not start with commentary or inter-titles on the importance of Benares to Hinduism, invites us to put this particular set of expectations away, and react to a different kind of film.

As the film develops, it became clear to me, and to some other viewers (e.g. Ostor (1989), Chopra (1989), Oppitz (1989)) that it is neither about 'death in Benares' in an ethnographic sense nor 'Benares as a city'. The film uses Benares but as a microcosm, in all its particularity, for a meditation in images and sounds on the intertwining of life and death, the cycles of ageing and youth, the interdependence of bodily life and spiritual attempts to control dissolution. Ambiguity, movement, process, the passing of time, purification, pollution, are all expressed as recurrent themes, but as images, rather than conceptual statements: a very brief shot of sand blowing off a ledge; an empty courtyard; an empty scale; a still patch of ground with smoking coals. These images are intended to convey dissolution, emptiness, absence, the condition of the person after death. Just as Chekhov ends *The Cherry Orchard* with the sound of an axe falling on the trees, to mark the passage of a social order, so Gardner uses hammering, rowing, bells ringing, and many other sounds to suggest the passage of time. The aim is to evoke thoughts in us by sounds and images, but not to tell us in formal conceptual terms what to think, or what to make of it. If we are reminded of Needham's thoughts on 'Percussion and Transition'(1967) we can see why Gardner has chosen highly appropriate sounds to make us aware of time, life, passing.

Parry's third criticism suggests the possibly harmful impact upon audiences. This is a minefield, and I would not be rash enough to assert that this, or any other film cannot evoke negative, dismissive reactions in some people. If the film denied people the power to think, or read, or it was the only exposure they would ever have to any form of knowledge about India, I might begin to share Parry's concern. But in my view, those likely to be hostile to Hinduism and its funerary customs would not be rendered less hostile by explanations about what is going on in the film. Precisely because it is *not* the only available source of information about Benares, neither Benares nor Hinduism require 'protection'. The genuinely curious viewer has, after all, Parry's ethnography for guidance, and many other scholarly works. We can read Parry on Benares, and we can watch Gardner's film. It does not matter which we do first, and we do not have to chose between them, although we will prefer one or the other for different purposes, and different constituencies.

It has simply been an error of judgement, and a category mistake, to treat this film as an ethnographic film gone wrong. It never tried to be one. The mistake is like mistaking a novel for a medical treatise, a racehorse for a work-horse, an orchid for a lettuce. Gardner is more like a Symbolist painter than a recording angel, more like Gauguin painting Tahitians than Goya recording the horrors of war. It makes better sense to understand how his films are made, and how they depart from the documentation and explanatory modalities of film than it does to mis-read them and inveigh against him.[5]

## Context enrichment

My fourth film modality can be thought of as '*research context-enrichment*'. I prefer this to the heavily-used term 'reflexivity', because it directs our attention away from the observer, back towards the process of inquiry, and the fruits of inquiry. It was probably the Rouch and Morin film *Chronique d'un été* which made us see that film need not take a passive recording role, but could be a catalytic agent. Another example is *Waiting for Harry* by Kim McKenzie, Les Hiatt, and Frank Gurramanamana.

The plot involves a group of people have come together to complete a reburial on clan lands of an Anbarra man who had been previously buried somewhere else. Anthropologist Hiatt is there both as a relative of the chief mourners, Frank Gurramanamana and Harry Diama, and to continue his inquiries. The film is mostly about the fact that Harry, absolutely essential for the completion of the ritual, is continuously called away on business, and the ritual is threatened with the defection of other participants, particularly a group who arrive by boat from Cape Stewart, and who left in a huff at a previous funeral because the drawings were not good enough. In the course of telling this story, the film also manages to get across to us, in a thoroughly informal and undidactic manner, some very attractive features of the ritual – the painting of the coffin, the highly poetic clan songs, and the slow rhythms of life among this group. At one point, Hiatt's commentary voice explains that although the ceremony was nearing a climax, Harry went off to town again:

The gannet dance seems to be a signal to the women and children that the ceremony is reaching a climax. But Harry returned to Maningrida again. In two days he was due to attend a court case involving his son. The next day his absence caused problems, because the Cape Stewart men were pressing for the ceremony to end as soon as possible.

These follow a shot of Frank, alone, looking perplexed and worried.

*FG* Harry would be angry with me. Not just a little bit, but arguments, fights. No good. If Harry comes, we could finish . . . [he starts to walk out of frame to the left, and the camera pans right to find Les Hiatt, who starts walking away, slowly, thoughtfully, right, past the Toyota truck.]
*FG* You go and get him. Or the cameramen. Pick him up and come back.
[*LH* nods, but also grunts, wearily, and worriedly.]
*LH* Aaaaahhhh, dear . . .
[two-shot, Frank and Les.]
*FG* [speaking Anbarra] If Les goes now in his car, we'll be ready to break the bones when Harry comes. We'll take the coffin, put in the bones, then go to the camp straight away. In daylight . . . we'll finish . . . then people can return to wherever they live. Like that.
*LH* Suppose I go to Maningrida and Harry says to me,But the court case isn't finished?
*FG* Come Back.

*LH* By myself?

*FG* By yourself. [he laughs]. That's it, Les. We've talked enough. We'll finish . . . there'll be nobody left here.

*LH* [addressing the sound recordist, in English]: It looks as though I'll have to go to Maningrida. And try and get Harry. No-one's going to do anything till he comes. Frank's given an order – he's given an order to me, now. We can't do anything until I go into Maningrida. If Harry won't come back . . . [the camera pulls back from a tight shot on L.H. to find F.G., and a group of five or six listening men] Well, we can't help it. But, only one thing . . . [speaking now in Anbarra language and looking rather tense]: I don't want to miss anything. I want to see the lot!

*FG* [smiling, in Anbarra]: Calm down, Les. These bones are yours . . . the bones of your brother.

*LH* O.K., but if I miss anything . . . [his face starts to break from tension into a smile] I'll . . . *swear at the lot of you*! [General laughter . . . He rises to his feet to go.]

A shot of the Toyota driving off towards Maningrida ended the extract.

This film provides us with insights into the nature of field research, filming, the organisation of death ritual and the politics of Aboriginal group management.

On field research, we are able to see some fruits of Hiatt's 22-year association with this group, and the way it has placed him in a specific kinship status. We can appreciate the sense in which he gains information by participation, but also the sense in which the method dictates its own peculiar constraints. He is in no sense a free agent. When ordered to do something by a senior man, he does it as cheerfully as he can. The image of the anthropologist as ruthless exploiter is put into serious question, for this situation at least.

The insight into filming concerns the need for patience, for filming what is going on as it unfolds, rather than 'waiting for the ritual to start' and then starting to film. The preparations are part of the event, and any line between ritual performance and essential preparations would be intellectually somewhat arbitrary. In a sense the film could help us theoretically towards a more holistic view of what constitutes 'the ritual'.

The third insight is the broadening of our understanding of what it means *to perform a ritual properly* in this sort of society. There are preparations; they have to be executed to certain standards; the essential personnel must be present. When all these things have happened, the ritual has been properly performed.

The fourth insight concerns the politics of leadership and management. The precariousness of the process and the event come through clearly. We get a sense of the pull of externalities; of the outside world pressing in on this group's attempt to constitute itself as a modified traditional society.

The film as research method, recording, probing, and sometimes being an agent or actor in the events allows us, through the addition of subtitles, to form a better understanding of the nature of the inquiry, and therefore of the quality of the material obtained. It makes field inquiries more accessible, and 'thicker' in Geertz's sense. We have words, plus intonations, plus pauses, plus facial expressions, and even a suggestion of the elusive quality of the relationship between anthropologist and informants, matters which an anthropologist alone might have difficulty writing about. Since the participants refer so often to the film and its importance, we may at some point have to decide whether this is a 'simple' document, or more plausibly, a 'metadocument'. But that is true of much written ethnography, too, which is normally something much more complex than a selection of field notes (primary documents) between two covers. The process of inquiry needs to be understood if we are to appreciate that which we are pleased to call, our information.

Context-enrichment is, surely, one of the great strengths of ethnographic film. We learned from *Chronique d'un été* not to be afraid to allow the film-making process to lead an inquiry, provided it does not, to change the metaphor, lead the witnesses, and bamboozle the jury. If we make it fairly plain how we have gone about asking our questions, and editing the responses, then film and video take rather good quality fieldnotes, alongside their documentation and explanation modalities.[6]

### Experience and theoretical understandings

The fifth kind of film modality involves engagement with individual experience, not experience in some transcultural vacuum, since all experiences are culturally mediated and constrained. We can be bicultural, and if particularly versatile, tricultural but never transcultural!

The presentation of experience increasingly demands our attention both as writers and film-makers, firstly, perhaps, because it helps us bring human subjects into a thinking which is otherwise too easily dominated by abstract, formal categories. There are good theoretical reasons why we should do this, too: it is not a matter of a misplaced enthusiasm for warm-blooded people: scepticism, non-conformity, and innovation as agents of change in social systems may be more identifiable through the experiences of singular persons, considered one at a time. One classic case of showing this is in cargo cult leadership in Melanesia. Why do cults arise? For all kinds of reasons, but partly because individuals prophesy. Who are the individuals who do this? Social actors with untypical life experiences, who have lived among Europeans, travelled beyond the local area, and so forth.

Instead of getting myself into difficulties by trying to stipulate what I mean by 'experience' I shall simply point at an example, and discuss its claims to our attention at some length. The film is *Goodbye Old Man* (1977), filmed on Melville Island off the coast of Australia. It was the second film produced by the Australian Institute of Aboriginal Studies about Tiwi death rituals. The first was made by Curtis Levy, with the same group of people, and was a strong explanatory documentation film which the Tiwi were keen to have made. Levy then took David MacDougall to Melville Island, which resulted in the second film, which has a markedly different style and concentrates on more subjective aspects of the ritual.

The film begins by identifying a number of people who have been bereaved by the death of an elderly kinsman. We then hear from Eleanor Brook, who tells the Tiwi myth of the origin of death, which arose when the culture hero Prokuparli's wife committed adultery with the Moon man, after which her son died. We then follow a party of people getting ready for a second burial ceremony. The film then returns to Eleanor Brook, a niece of the dead man. It is important to understand that Curtis Levy is present in this extract, screen right, and Eleanor Brook speaks to him some of the time and reminds him of things which happened while he was filming previously. David MacDougall is operating the camera, and he asks Mrs Brook several questions. Mrs Brook becomes more relaxed and confiding as time goes by.

Speaking to the camera, while pointing to persons in a photograph, she recalls them by name, and adds that they are now all dead:

Ah, dear. Wish my father was alive. You know, he was the same like Prokuparli – he used to worry about his younger son. Do you know, my youngest brother, he died when he was 13, of a heart attack. He took the same path like Prokuparli did – he followed his son . . .

I still remember, you know, it was Monday morning. He was lying on (his) bed. He told me, 'Go on, fix my breakfast'. And I said, you promise me you won't die, you won't die when my back is turned? And he said, no, I won't die. I'll wait for you when you come back, and bring my breakfast. So I went and brought 'im breakfast. I sat on his bed and watched him eat and he made me eat (some)thing, and then he told me to get up and get those medals, those ones he wore on his shoulder. I got those medals, and he said, 'You keep them'. And then he gave me a big smile before he died. (I) just can't believe it . . .

*David MacD.* He just knew?

*EB* He just knew. He just told me to get up and get those medals, and he told me to keep them and those spears, but I broke those spears at Carslake last year, you know, the first-time ceremony. He saw me breaking those spears, Curtis. [she nods towards Curtis Levy, screen right]

*David MacD.* Did he say he was following his son?

*EB* Yes, he often told me when he was in bed. 'You know, I'm always hearing your brother's voice calling me to come. People when they're sick, they hear dead people call them, you know, their relatives.'

[She looks down at the photograph, and there is a long silence. She draws the photo closer to her face, and stares intently at it]

For me this sequence has a special quality for an appreciation of innovation in ethnographic film, because it brings me into contact with a person who speaks directly, and relaxedly about what she herself sees as a very important personal experience. We are accustomed to the representation of death rituals among Australian Aboriginal peoples, but these tended to have been filmed as collective actions of a formal nature, with an emphasis on performance. You might have been forgiven had you thought on the evidence of the previous films, and most written ethnography that Aboriginal peoples dealt with death entirely through ritual, and that this somehow dissolved the more individual feelings of grief and loss which Europeans tend to associate with death.

There is, of course, a problem here which I shall point to and pass hurriedly by. It also arose with the Meo film extract. It is a dangerous short-cut for me as an anthropologist to assume I understand what Eleanor Brook felt about the loss of her father. First, she is speaking in my language, and in her own language something significantly different might be expressed. Secondly, there are aspects of Tiwi views of the afterlife which may be so different from my own that my supposed empathy with her may be simply a misunderstanding. So, although empathy has a positive value in my culture, like many other ideas we live by, it carries a warning, 'Handle with caution'. But let me take a risk, and say that her account of her father's death suggests to me that no matter how different our cultural modes of dealing with death, we may both experience the memory of an important death at work within us. Cultural differences make empathy a more complicated emotion, but not an impossible one.

If, however, we are to get this small portion of personal experience back into the frame of social research, we cannot treat it in isolation. What *is* the value of such recorded experiences for formal social theory? Accounts of Tiwi cultural life which ignore experiences like Eleanor Brook's memory of her father's death, are clearly technically 'incomplete', and also run the risk of representing their social actors as Durkheimian robots who perform ritual obligations with a mechanical precision but lacking in appeal, emotions, or, indeed, in distinctive personalities.

There is another way of linking such focal experiences to the concerns of mainstream anthropology. One of the reasons I find Eleanor Brook's account so involving is that it helps me relate intellectually to some otherwise rather abstract ideas which are of theoretical importance, on the cross-cultural understanding of death, particularly the contrast between 'good' and 'bad' deaths. Eleanor Brook's account of her father's death seems to crystallise what might be meant by a good death, and is a properly contextualised piece of ethnographic evidence. And, if we remember the film's opening we will recall that Prokuparli, the Tiwi culture hero, brought death into the world because his wife, through her casual adultery, neglected their infant son, who died as a result. This linking of death to 'irresponsible' female sexuality is, it turns out, a common theme in many cultures. So, the film and its resonances invite me to inform myself further about Tiwi culture, and give substance to my appreciation of a comparative theoretical argument.[7]

## Conclusion

My purpose has been to emphasize some of the things films can do, so that we can think about them more confidently as contributions to mainstream anthropology. That seems to involve some unpacking of the modalities of film as an intentional communication medium. I have been concerned to suggest that the approach to films for anthropology which treats them as one-off, stand-alone texts is too limiting, belonging to the purely entertainment film, to 'going to the cinema', and we should be more ready to think of them as texts gaining depth from their connectedness to other texts.

My last point concerns the challenge of plural learning systems, in the 1990s. We have learned to see film's capacity for making distinctive contributions to our understanding, which do not necessarily give priority to formal conceptual thinking. Paintings and songs do not reach us through quite the same processes as lectures on social theory, or economics textbooks. Learning and understanding occur through a plurality of channels, and film bears some similarity to 'hands on' learning techniques. I am not suggesting that we ever finally escape the conceptual, but we have a plurality of modes of reaching conceptual understanding, and film has a particular value in this. Nor are film and writing in competition: any struggle for domination would be a distortion, caused by a need to dominate, located in practising academics, and academic practices. The varied capacities of film are subtle, and rich enough that they should commend themselves to all anthropologists, once they unlearn the idea that formal conceptual analysis rules the academy – and rules alone.

### Notes

This is the text of the third Forman Lecture, delivered in Manchester on 24 September 1990 to inaugurate the RAI's International Festival of Ethnographic Film. A slightly shorter version was published in *Anthropology Today*, Vii, 1, February 1991. It is reprinted here with the permission of the editor of *Anthropology Today*.

I am grateful to Paul Henley, Peter Crawford, and David Turton for most helpful criticisms of earlier drafts of the lecture and to Jonathan Benthall and Gustaaf Houtmann for their editorial assistance in preparing the manuscript for publication in *Anthropology Today*. The Humanities Research Centre of the Australian National University gave me a chance to think about films in intellectually stimulating company. My thanks to all.

1   In this I am following a tradition of anthropologists and film-makers who argued for the importance of study guides and laboured to produce them. John Marshall, Timothy Asch and Karl Heider are notable early missionaries, as is the Gøttingen Institute for Scientific Film.

2   Moser and Granada had, with the help of anthropologist Bernard Arcand, already contributed one important document of a civil war in miniature, *The Last of the Cuiva*.

3   This crucial negative was left out of the original version of this article, published in *Anthropology Today*.

4   I am indebted to Peter Crawford for helping me see this point clearly.

5   There have been other notable attempts to give ethnographic films textual support. Some are deliberately convergent, like the Marshall/Asch texts for the San (Bushmen) films, and the Asch/Connors/Asch material on Jero; others are parallel, such as Chagnon/Asch examples, and others fairly independent and divergent, such as Dunlop's Baruya films and Godelier's writings.

6   I have written at greater length about Gardner's films, and how to get most out of them, in a book about innovation in ethnographic film, to be published shortly by Manchester University Press.

7   I would not propose that they *replace* conventional written fieldnotes, rather, that the

field worker can obtain high quality field data by judicious and selective video recording, used after sufficient conventional fieldwork.

8    I have in mind the introductory essay in Bloch and Parry (1982).

### References

*Books and articles*

Bloch, M., and Parry, J. (eds.) (1982) *Death and the Regeneration of Life*, Cambridge University Press, Cambridge.

Chopra, R. (1989), 'Robert Gardner's *Forest of Bliss*: a review', *Society for Visual Anthropology Newsletter*, V, 1. pp. 2–3

Morphy, H. (1984) *Journey to the Crocodile's Nest: An Accompanying Monograph to the Film 'Madarrpa Funeral at Gurka'wuy'*, Australian Institute of Aboriginal Studies, Canberra.

Needham, R. (1967) 'Percussion and Transition', *MAN* (NS), 2, pp. 606–14.

Oppitz, M. (1988), 'Review of *Forest of Bliss*', *Anthropos*, LXXXIII, 1–2, pp. 210–11.

Ostor, A. (1989), 'Is that what *Forest of Bliss* is all about ? A response', *Society for Visual Anthropology Newsletter*, V, 1, pp. 4–8

Parry, J. (1989), 'Comment on Robert Gardner's *Forest of Bliss*', *Society for Visual Anthropology Newsletter*, V, 1, pp. 4–7.

*Films*

Dunlop, I. and H. Morphy 1979, *Madarrpa Funeral at Gurka'wuy*, Film Australia, Sydney. Colour, 42 mins.

Gardner, R. (1986), *Forest of Bliss*, Film Study Center, Harvard University, Cambridge, Mass.. Colour, 90 mins.

MacDougall, D. and J. MacDougall (1977), *Goodbye Old Man*, Australian Institute for Aboriginal Studies, Canberra. Colour, 70 mins.

Mckenzie, K. and L. Hiatt (1980), *Waiting for Harry*, Australian Institute for Aboriginal Studies, Canberra. Colour, 57 mins.

Moser, B. and J. Lemoine (1972), *The Meo. Disappearing World* series, Granada Television, Manchester. Colour, 53 mins. (Anthropologist; J. Lemoine)

# Film as discourse: the invention of anthropological realities

Ethnographers are more and more like the Cree hunter who (the story goes) came to Montreal to testify in court concerning the fate of his hunting lands in the new James Bay hydroelectric scheme. He would describe his way of life. But when administered the oath he hesitated: 'I'm not sure I can tell the truth . . . I can only tell what I know.' (Clifford 1986, p. 8)

It may be [objected here] that the other societies did not develop the flexibility to know how to survive modern capitalism, but then as yet we don't know how to survive it either. (Wilden 1987, p. 105)

Recent developments in visual anthropology and ethnographic film-making seem to signal that the ethnographic film has established itself as a common, increasingly widespread, and accepted form of discursive practice within anthropology, alongside other discursive practices, most notably writing. The alleged so-called representational crisis of anthropology (Clifford and Marcus 1986; Marcus and Fischer 1986) has presumably boosted the significance of film-making as an alternative form of representation, competing with alternative literary practices in attempts to overcome what some critical approaches dub as the apparent shortcomings of 'traditional' and 'scientific' conventions of ethnographic writing.

In this chapter I explore the differences and similarities between ethnographic writing and filming or rather between textual and cinematic anthropology, whilst attempting to avoid the common simplifications entailing a perception of the relationship between filmic and written anthropology as that of a dichotomy between 'image' and 'word'. Although it is acknowledged that the word preceded the text and the photographic image the film, one of the main objectives is to demonstrate that film as well as text exist neither as pure image nor as pure word and hence to cast doubt on the frequent treatment of these phenomenon as if they did (see for example Hastrup and Pinney, above).

In spite of the discussions of the representational crisis referred to above, discussions which have led to distinctions between a multiplicity of genres of writing, matters are still presented as pure dichotomies as soon as the relationship between film and text is evoked. Hence, a second objective is to explore how one may distinguish between different styles or maybe even 'genres' in ethnographic film-making, styles which have parallels in the act of writing. The employment of various devices and conventions, such as narrative, in ethnographic film-making, enable us, as Loizos (Chapter 3) shows, to distinguish between a wide range of 'modalities'. In some cases it may be argued that these modalities constitute different types, or genres, leading to assertions about the degree of 'ethnographicness' of particular genres.

Although the concept of modalities, in many ways, and rightfully so, undermines attempts to schematically produce rigid classifications of ethnographic films, these attempts prevail and a third objective of this chapter is to explore in what sense and to what extent these classifications make sense. Referring to previous work (Crawford 1984; 1990) this is done by introducing a distinction between 'small format' and 'large format' ethnographic films on the basis of seven different types of ethnographic film. Basically this distinction coincides with a distinction between two very different audiences for the ethnographic film: that of the general public, notably the 'victims' of broadcasted anthropology, and that of the professionals, i.e. the world of academic anthropology and of film-making. Three modes of ethnographic film are discussed, the perspicuous, the experiential and the evocative, modes which overlap with three filmic approaches I have called the-fly-on-the-wall, the-fly-in-the-soup and the-fly-in-the-I.

The fourth and final objective of this chapter is briefly to comment on a discourse of critique which has described visual anthropology in general and the category of ethnographic film in particular as becoming fossilised and analytically impotent due to the focus on representation and authenticity. Recent examples of challenges, namely the work of Robert Gardner and Trinh T. Minh-ha, to what was apparently becoming stigmatised conventions of ethnographic film-making will be used to illustrate the critical points. The question is whether these new challenges will result in a move within anthropology from representation to evocation (cf. Tyler 1986).

## The word/image juxtaposition

The fundamental problem in all social science is that the facts are always distorted by the person who asks questions. You distort the answer simply by posing the question. (Rouch 1978, p. 22)

Authenticity has been a key concept in discussions concerning the representational crisis of anthropology. The point of departure has been criticism of realism in ethnographic writing and attempts to overcome the pitfalls of scientism and objectivism by, for example, reinstating the subject and allowing for reflexivity –

which (paradoxically) is the only way in which 'proper' authenticity may be achieved. It seems apposite to explore whether, or rather how, these problems are reflected in the practice of ethnographic film-making and in the theoretical debates of visual anthropology. Does authenticity constitute a predicament shared by both written and filmic ethnography and what are the similarities and differences between the various discursive practices of anthropology?

One thesis governs my exploration of the similarities and differences between textual and cinematic anthropology: the two discursive practices or forms of representation are two different *products* of the same (anthropological) *process*, the *producers* of which are engaged in and governed by the communicative conditions of human intersubjectivity. The repercussions of Fabian's often quoted triadic model (Fabian 1971; see for example Ruby 1980 and 1982; Banks, in this book), producer-process-product, are evident.

Following Fabian (1983; 1987), I find it fruitful to suggest a distinction between representation*s* (in the plural) and Representation. This reflects the common usage of the concept in the social sciences and in anthropology in which 'representations' is, or at least was, most often used in the plural. The singular form emphasizes an activity or *process*. By giving priority to the plural, we are talking about entities, *products* of knowledge or culture. Thus, when speaking of anthropology as a process of representation, the product of this process is the Other. Phrasing it in these terms we are operating at an abstract level which we may call epistemological or meta-communicative. At another level, which we may then call an ontological or communicative level, the anthropological process is no longer one process but (at least) two. These processes, which I call *Othering* and *Becoming*[1] have to do with the absence or presence of the anthropological subject and/or object – in other words, with the distance between the subject and object. They are fundamental processes in both written and visual anthropology, the products of which are written or filmic texts. Texts are here defined widely as the *products* of a *process* which may be called context. At yet another level, which is not treated explicitly in this chapter, and which one may call the methodological level, we find several parallel and simultaneous processes taking place in research projects or indeed film projects.

The representational processes of both anthropology and film are paradoxical in the sense that they both require *presence* and *absence* in order to produce meaning and text. In other words, a distance is necessarily imposed between the knower and the known (Fabian 1987, p. 1). The typical example of this in anthropology is, of course, the relationship between the ethnographic field work, when the anthropologist is in the process of 'becoming' the other, and the final anthropological product, the monograph. In the former 'sub-process' the anthropologist is *distancing* him/herself from his or her own culture and in the latter from the culture under study. Hence the anthropological process can be seen as the relationship between 'becoming' and 'othering':

'Becoming' ◄─────► 'Othering'

Although in *practice* these two processes are temporally and spatially divided, as processes of knowledge they are simultaneous or, rather, one cannot pinpoint when the process begins or ends. In other words, what is interesting is not the two poles of the axis depicted above but the relationship between them. Leaving aside for a moment the question of whether the ethnographic film is in itself a process of *knowledge* or merely a technical aid in the anthropological *process* of knowledge, the diagram below attempts to map the ground covered so far and to anticipate what is at stake when drawing parallels between anthropological and filmic processes.

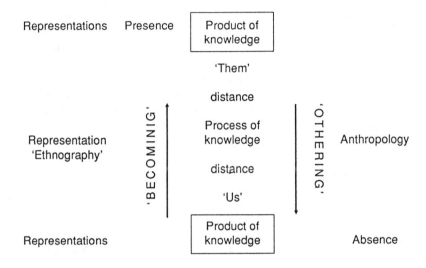

If both anthropology and film are seen not only as processes of knowledge but also as processes of *communication*, we must go a step further and try to understand how the products, which we may choose to call 'texts' or 'messages' are related to the process. Moving to what we can then call the textual level, it is important to bear in mind that this level is context-dependent. Communication covers, here, both communication as a representation *of* reality and communication as *part* of reality.

Wilden's distinction between analog and digital communication has proved to be fruitful when distinguishing between the qualities and characteristics of ethnographic film *vis-à-vis* ethnographic written texts (Crawford 1989). The concepts are derived from cybernetics and the difference between analog and digital 'computers' (Wilden 1972, ch. VII), where the analog computer is defined as any device which computes by means of an analog between real, physical, *continuous* quantities and some other set of variables, whereas the digital '... involves DISCRETE elements and discontinuous scales' (Wilden 1972, p. 156 emphasis in the original). The analog thus pertains to a continuum, a both/and or rather a more-or-less, and the digital to a discontinuum, an either/or. In his later work Wilden adds on a third level, the iconic (1987).

The analog, the digital, and the iconic can be seen as three levels constituting all knowledge and all information. In other words they cover the sensuous (mainly 'governed' by 'brain' = 'nature'), the intelligible (mainly 'governed' by 'mind' = 'culture'), AND the relationship between them. Whereas film predominantly, or at least ideally, exhibits *sensuous* capacities, the written text, especially that of academia, is characterised by its *intelligibility*. Referring to hermeneutics, one could say that film tends to communicate an *understanding*, whereas the written text procures some sort of *explanation*. Referring again to Wilden, these distinctions are coupled with the notion of film being *semantically* rich but *syntactically* weak, whereas written texts are the opposite (1987, p. 138). Relating these simplified distinctions to the models proposed earlier, the filmic text has some intrinsic capacities which convey to the audience a sense of *becoming* (again, of course, ideally) whereas the written text tends to engage in *othering*.

The word/image juxtaposition would suggest, if used to characterise the difference between writing and filming, that words constitute an articulation of reality whereas images are an expression of reality. At an abstract level, the level of language and communication in general, this may be an appropriate distinction but when it comes to actual writing and filming as discursive practices this is no longer the case. In order to be intelligible and explanatory (or articulate) film has to distance itself from its intrinsic 'presence' established by the image's insistence on 'being there'. Writing, on the other hand, wrestles with its intrinsic 'absence' in attempts to diminish the imposed distance between itself and the 'Other' and hence convey a sensuous understanding of what 'being there' is like. In the case of film, distancing is most often achieved by employing digital devices, most notably *words* (for example, narration). In the case of writing, a sensation of presence is conveyed by means of analog elements of communication. This often implies the use of *images*, either in the literal sense, in which photographs are inserted in the text, or by adopting a writing style which loosens the digitalised straightjacket of academic jargon through extensive use of metaphors, word-images (!) and poetics (or, as in this chapter, the stylistic use of epigraphs). In many ways this is what is at issue when Fabian (1983) criticises the visualism of ethnographic writing and when ethnographic film-makers criticise documentary films (especially television documentaries) for being too heavily narrated.

In other words, both ethnographic film and ethnographic writing try to cope with problems arising from the distance between the subject and the object in order to produce better accounts and analyses of other cultures and, paraphrasing Fabian, to avoid the circumvention and pre-emption of coevalness by (re)presenting themselves as the products of human intersubjectivity (Fabian 1983, p. 40ff). Both forms of representation are thus, admittedly from 'opposite' directions, as it were, struggling with an inherent paradox of anthropological theory and practice constituted by the imposition of a distance between 'presence' and 'absence', forcing the anthropologist into a continuous oscillation between 'becoming' and 'othering', between detachment from and attachment to the culture under study. A similar paradox applies to documentary film-making and is eloquently expressed by, I believe, Dai Vaughan when he stated that in order to analyse a film properly one should not mistake it for reality but if one does not mistake it for reality no analysis is possible.[2] Geertz, and others, seem to believe that hermeneutics may provide the means by which anthropology can overcome these paradoxes, the mediator between understanding and explanation being 'interpretation'. This, however, does not *solve* the problem although it admittedly contributes to an awareness of its existence. Scholte has probably given the best description of the interpretative turn of anthropology when referring to 'the charmed circle of Geertz's hermeneutics' (Scholte 1986).

The criticisms made of 'traditional' ethnographic writings are based on their lack of the sensuous, on their digitalised bias. Sensuality has been regarded as unscientific, thus forcing people to write both scientific and 'unscientific' accounts of their findings, through the novel, for example or poetry. On the other hand, some films, such as *Forest of Bliss* (Gardner 1986), have been criticized by anthropologists for being too sensuous, having too little explanation. Hopefully the current debate will establish that the distintions made above *are* analytical, that they are not dichotomies or binary oppositions but relationships. This implies that the word/image juxtaposition may be valid and appropriate when operating at the analytical level of language in general but that when it comes to discourse (film or text), which by definition involves both a subject and a subject-matter (Wilden 1987, p. 132), words and images are constituent elements of both visual and verbal processes of representation. The present focus on key concepts such as reflexivity and subjectivity certainly demonstrates the processual character of representation and the necessity of contextualizing both the text and the producer of the text, the 'author'.

## The verisimilitude of ethnographic film

Film with words is much better at doing most things than it was without words; words (and other sounds) are therefore part of its repertoire and not something inimical to its nature. Film is, to sum the point up, not primarily a visual medium. It is a medium that operates on two of the five senses at once, and it is an uninteresting question to discuss whether or which one of these senses is dominant. (Jarvie 1987, p. 236)

New ways of combining words and images (and sound) in ethnographic writing and filming undoubtedly signal an attempt to include dimensions of the anthropological enterprise which until recently were not acknowledged or regarded as being important in academic circles. The so-called representational crisis of anthropology and the ensuing debates are redefining and reconsidering the forms of what may serve as admissible (or permissible) evidence (see Loizos, Chapter 3 above) in anthropology. 'Objectivity' and 'facts' are being challenged by subjectivity and 'points of view' in the quest for anthropological authority. It has become almost *comme-il-faut* not only to reinstate the subject, the ethnographic 'I', but also, it appears, to ensure that the 'native's point of view' is part and parcel of any ethnographic account. Turning anthropology into a story-telling activity (among other story-telling activities such as film) appears to have been a prerequisite for enabling anthropology to deal with the dialogic, heteroglossic and polyphonic aspects of its encounter with the 'Other'. Ethno-graphic poetics, novels and films are seen as possible alternatives to 'traditional' ethnographic accounts which 'have failed to convey cultural differences in terms of *full-bodied experience*' (Marcus and Fischer 1986, p. 73, emphasis added). Where ethnographic accounts were previously regarded as admissible evidence if they complied with certain scientific rules, it seems that they are now considered permissible evidence if they comply with various conventions of ethnographic discourse.

Whereas ethnographic writing has been renewed, during the 1980s, through inspiration drawn mainly from literary theory and practice, the parallel changes taking place in ethnographic film-making seem to be the result of, on the one hand, new trends in documentary film-making as such and, on the other, the auto-didactic implementation of new cinematic strategies. Although reflexivity, subjectivity, authnticity and the need to listen to 'indigenous voices' have been discussed in ethnographic and documentary film-making for at least thirty years, this seems to have had very little impact on the more recent discussions of ethnographic writing. These discussions, on the other hand, do not seem to have served as an obvious source of inspiration for ethnographic film-makers. The reluctance with which visual anthropology has been accepted as a sub-discipline by 'mainstream' anthropology is probably one of the main reasons for this lack of 'exchange'. Ethnographic film-making has always run the risk of falling between the two stools of anthropology and cinematography. Recent debates and articles, however, seem to indicate that radical changes are taking place. Several 'main-stream' anthropologists[3] have started to intervene in discussions concerning ethnographic film and many visual anthropologists are committed to *writing* about their particular sub-discipline.[4]

If the fundamental similarities between the processes of filming and writing, described above as the oscillation between 'othering' and 'becoming', are accepted and if it is also accepted by now that both forms of representation are engaged in 'story-telling', why is it that film, until recently at least, was treated with suspicion and disbelief by anthropologists? This question becomes even more pertinent once it is realized that many of the issues regarding 'textuality' and 'authenticity' were being discussed by film-makers long before similar questions were raised within anthropology (McDougall 1992).

The relationship between 'reality' and the record, constituting what I call the verisimilitude of ethnographic film, is probably established in the very first phase of the film-making process, the shooting of footage. Unedited footage[5] already contains much of the meaning that will finally exist (if edited) in the final product, the film. The dual nature of film (described by Vaughan in this book), film being both record and language, is evoked as soon as the shooting begins. In the process of ethnographic writing the equivalent of footage would be 'data' stereotypically existing in the form of words in the ethnographer's notebook. At this stage no meaning has emerged (except in the mind of the ethnographer). Meaning is established through textualisation by transforming words into utterances and sentences which are combined in particular ways in the final product (book or article) to convey particular 'meanings'. In film 'utterances' have already been formed in the footage, the image not being the word but the utterance (Heath 1981, p. 109). Unedited film footage may be shown to an audience able to decode the images whereas the data providing the raw material for ethnographic writing needs to go through some degree of codification in order to make (any) sense to others than the producer. This is what I was referring to above when I wrote that film is semantically rich but syntactically weak, the opposite being true of language.

The fundamental difference between the process of ethnographic writing (data → textualisation → text) and filming (footage → editing → film) explains why the 'authority' (or verisimilitude) of written ethnography rests solely on the anthropologist. He or she is responsible for the codification of the final product, the book or article, the raw material of which is uncoded. In film-making, the raw material is already heavily coded. Although the responsibility in the last instance rests upon the director (anthropologist or not), codification relies very much on the contribution of the cameraman, the sound recordist and, most notably, the editor. To use observational film as an example, one of the main points of observational cinema is to leave open the interpretation of the codes that form an inherent part of the film material. This explaines why Richard Leacock once praised observational cinema for allowing the audience to 'see' (for themselves), this being made possible by the camera's 'watching how things really happen' (Leacock, quoted in Blue 1965, p. 18). As MacDougall expresses it, observational cinema shows a 'stance of humility before the world':

Observational films are frequently analytical, but they also make a point of being open to categories of meaning that might transcend the film-maker's analysis. This stance of humility before the world can of course be self-deceiving and self-serving, but it also contains the implicit acknowledgement that a subject's story can often be more important than the film-maker's. (MacDougall 1992)

Observational film with its emphasis on objectivity, neutrality and transparency, has provided anthropological cinema with a filmic strategy which complies with the requirements of modernist ethnographic representation, which presumably is why, to use the words of Banks (p. 124 below), 'observational films form the jewels in the crown of the ethnographic film canon'.

## Ethnographic film as representation

When a movie shows a fairy with seven dwarfs in a flying coach, one knows that such a situation is fictional, even though one trusts the faithfulness of the recording apparatuses shooting it. (Eco 1986, p. 231)

The products of anthropological cinema are usually filmic texts, which means film material edited into a more or less coherent whole. The raw material is footage which, of course, may be used anthropologically, for example, for research purposes. I have chosen to call these products ethnographic films, a category which may be sub-divided into (at least) seven categories according to differences in form, content, purpose, intended audiences, methods, degree of anthropological relevance, and so on.

1. Ethnographic *footage* is unedited film material, which may be used in its unedited form for research purposes or eventually be edited into a film.
2. *Research* films are edited films made specifically for research purposes and hence not intended for public screening or an audience other than a highly specialized academic audience.
3. The ethnographic *documentary* is a film which has a specific relevance to anthropology but which is in one way or another part of documentary film-making in general. I have in mind what one may call 'large format' films, made for the cinema and ideally intended for a wide audience, which means both a specialized and a non-specialized audience.
4. The ethnographic *television* documentary is a film made for, and very often by, a television company, with the intention of reaching a wide non-specialized audience. I call these 'small format' films.
5. *Education* and *information* films are made for educational purposes and meant for classroom audiences or general audiences. They include, for example, films made for instructional purposes in development communication projects and films used in various community contexts.
6. Other *non-fiction* films include journalistic reports, newsreels, travelogues and so on. Today they are mainly made for television but previously were also made for the cinema.
7. *Fiction* films and drama documentaries may be labelled ethnographic because of their subject matter. In recent years, several fiction films have dealt with 'typical' anthropological topics.[6]

The boundaries between the seven categories are obviously fluid and any one film may well fall into several categories. It may, therefore, be more fruitful to follow Loizos's suggestion (Chapter 3 above) and distinguish between different 'modalities' which may be employed in any one film. In the following I shall distinguish three 'modalities' of ethnographic film which tend to overlap the five mentioned by Loizos. These three modalities belong to categories 3 and 4 above. The first two belong to ethnographic film as a representation of culture, whereas the third corresponds to attempts to overcome the limits of representation through 'evocation' in the sense described by Tyler (1986, p. 130). Finally, these modalities roughly coincide with three descriptive categories: the-fly-on-the-wall, the-fly-in-the-soup and the-fly-in-the-I (Crawford 1991).

If, following Metz (1971), we accept that cinematic language consists of five different components (moving visual images, phonetic sound, non-phonetic sound (including 'noise'), music, and writing or written text) the combination of these components determines the ways in which a given film communicates its message or in other words, how it comes to terms with the problems concerning understanding and explanation described earlier in this chapter. The differences in how this is accomplished constitute the differences between the three modalities I have in mind.

I have chosen to call the first two modalities the *perspicuous* mode and the *experiential* mode respectively, indicating that the former tends to emphasise explanatory clarity whereas the latter conveys to the audience an understanding open to interpretation. The perspicuous mode is usually employed by television in its attempts to cater for the needs of a non-specialized mass audience. The visual images, which are handicapped by the size and quality of the television screen,[7] are 'boosted' by the use of, for example, commentary/narration/voice-over, often provided by a 'talking head'. Contrary to what some critics seem to think, this is not necessarily because television people find images inadequate. Apart from the fact that images have less 'punch' in the small format, they are very often ambiguous. In the case of ethnographic film, 'exotic' images standing alone could lead to misinterpretation. The problem, of course, is how to provide the audience with adequate contextual information on the assumption that it would be very difficult to persuade television viewers in general to read ethnographic monographs before watching an ethnographic film. Television as a mass-audience medium must always try to relate 'their' societies to 'ours'. In a sense this means that television is intrinsically 'ethnocentric'.

Whereas the images often tend to emphasise the differences between 'us' and 'them', the verbal information provided by television, often assisted by professional anthropologists, tends to emphasise the similarities between different cultures by using formulas to which we can all relate. Broadcasting companies, being commercial enterprises, also depend on what is regarded as fashionable among their viewers. Very often this means that the general topics of broadcasted anthropology are selected accordingly and explains why many recent ethnographic television programmes[8] have been on issues such as the environment and gender.

To exemplify some of the points made here I will use three examples from Granada Television's *Disappearing World* series, together with one I have invented. Granada Television has in recent years published written material to accompany the programmes in the series. This material has been written by the anthropological consultants to the programmes in a colourful illustrated brochure. My first example is from the accompanying text for *The Kalasha: Rites of Spring* (Sheppard 1990):

Women may be treated as ritually 'impure' in respect of goats and sanctuaries, *but they do have much personal freedom and influence in community affairs*, in marked contrast to the domestic seclusion of women among surrounding Muslims. (Parkes 1990, p. 14, emphasis added)

The following quotation is from the accompanying text for *The Trobriand Islanders of Papua New Guinea* (Wason 1990).

To accumulate huge amounts of bundles [of banana leaves, PIC], a woman needs far more than she can make herself. *Surprisingly*, it is her husband who must spend hundreds of kina to supply her with the surplus she needs. (Weiner 1990, p. 11, emphasis added)

My third example is from the accompanying text for *The Mende of Kpuawala Village* (MacDonald 1990):

But, in spite of their formal subordination to male authority, women do have ways of achieving their goals and protecting their interests. (Ferme 1990, p. 5)

All three films exhibit stunning imagery of the respective cultures, as most *Disappearing World* films do, and, compared with many other ethnographic programmes on television, are informative and interesting. The accompanying texts, however, with their didactic and normative interpretations, using either stereotypes of personal convictions of what is wrong or right, seem to close the avenues open for interpretation by any critical viewer. My final example is an entirely fictional one: a *Disappearing World* programme set in Milton Keynes (a setting very exotic to a Mende or Trobriand Islander): *The English of Milton Keynes*. In the accompanying text, the anthropologist writes:

Although women are in general subjugated by male society, they are allowed to vote at general elections and extra-marital affairs are almost a norm. This, of course, stands in sharp contrast to the social seclusion of Muslim women in Bradford.

Television tends to mediate its exotic images of otherness by using verbal information to relate the images to a conceptual frame recognised by the audience. The 'expertise' of the anthropologist is used not only as an 'entry card' to the portrayed culture but also as an interpreter for an audience which is assumed to be unable, or to lack the time, to carry out this task on its own. The perspicuous mode of ethnographic film is 'ready-made' with a nice wrapping and detailed instructions for use.

Authenticity is conventional (and contextual) in the sense that the devices and conventions employed in ethnographic film-making in, for example, the 1930s, in order to achieve an optimal degree of authenticity, are different from those employed decades later. New technologies have, of course, widened the options open to the film-maker. To appreciate this one need only contrast Bateson and Mead's *Childhood Rivalry in Bali and New Guinea* (1940), an early example of the perspicuous mode where 'authenticity' is achieved through a combination of an unintrusive camera at social distance and a sincere scientific narration by the guarantor of authenticity herself, Margaret Mead, with the work of the MacDougalls in East Africa in the 1970s. In films such as *To Live with Herds* (1972) and *A Wife among Wives* (1981) the intrusiveness of the camera was acknowledged by revealing the presence of the film crew and diminished by a long stay in the field in which people became used to the camera. The authenticising voice no longer belonged exclusively to the film-maker or anthropologist ('exterior' commentary was kept to a minimum by using concise explanatory captions) but was shared by the people filmed, now that subtitling had been introduced.

The use of images in the experiential mode often emphasises the similarities between 'us' and 'them' whereas the verbal components may underline the differences. The hilarious (to a European) dialogue of the film *Under the Men's Tree* (MacDougall 1974) would have an exoticising effect on the audience were it not coupled with the visual images of the facial expressions and gestures of the people involved. What I here call the experiential mode incorporates the use of a number of conventions, many of which have been developed in observational cinema and have almost become rules of ethnographic film-making. Here are some of these 'rules':

— Strong emphasis is given to the visual images that are considered the bearers of the film's meaning. Examples are Jerstad's *A Tibetan New Year* (1987) and *Forest of Bliss* (Gardner 1986), the latter of which exhibits many of the characteristics of the evocative mode I shall briefly describe later.
— A very limited use of narration or commentary and other 'digital' and 'authoritative' devices.
— No or very little use of non-synchronous and unauthentic sound.
— Long takes and no jump cuts. This gives the film a slow pace and rhythm which may accommodate the rhythm of the filmed event. A good example is *Under the Men's Tree* (MacDougall 1974).
— The use of the camera for 'primary' editing, which gives a low ratio of footage to final film.
— When explanation is needed, culturally neutral techniques are employed, such as brief captions, or what MacDougall has called 'interior commentary', where the protagonist or another person in the film or of the filmed culture is used as narrator.
— Subtitling of indigenous dialogue, as in the MacDougalls' *Turkana* films or Marshall's *N!Ai, the Story of a !Kung Woman* (1978).
— The use of the wide-angle lens and avoidance of close-ups.
— Exploratory or intuitive use of the camera, which means no scripts.
— Reflexivity, underlining that 'this is a film' by revealing the presence of the camera and the film crew. *Chronique d'un Été* (Rouch & Morin 1961) is a classical example, *A Wife Among Wives* (MacDougall and MacDougall 1980) a more recent example.

If the perspicuous mode of ethnographic film can be said to reach its audience by means of explanatory devices, the experiential mode invites the audience to understand and sense other cultures by emphasising analog forms of representation open to interpretation. This, of course, does not imply that some films are strictly explanatory while others are merely sensous. All films rely on the relationship between explanation and understanding, a relationship which may be established within the film itself, through links to external accompanying written texts or through 'intertextual' links to other films. Most films of the experiential mode provide contextualisation using all three approaches.

Contextualisation within the film itself may be exemplified by *The Feast* (Asch and Chagnon 1969), the first few minutes of which consist of heavy narration illustrated by still photos, thus 'preparing' the audience for the latter part of the film which provides very little additional explanation. *The Feast* also relates to external written texts, both professional academic texts, the work of the film's anthropologist, N. Chagnon, and texts made specifically to accompany the film. The contextualisation of some experiential films is established only if they are viewed in correlation with many other films in what, in fact, constitutes a series. This is the case in the so-called sequence filming carried out by Marshall among the Ju/wasi of the Kalahari as well as in his Pittsburg police films (Marshall 1991).

The experiential mode, adhering to the conventions listed above, which have almost assumed the status of doctrine, is employed by two filmic approaches which I have called the-fly-on-the-wall and the-fly-in-the-soup (Crawford 1991).[9] The former is used to label observational cinema in which the camera acts as a passive recording device which, as already noted, allows the audience to see and the events to speak for themselves. The latter refers to a filmic approach in which the camera is not merely serving as a passive recorder but intervenes actively in the film process. The intervention may take the form of either catalysing events, as is the case in *Chronique d'un Été*, and/or confer to the film a stance of reflexivity as in *A Wife Among Wives*.

### The fly-in-the-I: from representation to evocation?

Language is not an impediment that gets in the way of our expression, estranging us even from our own passion and pain, nor something we could perfect by transforming it into mathematics. It is not in the way, but on the way, as Highdigger sez. (Tyler 1991, p. 90)

The criticisms launched against traditional modes of ethnographic writing and representation, referred to earlier, seem to be parallelled by new trends in cinema that challenge the doctrines held by the practitioners of the two modes of ethnographic film described above. The perspicuous and experiential modes of ethnographic film both subscribe to a notion of mimetical representation in which concepts such as authenticity, truth, contextualisation and meaning are still regarded as pertinent and desirable. If the advent of Gardner's *Forest of Bliss* confirmed his status as the principal *provocateur* of ethnographic film-making, the recent impact of, and interest in, the work of Trinh T. Minh-ha demonstrates that he is not the only person challenging the doctrines of ethnographic film-making.

Ridicule and irony are significant elements of the films and writings of Trinh T. Minh-ha,[10] which reject the search for authenticity, truth and objectivity embedded in ethnographic representation. If evocation is a feature of post-modern anthropology, transcending the alleged limits of representation, Minh-ha's first film, *Reassemblage* (1982), may be considered a contribution to a postmodern ethnographic film practice which we could label the evocative mode.

In the film she (deliberately) breaks all the 'rules' of ethnographic film. Apart from being a *collage* of image, sound and poetic narration evoking a sensuous impression of Senegal, the film functions as *critique*. The film, as well as her writing (1984), derides many of the conventions of documentary film-making: the long take, for example, and its assumption of life being an uninterrupted process and therefore 'the longer the truer'; the use of hand-held or shoulder-born camera; the use of the wide-angle lens and avoidance of close-ups; the use of synchronous sound; the paternalistic 'giving voice' to the 'Other', 'letting them speak for themselves'.

Minh-ha's evocative alternative to filmic representation may be described as the-fly-in-the-I, in which the camera is used to comment on and 'deconstruct' Western conventions of representing other cultures. It is pure critique of the 'I' of the Western eye. It exaggerates reflexivity to an extent where the boundaries between fiction and non-fiction no longer exist. *Reassemblage* is a critique which may offer, in its deconstruction, constructive solutions to some of the problems with which ethnographic film and writing are trying to cope. Its rejection of contextualisation, as noted by Moore (1991), however, implies that the critique can hardly eradicate the paradoxes described at the beginning of this chapter.

The question is whether the criticisms of ethnographic representation made by Minh-ha and others, themselves make up a discourse of critique, which, in Tyler's words, 'is already and inextricably involved in what it criticises' (1991, p. 91). If so, then we are merely offered yet another contribution to the invention of anthropological realities.

## Notes

1 The concept 'othering' is derived from the work of Fabian (1983; 1987) while 'becoming' is borrowed from Hastrup (1986). Neither concept, however, is used here in exactly the same way as by these authors and definitely not in the same context.

2 I have discussed the significance of 'paradox' in further detail elsewhere (1985; 1989). In a broad scientific sense the problems concerning 'paradox' were the core of the discussions taking place in the natural sciences in the early part of this century, most notably in the work of Bohr, Einstein and Heisenberg. Postmodernism in many ways signals a renaissance of these discussions, albeit in a different context. George Devereux has probably provided us with the clearest example of the problem by referring to the difficulties involved in analysing sexual orgasm:

> 1. A fully experienced orgasm produces a clouding of consciousness which makes the self-observation of the orgasm imprecise.
> 2. If in order to observe it better, one makes an effort to prevent this clouding of consciousness, that which one observes will no longer be a true orgasm, experienced in all its plenitude, but simply a physiological spasm which culminates in an ejaculation. (Devereux 1978, p. 10)

3 Hastrup's contribution to this volume is an evident example as is Marcus's discussion of cinematic montage (1990).

4 Apart from Heider's *Ethnographic Film* (1975) and the book which has been considered the 'bible' of visual anthropology (Hockings 1975), very few books have been published on ethnographic films. The present volume and several recent books (for

example, Hockings & Omori 1988; Rollwagen 1988), as well as an increasing number of journals and newsletters seem to indicate that visual anthropologists have faith in both the pen and the camera.

5  I leave aside here the intrinsic problem that footage has already been edited in the camera.

6  See, for example, Tomaselli's discussion of a number of so-called Bushman films (Chapter 10, below).

7  This, of course, may all change with new technologies which will enable television reception on very large screens with high definition.

8  I use the term 'programme' deliberately to distinguish it from 'film'. For a discussion of this point see Turton (Chapter 17, below).

9  The fly-on-the-wall has become, in the jargon of documentary cinema, a concept describing observational or direct cinema. The term 'fly-in-the-soup' I have borrowed from Breitrose (1986, p. 47).

10  I am indebted to Naomi Vera-Sanso who introduced me to Trinh T. Minh-ha's films *Reassemblage* and *Naked Spaces*.

## References

*Books and articles*

Blue, J. (1965), 'One Man's Truth. An Interview with Richard Leacock', *Film Comment*, 3, pp. 15–22.

Breitrose, H. (1986), 'The Structures and Functions of Documentary Film', *CILECT Review*, II, 1, pp. 43–56.

Clifford, J. (1986), 'Introduction: Partial Truths', Clifford, J. and G. Marcus (eds.), *Writing Culture: The Poetics and Politics of Ethnography*, Berkeley, California, pp. 1–26.

Clifford, J. and G. Marcus (eds.) (1986), *Writing Culture: The Poetics and Politics of Ethnography*, Berkeley, California.

Crawford, P. I. (1984), 'Hvad er antropologisk film – et definitorisk essay', *Årsskrift for Etnografi*, 1983/84, Aarhus University, pp. 39–57.

Crawford, P. I. (1985), Nødvendighed og Tilfældighed, Marxisme og Antropologi: På sporet af den antropologiske totalitet, MA Thesis, Department of Social Anthropology, Aarhus University.

Crawford, P. I. (1989), *Anthropology and Paradox: Introducing Anthony Wilden*, seminar paper no. 10, Department of Social Anthropology, Aarhus University.

Crawford, P. I. (1990), *Ethnographic Film as Popular Text*, paper presented at seminar 'Texts in Action', April 1990, University of Manchester.

Crawford, P. I. (1991), 'The-Fly-in-the-I: Reflections on Ethnographic Film-making', paper presented at the 12th. NAFA Conference, Oslo.

Devereux, G. (1978), *Ethnopsychoanalysis: Psychoanalysis and Anthropology as Complementary Frames of Reference*, London.

Eco, U. (1986), 'Mirrors', Bouissac, P., M. Herzfeld and R. Posner (eds.), *Inconicity! Essays in the Nature of Culture. Festschrift for Thomas A. Sebeok on his 65th birthday*, Tübingen.

Fabian, J. (1971), 'Language, History and Anthropology', *Phil.Soc.Sci.*, I, pp. 19–47.

Fabian, J. (1983), *Time and the Other: How Anthropology Makes Its Object*, New York.

Fabian, J. (1987), *Presence and Representation: The Other and Anthropological Writing*, paper presented at the 85th Annual Meeting of the American Anthropological Association, Philadelphia.

Ferme, M. (1990), 'The Mende of Kpuawala Village', *Three films from the series Disappearing World*, Granada Television, Manchester, pp. 2–6.

Hastrup, K. (1986), 'Veracity and Visibility: The Problem of Authenticity in Anthropology', *FOLK*, 28, pp. 5–17.

Heider, K. G. (1976), *Ethnographic Film*, Austin, Texas.

Hockings, P. (ed.) (1975), *Principles of Visual Anthropology*, The Hague.

Hockings, P. and Y. Omori (eds.) (1988), *Cinematographic Theory and New Dimensions in Ethnographic Film*, Senri Ethnological Studies, no. 24, Osaka.

Jarvie, I. (1987), *Philosophy of the Film. Epistemology, Ontology, Aesthetics*, New York and London.

MacDougall, D. (1992), 'Whose Story Is It?', Crawford, P.I. and J. K. Simonsen (eds.) (forthcoming), *Ethnographic Film, Aesthetics and Narrative Traditions*, Proceedings from NAFA II, Intervention Press, Aarhus.

Marcus, G. (1990), 'The Modernist Sensibility in Recent Ethnographic Writing and the Cinematic Metaphor of Montage', *SVA Review*, VI, 1, pp. 2–12.

Marcus, G. and M. M. J. Fischer (1986), *Anthropology as Cultural Critique: An Experimental Moment in the Human Sciences*, Chicago and London.

Marshall, J. (1991), *Filming and Learning*, unpublished manuscript.

Metz, C. (1971), *Langage et Cinéma*, Paris.

Moore, H. (1990), 'Anthropology and Others', *Visual Anthropology Review*, VI, 2, pp. 66–72.

Parkes, P. (1990), 'The Kalasha: Rites of Spring', *Three films from the series Disappearing World*, Granada Television, Manchester, pp. 13–19.

Rollwagen, J. (ed.) (1988), *Anthropological Filmmaking*, Chur.

Rouch, J. (1978), 'The Politics of Visual Anthropology. An Interview with Jean Rouch', by Georgakas, D. *et al.*, *Cineaste*, VIII, 4.

Ruby, J. (1980), 'Exposing yourself: reflexivity, film and anthropology', *Semiotica*, 3, pp. 153–179.

Ruby, J. (ed.) (1982), *A Crack in the Mirror: Reflexive Perspectives in Anthropology*, Philadelphia.

Scholte, B. (1986), 'The charmed circle of Geertz's hermeneutics. A neo-Marxist critique', *Critique of Anthropology*, VI, 1, pp. 5–15.

Trinh T. Minh-ha (1984), 'Mechanical eye, electronic ear and the lure of authenticity', *Wide Angle*, VI, 2, pp. 58–63.

Tyler, S. A. (1986), 'Post-Modern ethnography: from document of the occult to occult document', Clifford, J. and G. Marcus (eds.), *Writing Culture*, pp. 122–140.

Tyler, S. A. (1991), 'A post-modern in-stance', Nencel, L. and P. Pels (eds.), *Constructing Knowledge: Authority and Critique in Social Science*, London, pp. 78–94.

Weiner, A. B. (1990), 'The Trobriand Islanders of Papua New Guinea', *Three films from the series Disappearing World*, Granada Television, Manchester, pp. 7–12.

Wilden, A. (1972), *System and Structure: Essays in Communication and Exchange*, London.

Wilden, A. (1987), *The Rules Are No Game: The Strategy of Communication*, London.

*Films*

Asch, T. and N. Chagnon (1969), *The Feast*, Documentary Educational Resources, Watertown, Mass. Colour, 29 mins.

Bateson, G. and M. Mead (1940), *Childhood Rivalry in Bali and New Guinea*, New York University, New York. Black and white, 17 mins.

Gardner, R. (1986), *Forest of Bliss*. Film Study Center, Harvard University, Cambridge, Mass. Colour, 90 mins.

Jerstad, J. (1987), *A Tibetan New Year*, The National Film and Television School, Beaconsfield. Colour, 43 mins.

Macdonald, B., (1990), *The Mende of Kpuawala Village, Disappearing World* series, Granada Television, Manchester. Colour, 52 mins. (Anthropologist: Marian Ferme)

MacDougall, D. (1972), *To Live With Herds*, Film Images, New York. Extension Media Center, Berkeley. Black and white, 68 mins.

MacDougall, D. (1974, *Under the Men's Tree*, University of California Extension Media Center, Berkeley. Black and white, 17 mins.

MacDougall, D. and J. MacDougall (1980), *A Wife Among Wives*, University of California Extension Media Center, Berkeley. Colour, 70 mins.

Marshall, J. (1980), *N!Ai: The Story of a !Kung Woman*. Documentary Educational Resources, Watertown. Colour, 59 mins.

Rouch, J. and E. Morin (1961), *Chronique d'un été*, Argos Films, Paris. Black and white, 90 mins.

Sheppard, J. (1990), *The Kalasha: Rites of Spring, Disappearing World* series, Granada Television, Manchester. Colour, 52 mins. (Anthropologist: Peter Parkes)

Minh-ha, Trinh T. (1982), *Reassemblage*, Women Make Movies, New York. Colour, 40 mins.

Wason, D. (1990), *The Trobriand Islanders of Papua New Guinea, Disappearing World* series, Granada Television, Manchester. Colour, 52 mins. (Anthropologist: Annette Weiner)

Part Two

# Image, audience and aesthetics

# Introduction

In Jean-Luc Godard's film *Les Carabiniers* (1963) one of the protagonists, a poor and simple peasant, goes to the cinema for the first time in his life. Curiously enough, he even happens to see one of the first films ever produced, Louis Lumière's *The Arrival of the Train at the Gare de Lyon* (1895). This one-minute, unedited film shows the train coming from afar, approaching and approaching, and finally arriving in a medium shot (felt as a close-up). Just like the original audience, the hero gets scared. He feels that he will be run over by the train; he does not distinguish film from reality.

Shortly, however, he learns to do so. The next film in the program happens to be an innocently pornographic movie about a girl bathing. Wanting to join the nude in the bathtub, the hero jumps to the stage. But unable to get into the tub, he pulls down the screen, and the rest of the film is projected on the bleak wall – and on him. He has been forced to realize that film is not reality, even though it may offer a semblance of reality. He has been forced to realize that film is a symbolic medium, a visual language. (Kjørup 1977, p. 20)

This quotation from Kjørup's article on film 'as the meeting place of multiple codes' succinctly describes the scope of the subject matter of Part Two. It illustrates the point in MacDougall's emphasis on the necessity of 'complicities of style', a necessity embedded in the film medium's multiple coding coupled with a culturally conditioned diversity in 'encoding' practices and capacities. It also illustrates the point of Vaughan's emphasis on the dual nature of film specified in his initial distinction between 'film as record' and 'film as language', a distinction which our hero above fails to recognise. The same applies to Banks' distinction between the 'object' and 'concept' of film, the former referring to the documentational capacities of the celluloid strip and the latter to the cinematic products, films. Finally, the reactions of our hero highlight Martinez's emphasis on film spectatorship, since they demonstrate the significance of the relationship between film and reality on the one hand and between the film and its audience on the other. In this sense all four contributor's to Part Two deal with the tension between anthropology as a process (and product) of knowledge and film as a process which may be described as aesthetic, even when it comes to ethnographic filmic 'texts'. In a more general sense, the issue refers to a tension within academia between record and exposition, knowledge and aesthetics or science and art, a tension which Firth has described as follows:

A systematic record, based upon observation of the institutions, behaviour patterns, and concepts of the people of a society or community is looked upon in a sophisticated way, not given any particular authority but seen as a reflection or illustration of the ethnographer's personal interpretation of the situations observed. It has long been realized that any ethnographical text is a *crafted* job. (1989, p. 48, emphasis in original)

That this has 'long been realized' confirms that 'craft' is a legitimate component in the production of *written* ethnographic texts although *filmic* texts, which are even more overtly products of a craft, have not yet achieved the status of being legitimate means by which anthropological knowledge is established (MacDougall, p. 91).

Ethnographic writing has followed a set of conventions and particular formulae which until recently meant that ethnographic texts were very similar, in form and structure, even in cases where the societies and cultures under study differed considerably. MacDougall forcefully argues that one of the main lessons to be learned from ethnographic film-making is that a successful approach in one society may prove impossible to follow in another:

I would suggest that the dominant conventions of ethnographic film make some societies appear accessible, rational and attractive to the viewer, but applied to a society with a very different cultural style they may prove quite inadequate and inarticulate. (p. 92)

Problems arise when the film style, based on the current repertoire of cine-matic conventions and technological options, is not compatible with the 'cultural style' of a given society. The MacDougalls encountered these problems when they began filming Australian Aboriginals, using an approach which had been developed during their long period of filming in East Africa. The lack of compatibility between 'film style' and 'cultural style',

. . . not only affects the success or failure of individual films but may predispose film-makers . . . to make films in certain kinds of societies rather than others or, if they have less choice in the matter, to focus on a particular selection of cultural features, such as ceremonial events and technology. These can take on an exaggerated importance simply because they appear more 'filmable', just as language and kinship have perhaps figured more prominently in anthropology because they are more easily written down. (*loc. cit.*)

Taking MacDougall's point we may even find examples in which the 'cultural style' determines the film style, as in Cooper and Schoedsack's classic, *Grass* (1952), where the 'narrative structure' of Bakhtiari society provided the narrative structure of the film (Crawford 1991).

The diversification of film styles, catalysed by the need to employ different conventions in different contexts, may, as MacDougall argues, result in the development of a new concept of film-making which he labels 'intertextual cinema'. Intertextual cinema, apart from reflecting the complicity and diversity of cultures, will have to take into account the 'multiple voices', which 'speak' about cultural representation as well as the multiple audiences for whom the films are made.

The present trend towards openness and multivocality is reiterated in Vaughan's article, even though it was written twelve years ago (it is published here for the first time). Focusing on the differences between documentary and fiction, Vaughan addresses many central issues in documentary film-making. Acknowledging that, 'all events, at least in human affairs, are *events perceived by somebody*' (p. 101) Vaughan places the definition of documentary firmly in the hands, or rather the eyes, of the viewer: 'documentary is what we-as-viewers can perceive as referring to the pro-filmic, it being presupposed that we can construe it as meaningful'. One hears echoes of Young's often quoted dictum: 'the camera tends to lie but the audience tends to believe' (Young 1975, p. 66). This ambiguity, which Vaughan ascribes to the dual nature of film as both 'record' and 'language' (p. 99), marks the difference between documentary and fiction. Not in the simplistic sense that fiction is language and documentary is record but in the basic sense that the language of documentary is always directly related to what it records or as Vaughan puts it, 'the documentary response is one in which the image is perceived as signifying what it appears to record' (p. 101). In semiotic terms this means, in documentary, that the sign (in this case the image) coincides with the meaning, as opposed to fiction where meaning is constructed by a sign which has no (necessary) connection to empirical reality but which nevertheless may be extremely 'authentic' due to what de Man has called the 'self-reflecting mirror effect' (1983, p. 17): fiction creates its own reality.

As for the relationship between anthropology (and film) and reality, Vaughan is puzzled by the fact that observational cinema has been the approach preferred by 'mainstream' visual anthropology:

Many of the prescriptions of ciné-anthropologists have rested upon an assumption, implicit or explicit, that the inevitable selectivity of shooting may be counteracted – or perhaps atoned for – by a refusal of selectivity in the editing: that the minimum of structuring will afford the maximum of truth. But the antithesis of the structured is not the truthful, or even the objective, but quite simply the random. We may, indeed, find it a little puzzling that anthropology should have taken so readily to observational modes of film-making at all, when it might, as a science, have been expected to prefer the traditional patterns whose tight organization of proto-fictional (or at any rate proto-demonstrative) materials promises to raise the general principle above the vagaries of the particular instance. (p. 100–101)

This leads us to Banks's question, 'which films are the ethnographic films?' (Chapter 7). His point of departure is that any film is governed by a triadic process constituted by three phenomena, intention, event and reaction. 'An intention – to make a film – results in an event – the filming process – which leads to a reaction – the response of the audience to the physical manifestation of the event (the film).' (p. 117). Banks confirms Vaughan's claim that anthropologists have seen observational cinema as closely representing their own interest and, quoting the work of the MacDougalls, Gary Kildea and Robert Gardner, offers an explanation of why this is the case:

It seems to me that this is because the films of these directors most closely adhere to a set of genre conventions established by a certain kind of anthropological writing. One could argue, however, that these films only accidentally accord with the anthropological agenda – their claims to ethnographicness are brought about by mimicry of what the fieldworking anthropologist sees and hears, not by their ability to perform the anthropological task directly. Occasionally, the mimicry is sufficiently flawed to be perceptible and to allow anthropologists to deny certain films the status of being ethnographic (as in the case of Gardner). (p. 124)

And he adds that:

. . . observational films form the jewels in the crown of the ethnographic film canon, apparently because their ethnographic qualities are most clearly seen to shine in the 'event' category of the process, a category which we tend to privilege over intention and reaction because it appears most objective, neutral and transparent. (*loc. cit.*)

In his conclusion Banks warns against films which 'stress the location of ethnographicness in event' due to their intrinsic mimetical trend which may result in the production of pastiche. If anthropology were to locate ethnographicness in intention instead, it would enable the anthropologist to control the overall process to the advantage of both the anthropologist and the non-anthropological audience and readership (p. 127).

The emphasis on 'audience', a category which has, until recently, received very little attention in visual anthropology, is further accentuated in the final chapter of Part Two in which Martinez adds theoretical substance to his previous study of student reaction to a number of ethnographic films (Martinez 1990). Stressing the 'need to move from the dominance of author-text to a theoretical consideration of the viewer/reader as a powerful source of signification in the construction of anthropological knowledge' (p. 132), Martinez, in this very ambitious and far-reaching chapter, explores the relevance of theoretical approaches in literary studies, reception theory, reader-response studies and theories of the text. One of the results is a distinction between 'closed' texts, which carry specific instructions as to how they should be read, thus limiting the scope of the reader's interpretations, and 'open' texts which explicitly invite the reader to carry out his or her own interpretations, thus being 'suggestive and susceptible to a virtually unlimited range of possible readings' (p. 135). In his empirical study of students' responses, Martinez discovered that the 'strongest pattern of aberrant readings' seemed to emerge in cases where the films followed a 'closed' strategy, whereas more 'open' films, 'those using narrative, experimental, or reflexive styles . . . empower viewers by allowing them space to negotiate meanings in a more dialogic, interactive way of reading, generally resulting in more complex interpretations' (p. 135–6).

All four chapters demonstrate the complexity of ethnographic film-making when viewed as a *process* which necessarily relies on conventions and knowledge emanating not only from the particular sphere of anthropology but also from cinematography, literary studies, aesthetics and, indeed, the consumers of ethnographic film, the audience.

## References

*Books and articles*

Crawford, P. I. (1991), 'Baba Ahmedi and *Grass*: the visual narrativity of pastoral nomadism', Danish version in Dybbroe, S. *et al.* (eds.), *Klaus Khan Baba*, Aarhus University Press, pp. 286–300.

De Man, P. (1983), *Blindness and Insight*, New York.

Firth, R. (1989), 'Fiction and fact in ethnography' in Tonkin, E., M. McDonald and M. Chapman (eds.), *History and Ethnicity*, ASA Monographs 27, London, pp. 48–52.

Kjørup, S. (1977), 'Film as a meetingplace of multiple codes' in Perkins, D. and B. Leondar (eds.), *The Arts and Cognition*, Baltimore, pp. 20–47.

Martinez, W. (1990), 'Critical studies and visual anthropology: Aberrant versus anticipated readings of ethnographic film', *Commission for Visual Anthropology Review*, Spring 1990, pp. 34–47.

Young, C. (1975), 'Observational Cinema' in Hockings, P. (ed.), *Principles of Visual Anthropology*, The Hague, pp. 65–79.

*Films*

Cooper, M. C. and Schoedsack, E. B. (1925), *Grass*, Paramount Films, USA. Black and white, 66 mins.

# Complicities of style

I will begin with what may turn out to be one of the stranger footnotes in the history of visual anthropology. A number of years ago, a researcher in psychology was devising an experiment to measure castration anxiety among American men (Schwartz 1955). In order to trigger the anxiety he hit upon the tactic of putting his experimental subjects in a theatre and subjecting them to screenings of film footage of Aboriginal subincision operations in Central Australia. We may find this disturbing for several reasons, but not least of all because we simply aren't used to seeing culture shock being dealt out quite so cavalierly. It tends to alarm whatever remains of our sense of cultural relativity.

But in retrospect the researcher's methods may have a crude message for us. For quite some time, and again in a recent study (Martinez 1990), we have seen mounting evidence that many films designed not to shock, but to bridge cultural differences, have quite the opposite effect when shown to at least some audiences. Most anthropological and ethnographic films are not made exclusively for anthropologists, and, if one of the underlying metaphors of anthropological endeavour is to cure the disease of cultural intolerance, then it is clear that for some recipients, the medicine may be wrong or too strong. We are finally beginning to take more seriously how audiences interact with film texts to produce meanings. But that is only one of the issues. We need to pay equal attention to the prior issue of how the implicit texts of representation used in making films overlap and interact with the cultures they seek to portray.

It is a commonplace that when Flaherty went to Samoa and the Aran Islands he failed to find the dramatic conflict of *Nanook of the North* and had to invent it. Granted that he may have invented much of the drama of *Nanook* as well, this is the kind of obvious, large-scale observation which may keep one from going on to related questions, such as why some societies (the Inuit, for example) are so heavily represented in ethnographic film as compared to anthropological writing; why some societies are represented largely by films on ritual and material culture;

and to what extent ethnographic films are influenced by their search for (or creation of) strong central characters. In this regard one thinks immediately of the 'stars' of the ethnographic cinema, among them Nanook, Damouré, N!ai and Ongka.

The relation between knowledge and aesthetics is always tricky, and that between anthropology and film especially so, in part because the legitimacy for anthropology of a kind of knowledge expressed in images has yet to be addressed. Defining the world in writing may appear better understood, but that is often because this older method assumes a literary and linguistic tradition in common with a cultural one. When the subject is another culture, a different and less well explored set of problems arises.

Gilbert Lewis, in a paper called 'The look of magic' (1986), has described how in *The Golden Bough* Frazer's accounts of unfamiliar cultural practices give them an oddness bordering on the surreal, making them more likely to be ascribed to magical beliefs than to everyday rationality. Indeed, he suggests that anthropological writing may make the ordinary strange simply because it *is* writing, unable to contextualise certain details sufficiently to prevent them from emerging in a lurid isolation. Pictures can help to solve this particular problem but they will inevitably introduce problems of their own. For each form of representation, Lewis says, 'the conventions may need to be modified for new and unfamiliar subjects' (p. 416).

## Film style v. cultural style

One of the difficulties in developing a coherent discipline of visual anthropology has been pinning down basic principles from a film-making practice which is both slender in output and which undergoes a major technological and stylistic shift every few decades. These shifts occur because ethnographic film is not simply an alternative technology for anthropology but has its own history as part of a larger cinema culture. Compared to the rate of chopping and changing in ethnographic film-making, the methods of anthropology sometimes appear to have remained in a steady state.

For all that, the fickleness of ethnographic film method is in many ways illusory. Despite certain injections of anthropological ideas, its origins lie in the essentially European invention of documentary cinema, which embodies in its stylistic conventions still earlier European inventions and assumptions about behaviour and discourse. Compared to the potential stylistic diversity of human cultures, this makes it quite steady and specific in its cultural outlook. If new subjects require new conventions, it can be said that ethnographic film has often failed to find them. This stylistic narrowness has led to an unevenness in how films represent the social reality of other societies, rather like the troughs and ridges that a particular wave system creates by reinforcement and cancellation as it passes over other wave systems beneath it. Such an imbalance may also mean that as documentary film conventions are diffused into an international film language, particularly by television, they are likely to have a differential effect on the self-expression and survival of local cultures.

I would suggest that the dominant conventions of ethnographic film make some societies appear accessible, rational and attractive to the viewer, but applied to a society with a very different cultural style they may prove quite inadequate and inarticulate. They may indeed make the society look strange, and in terms even stronger than Gilbert Lewis describes. And no amount of external explanation or contextualisation may make much difference.

This is not simply a matter of the cultural gap between film-maker and subject or subject and audience. The cultural incompatibility is more deeply embedded in the representational system itself, including its technology; and without radical changes, the result will be much the same whether it is used by a First, Third or Fourth World film-maker.

Film has a psychological plausibility which tends to naturalise many of these conventions into invisibility. Film-makers may be aware that alternative approaches to film-making are possible – Sol Worth, John Adair and the late Eric Michaels have been at pains to show this – and yet not be fully aware how their own film-making practice channels their efforts in certain directions and frustrates them in others. This not only affects the success or failure of individual films but may predispose film-makers (and need I add, television companies) to make films in certain kinds of societies rather than others or, if they have less choice in the matter, to focus on a particular selection of cultural features, such as ceremonial events and technology. These can take on an exaggerated importance simply because they appear more 'filmable', just as language and kinship have perhaps figured more prominently in anthropology because they are more easily written down.

The problem is often declared by an absence, or by an awkward or bizarre stopgap solution. Many films give evidence of the bafflement which has confronted their makers – films which suddenly resort to romantic imagery, narration, or a 1940s Hollywood montage when they are unable to follow a subject where it would otherwise lead them. Other films betray a hollowness behind the devices they employ. People are followed almost by reflex, doing things as though those things had a cumulative significance, but the significance never materialises. The camera zooms in on a face which reveals precisely nothing. Worse than just showing nothing, these false emphases contribute to an image of a world which is mute and off-balance.

Such strangeness is the overriding quality to me of a considerable number of films on Australian Aboriginal society, including some of my own and some made by Aboriginal people themselves. They give off a characteristic cultural tone, like a tuning fork, but it is like a sound heard at a great distance, or the spectral signature of a star. Sometimes the film-maker's unfamiliarity or lack of sympathy with Aboriginal society can be blamed, but often it seems to have more to do with complexities in the subject and styles of cultural expression unmatched by a comparable cinematic style.

William Stanner, probably the most perceptive and politically engaged anthropologist writing about Aboriginal society in the 1950s, linked the problem to Aboriginal frames of reference. '[The] fundamental cast [of Aboriginal thought]', he wrote, 'seems to me to be analogical and *a fortiori* metaphorical. . . . I am suggesting that the association of European and aboriginal has been a struggle of partial blindness, often darkened to sightlessness on our part by the continuity of the aborigines' implicit tradition' (1958, pp. 108–9). That sightlessness, he might have added, extends as well to the implicit pre-suppositions of our own habits of description.

If such difficulties cripple some ethnographic films, it is also true to say, without belittling the film-makers, that other films have benefitted from cultures which seem positively to lend themselves to the codes of Western film-making. Peter Loizos has praised the special cogency of the interviews in Melissa Llewelyn-Davies' excellent film *The Women's Olamal* (1984) and has noted how, without intruding on events, the film observes the unities of time, place and person of classical Greek tragedy (1989). We get just the information we need to interpret the events, and these explanations come from the Maasai themselves, either in direct address to the camera or in observed interactions. The drama is Aristotelian and the Maasai are found to be superb explicators of events in their lives and their own social system. Other film-makers, including myself, have found a similar openness and eloquence in the cultural style of other East African pastoralists, at a time when the aim was to get away from *ex cathedra* explanations and rely instead upon the self-revelation and social interactions of the people portrayed.

That aim reflected a Western realist tradition dependent upon a certain literalness of words and deeds and a focus upon events which crystallised deeper social issues. But for this to work requires that the social actors conduct them-selves in the world in somewhat the same terms. It requires a society in which there is a positive value placed upon explicitness of speech, expression of personal emotion and opinion, and the public resolution of conflict – although not necessarily to the extent of public adversarial debate, as in *The Women's Olamal*.

But I think these assumptions penetrate to another level as well. Even when ethnographic films do not follow models of classical dramaturgy – and most in fact do not – they make use of certain formal conventions of camera work and editing which derive from it. Thus even a film guided by an anthropological commentary and concerned with economics or politics will do so in visual terms which reflect European expectations of causality, chronology and interpersonal behaviour.

## The look of documentary

If ethnographic writing assumes we can be told, even if we cannot always experience, ethnographic films, even when they include explanatory narration, assume that we will learn something experientially from the images, and in some sense make them our own. Films attempt to create a trajectory of understanding, beginning with images which make certain claims upon us. These claims are typically produced through acts of disclosure which create a sense of obligation in the viewer towards the viewed, and this can be compared to a kind of submission or display of vulnerability in which the subject invites our protection or interest. That is why the term 'exposition' must be taken not only in the sense of setting out the subject and its context but in the literal sense of self-exposure. From the privileged knowledge that results, the audience embarks upon a problem or a journey.

The repertoire of shooting and editing techniques in both fiction and non-fiction films is employed in the first instance to gain the viewer's complicity, by disarming and penetrating the subject from every angle. It is a repertoire of exaggeration, overstepping the bounds of normal vision. There are wide-angle shots and close-ups for expansiveness or intimacy; montage and continuity editing to condense and intensify significant actions; and sequence-shots to direct an unwavering gaze at nuances of behaviour. In documentary, various kinds of direct and indirect address have been added to these expository techniques, perhaps in recognition of the fact that although self-disclosure can be written into a script, special conditions, such as the interview, must be created to extract it in real life.

Some conventions seem related to implicit expectations about behavioural style, such as the assumption that characters will assert their personalities and desires visually, in ways that can be registered in close-ups of the face. The reaction shot, the over-the-shoulder shot and the point-of-view shot all show a preoccupation with expressive behaviour and response, designed to convey information about inner states and invite identification. These techniques reflect the Western interest in developing an ideology and psychology of the individual, usually in preparation for some test. As cinema relies more and more on easily-recognisable 'types' it rejoins other theatrical traditions and is capable of more long-shots, just as the masks and costumes of Kabuki theatre and Greek tragedy, and certain sports, permit a huge stage and viewing at great distances. A further implication of the close-up – as it is used in interviews with 'experts', and especially in the case of the television talking head – is the assumption of a hierarchical and specialised society in which certain persons have the authority to define social realities and speak for others.

Interiority and the character-narration of Western cinema are not only encoded in the close-up but in devices such as the shot/counter-shot, or reverse angle, designed to construct an imaginary geography in which the characters can move and which can become the temporary home of the viewer, or what Nick Browne has called the 'spectator-in-the-text' (1975).

Other kinds of structures, such as sequence construction, point to cultural assumptions which perhaps have more general implications. For example, it seems to me that the condensation of time characteristic of classical Hollywood continuity editing, and the similar reduction of physical processes to a series of key steps in much documentary editing, point to an essentialist rather than an elaborative view of knowledge which may have repercussions in how films represent the discourse and activities of other cultures. It may well be that what is important to members of those cultures lies between the shots, or in the unbroken continuity of part of the action, even if the whole process is never shown. The linearity of such editing may also go against the grain of a way of thinking which is fundamentally multidirectional in recognising the different manifestations of objects and events. Western conceptions of causality are also implicated in such structures, as well as in the emphasis upon strict chronology in reporting events, which we can see in the predilection for characters making formal entrances and exits from the frame, and in lapsed-time markers like the fade and the dissolve.

An exception, but a significant exception to this temporal linearity, is the convention of parallel action cutting, in which the film alternates between two actions so that they appear to be happening simultaneously. On the micro-level this kind of editing results in the simple cutaway, whose overriding purpose is commonly to bridge a temporal gap. But when it is used on a larger scale, parallel cutting tends to imply a convergence of the two lines and an eventual collision. This can be taken as the visual analogue of the conflict structure around which so much of Western film-making revolves.

For Western film-makers, conflict is almost an essential discursive principle, if not in obvious form then in the form of issues or problems requiring resolution. It is like the carrier frequency of all other matters. Conflict structure in ethnographic films tends to mean filming events in which conflict, real or potential, brings cultural imperatives to the fore. An initiate passes a test and reconfirms a hierarchy. An episode of childhood rivalry explains how personalities are formed. Whether or not Ongka's *moka* ever comes off or Harry ever turns up, events have occurred which reveal the principles by which people live. At a deeper level, such events reveal the unresolved paradoxes within a society which generate conflicting messages about the management of authority, allegiance and desire.

The strategies of ethnographic filming often involve seeking out significant rents in the social fabric, such as N!ai's rejection and alienation in !Kung society. There is an echo in this process of the propensity of observational cinema to lie in wait for the moments in life when people let their social masks slip and literally 'give themselves away'. The focus may be on traditional sources of tension, or contradictions between 'correct' and actual behaviour, or even on a person who is so specialized or marginal in the society as to provide a revealing perspective on it. These approaches may sometimes make more sense to the anthropologist/film-maker than to the people being filmed; but in many societies conflicts are perfectly legitimate topics of attention and often focus issues for local people as well. They may even be seen in some sense as therapeutic eruptions which provide opportunities to readjust the social landscape.

But the reliance upon conflict structure also presupposes a society in which people typically get embroiled in contradictory sets of obligations and in which some benefit is seen in living through the consequences. In another society this might be deemed sheer foolishness. My experience of Aboriginal society leads me to think that it systematically resists approaches based on conflict structure and most of the other expository conventions of ethnographic cinema. This is partly due to a style of discourse which, as Stanner noted, is highly allusive and, when not formal, is often laconic and multi-pronged. Speech here does not provide an open channel to personal feeling and opinion, nor does the close-up of a face. Personal reticence is deemed a virtue and language is only one of the surfaces of a complex spiral of art, reference and ritual in what I have increasingly come to think of as a 'heraldic' culture.

Thus, from a film-maker's perspective, it would perhaps be hard to find a greater contrast to the outspoken and sceptical pragmatism of East African pastoralists than the style of Aboriginal social interaction. Conflict is carefully contained behind the scenes and, should it break out of formal control, is considered far from therapeutic and highly dangerous. Contentious issues are systematically avoided or dealt with in parables. This is not to say that Aboriginal people are not personally ambitious or contentious, but the public weal resides in the constant reinforcement and repair of personal relationships.

It could also be said that Aboriginal self-expression is more typically one of inscription than explanation. A film consistent with Aboriginal culture would tend to be enumerative rather than comparative and might typically consist of a demonstration of rights to land, knowledge or other cultural property. For Aboriginal people, *showing* is in and of itself a sufficient act and can constitute a transmission of rights. Thus a film in these terms need not explain anything or develop any argument or analysis; rather, by simply existing it has the potential to be a powerful political or cultural assertion.

### The voices of ethnography

To be helpful, recognising the interactions of different cultural styles must be seen in relation to the larger purposes of ethnographic representation. Ethnographic film is different from indigenous or national film production in that it seeks to interpret one society for another. Its starting point is therefore the encounter of two cultures, or if you will, two texts of life; and what it produces is a further, rather special cultural document. Increasingly, though, ethnographic films cease to be one group's private notes or diaries. They reach multiple audiences and I think must now be made with this in mind. They will certainly be seen and used by the societies they portray. One consequence, therefore, is that they should become more precise – and perhaps more restrained – about what they claim to be. (There is a corresponding obligation on viewers to read these limits more accurately.) Another is that they should begin looking in two directions instead of one.

This is really a question of how ethnographic film conceives and frames its subject. Since 1896 ethnographic film-making has undergone a series of revolutions, introducing narrative, observational and participatory approaches. With each, a set of assumptions about the positioning of the film-maker and the audience has crumbled. Now it is the single identity of each of these that is under review. If we are in the midst of a new revolution, as I believe we are, it is one which is interested in multiple voices and which might be called an *intertextual cinema*.

I think we are already seeing the changes in a new emphasis on authorship and specific cultural perspectives. Films are less often posed as omniscient or definitive descriptions, but equally, film-makers are less likely to claim a spurious oneness with their subjects. Societies are no longer portrayed as monolithic, or unpenetrated by external and historical forces. But this is only the beginning of changes which could affect both the conventions and larger structures of ethnographic film-making.

The focus on authorship can have two important consequences: first, in clarifying the provenance of film texts, and second in opening up new directions in film strategy in ways more understandable and acceptable to audiences. (A film with declared interests can more easily afford to be unusual.) Other modifications of film conventions will come from cultural borrowing or from explicit responses to conflicts in cultural style. I think we will increasingly regard ethnographic films as meeting places of primary and secondary levels of representation, one cultural text seen through, or inscribed upon another. In place of the centred and linear models of the West may also come more films employing repetition, associative editing and non-narrative structures. The decentreing of subject-matter could result in films that look at the environments or peripheral activities of what were previously taken to be the 'significant' events.

The other implication of these shifts, and probably the more important one, is the recognition that ethnographic films for multiple audiences must confront contending versions of reality. Further, they must acknowledge historical experiences which overshadow any text and which inevitably escape from it. I think we will therefore see films which become repositories of multiple authorship, confrontation and exchange. We will see more ethnographic films which re-deploy existing texts and incorporate parallel interpretations. We will see more films which begin from different directions and converge upon a common subject.

In recent years ethnographic films have become less insular in opening themselves to the voices of their subjects, but one can now foresee films which are produced by and belong equally to two cultures. This should not in my view result in cultural relativity run wild, nor mirrors within mirrors and unending nesting boxes, nor does it imply an abandonment of anthropological analysis. It may instead help us to recast the problem of Self and Other more productively as a set of reciprocal relations in which film, when all is said and done, plays only a very small part.

## References

*Books and articles*

Browne, N. (1975), 'The spectator-in-the-text: the rhetoric of *Stagecoach*', *Film Quarterly*, 29, pp. 26–38.

Lewis, G. (1985), 'The look of magic', *Man* (NS) 21, pp. 414–47.

Martinez, W. (1990), 'Critical studies and visual anthropology: aberrant vs. anticipated readings of ethnographic film', *CVA Review*, Spring, pp. 34–47.

Loizos, P. (1989), *Through a Glass Darkly* (working title), unpublished ms.

Schwartz, B. J. (1955), 'The measurement of castration anxiety and anxiety over loss of love', *Journal of Personality*, 24, pp. 204–19.

Stanner, W. E. H. (1958), 'Continuity and change among the Aborigines', *Australian Journal of Science*, XXI, 5a, pp. 99–109.

*Films*

Flaherty, R. (1922), *Nanook of the North*, Révillon Frères, Paris. Black and white, 70 mins.

Llewelyn-Davies, M. (1984), *The Women's Olamal: The Organization of a Maasai Fertility Ceremony*, BBC Television. Colour, 120 mins.

# 6 *Dai Vaughan*

# The aesthetics of ambiguity

*In Plato, art is mystification because there is a heaven of ideas; but in the earthly domain all glorification of the earth is true as soon as it is realised.'*
Simone de Beauvoir *The Ethics of Ambiguity*, Citadel Press, New York, 1962, p. 157

Recently I cut a film about two women in their suburban London ménage.* After the completion of the editing, I came to know these people personally, and visited them in their home. When the film was eventually transmitted on television, I found myself perceiving it in an unnervingly bifocal manner. To the extent that I fed into the images my subsequent knowledge of the characters and location, the film broke down into incoherence. To the extent that it did cohere, it projected a world which repudiated any connection with the people and place as I now knew them. Such an experience is the subjective correlative of the dual nature of film, which exists both as record and as language; and this duality, a source of paradox, has generated much confusion in the debates surrounding 'observational cinema'.

The problems we face are not new in principle; but the terms in which they must be resolved have changed radically within the past fifteen years. Beneath the many styles in which documentary has historically manifested itself may be discerned a common purpose: to enable the character of film as record to survive, so far as is possible, its metamorphosis into language. But the development of lightweight cameras and tape recorders, mobile and relatively inconspicuous, has brought documentary to a crisis which is largely one of confrontation with its own being. It is as if, having long watched itself approaching, it were now almost near enough to reach out and shake itself by the hand. Almost, but never quite.

The crisis has been most acutely registered in that realm of subject-matter which may be termed the domestic. At a calculated risk of question-begging, I shall offer a filmic rather than an ethnographic definition of the domestic realm as comprising those areas of human activity which are (a) most difficult to shoot without interference, since they are not public, and (b) least susceptible to

---

* This paper was written in 1978/79. We are grateful to Dai Vaughan, who was unable to attend the Manchester conference, for allowing us to publish it here (in a slightly shortened form) for the first time. Editors.

re-enactment, since they are not in any simple way repetitive. The purpose of this somewhat negative phrasing is to denote an area of personal, intimate though not quite clandestine behaviour in explicit contrast with those repeatable or public events which have formed documentary's traditional sources – events on which the paraphernalia of film-making has been assumed not to exercise any significant influence. Repetitive actions – such as the operating of a lathe – can be performed in front of the most cumbersome of cameras once the subject has overcome self-consciousness. With public events – such as political speeches – it is different. We cannot say that the presence of the camera necessarily has no effect, for there is a whole category – once known fashionably but misleadingly as *non*-events – where the attention of the media is held responsible for their very existence. An early example might be the 1934 Nazi Party convention which, we are told, was organised largely with a view to supplying Leni Riefenstahl with good shots. But it is difficult, in such cases, to charge the camera with 'distortion'. Rather it is in the nature of public events to *change* their nature according to expectations of public response.

It was a consequence of the character of these traditional source materials – materials which contained already, in their being rehearsable and/or audience-directed, something of the quality of such events as exist only for the purpose of being filmed and of being wholly assimilated into the fabric of a discourse – that documentary seemed, in its classic period, to be concerned only with the general truths of the human situation as opposed to the 'individual psychology' of acted fiction: a dubious distinction being thus implied between people as individuals and as social creatures. It is not surprising, then, that the prime enticement offered by the new equipment should have been the possibility of opening up domestic behaviour to the record without first translating it into something other than itself (i.e. the scripted behaviour, or at least improvised performance, into which classical documentary had sometimes gingerly ventured in an attempt to transgress its limits); that the problems entailed should have been seen as clustering around the ideas of 'influence' or 'distortion' within the pro-filmic; and that those immediately exercised by such problems should have been the fieldworkers – directors, camera operators and, above all, anthropologists already committed to a notion of academic 'objectivity'.

While most practitioners would claim to be aware that film is not an open channel to 'reality', they have nonetheless tended to see the difficulties as centreing on their own attitudes and the fear that these may somehow mar the neutrality of the material. Many of the prescriptions of ciné-anthropologists have rested upon an assumption, implicit or explicit, that the inevitable selectivity of shooting may be counteracted, or perhaps merely atoned for, by a refusal of selectivity in the editing: that the minimum of structuring will afford the maximum of truth. But the antithesis of the structured is not the truthful, or even the objective, but quite simply the random. We may, indeed, find it a little puzzling that anthropology should have taken so readily to observational modes of film-making at all, when it might, as a science, have been expected to prefer the traditional patterns whose tight organisation of proto-fictional (or at any rate proto-demonstrative) materials promises to raise the general principle above the vagaries of the particular instance. (Flaherty's method, for example, with its heavy use of reconstruction, may be said to have been based on the idea that the better we familiarise ourselves with the lifestyles of our subjects, the more of the elements of those lifestyles will be gathered into the realm of the repeatable – repeatable by virtue of our-the-film-makers' understanding of what constitutes their essentials.)

All events, at least in human affairs, are *events perceived by* somebody. What may seem to be at stake, from the film-makers' viewpoint, is to prevent their own perceptions from intervening between the viewer and the pro-filmic. But the film-makers' intentionality is not within the viewer's ken; and their abdication of it will, conversely, do nothing to prevent the camera from transposing the world into what will function for the viewer as imagery. It is to the nature of this imagery that we must look for clarification.

The photograph is a physical imprint of the world. Like the photograph, film stakes a claim on reality which has nothing to do with 'realism' in any literary sense; and it is this claim which documentary aspires to fulfil. If it has proved notoriously difficult to define documentary by reference to its constantly shifting stylistic practices, it is because the term 'documentary' properly describes not a style or a method or a genre of film-making but a mode of response to film material: a mode of response founded upon the acknowledgment that every photograph is a portrait signed by its sitter. Stated at its simplest, the documentary response is one in which the image is perceived as signifying what it appears to record; a documentary film is one which seeks, by whatever means, to elicit this response; and the documentary movement is the history of the strategies which have been adopted to this end.

A crucial fact about the definition of documentary as a mode of response is that it places the attribution of documentary significance squarely within the province of the viewer. Any fiction film can, albeit with difficulty, be perceived as a documentary on its own making. Of course, it is perfectly possible for a film to 'be' a documentary in that it will achieve greater coherence on this than on any other interpretation; and it is certainly more than possible for the makers to have intended it in this sense. But the fact remains that documentary is what we-as-viewers can perceive as referring to the pro-filmic, it being presupposed that we can thus construe it as meaningful. If, however, we are to treat documentary as so-defined by the viewer's perception, we must face up to certain difficulties which this raises concerning the identification of the images.

The photograph – once we are sure that it *is* a photograph – cannot lie. But it can be wrongly labelled. This so-called photograph of King George VI is *in fact* a photograph of someone else. If we accept that documentary is best defined as a way of perceiving images, we cannot evade the implication that it is blind to the falsity of labels. Documentary will be consequent upon what it appears to show, rather than upon what it necessarily does show; and the relationship between the two is a matter for the film-makers' ethics, inaccessible to the viewer. Yet the assumptions which the viewer makes about this relationship, on the basis of signals intended or unintended, will inform his perception of the film. To make a documentary is therefore to persuade the viewer that what appears to be *is*.

Film is not unique in this demand for a response based upon an ethical assumption which it cannot substantiate. Jazz, for example, may be considered documentary music in that it claims to be predominantly improvised and therefore to represent the actual moment of musical creativity. Likewise functional architecture, in its requirement that appearance should express use and structure, is assumed not to cheat. What appears to be a load-bearing pillar must not be simply the outer facing of a ventilation duct. It is possible for documentary to be labelled as such in a bald, extrinsic manner with some caption or billing or publicity which, whilst overtly just requesting us to construe the images in a documentary sense, carries also the implication that they may be taken on trust. (Here again, Flaherty may offer us an example: for the *myth* of Flaherty, to which he never quite lived up, was taken as an extrinsic tag of 'trustworthiness' under whose credential he felt able to engage in a degree of manipulation of the pro-filmic which most people today would consider a transgression of anthropological ethics.) Most film-makers, aware of the implicit circularity of this – 'Believe me when I say that I'm telling you the truth' – prefer to rely upon intrinsic signals as indications of how the film is to be understood. The labels are swallowed. The ethics become buried in the style.

Documentarists, tracing their genealogy proudly from Lumière, like to believe that documentary is the 'natural' form of cinema. But fiction film, like painting and literature, rests no special claims upon the provenance of its linguistic elements. It must surely be clear that it is documentary which is the paradoxical, even aberrant form. True, the first films were of a 'factual' nature; but the medium was not out of its immobile, one-shot infancy when someone saw the possibility that it might be employed to signify something *other* than that which it recorded, this step being taken by Méliès, a prestidigitator. From now on, it was non-fiction films which were to be distinguished by a special name: actualities.

The problems latent in the idea of actuality become compounded at precisely the point where this name becomes inadequate and must be replaced by the more evasive one, 'documentary': the point at which the primordial image becomes articulated as language. (It is interesting, though futile, to speculate on how differently the syntax of film might have developed had Méliès' irreversible step – the original sin of the cinema – not been taken.) The difficulties are twofold. Firstly, this is the point at which it becomes possible for the articulations to be used – and perhaps inevitable for them to be perceived – as implicit indications of the nature and status of the component images. Secondly: there is clearly no sense in which the one-to-one relation of shot to prior event may be said to hold good for a structured sequence, let alone an entire film. The activity of an editor is in this respect more akin to that of a painter than to that of a photographer, whose apparatus may be held to ensure a certain 'objectivity' even when it does not produce a good – or a recognisable – likeness. In what sense, then, is it meaningful to claim any privilege at all for such structures?

These two difficulties – the status imputed by structures to their elements and the status claimed for the structures themselves – may be seen as the 'vertical' and 'horizontal' aspects of the problem. They are not entirely separable, as one example will suffice to demonstrate. Consider a group of synchronous shots taken from various distances, with or without simultaneous cameras, at a cricket match. An essential factor in this record, as indeed of the 'atmosphere' of the occasion, will be the delay between sound and vision as the ball makes contact with the bat. This delay will vary in proportion to our distance from the batsman. If, then, we wish to cut from midshot to longshot immediately after the batsman's stroke, in order to show where the ball goes, the sound on the former shot will be almost instantaneous with the image, whilst the sound on the latter will be noticeably retarded. Thus the sound on the former may occur before the cut, whilst that on the latter may occur after it: in which case we should hear the impact twice. Conversely, if we cut from longshot to midshot to follow the subsequent movement of the batsman, we ought not to hear it at all. What the editor will in fact do is to iron out these anomalies by laying all the sounds in apparently simultaneous synch with the pictures. In so doing, however, he is allowing a syntactic relation between two elements, a relation whose claim to documentary privilege might properly be discussed in the context of alternative 'horizontal' strategies, to determine a shift in the actual relation of the image to the pro-filmic. (It need hardly be added that the problem becomes more vexed when we are dealing not with true variations in camera position but with variations in the setting of a zoom lens from a static viewpoint.)

With this proviso in mind, however, let us examine first the 'vertical' question. To face it directly: when, in our watching of a film, do we 'know' that it is a documentary, i.e. that its constituent images are to be read in a documentary sense, and how? What is the nature of those buried stylistic signals to which we are responding? The answer to this question will vary from film to film and also, perhaps, from person to person; but what is probable is that these signals, in fact no more than reading instructions preferred to extrinsic labels for their very inexplicitness, will take on, through our-the-viewers' acquiescence in them, the misleading and contentious character of guarantees of the film's veracity. The reasons for this lie in the nature of the documentary idiom.

Just as jazz and functional architecture are identified by certain characteristics consequent upon their mode of manufacture, so most of what one might designate the stylistic indices of traditional documentary have been the product of practical constraints: the physical difficulties of filming, the demands of a theme not wholly tailored to the pre-given technology, or simply the usual inadequacy of the budget. These find their objective expression in: a predominance of location shooting; a graininess due to the absence of studio light; a customary linking of diverse images through verbal narration; a woodenness in rehearsed performances due to the use of non-actors, and a consequent tendency for rehearsed material to be broken into short units; a wobbliness in spontaneous material due to hand-holding of the camera, and a toleration in such material for temporary lapses of focus or framing and for imperfect continuity in the cutting of supposedly matching actions; and a tendency to define complementarity of shots (in a cross-cut conversation, for example) according to the framings obtained by panning the camera from a fixed position.

In fiction film, by contrast, the stylistic characteristics are not directly determined by the exigencies of production. Thus, for example, a cross-cut conversation will typically be constructed from an alternation of over-the-shoulder shots involving a re-location of the camera, as often as not in mid-sentence. Generally speaking, classic fiction style wilfully avoids the construction of its space from what might be thought credible positions for one casual observer. It is as if the very arbitrariness of the conventions were itself an index of the fictive predisposition of the elements – a signal that what actually happened during filming had no priority over the *fact* of filming, and need not concern us.

But if the idioms of documentary are not arbitrary, that certainly does not mean that they are trustworthy. There is scarcely one of them (the only obvious exception being the un-actorly performance) which has not at some time been appropriated by the fiction film, in which context it becomes an *arbitrary* signifier of real*ism*. Indeed, it is difficult to think of a style of realism in film fiction which does *not* call upon some quality thrust upon non-fiction by circumstance. It is almost as if verbal realism were to find it necessary to sport the mis-spellings, erasures and shaky grammar of a hastily-jotted dispatch. But the traffic has, of course, been two-way. Documentary has usually sought, in its more premeditated sequences, to approximate to the arbitrary conventions of fiction, since these constitute, after all, our received and shared film language for the articulation of time and space. The strangest of transactions, however, are documentary's borrowings from itself. We have all seen the shot where a reporter knocks on a door and is admitted, camera atilt, mike in picture and hand-held lights slewing drunkenly, to a house whose occupants show not the slightest surprise at this invasion. At this point the documentary ethic is buried in more senses than one. (No doubt this sort of thing happens less in academic film-making than in television; but only in the most Utopian of fantasies can we neglect entirely the possibility of fraud.) What this amounts to is an attempt to invest documentary realism with literary realism: a superimposition of idioms which, ethics aside, can lead only to a blurring of perception.

What we have seen in recent years has been a narrowing of the gap between the languages of documentary and fiction. On the documentary side, this convergence has resulted from precisely those technical developments which have been hailed as opening up the domestic realm to scrutiny, and from the skills developed by technicians in response to their challenge. Those same lightweight, silent-running cameras and recorders, plus film emulsions whose sensitivity obviates the need for extra lighting in most situations, have led to the production of films whose fluency of camerawork and naturalness of 'performances' rival the most polished of studio achievements; and the high shooting ratios now frequently available for such film-making have opened up an unprecedented range of stylistic choice for the editor.

What 'observational' technology in fact offers us, when we turn our attention from its mere data-gathering aspects, is a film grammar almost free of such technical limitations as have in the past characterised documentary, and have indeed virtually defined it in contradistinction to fiction. If documentary is a form fractured by paradox, what are we to think of a fulfilment whereby it divests itself of what have hitherto been, for the viewer, its definitive and delimiting features? There have, after all, been earlier casualties of the discovery that a stylistic label guarantees nothing: witness that 'immediacy' which, as a cant word in the formative years of television, carried an implication that the quality of being immediate, rather than simply of looking spontaneous, might magically be conveyed across the airwaves. This concept did not survive the introduction of videotape recording. Does documentary face a similar dissolution?

Some people would argue that any distinction between documentary and fiction diminishes rapidly to zero as a film increases in complexity, and that such problems of language and labelling as have been seemingly posed or exacerbated by recent technical advances are no more than the reaffirmation of this under-lying contradiction. If they are right, then documentary is indeed a false calling. It is here that we shift from the 'vertical' to the 'horizontal' dimension: from the question of the labelling of elements to that of the relation of a broad text (and, by implication, of the elements considered as subdivisions of that text) to the pro-filmic. For to make documentaries is to engage with precisely this paradox: to seek structures in which the aspect of film-as-record may retain (or perhaps reassume?) its significance.

The definition of documentary in terms of the viewer's perception, i.e. as material perceived as signifying what it appears to record, avoids some of the wilder consequences of attempted definitions in terms of productive method, which, with their stress upon the status of the pro-filmic, inevitably end up in disputes about whether this or that reality is as real as it might be. It is in this light that we may understand why the appropriation of the domestic realm – the conquest of an area hitherto 'accessible' only to fiction – should constitute both a fulfilment and a crisis for documentary. The crisis, unfathomable from either of the extreme viewpoints grounded in the conception of film as either purely language or purely record, is one not primarily of field ethics – of how to register behaviour with the minimum of intrusion – but of how to structure material so that whatever it may become as experienced language may in some sense keep faith with its character as pro-filmic fact. For, whilst the attempt to ensure that things are what they seem will present itself to the location crew as an ethical problem, the implications will be present to the viewer only in so far as they manifest themselves in terms of the aesthetic. In the sense that the crisis is located in the transition from the film-makers' terms of reference to the viewer's it is a crisis of editing, for it is at this interface that the editor works.

If, as has been suggested, the repetitiveness and public nature of the elements of classic documentary may be said to mark the outset of their own self-symbolism, it is clear that the reality contrived upon such elements must take on the character either of a generalisation from a multitude of possibilities, super-imposed and scarcely distinguishable, or of a symbolic entity towards which the pro-filmic was already in incipient project. Even when individual behaviour was essayed, these guidelines were usually respected. The stilted speech of the groundcrew awaiting the safe return of F for Freddie was a clear signal (an 'intrinsic label') that these were to be construed not as characters (acted) but as people (act*ing*): that this record of their actions, though structured according to the familiar canons of realism, was to be seen as articulating a *demonstration* in the Brechtian sense – a generalised statement about their own lives. Now, deprived of the support of those conventions which no doubt at the time seemed the most grievous of limitations, condemned to a treacherous fluidity by the spontaneities of observed behaviour, documentary must ask itself what may be the structures which will arrest the settling of this fluidity into the ever-accommodating moulds of rhetoric. Seen in this 'horizontal' perspective, however, the prospect is not encouraging. A mere juxtaposition of two shots will demonstrate the proliferation of the difficulties.

In an American senate committee hearing, a senior public official faces accusations of misconduct. As he listens to the development of a hostile line of questioning, we cut to his hands playing nervously with a paper clip, the voice of his interrogator continuing off-screen. This simple cut opens up a range of possibilities:

1. The sound continuity is genuine and the second shot is also genuinely synchronous, i.e. it was taken with another camera.
2. The sound continuity is genuine, but the second shot is a 'cutaway' taken from a similar context elsewhere in the rushes.
3. Both shots are synchronous, but taken with one camera; and there is a concealed cut (perhaps not *exactly* matching the picture cut) in the sound.
4. The second shot is a cutaway designed to conceal the fact that the sound is discontinuous.
5. The cutaway is taken from a *dis*similar context elsewhere in the rushes.
6. The cutaway was re-enacted after the event by the character in the film.
7. The cutaway was set up with an actor.

And so forth. These may be said to represent varying levels of ethical probity – assuming, that is, that some ethical claim has been implicitly made – or, alternatively, to represent a range of statements whose verbal equivalents would be somewhat as follows:

a) This man is made nervous by this question.
b) This man is made nervous by this type of question.

c) This type of man is made nervous by this type of question.

But the implicit signals whereby we-as-viewers evaluate the material will, even if we consent to trust them, be too coarse to enable us to discriminate between such alternatives. Not only will we be unable to judge the truth of the film's statement; we will be unable even to determine with any precision what sort of statement it is. However carefully the film-makers may have matched the nature of the cut to the nature of the statement they wished to be seen as making, however scrupulously they may, under the banner of *vérité*, have selected their options only from the upper reaches of the above lists, neither the sincerities nor the choices made in sincerity will be truly legible in the product. From the standpoint of the viewer, the practices of 'observational' cinema cannot be legitimised by the ethics of fieldwork. Yet it is only from the standpoint of the viewer that documentary can be understood.

How, then, are we-as-viewers to take such a sequence? If we perceive it as a transparency (selecting, that is, from the upper parts of the above lists), we stand in danger of being cheated; if we perceive it as an argument (i.e. selected from the lower parts), then the aspect of film as record, with its implication of uniqueness and contingency, dwindles into insignificance and the particular becomes only the exemplar of the abstraction which it articulates. The latter option leaves us little better off than we were in the days of classical, 35mm documentary.

This problem can only be compounded by the use of film as a mode of disquisition (and I am not convinced that retreat into the idea of film as a mere research tool is any more than an evasion of it) in anthropology, whose whole bias is to regard the pro-filmic – in the form of ritual, kinship, mythic representation, everyday behaviour – as itself a structure for the articulation of social meanings. If an event is itself an element in a linguistic structure, what is the status of a film which linguifies it into an element of an altogether different discourse – and, worse still, tries to make this discourse accessible to those who do not speak the original 'tongue'?

Consider another example of what occurs in the editing process: an example taken, for simplicity's sake, from our own culture. The event is an argument between two people in a small office. The argument lasts for an hour and a half, out of which the camera is running for approximately fifty minutes, panning between the two people and occasionally shifting position to favour one or the other. The attitudes of the characters emerge only slowly, with much repetition of key points, though with a gradual overall rise in the emotional temperature. The relevance of this sequence to the theme of the film does not justify allowing it more than about twelve minutes of screen time: but this, irksome though it may be, does no more than stress the inherent selectivity of cutting. The problems confronted by the editor therefore present themselves in the form of such questions as: 'Does this sequence, whilst avoiding undue repetition, reproduce the spiral nature of the interaction? Does it do justice to both positions whilst also conveying the subtleties of the psychological tactics in use on both sides? Does it respect the integrity of each participant, in the sense of not allowing a change of emotional state to appear unmotivated (so that anger, for example, might come across as mere petulance), or of presenting someone's line of argument in a form less rational – or even more rational – than that which it took in the actual debate?' And beneath these, of course, lie more fundamental questions. Are we trying to be fair to the people as individuals or to their strategies, or to the institution of whose ethos they are the temporary embodiment? Are we seeking to demonstrate the arguments used or to clarify the actual intellectual positions which these partly express but partly mask? Is the tedium of the event's repetitiousness – a quality it may posses only for the observer uncommitted to either viewpoint – something which should be retained or avoided? Such things need to be asked not just in a liberal spirit of impartiality, but in an attempt to ground the film's putative meanings – even, where appropriate, its polemic – in a correct apprehension of the world. Throughout the process, the editor is engaged in a curious mental exercise: to attempt, from the rushes and from the testimony of those present, to form an intuitive impression of the event as if it were first-hand experience (granted that all such experience is itself partial and selective); and then, in settling upon the presumptive happening 'behind' the material, to use that material to *say* it.

The difficulty with all this lies not in the fact that it is a matter of personal judgment (as of course it is), nor that people are having scripts written for them out of their own words, and performances drawn from the repository of their own unguarded gestures (for it cannot be otherwise), nor even that, in the process of compression, certain of the 'themes' may have to be sacrificed to the coherence of others (the given becoming the data); but in something less obvious. In our anxiety to keep faith with the event as we have understood it, in our careful attention to the mutual respect of the two characters and the behaviour appropriate to their relative status, in our assessment of the degree of eye-to-eye contact which may be permitted across a given cut, the alacrity with which one party may press home an advantage or the pause to be allowed before the other climbs down or gives way to fury, how much interruption is permissible, how much non-sequitur will be tolerated . . . in all these judgments we are resorting to a multiplicity of social behavioural codes: and we are resorting to them not in the sense of requiring to encode them as pro-filmic matter to be demonstrated, but in the sense of recruiting them for use *as filmic codes* in the articulation of the sequence.

The dangers of such a procedure in the portrayal of unfamiliar societies, whose codes of body-language, etiquette and protocol lie outside the competence of editor and viewer, need scarcely be emphasised. I have myself required expert help in the editing of a conversation between two Tuareg, where the constant microscopic adjustments to the height of the veil carry a great weight of social significance. But it is not simply a question of 'getting it right'. What was in effect happening here was that we were allowing the known conventions of dialogue cutting to feed significance back, as it were, into the gestures which had cued the cuts, so that these gestures might be understood retrospectively by the untutored viewer. And the deeper danger lies precisely in the elision of such known conventions – concerning matching of eyelines, continuity of dialogue over cuts and so forth – with the capacity of film to swallow the world into its own syntax, since these conventions have been developed specifically for the articulation of the world as realist fiction.

A more extreme example may be taken from a film about a video-dating service. Here, in a sequence where a man watches the videotape of a potential girl-friend, I found myself able to impart an emotional coherence and momentum to the action by employing intuitively-understood conventions of eye-contact and its avoidance; but in this case the interaction thus narrated from the documentary elements bore a purely illusory relevance to those elements, since the glances of the man were directed not at the girl herself but at a television screen, whilst those of the girl had been directed not at the man, nor even at her unseen interviewer, but at the video-camera. What was happening in this sequence, then, was the deliberate narrative pre-figuring of a relationship which was to develop later in the story – an excursion into that treacherous terrain between documentary and fiction which it was our conscious intention in this film to explore. But, whilst one might hesitate to use such methods in a film claiming strictly observational status, we must face the fact that the alternative to using these social codes to imply a relationship might have been to allow them, by default, to deny one.

To put it crudely: we have learned that, when a mid-shot of someone lowering a cup is followed by a close-shot of a cup being placed on a saucer, this is to be construed as signifying not two separate actions but one continuous one. Such a convention – some twenty years younger than the cinematograph itself – functions to efface the pro-filmic (where there actually *were* two actions) in the projection of a hermetic reality, a closed diegetic world defined only by the narrative which it calls into being to inhabit it and, though masquerading as everybody's world, intelligible only from the standpoint of its narrator.

Furthermore, it is arguable that recourse to such conventions serves not only to define a quasi-literary realism but to inhibit the documentary response altogether: for it is difficult to see what, other than their cumulative presence, may be said to alert the viewer to the fact that material is to be construed in a fictional mode, that we are to see not Christopher Lee mounting some plaster steps in a low-key-lit studio but Count Dracula returning to his castle. Just as, in the documentary response, failure to construe an element as signifying what it appears to record leads to breakdown of meaning, so, in the fictive response, perception of an element as recording other than what it appears to signify is consigned to irrelevance. In other words, it is not merely incidental to but definitive of fiction that its nature as record should be negated; and one of the functions of received film syntax is precisely to ensure such negation.

In our case, however, the fiction is not a true fiction, acknowledged by the viewer as such, but the insinuation of a demonstrative position – a pseudo-

narrative omniscience achieved by the elision of filmic and pro-filmic languages –
into the viewer's construction of the film's meaning: a replacement of documentary's once frank demonstrativeness by a demonstrativeness covert and
shifty: an attempt to pass off a meta-reality as a reality of some transcendent
make. The viewer will refer the film back to the events filmed; but such return
will constitute not the fleshing-out of understanding from the fund of his
experience but the superimposition of fictive representation upon the disorder of
the pro-filmic. One might posit a form of crypto-fiction: a mode in which, though
the relation of the material to a prior world is intellectually acknowledged, such
relationship remains marginal or irrelevant to the meaning we-as-viewers
attribute to the whole. Conversely, it is possible that such meaning may be
re-invested in the world in ways the material does not warrant: that an argument
may be concealed within the structure of the diegesis such that our construction
of the latter will entail endorsement of the former.

Ought we then to regret the invention of the equipment which, erasing the
signatures of documentary's previous (if limited) credibility, have enabled us to
weave our dubious assertions into the semblance of unanswerable reality?
Perhaps. But the problem as we have stated it offers at least a clue to its own
solution, hinting at strategies which must be adopted if documentary is to escape
its former demonstrative limitations, its confinement to the general, without
being willy-nilly sold into realism. What are needed, broadly speaking, are
methods whereby the various strands of the discourse – the referential nature of
the images, their demonstrative disposition, the construction of narrative con-
tinuities in time and space, the filmic and extra-filmic codings – may be denied
elision and offered as separable to the viewer's security. Many approaches are
possible. Indeed, the creativity of future documentary must consist largely in
exploring them. One – perhaps not too promising – might consist in pushing the
received conventions to the point of parody so that, whilst still functioning to
articulate the material, they would be perceived in their arbitrariness. Another
would be to employ methods of selective jump-cutting whereby one theme – the
logic of an argument, perhaps, or the local narrative of one character's actions –
would be articulated as a continuity whilst the remainder respected the dis-
continuity of the pro-filmic. Where commentary must be used, it might take the
form of two voices disagreeing as to the proper interpretation of the evidence. If
cutaways are needed, perhaps they should be graded differently or wear different
clothing from synchronous shots of people listening, as a mark of their different
grammatical status. (I once heard an anthropologist-film-maker being taken to
task by a colleague for having constructed a bargaining sequence by intercutting
material of a stall-holder and customer shot on different days. A distinction in
grading between the two components might have satisfied the requirements of
both differentiation and synthesis.)

An interesting pendant to these considerations is that even the received
conventions of fiction are not immutable, and do not always retain their
significance when the responsive context is changed. This fact may act against us

or in our favour. On the one hand, I have made the mistake of trying to use a dissolve in a documentary for its classical fiction purpose of indicating a tele-scoping of narrated time (which in documentary means a telescoping of pro-filmic time), only to find that viewers simply failed to read it in this sense, or even to notice it at all. On the other hand it seems likely, once the documentary response is firmly established, that a continuity-cut which in fiction would certainly signify a single action may take on the force of a jump-cut signifying two.

Some of the above suggestions may, I confess, have their origin in the editor's preference for scratched, unmatched picture and non-equalised sound of the cutting copy over the harmonious fluency of a finished print. However, I am not here trying to outline all the possibilities, but merely to suggest that the puritanical caution advocated by many anthropologists as an appropriate attitude to their records is unnecessary. There are certain jokes which we assume to be true stories because there would be no point in telling them if they were not. Perhaps film-makers should aim towards forms of construction which, in achiev-ing this sort of credibility, would circumvent the need for stylistic labels. Back in the early fifties I saw a television programme about George Bernard Shaw, doubtless shot with the full panoply of 35mm equipment and its attendant hordes of technicians. A mid-shot of Shaw sitting down at his typewriter was followed, in classic fashion, by an over-shoulder shot as he began to type. What he typed was, 'I don't normally behave like this at all.'

We have only to look at some of the best in ethnographic film to see both the meaninglessness of claims to supra-linguistic objectivity and the subtlety of the methods whereby documentary may yet insist upon the pro-filmic. In a film such as *Lorang's Way*, by David and Judith MacDougall, we may perhaps respond first to its formal discipline and to the sureness of its control. We may be inclined to point out that the long-sustained shots, whose exclusion of off-screen activity becomes at times almost oppressive, constitute as much the imposition of a filmic rhythm as would constant cutting to the objects of the characters' gaze. Yet it is also true, not only that the presence of the camera is acknowledged in each sequence, but that it is acknowledged by successive sequences in contrasting ways – as companion during a walking track, as interlocutor during a formal interview, as casual nuisance in an occasional verbal jibe, as maintaining-a-respectful distance in a long telephoto hold – and that the juxtaposition of these modes of acknowledgment sustains a constant interrogation of the status of the film unit, both technical/aesthetic and social, which inhibits the semantic closure to which realism constantly tends. And it does this, furthermore, in a way which can have no precise equivalent in fiction.

In short, then, we must beware of treating film from an Olympian standpoint as if, solely by declaring ourselves outside the process, we were able to span that dichotomy between film-makers' perspective and viewer's perspective which is the concrete presence of film. We may ask only what options face the film-makers for the structuring of their perceptions as recorded, and what options face the viewer for the deciphering of this structure as a text. Indeed, as an extreme statement of this position one might suggest that the film-makers' responsibility is fulfilled in an attempt to reverse the polarity of the filmic signs so that their sense is towards their material sources – their object-matter understood as their subject-matter. Certainly it is the case that, since documentary reality is the viewer's construction, any suggestion of interpretations being 'forced on us' represents an abdication of responsibility by the viewer. Wilfully or by oversight, some materials may be wrongly labelled. Some things may have been less rehearsed or more rehearsed, less spontaneous, less calculated, less un-influenced by the camera's presence than we-as-viewers suppose them to have been. But there is no sharp demarcation between the misunderstandings of documentary and the misunderstandings of life. And the documentary stance is essentially one of interrogation.

I have suggested ways in which complex structures may draw upon, rather than efface, the aspect of film as record; but I have not yet found a justification, within the viewer's perspective, for those 'observational' practices which, in the film-makers' perspective, represent themselves as exploring the potential of the new technology in the appropriation of the domestic realm. (By 'observational practices' I mean the extreme precautions frequently taken to minimise the crew's influence upon the pro-filmic and/or, within the acknowledged fallibility of the medium, to signal the degree of such influence to the viewer: such practices as lengthy acquaintance with the subjects before the start of shooting and/or the inclusion of crew members or camera gear in the shots.) Anthropologists have been mistaken in imagining that *vérité* might herald a return to the pre-lapsarian innocence of the actuality. But have they been altogether wrong in the methods they have evolved in this belief?

Let us look again at the dichotomy film-as-record/film-as-language with whose subjective aspect we began. If documentary were merely record, then editors would not be needed to order it, since to grant significance to the order in which records are presented is to impute to it a linguistic nature; yet if documentary were language pure and simple, editors would not be needed to manipulate it, since there would be no meanings generated other than those commonly available, to film-crew and viewers alike. Clearly these twin aspects of the medium are not to be understood as alternatives: for, quite apart from its possible articulations as fiction, the record can only function as a record to the extent that it is *legible* as such. Of course, there may be mementos so poignant and personal that the linguistic element scarcely rises even to the rudimentary; and we may well, at the other extreme, care to ask exactly what 'record' can mean to someone who was not present at the original event. Whether at the cellular level of the photograph or the complex one of a structured communication, whether in one-to-one relationship with the pro-filmic or otherwise, an act of decipherment is what is called for. As viewers, in electing to perceive a film as documentary, we do not reject a fictive option for a known non-fiction, but rather select a mode of apprehension in full knowledge of our own ignorance.

There are in *The Battleship Potemkin* sequences in which minimal human activity – sailors asleep in hammocks, others on watch – is intercut with details of the ship and with seascape material such as buoys, gulls, other vessels and views ashore. At our present distance in time we may construe such material as a portrayal of Odessa harbour either in 1905, when the story is set, or in 1925, when the film was made. This distinction, between the fictive and the documentary construction, is subtle but absolute: and it would remain absolute even if the action of the fiction had been set in 1925 also. It depends not upon our prior knowledge of the look of Odessa at these dates but upon the mode of our interrogation of the images. A reality, like a fiction, must be articulated. But the difference between an account and a narrative lies, for us-as-recipients, in the relationship we posit between the linguistic elements and the total discourse. In fiction, the elements are exhausted in the production of the overall meaning of the text; and anything which cannot be read as contributing to this meaning is consigned to a limbo of insignificance. In documentary, by contrast, the elements are seen as always exceeding their contribution to any given meaning; and they remain always open to scrutiny either for their own sakes or for their potential in the generation of new meanings oblique, peripheral or even antagonistic to the text as understood.

As will be recognised, the analogy of an 'account' is inadequate beyond a certain point: for in a verbal account of something, a piece of journalism, say, the excess by which we interpret the prior world as outspanning its description is present to the reader only as a subjective coloration to the words, a sense of their striving after what they cannot wholly comprehend; whereas in documentary that excess is present in the images, in their potential always to reveal – under different interrogations – aspects of the pro-filmic hitherto unremarked. In this respect, then, the verbal affinities of documentary are with poetry, since the resistance of its elements to total absorption in the discourse represents a resistance against the drift towards pure symbolism. Verbal poetry seeks to dissolve the symbolic fixity of the word by undermining the rules of syntax – either relaxing them, as in free, surreal or rhapsodic verse, or subordinating them to other and more arbitrary structures (alliterative, metrical, syllabic, quantitative . . .) which, whilst preserving, mock them. Freed of the absolute grip of those grammars with which its symbolic precision is held in mutual support, the word offers the full range of its ambiguities and connotations for the generation of a flux of meaning which will be set in resonance by the reader's experience. All film aspires towards the poetic in that it has neither a wholly predetermined syntax nor a precise, delimited symbolic vocabulary. But to grant a film documentary sense is to respect in its images the density, the plenitude of the pro-filmic: a plenitude which defies its reduction towards the symbolic and thus defies also, by implication, its articulation into a simple, linear statement approximating to the condition of prose. Documentary faces us with the paradox that, whilst in its elements it is capable of falsehood, since its labels are swallowed, in its totality it is not capable of falsehood, since its articulations are those of poetry.

Thus whilst its elements may be misread though not miswritten, its totality –
conceived as prose but perceived as poetry – may be miswritten but not misread.

Very well, perhaps this formulation is a little exaggerated. I do not wish to
suggest that there is *no* sense in which documentary may be read as prose. To the
extent that it uses unambiguous constructions to make statements capable of
falsehood, clearly it may. By editing, I could show the 'wrong' side carrying a vote
or winning a battle; and even those who insist that there is no absolute, or at least
absolutely knowable, 'real' event against which its 'representations' can be
judged would surely agree in finding such editing reprehensible. But today's lie,
differently regarded, may be tomorrow's evidence. A notorious film of Pygmies
building rope bridges becomes, when we are told that they do not build such
bridges and had to be taught to do so by the film-makers, a film about Pygmy
adaptability and helpfulness. Old documentaries are constantly being ransacked
for new compilations; yet such re-cycling seems always to enrich rather than
diminish them. Documentary, unlike fiction, welcomes its own displacement.

Another way of putting this would be to say that documentary always exceeds
its makers' prescriptions. (If it did not, ethnographic films might as well be made
in the studio with actors.) It is such a recognition which lies behind the wish
expressed by many anthropologists that every last frame of ethnographic rushes
should be catalogued and preserved in a gargantuan *Monde Imaginaire* for the
benefit of researchers yet unborn – an idea which at first may seem as crazy as
making a collection of good sentences in the hope that somebody will one day
shuffle them into a book. Resistance to this recognition, on the other hand, is
frequently encountered in the form of politically reactionary claims of privilege
for the source of discourse, whether personal or (by surreptitious proxy) institutional. Superficially reasonable demands that our films be comprehensible are
often in effect demands that the viewer be browbeaten into sharing *our* understanding of them. Documentary's images are, ideally, not illustrative but constitutive. They are constitutive of the viewer's meanings, since it is the viewer who
constitutes them as documentary.

It has always been so. Of course, in the post-Méliès era, the documentary
impulse had to satisfy itself with what amounted to an act of retrenchment,
sustaining the Lumière actuality-values in this limited area and that – the locations, 'real' people, confinement to the 'facts' of known incidents – all of which
became, as it were, tokens of a fidelity to be rewarded at some later consummation, endlessly deferred.

But if the technical developments of the past decade-and-a-half have announ-
ced that consummation, the announcement has been widely misunderstood.
What the new equipment can recover of actuality is not its innocence but its
plenitude: or rather, it can extend to most realms that plenitude which was
previously available only in those of public or of non-spontaneous behaviour.
'Observational' practices increase the margin of 'excess' whereby the film out-
strips its makers' intentions: and it is by this argument – by this argument alone –
that they may be justified within the viewer's terms of reference. In our example

of the hands fiddling with the paper clip: once the viewer has accepted our assurance of its significance, it is its significance, not our assurance of it, which will be effective. The plenitude of the image, its polyvalency, is experienced by the viewer as a play of connotations. Just as the ethics of the film-makers are experienced as aesthetics by the viewer, so the anthropologist's objectivity translates into ambiguity, and the 'real-life' density commonly attributed by the viewer to such film is our experience of active engagement in the generation of meaning. All film is a trace of the world: and, whilst it may be true that the very articulations whereby we are enabled to perceive it as such commit us to ethnocentricity, this truth may at least arguably be suspended in that zone of flux at the leading edge of communication where poetry is forever congealing into prose, insight into dogma. If not, documentary is unjustified.

## References

*Films*
MacDougall, D. and J. MacDougall (1978), *Lorang's Way*, University of California Extension Media Center, Berkeley. Colour, 70 mins.
Eisenstein, S. (1925), *Battleship Potemkin*, First Studio Goskino, USSR. Black and White, 75 mins. (silent).

# Which films are the ethnographic films?

The name of the (ethnographic) game now is . . . pastiche
(Caplan 1988, p. 8)

There are good grounds for thinking that the discipline of visual anthropology is now at some sort of turning point, at least in Britain. As anthropology in general shudders under the impact of largely American-inspired postmodernism, so that part of anthropology which is concerned with visual representation and visual communication is seeking to assert for itself some kind of identity that can be easily summarised in course prospectuses and imparted to new students. Within this, the role of film still continues to dominate the scene and it therefore seems timely to consider what exactly we mean by ethnographic film and what we intend to do with it. Numerous surveys of ethnographic film in general have been published in recent years (e.g. Banks in press; Chiozzi 1989; Ginsburg 1988; Henley 1985), but most have sought to describe films that are self-identifyingly 'ethnographic'. With reference to some of the articles mentioned this seems a worrying tendency when it is television companies rather than anthropologists that are applying the label 'ethnographic'. It would seem that, in these days of ever higher production standards and the need to cater for a television audience, a division of labour is developing whereby 'ethnographic' films are produced for anthropologists by others, the anthropologists merely acting to set a seal of authenticity upon the finished product. I feel that it is time to challenge this tendency and for anthropologists to redefine what it is they consider to be important in film, that we should not be afraid to say a polite 'no, thank you' to certain productions and to welcome instead those which might be scorned by the media professionals.

## Terms of reference

When one comes to define what an ethnographic film might be there are three angles or perspectives to consider. For clarity, I will present these diagrammatically:

Any film can be considered as the outcome of these three phenomena and they are linked, as in my diagram, in a chain to form a process.[1] An intention – to make a film – results in an event – the filming process – which leads to a reaction – the response of the audience to the physical manifestation of the event (the film). For different films and among different audiences, one or other aspect of the process may be foregrounded. For example, film critics espousing some form of auteur theory will be primarily interested in the intention of the director: who is Peter Greenaway and why does he make films like *The Cook, The Thief, His Wife and Her Lover* (1989)? Similarly, non-film-making viewers of a *verité* documentary may be primarily interested in the event (both the filmic event and the event of film-making – the Maysles brother's film *Grey Gardens* (1975) would be a good example of this). Finally, the reaction may itself evoke interest among, for example, academics working in media studies (why do so many people watch *EastEnders*? Do pornographic films precipitate violence against women?). Of course, all three stages of the process may be evinced (or conjectured) from the study of any particular film, and I do not wish to suggest that one may find evidence of one to the exclusion of the others.

Thus, when we turn to so-called ethnographic films it would be instructive to consider where it is that the criterion of ethnographicness is supposed to reside and then to make a judgement – on the basis of my remarks above – as to which anthropologists might consider most suited to their purposes. I shall do this by considering each of my three process categories in turn, without wishing to suggest that analysis of this process is a way of evaluating the ethnography enshrined. For the moment at least I am unconcerned with whether one can call the ethnographic insights 'good' or 'bad'.

## Intention

The overt reasons for creating an ethnographic film constitute an aspect of intentionality that I shall return to in my discussion of the third category, reaction. That is to say, questions of intentionality such as 'Why was the film made?', 'Who was it made for?', 'What can it be used for?', are questions that can only be answered when the response or reaction is considered. In this section I am rather concerned with intentionality as an aspect of agency. The intention is to stimulate an ethnographic event (however this may be defined or received) and thus the cause of such an intention must be the ethnographic agent.

One obvious locus of intentionality would be in the person of the film's director; if he or she were an anthropologist, then it would seem fair to call the film anthropological or at least ethnographic. Of course, this discounts any instances (although I know of none) of an anthropologist making a film which has no obvious connection with anthropology: a madcap comedy, for example (there aren't many jokes in anthropology). There are, however, a few directors of non-self-identifying ethnographic films who have had some anthropological training in the past. In Britain it is rare for active anthropologists to have made their own films and those that do usually make a single film about a culture they know well. As far as Britain is concerned, anthropologists are more usually involved as consultants, often with television productions, but this means that they are rarely the initiators of the project, but rather the agents by which the project is realised.

Narrowing the locus of intention down to the initiator and initial facilitator of the project (the producer or producing company) leaves us with rather a small range of films to consider. Leaving aside the corpus of work of certain 'big men' (Asch, Dunlop, MacDougall, Rouch) we are left with a residual category which could loosely be described as 'research footage'. In this I would include the work of the Institute of Scientific Films in Göttingen and those bits of footage which many anthropologists turn out to have shot and then modestly shelved under their desks.

First, however, let me raise another idea: the difference between the two meanings of the word 'film', the object and the concept. On the one hand we have the physical object, the celluloid film strip: consideration of this leads to the ideas of 'documentation' and 'research footage'. On the other hand we have the concept (usually referred to as 'cinema' to avoid confusion): consideration of this leads to 'films' (documentary, ethnographic, feature and all combinations).

In the first approach, that of the celluloid film strip, there is a primary focus of interest, the 'reality' which appears to be directly encoded upon the emulsion of the celluloid. In the anthropological world we would find footage of house-building, dances, rituals and so forth. These documents carry with them inherent functionalist dangers – bounded, linear representations, monovocal and a-contextual. If we take as a metaphor the idea of a cinematic plane, analogous to the flat plane of the film surface, then this 'documentation' approach to film is concerned only with a plane of representation that transparently reveals the action that went on in front of the camera and which was recorded by the light-sensitive film.

In the second approach, that of 'film as cinema', a further plane, the cine-matographic plane, intervenes between the transparent plane of 'reality' and the viewer. This cinematographic plane, which is denied or ignored by the first approach, is the one in which the technological processes of filming reveal themselves – camera-work, lighting, sound mixing, editing – in short, all the transformations that the raw film and the raw 'reality' captured by that film (inevitably) undergo before they are seen by the viewer. While the first approach, film as document, is necessarily limited, film as cinema (the second approach) can head off in a huge number of directions: feature films, documentary film, ethno-graphic documentaries, drama documentaries, animation and so on and so on.

When we consider the idea of ethnographic intention it appears that it is most clearly seen when the desire is to encode 'reality' directly upon the film strip. When the cinematographic plane intrudes or is emphasised, criteria other than ethnographic intention may intervene. That is, values from the domains of cinema or television ('good' shots, exciting cutting, the division of material to allow for commercial breaks, strong narrative content, engaging personalities) may obscure the original ethnographic criterion. Thus some anthropologists call for the cinematographic plane to be excised or minimised into oblivion. This is the position of Karl Heider and of Peter Fuchs and his colleagues at Göttingen.

Heider's milestone work, *Ethnographic Film* (1976) seeks to lay down clear, if over-rigid, guide-lines by which one could judge the ethnographicness of certain filmic texts. His schema has the virtue of simplicity and of being rooted in anthropological ideas. In particular he is concerned with 'wholeness': ethnographic films should reveal whole persons, whole objects, whole actions. Of course, there are problems with this approach, especially the positivist naïvety of the traditional functionalist perspective – how 'whole' is 'whole'? Can one see (in an analytical sense as well as a visual sense) all of everything anyway? Nevertheless, the ideal of ethnographic intentionality is to the fore. Heider recommends the privileging of material for its intrinsic ethnographic worth rather than for its cinematographic merit. For example, he gives two examples of film sequences which contain soft focus shots (pp. 47–8) and defends the decision of the film-makers (one of them himself) to include these shots: '. . . ethnographic considerations overrode cinematographic considerations' (p. 48).

Similarly, Peter Fuchs and his colleagues at Göttingen adopt a 'purist' line (perhaps more so than Heider) by rejecting cinematographic, or aesthetic, considerations: 'A scientific ethnographic film documentation must satisfy the following requirements: unity of place, time, group, and action, together with strict obedience to the chronology of action in the final version of the film. Artificial manipulation in either shooting or cutting is not permitted. A scientific film also rules out the use of staged scenes.' (Fuchs 1988, p. 222). From this perspective, a film (or rather, a piece of footage) is ethnographic if the intention is to portray an area of established anthropological interest – a dance, a ritual, house-building, political debate – so long as it is objective and the cinematic plane wholly transparent. In so far as this goes this is quite laudable: by watching such a piece of footage over and over again in the privacy of one's study or cutting-room, sheer information can be amassed and examined in meticulous detail. This information can then become the data for more conventional forms of analysis. The limitations are that no analysis can be enshrined within the film itself, the cinematic plane of film is denied. Both Fuchs and Heider claim that ethnographic film is not free-standing: it must be supported by written texts (Heider 1976, p. 127; Fuchs 1988, p. 223).

There are exceptions. Jack Rollwagen's edited collection, *Anthropological Filmmaking* (1988) contains two articles by anthropologists who claim that it is possible to carry the ethnographic intention through into the cinematographic plane of the film. Peter Biella and Don Rundstrom each discuss their own films and claim to demonstrate how the construction of the cinematographic plane (especially through predetermined composition at the time of shooting) encodes some degree of specifically anthropological analysis.[2] These are instances where intentionality would seem to transcend the second aspect - event – that I discuss below. Of course, the fact that Biella and Rundstrom have written their articles indicates that they feel a need to amplify upon the analysis contained within their films. Rundstrom at least has also written a study guide to his film (Rundstrom *et al.* 1973).

Thus intention, in terms of stimulating an ethnographic event as recognised by anthropologists, may produce a document which is of further use to anthropologists (the approach of Fuchs and his colleagues) or a document which directly enshrines some form of anthropological analysis (the approach of Biella and Rundstrom).

## Event

If by event we mean the action content of a film then we open ourselves to considering a huge variety of documents as ethnographic films. That is to say, any film which represents the normative subjects of ethnographic enquiry – non-western people doing non-western things (such as gift-exchange, or 'tribal' dancing) – is inherently ethnographic. Heider (1976) warns against such interpretations by his stress on 'wholeness'; just because it is a Nuer who is in the frame doesn't mean that it is an ethnographic film we are watching. Similar arguments have been used to deny ethnographic film status to many of Robert Gardner's films. These films are 'about' non-western people – Dani, Hamar, Hindu Indians, Ika – but are not ethnographic films, because they lack context, or are manipulative, or because Gardner doesn't 'really' understand what is going on.

However, by 'event' I mean instead the filmic event and include the fact that a crew has arrived somewhere and has selected some aspect of someone else's life to enshrine on film. Event is thus a category which is precipitated by intention. This category can thus be examined as a potential container for ethnographicness.

Incorporating the presence and actions of the film crew as part of the 'event' category brings us close to Jay Ruby's reflexive position (Ruby 1980; 1988). Ruby argues that one of the most important things happening in any ethnographic film is the fact that the film is being made at all. This is the 'process' element of Fabian's 'producer-process-product' triad (cited in Ruby 1980, p. 155). As the revelation of the 'process' element is that which validates the findings ('products') of (natural) science research (*ibid.*, p. 164–5) so too such revelation might aid in legitimating the findings of anthropological research. Thus self-declaring ethnographic films which do not reveal the details of their production are no more than impressionistic documents, lacking scientific and analytical validity. Ruby goes on to stress the importance of Rouch and his work in continuing Dziga Vertov's experiment; *Chronique d'un eté* (1960), for example, clearly sets out its methodology within the film text, while the vast majority of other ethnographic films draw legitimation from without the film text, in the form of study guides and the like (*ibid.*, p. 169). Ruby's position is difficult to assess. Since first writing on the topic in 1977 more 'reflexive' films have appeared (even Granada's staid Disappearing World series has flirted with reflexivity in recent years, John Shepherd's *The Herders of Mongun Taiga* (1989) being one example, David Wason's *The Trobriand Islanders of Papua New Guinea* (1990) being another), but they have also revealed certain difficulties, not least, the question of how much information needs to be revealed and of what type. Part of the problem, I think, lies in seeking to extract information about the film-making process from the ethnographic context that any film purports to portray (one of the reasons that I prefer my broader category of 'event' to Ruby's use of Fabian's 'process' category).

Let us then consider a more obvious locus for ethnographicness, lying, as mentioned above, in the speech, action and character of the filmed subjects. If they look like the kind of people anthropologists normally study then a film about them must be ethnographic. Does this then mean that all documentaries shot outside Western Europe will be ethnographic?

One way of approaching this might be to examine the criteria which mark ethnographic writing off from other forms of descriptive writing, travel writing for example. Anthropologists, not surprisingly, are keen to establish and maintain the professional boundaries of the discipline, while at the same time paying lip service to other disciplines considered useful – sociology, linguistics, history, philosophy. Most are agreed, however, that the untrained traveller is hopelessly naive and that travel writing has little to offer beyond a basic 'scene-setting' function for students. I make this comparison with travel writing because the more exotic and non-Western a group of people are, the more anthropologists can claim them as their own. Hence the temptation to see any documentary film about non-western people as intrinsically ethnographic.

The ethnographer is distinguished from the travel writer on a number of counts: the ethnographer is fluent in the local language, while the travel writer at best will know only a few words; the ethnographer stays for a long time, the travel writer for shorter; the ethnographer can seek out and examine abstract phenomena – kinship systems, moral knowledge, the travel writer is concerned with surface – the look of things, material culture; the ethnographer participates (the philosopher's stone of participant-observation), the travel writer only observes; crucially, the ethnographer sees the essential interconnectedness of things, the travel writer sees only incidents and social facts in isolation. But of course, most of these differences are of a quantitative rather than a qualitative kind, the length of time spent in the culture, for example, or the degree of participation. Instead, the difference is revealed by the fact that most ethnographers today return from the field and then do something with the data which places them in a common discourse shared by like-minded others – analyse them, in short – while the travel writer presents the raw data with a few personalised observations (indeed, the more personalised and idiosyncratic the observations the more the travel writer stands to gain acclaim; Bruce Chatwin is an obvious example). There are thus a number of genre conventions that mark off ethnographic writing from travel writing (see Clifford and Marcus 1986), just as genre conventions mark off the western from the horror film.

There are of course, a number of other features which could serve to mark ethnographic film off as a subset of documentary: for example, an attempt to 'anthropologise' visual ethnographic data by, for example, adding a commentary track to a film which contains certain words and turns of phrase from the anthropological discourse established by anthropological writing – 'ethnic group', 'moiety', 'kinship system', 'clan-based factions', and perhaps illustrative diagrams and such like (the Yanomami films of Chagnon/Asch, for example). In fact, these are all techniques by which the genre defines itself, features that we learn to recognise by force of convention as denoting an 'ethnographic film'.

As a footnote to the above comment on words and phrases from the anthropological discourse I would suspect that these are, by and large, phrases from a structural-functionalist discourse, although I have not tested this in any systematic way. It was the functionalism of Malinowski and Radcliffe-Brown which underpinned the professionalism of what had previously been a gentleman amateur's occupation; Lévi-Strauss's structuralism adds a few more terms to the discourse (for example, 'symbolic', 'structured opposition', 'dual') without removing any of the old ones. However, the buzz words of the post-structuralist, postmodernist discourse (such as 'gendered subjectivities', 'self and other', 'hermeneutic tradition' and indeed 'discourse' itself) would be dangerous to use in the commentary of a self-identifying ethnographic film: most of the terms themselves have come from other disciplines or from outside academia alto-gether and are therefore poor allies in establishing the distinctiveness of an anthropological discourse.

This is an example of self-identifying ethnographic films drawing upon key terms (and hence, paradigmatic features) of academic anthropology as a strategy of legitimation. There is, however, another strategy by which ethnographic film seeks to claim its authority and this is through mimesis. The preferred style of ethnographic film-making, the observational style, can be viewed as being mimetic of anthropological practice. To give some wider context to this claim, it is necessary to examine the genre of documentary cinema more generally.

Three labels stand out in the cinema of documentary: *cinéma verité* (the involved camera acting as a catalyst), direct cinema (the invisible camera) and observational cinema. Confusingly, some commentators on documentary will use these as synonyms, while others insist on clear distinctions between them. Such distinctions may relate to external criteria, for example, that certain 'schools' should be given one label and not another. If it's French it must be *cinéma verité*. If it's American it's direct cinema. Or else the distinctions relate to criteria internal to the film. If the film-makers interact with and talk directly to the subjects on camera then it's direct cinema, if they don't then it's observational. Still more confusingly, there are further terms which may or may not be synonyms for the three already mentioned – participatory cinema, fly-on-the-wall documentary, fly-*off*-the-wall documentary and so on. Those who regard these labels as marking significant differences between types of film are usually doing so to advocate one label (and hence style of film) as better than the rest, and better often means purer – closer to the action, more real, etc.

Regardless of the fine distinctions, film-makers who support any of these labels tend to share a common core of beliefs, like a set of vaguely overlapping Venn diagrams. The prime one is a mistrust of television and all its doings. The TV documentary, with its pervasive commentary, its staged and directed events (significant or trivial), its lowest common denominator values, is a smiling tempter to be approached with caution, corrupting, as it does, the purity of the documentary form. TV production values are also scorned; the ideal for the 'pure' documentary is a two person venture, which conceives, executes and edits the project, in place of the TV values where conception, execution and completion are highly separated tasks and where even during the shooting it is inconceivable to have less than three people present and usually more (director, researchers, electricians, camera, assistant camera, sound, assistant sound, etc.).

The rest of the core beliefs are related to these. In no particular order we could list the following:

1. The film-makers should follow action, rather than provoking it, but at the same time guard against the fallacy that the camera and crew can ever become invisible.
2. A vast amount of film should be shot and then edited to preserve whole sequences in their entirety while rejecting others completely, rather than taking a little bit of this and a little bit of that; the film-makers should film everything rather than just the highlights – the trivia are often the most revealing.
3. Following from this, the less obvious a 'subject' a film has, the better; famous people or historic events should be avoided (unless approached tangentially, as in, for example, Chris Marker's *Le Joli Mai* (1963) which crucially does *not* deal with the Algerian war, although this provides the background to much of the film's action). Eschewing such key figures and events prevents the film becoming preoccupied with surface appeal (many 'purists' were upset when members of the famous Drew Associates group of film-makers began to make films about celebrities: *Primary* (Drew/Leacock 1960) being one of the first; *Don't Look Back* (Pennebaker/Leacock 1966), a record of Bob Dylan's 1965 tour of Britain, was the first of several pop-celebrity documentaries).
4. There is a great belief in so-called 'magic moments', when a character being filmed drops his or her carefully constructed persona and bares his or her innermost soul; this is often connected with tears, memories, moments of personal crisis etc. For this reason, some film-makers often continue filming after the obvious moment has passed, when, for example, the subject has

made some speech or committed some deed and then paused to reflect on his or her speech or action.

I reel off this list somewhat cynically and indeed, there is a sense in which the advocates of observational cinema and its variants have cast off one straightjacket of formulae in favour of another. There is, however, a startling similarity between the features which are held to bound off such documentary cinema and, indeed, mark an advance on other forms of documentary, and the features which distinguish anthropological research and writing from any other form of human observation. Anthropologists are less intrusive than other visitors (by their participation and linguistic fluency); they tend to ignore the rich, powerful and well-known in favour of obscure corners of obscure countries; they follow action and record masses of data, many of which may never be used; they are concerned, following Malinowski, with the minutiae of daily life, with gossip and apparent trivia; they believe in getting to the heart of things, of moments of revelation; they believe in waiting. It is for these reasons that I wrote above of observational cinema as having a mimetic quality and it is thus that the preferred form of ethnographic film is one of the variants of observational cinema.[3]

Away from the arena of television (which in general has difficulty in accommodating observational film) anthropologists have raised up the work of certain film-makers – David and Judith MacDougall, Gary Kildea, even Robert Gardner – as most closely representing their own interests. It seems to me that this is because the films of these directors most closely adhere to a set of genre conventions established by a certain kind of anthropological writing. One could argue, however, that these films only accidentally accord with the anthropological agenda, their claims to ethnographicness are brought about by mimicry of what the field-working anthropologist sees and hears, not by their ability to perform the anthropological task directly. Occasionally, the mimicry is sufficiently flawed to be perceptible and to allow anthropologists to deny certain films the status of being ethnographic (as in the case of Gardner).

Along with television's ethnographic films which I discuss briefly below and have discussed at length elsewhere (Banks 1989 and in press) observational films form the jewels in the crown of the ethnographic film canon, apparently because their ethnographic qualities are most clearly seen to shine in the 'event' category of the process, a category which we tend to privilege over intention and reaction because it appears most objective, neutral and transparent (intention can largely only be guessed at, reaction is variable).

## Reaction

The response to the physical manifestation of the event ('the film') is an area with which anthropologists seem to have least concerned themselves. One way of measuring it might be through certain apparently objective criteria. Which films win prizes at festivals of ethnographic film? Which films are chosen for inclusion in ethnographic film libraries? Which films are reviewed and where? There are two problems with using such criteria. First, factors other than pure ethnographic quality may come into play which influence such decisions (favouritism, budgetary constraints, regional bias). Secondly, and more importantly, the loop of discourse is a closed one. If a self-identifyingly ethnographic film is submitted for judgement to an individual or panel who recognise (but do not question) the conventions by which such films declare themselves to be ethnographic, then the ethnographicity (to coin a word) is accepted *a priori*. Only in certain unusual cases (I would again cite Gardner's films as an example) are the conventions so flagrantly breached that the response is to recoil and to challenge. But this is rarely a question of considering any intrinsic ethnographic worth or merit, or of considering the film anthropologically, rather it is a matter of style and convention, of measuring the physical manifestation of the filmic event against other such manifestations which have already been accepted.

Paul Henley has noted that there are grounds for considering even the most unlikely films as ethnographic. One particular example he gives is of a television documentary about a well-known steeplejack (Hayworth, 1979), but unfortunately he gives little indication of his criteria and indeed then goes on to narrow his focus to include only those films which 'deal with . . . non-Western and/or non-industrialized societies' (Henley 1985, pp. 5–6). It is obvious, however, that in such instances the ethnographic attributes may be located in the response, rather than in the intention or even in the event. This is clear when we consider that anthropologists have responded to some fiction films that have no apparent ethnographic intention, nor – arguably – any ethnographic content.[4]

When we turn to self-identifyingly ethnographic films, the response (as far as it can be ascertained) may nonetheless be ambiguous. The reaction to Granada Television's Disappearing World series is a good case in point. In a deservedly important article Peter Loizos defends Granada from the criticisms certain films have drawn from professional anthropologists:

Quite simply, the failure of much evaluation of the series by anthropologists has been a failure to judge the films as mass-audience films *and to apply appropriate criteria*. Mostly, the critics list the questions they would ask of a monograph, or as examiners of a doctorate. No film which could also hold a mass audience could possibly include the amount of analysis or detail they seem to be seeking. (Loizos 1980, p. 589).

The anthropological reviews quoted by Loizos consistently criticise the apparent shallowness of the films' information content and demand more 'facts'. More importantly, many of the reviewers he discusses appear to be specialists in the ethnography of the people filmed, but to have little experience of how television as a medium works. Thus, while certain anthropologists may demonstrate a reaction of disappointment, the fact that some several million viewers consistently tune in to these programmes would seem to indicate some other kind of reaction. One must not confuse the act of watching with approval, however. The fact that several million people watch a television ethnographic film does not allow us to know the nature of their response. We can, however, assume that they must derive at least some satisfaction from the films and it is here that we should seek to locate the criterion of ethnographicness. The anthropologist (or certainly those reviewers cited by Loizos) seeks ethnographicness in the event and is disappointed at the shallowness. The home viewer on the other hand is reacting to a different event (the same film but completely different context) and appears to derive the amount of ethnographicness (if such a thing can be quantified) that will bring satisfaction. Similarly, when used in teaching, my own experience of films such as Granada's has been that the post-screening discussion is the location of ethnographicness. This is not simply a question of the teacher (myself and my colleagues) filling in the missing ethnographic component of the event. Indeed, I often screen films which represent cultures of which I have very little knowledge. Instead, it is in the response that both I and the students situate a pool of ethnographic data, drawn both from the film and from other sources to construct contextually dependent (and hence contingent) ethnographic insights.

Wilton Martinez has recently claimed that far from provoking a positive response, certain ethnographic films may do exactly the opposite (Martinez 1990). In his analysis of student reaction to twenty well-known ethnographic films he discovered that several appeared to bring about an 'aberrant' reading, where the film evoked feelings of disgust or fear rather than inducing the (presumably) desired and desirable identification or empathy with the group represented and its culture. Generally, the less clothing worn by the subjects of the film and the less complex their material and political economy, the more likely an 'aberrant' reading seemed. However, the students' reaction – worrying though it might be to those who make such films – is nonetheless an ethnographic response and Martinez is right to seek the location of ethnographicness in that response rather than as objectively located within the films themselves (Martinez is, in fact, influenced by reader-centred literary theorists such as Bakhtin and Eco – see his chapter in this book).

The final aspect of reaction that I wish to mention takes us neatly back to the beginning: the reaction to a particular film or to ethnographic films in general may be for the viewer to locate ethnographicness in intention, as part of the desire to go out and make such films him- or herself. Here one could cite Ivo Strecker's reaction to the intention and event of Robert Gardner filming among the Hamar of southern Ethiopia, which led him first to recut Gardner's film (*Rivers of Sand*, 1974) and then to go on and make several of his own (Strecker 1988).

## Conclusions

To begin with, I should like to point out that different films are given the 'ethnographic' label for different reasons and, on the whole, each may be useful when that fact is recognised and desired. But my three categories (intention, event and reaction) are not intended as pigeonholes into which different films are to be slotted – this is an intention film, that is an event film, and so on. Rather they are potential containers or aspects of ethnographicness or of ethnographic response. Ethnographicness is not a thing out there which is captured by the camera but a thing we construct for ourselves in our relation to film (as well as in relation to a variety of other things, such as fieldwork). While the labels I have used were chosen to delimit an argument about ethnographic film, they can be transformed into a more general and more familiar description of process:

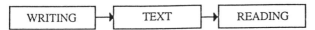

Here, of course, the terms do not relate solely to the printed word, but to all forms of cultural encoding. To do this, however, is to misplace the aspect of agency within the process as a whole, for it is usually substantialised as an essence either at the beginning or (following Bakhtin and others) at the end. In part I think this explains part of our confusion when considering which films count as the ethnographic ones or in trying to locate and legitimate their ethnographicness, for we define ourselves (or more rarely, our subjects) as the originators of agency and see ethnography as epiphenomenal. In my description of the process as defined by the terms chosen at the start of this chapter I would prefer to see ethnographicness itself as the agent which informs us of its presence to varying degrees in various parts of the process. Of course, as anthropologists it is we who empower the agent in the first place. Television is therefore a problematic area for us, given that it has a strong empowering capacity of its own.

As anthropologists it would seem that by choosing to locate ethnographicness in intention, rather than in event or reaction, we stand the most chance of controlling the overall process, certainly for our own benefit and thus helping us guide non-anthropological readers (students, television audiences). Following on from this we should therefore be wary of films which stress the location of ethnographicness in event. As I said above, there is a process of mimesis involved, perhaps even pastiche, so that we see films of people who *look like* the kind of people we study but who are not because they are differently constituted, or at least in a form which our bibliocentric heritage does not easily allow us to comprehend. With observational documentaries we have the added danger that the style of film-making itself is mimetic of our working practice. In neither case is there any particular cause for worry or alarm, simply there should be recognition of the fact.

There is nothing exceptional in what I have done above; I have really just spelled out the obvious. I certainly do not wish to use my criteria to establish a canon of films or to be used as a principle by which some films are awarded the label 'ethnographic' and others denied it. Nor do I wish to follow Heider (1976) in trying to create a sliding scale of 'ethnographicness' against which a film can be judged. Rather I wish the writers and readers of ethnographic film to be aware of the criteria by which ethnographicness is attributed to a film and to decide whether the attribution is in an arena which suits them. 'Ethnography' is not an absolute term, nor something unchanging (there are plenty of things that anthropologists do today that our forefathers would not have considered part of the discipline or which they might never have considered at all); rather it is a cultural construct, a product of the type of society which produces the very discipline of anthropology. As that cultural construct begins to mesh more firmly with another – cinema – so we may see a new product, a kind of ethnography which does not rely on mimesis nor legitimating attribution from a parallel field. This, however, is to be an evolutionary process.

## Notes

1  The conscientious reader will no doubt spot the similarity to Jay Ruby's use of Johannes Fabian's 'producer-process-product' term-triad (Fabian 1971; Ruby 1980, pp. 155ff). While initially inspired by this, I feel it ignores response to the product and I have thus collapsed the terms 'process' and 'product' into the single category 'event' and added the 'reaction' term. I also consider the entire triad to constitute a process which is amenable to anthropological investigation.

2  Biella's films – 'still in progress' in 1988 – were made with the anthropologist Peter Rigby and concern the Ilparakuyo Maasai of Tanzania; the article discussing them is referenced as Biella 1988. Rundstrom's film *The Path*, concerning the Japanese tea ceremony, was completed in 1971 and is discussed in Rundstrom, 1988.

3  The process works both ways: observational films made with no direct anthropological input whatsoever are regularly entered for ethnographic film festivals.

4  Two examples of this, admittedly rare, phenomenon are, first, Keith Tribe's structuralist 'investigation' of John Ford's *My Darling Clementine* (Tribe 1973) and, second, my own use of David Byrne's *True Stories* as a parody of documentary genre (Banks 1990).

## References

*Books and articles*

Banks, M. (1989), 'Retreating universes and disappearing worlds', *Journal of the Anthropological Society of Oxford*, 20, pp. 168–72.

Banks, M. (1990), 'Talking heads and moving pictures: David Byrne's 'True Stories' and the anthropology of film', *Visual Anthropology*, 3, pp. 1–9.

Banks, M. (in press), 'What's new on British television?', *CinémAction*, Paris.

Biella, P. (1988), 'Against reductionism and idealist self-reflexivity: the Ilparakuyo Maasai film project' in J. Rollwagen (ed.), *Anthropological Filmmaking*, Harwood Academic Press, Chur.

Caplan, P. (1988), 'Engendering knowledge: the politics of ethnography (Part I)', *Anthropology Today*, 4, 5, pp. 8–12.

Chiozzi, P. (1989), 'Reflections on ethnographic film with a general bibliography', *Visual Anthropology*, 2, pp. 1–84.

Clifford, J. and Marcus, G. (eds.) (1986), *Writing Culture: the Poetics and Politics of Ethnography*, University of California Press, Berkeley.

Fabian, J. (1971), 'Language, history and anthropology', *Journal of the Philosophy of the Social Sciences*, 1, pp. 19–47.

Fuchs, P. (1988), 'Ethnographic film in Germany: an introduction', *Visual Anthropology*, I, pp. 217–33.

Ginsburg, F. (1988), 'Ethnographies on the airwaves: the presentation of anthropology on American, British and Japanese television' in Y. Omri and P. Hockings (eds.),

*Cinematographic theory and new dimensions in ethnographic film*, Senri Ethnological Series 24, National Museum of Ethnology, Osaka.

Heider, K. (1976), *Ethnographic Film*, University of Texas Press, Austin.

Henley, P. (1985), 'British ethnographic film: recent developments', *Anthropology Today*, I, 1, pp. 5–17.

Loizos, P. (1980), 'Granada Television's Disappearing World series: an appraisal', *American Anthropologist*, 82, pp. 573–94.

Martinez, W. (1990), 'Critical studies and visual anthropology: aberrant vs. anticipated readings of ethnographic film', *CVA Review*, Spring, pp. 34–47.

Rollwagen, J. (ed.) (1988), *Anthropological Filmmaking*, Harwood Academic Publishers, Chur.

Ruby, J. (1980), 'Exposing yourself: reflexivity, film and anthropology', *Semiotica*, 3, pp. 153–79.

Ruby, J. (1988), 'The image mirrored: reflexivity and the documentary film' in A. Rosenthal (ed.), *New challenges for documentary* University of California Press, Berkeley.

Rundstrom, D. (1988), 'Imaging anthropology' in J. Rollwagen, (ed.), *Anthropological Filmmaking* Harwood Academic Press, Chur.

Rundstrom, D., Rundstrom, R. and Bergum, C. (1973), *Japanese tea: The Ritual, the Aesthetics, the Way. An Ethnographic Companion to the Film* The Path, Warner Modular Publications Inc, Mass.

Strecker, I. (1988), 'Filming among the Hamar', *Visual Anthropology*, I, pp. 369–78.

Tribe, K. (1973), 'John Ford's *My Darling Clementine* – an investigation', *Cambridge Anthropology*, 1, pp. 10–17.


*Films*

Byrne, D. (1986), *True Stories*, Warner Bros. Inc., USA. Colour, 90 mins.

Ford, J. (1946), *My Darling Clementine*, Twentieth Century-Fox, Los Angeles. Black and white, 97 mins.

Gardner, R. (1974), *Rivers of Sand*, Phoenix Films, New York. Colour, 83 mins.

Greenaway, P. (1989), *The Cook, The Thief, His Wife and Her Lover*, All Arts, London. Colour, 124 mins.

Hayworth, D. (1979), *Fred Dibnah: Steeplejack*. BBC Television, Manchester. Colour, 50 mins.

Leacock, R. and D. A. Pennebaker (1960), *Primary*. Drew Associates for Time-Life Broadcast, USA. Black and white, 60 mins.

Marker, C. (1963), *Le Joli Mai*, Sofracima, Paris. Black and white, 110 mins.

Maysles, A. and D. Maysles (1975), *Grey Gardens*, Portrait Films, USA. Black and white, 95 mins.

Pennebaker, D. and R. Leacock (1966), *Don't Look Back*. Drew Associates, USA. Black and white, 100 mins.

Rouch, J. and E. Morin (1961), *Chronique d'un été*. Argos Films, Paris. Black and white, 90 mins.

Rundstrom, D., R. Rundstrom and C. Bergum (1971), *The Path*. The Sumai Film Company, Los Angeles. Colour, 34 mins.

Sheppard, J. (1989), *The Herders of Mongun-Taiga*. Disappearing World series, Granada Television, Manchester. Colour, 50 mins. (Anthropologist: Caroline Humphrey)

Wason, D. (1990), *The Trobriand Islanders of Papua New Guinea*. Disappearing World series, Granada Television, Manchester. Colour, 52 mins. (Anthropologist: Annette Weiner)

8  Photo-montage by Stacey Rowe from a design by Wilton Martinez: photograph of spectators by Stacey Rowe, photograph of African woman by Lucien Taylor

# Who constructs anthropological knowledge? Toward a theory of ethnographic film spectatorship

In recent years, critical anthropology (Clifford and Marcus 1986; Marcus and Fischer 1986; Clifford 1988) has challenged the 'truthfulness' of 'realist' ethnographies and anthropologists are increasingly experimenting with partial, 'open' and evocative forms of ethnography, adopting 'self-conscious' and dialogic styles of writing (Crapanzano 1980; Taussig 1989 and others). The main concern of this critique is, to a large extent, still focused primarily on authorship, style and textuality. Although there is considerable debate over the impact of these alternative texts, little attention has been paid to their reception by the 'general public' or to their linkage with the larger process of the construction of cross-cultural knowledge and cultural identities.

An increasing number of studies in visual anthropology have focused on the politics of representation in ethnographic film, challenging the authority of film-makers (Pinney 1989; Banks 1990), their perpetuation of patriarchal views of other cultures (Kuehnast 1990), and their colonialist stereotyping of the 'primitive' (MacDougall 1975; Nichols 1981; Tomaselli *et. al.*, 1986; Lansing 1990). This recent deconstruction of ethnographic films has questioned their apparent stability, but only to a limited extent. Again, these critical studies tend to consider the text (i.e. film) as the fundamental source of meaning and to overlook the role of the 'reader' (i.e. viewer) in its construction.[1]

In the pedagogical practice of ethnographic film, it is the films that are generally seen as the exclusive vehicles of anthropological knowledge – with a relatively fixed set of meanings; many instructors teaching with ethnographic film continue to use an 'archaeological' approach assuming that 'meaning is a treasure that can be excavated through interpretation' (Iser 1978, p. 5). Despite the impact of films on an increasingly large viewership, there is a notable absence of studies of ethnographic film spectatorship. Films are still seen as the result of epic enterprises in 'the field', embodying a 'truthful' knowledge which viewers must come to understand one way or another. Underlying this attitude is the assumption that the construction of anthropological knowledge about other cultures is the exclusive domain of the anthropologist/author.

In this paper I explore the ramifications of various reader-oriented theories as a 'provocation' to the field of visual anthropology to redirect our attention to the spectator of ethnographic film. I believe we need to move from the dominance of author-text to a theoretical consideration of the viewer/reader as a powerful source of signification in the construction of anthropological knowledge. Undergraduate students, the primary users of ethnographic film, are by no means passive receptors; they are necessarily inscribed in the filmic text; they interact with films; they decode texts using their interpretive strategies and ideologies and they eventually constitute textual meanings.

What motivates this concern with the 'reader' is my finding of an interpretive 'gap' between the intentions of film-makers/instructors and student response (Martinez 1990a, 1990b). In a study of students' responses to a variety of films in an introductory anthropology course at the University of Southern California,[2] I have found that many students decode films in an 'aberrant' way (Eco, 1979), with relatively high levels of disinterest, 'culture shock' and/or alienation, and with a relatively low level of 'understanding' (correspondent with textual and pedagogical intended meanings). These readings were generally linked to the specialised format of conventional and 'factual' ethnographic film and to what was perceived as the 'bizarre' appearance and behaviour of the 'primitive'. In contrast, when students' interest was stimulated and 'understanding', analytic insight, and empathetic reflexivity maximised, it was generally in response to emotionally engaging films with humour and narrative drama, made-for-TV documentaries, films using a reflexive style, close-up portrayals of the lives of individuals, and/or filmic attention to topics of general concern (issues of gender, economics, etc.). This film preference and the more active spectatorship which it suggests was a product of stimulated curiosity for the 'primitive' combined with students' desire for entertainment, a need for self-empowering knowledge and pleasurable ways of seeing. Meanwhile more strictly informational and overtly educational films were commonly seen as 'dry' and 'boring' and, most disconcertingly, tended to leave students with reinforced and even augmented colonialist stereotypes of the 'primitive'.

These 'symptomatic' readings indicate more than a pedagogical problem; they suggest that the use of film has powerfully catalysed the crisis of representation in the classroom. Similar to results reported by Hearne and DeVore (1973), my findings indicate that we may be perpetuating the devaluing and stereotyping of other cultures. Moreover, by overlooking student responses, we may also be contributing to reconstituting anthropology as a univocal and hegemonic discourse. In the long run, students' constructed knowledge is re-inserted into the circuit of anthropological meanings, into the larger sets of cultural discourses of the 'primitive' and into the 'political unconscious' of the 'Other' in the West (Jameson 1981). In short, we need to listen to students' voices more carefully; they speak for more than just 'uninformed' readings.

## Understanding the ethnographic film spectator

Studies on the anthropology of visual communication (Worth 1981; Worth and Gross 1974) have elaborated on the interpretive strategies and semiotic mechanisms by which viewers decode and 'assign' meanings to films. In their view, good communication occurs when readers move beyond 'attributing' their own pre-assumptions to texts and learn to 'infer' authors' intended meaning. While this model is helpful for understanding the dynamics of stereotyping (via attribution), it retains an ultimately text-centred perspective by limiting the role of the reader to 'assigning' meanings to texts, rather than co-constructing signification and knowledge.

MacDougall (1978) has moved closer to theories that challenge the dominant role of the author in the construction of meaning. He has characterised 'modern' ethnographic films as open-ended 'texts' in that they incorporate and juxtapose multiple perspectives (e.g. author, film subjects, 'indigenous commentary'). His approach suggests displacing traditional forms of representation and ways of reading in favour of participatory film styles which allow for more complex forms of communication: 'The underlying insight of the film-as-text is that a film is a conceptual space within a triangle formed by the [film] subject, film-maker, and audience and represents an encounter of all three' (1978, p. 422). Although pointing in the right direction this approach has not evolved theoretically nor has it been applied in empirical studies of reception. Furthermore, MacDougall's advocacy of modernist texts carries with it an excessive optimism that overlooks the unequal power relations within the filmic triangle (cf., Martinez 1990b).[3] In the light of these limitations within our field, I shall turn to other disciplines which have developed complex models of interpretive processes and readership: literary criticism, film theory and Marxist 'cultural studies'.

In literary studies, the shift from text-centred theories (i.e. Formalism, New Criticism and structuralism) to reception theory (Jauss 1982a, 1982b; Iser 1978), reader-response studies (Gibson 1950; Holland 1968; Fish 1980; Tompkins 1980) and theories of the text (Barthes 1977; De Man 1979; Eco 1979) has been experienced as a veritable revolution (Holub 1984). These new paradigms have challenged the notion of 'objective' works and proposed a responsive and pro-ductive reader as the central role player in the constitution of meaning. Given their attention to the larger historico-cultural process of communication, recep-tion theories have been assimilated into mass media and film studies and have more recently merged with post-structuralist and postmodern perspectives.

Historically, film scholars have privileged the power of texts over spectators, generally reserving any critical role for specialised film analysts. Largely influenced by structuralist semiotics and Lacanian psychoanalysis (Metz 1977), film theorists have discussed the 'cinematic apparatus' and the unconscious mechanisms by which the spectator identifies with the gaze of the camera and is thereby constructed as 'subject' of the filmic text. More recently (Mulvey 1975; Dayan 1976; Miller 1977; Oudart 1977; Heath 1981) they have incorporated

Marxist and feminist approaches and a more radical Lacanian psychoanalytic perspective, focusing on the ways in which films, understood as products of ideology, 'interpellate' (Althusser 1971) and 'suture' (Miller 1976) spectators who are already constituted as the 'subjects' of dominant discourses (e.g. capital, patriarchy). Contemporary approaches are progressively assimilating theoretical influences from reception theories and 'cultural studies', focusing on the dialogic relation between film structures and spectator activity.

Marxist theories of mass communication have also switched attention to the reader. The Frankfurt School of the 1930s and 1940s (Adorno and Horkheimer 1944), and the later 'critical theory' (Gouldner 1976; Gitlin 1978) both saw viewers as alienated consumers dominated by an overpowering 'culture industry' able to orchestrate every aspect of the reception process. In response, 'cultural studies', a multidisciplinary perspective which combines social sciences, semiotics, film theory and feminism, has questioned the power of the text and elaborated on the role of hegemonic reinstation, equating the process of reception with the political 'struggle for meaning' (Williams 1977; Hall, 1980, 1985; Morley 1980; Bennett 1982; Fiske 1987). In this view, readers are 'overdetermined' (Althusser 1971) by their socio-historical position (class, sex, race, culture, etc.), which powerfully affects the ways they are 'interpellated' by textual discourses. Yet, given the multiple and contradictory nature of signifying practices, subjective experience and social relations, viewers nevertheless play an active role in negotiating meanings and contesting hegemonic ideologies. Postmodern and discursive theories of culture (Kuhn 1982; Grossberg, 1984) have further elaborated on the notion of 'difference', the multiple moments of resistance in the text and the viewers' potential to deconstruct dominant messages. Similarly, Fiske (1987) has emphasised the power of audiences to derive pleasure from texts by reading them oppositionally.

While these disciplines have primarily conceptualised the role and power of the reader in terms of (textual) 'dominance' or (reader) 'contestation', there is growing attention in each field to dialogic models of communication. My view is that neither of these extreme positions accounts for the complexity of ethnographic film spectatorship. Rather, we need to consider the student/spectator as both active, resourceful, motivated and critical *and* passive, submissive and alienated. These roles and stances, furthermore, will be situationally affected by the particular context of viewership (e.g. school setting, educational philosophies and strategies, film repertoire). We need to concentrate on the process of reception itself and on how anthropological knowledge is co-constructed in the interaction.

## The reader in the text

The reader is the space on which all the quotations that make up a writing are inscribed without any of them being lost; a text's unity lies not in its origin but in its destination. (Barthes 1977, p. 148)

Some of the most useful theories of the role of the reader have resulted from the convergence of semiotics with phenomenology in literary studies. Eco's 'model reader' (1979) and Iser's 'implied reader' (1974) are two of the most influential representatives, according to which the reader is inherent in the text. Eco conceives of the 'model' reader as a 'textual strategy', one 'supposedly able to deal interpretively with the expressions in the same way as the author deals generatively with them' (1979, p. 7).[4] Whether directly or indirectly addressed in the text, the reader is positioned 'in' and 'by' it, ideally matching semantic frames of competence, knowledge and ideologies shared by addresser and addressee. Iser's 'implied reader' is a 'textual structure' and a 'structured act' or a 'process' of meaning production: 'The term incorporates both the prestructuring of the potential meaning by the text and the reader's actualisation of this potential through the reading process' (Iser 1974, p. xii). Similarly, film theory distinguishes between the 'subject-position' prescribed by the text and that of the human agent who actually engages with that text (Heath 1981; Silverman 1983; Smith 1988).

Thus, we need to focus on the specific strategies texts use to 'create' their reader and to guide the reading activity. Eco's (1979) distinction between 'open' and 'closed' strategies proves helpful for considering the particular effect of different types of ethnographic film on communication. In short, 'open' texts carry, and generate, a high level of semiotic 'movement' (i.e. communicative and interpretive dynamics, active interaction of reader-text, intertextual relations) and thus carry an explicit 'invitation' for the reader to do the interpretive work. Generated with an 'ideal' reader in mind, 'open' texts are suggestive and susceptible to a virtually unlimited range of possible readings. Yet, some semiotic 'limits' are imposed precisely by the textual strategies: 'An open text, however "open" it be, cannot afford whatever interpretation. An open text outlines a "closed" project of its Model reader as a component of its structural strategy' (Eco 1979, p. 9).

In contrast, 'closed' texts carry specific instructions to be read in a particular way, thus significantly delimiting the variability of reader's interpretations. The forces of closure do not, however, necessarily ensure transparent communication, nor do they 'silence' readers who do not match the 'model reader'. Closed texts are still in semiotic 'movement', yet of a different kind; most critically, they are 'immoderately open' to *aberrant* decoding, resulting largely from a mismatch between the intended or 'model' reader and actual readers. Generally seen as a 'betrayal' of the author's intentions or a failure of communication (mostly at the level of denoted messages), aberrant readings should not, however, necessarily be viewed in a 'negative' way. They can also entail critical and even oppositional interpretations.

Perhaps one of the most significant findings of my study (1990b) is the high correspondence between films using 'open' textual strategies and more elaborated and reflexive responses. The strongest pattern of aberrant readings and reactions of disinterest, alienation and shock corresponded to more 'closed' strategies. Supporting MacDougall's (1978) position, these results suggest that the more 'open' films, those using narrative, experimental, or reflexive styles (e.g. *First Contact, Cannibal Tours, Number Our Days*), empower viewers by allowing them space to negotiate meanings in a more dialogic, interactive way of reading, generally resulting in more complex interpretations (as we shall see later). In contrast, the responses to conventional ethnographic film, those using the 'closed' strategies of 'factual' and distanced representations (e.g. *Trance and Dance in Bali*, Asch/Chagnon Yanomami films), suggest a closing of interpretive space and thus an apparent disempowerment of viewers. Although assuming a reader with considerable anthropological knowledge, these films generally work to reduce ambiguity by attempting to elicit the 'right' or 'truthful' response from spectators – and thus act as catalysts for aberration. At the same time, most ethnographic films convey representations of cultures largely foreign to spectators. They are thus potentially 'immoderately open' to cross-cultural meanings and interpretations and are a rich source of aberrant readings by those who do not match the 'model' reader inscribed in the text (extreme examples are *Les Maitres Fous, The Nuer* and *Forest of Bliss*).

Akin to Eco's conception of an 'outline' in the text that helps to curtail absolute arbitrariness in interpretive practices, Iser (1978) sees the literary text as a 'schematised structure' (also 'schemata' or 'structure of the blanks') to be completed by the reader. The 'blanks', or 'gaps', within the textual structure play a regulatory function by which the text exercises considerable control over the reader in a relation of fundamental *asymmetry*. Given this imbalance, the reader is generally unable to validate the 'correctness' of her or his interpretation, or to corroborate the ultimate intentionality of the author. This elusiveness, and thus dominance, of the text is based on the notion of 'contingency', which accounts for the unpredictability of reading situations. This is particularly relevant to the reception of ethnographic films which, due to the foreign, 'different' and 'unknown' nature of their content, and to their usually prescriptive/explanatory 'rhetoric of truth', confront student viewers with a more powerful and controlling schemata. The asymmetry of the ethnographic film text may be further augmented given that these films often constitute the only source of information for viewers about a given culture.

Iser distinguishes three levels ('blanks', 'vacancies' and 'negation') on which texts operate to guide the reading activity, a distinction which proves fruitful for analysing ethnographic film. On the first level, 'blanks' appear in the empty spaces between elements (e.g. utterances, gestures, objects) and perspectives (e.g. narrator's, characters') in the text. In ethnographic films, like fictional texts, the blanks are prestructured by the text to be filled in specific ways, for example, according to particular pre-coded and editorialised cultural patterns of behaviour. However, given both the cross-cultural nature of the message and the power of the visual image, the textual elements and perspectives are more resistant to authorial prestructuring and more open to idiosyncratic interpretations. We may find ourselves asking, 'What is the relation between Pua and the narrator in *Dead Birds?*' or 'What does the anthropologist's gaze at Dedeheiwa mean to the viewer of *A Man Called Bee?*' It is at this level that students' immediate impressions of cultural behaviour, appearance and interaction are configured by a politics of difference and the blanks get filled in aberrant ways: nudity is read as vulgarity; normative verbal communication as rude and angry confrontation; delousing as a manifestation of a despicable lifestyle rather than an act of communication and intimacy, etc. The blanks, once connected by viewers, become 'thematic units'.

At the second level, broader guiding devices, or 'vacancies', condition readers' views of new and previous themes, leading them to form the text's 'horizon'. The 'themes' of ethnographic films are generally narratives illustrating anthropological topics (e.g. daily life, social organisation, ritual) which are based, on or even motivated by, theoretical paradigms or explanations (i.e. the 'horizon' of ethnographic films). At this level, the 'filling' activity is more powerfully guided by anthropologists' rationalisations of a cultural 'logic', anticipating a closer correspondence between reader and text. Yet, in some cases, despite the contextual information provided in lectures, films and books, students fill not only the thematic 'blank' but also the text's 'horizon' in aberrant ways (Martinez 1990b). In response to *Trance and Dance in Bali*, for example, some students explained Balinese mythology and performance as mere 'superstition' and 'masochistic' behaviour. Similarly, a significant number of students interpreted the film-maker's intention in *The Ax Fight* as one of representing the level of extreme violence of a 'corrupted' and 'barbaric' society.

While blanks and vacancies operate at the syntagmatic level, Iser's third level, a more complex variety of 'blank' or *negation*, operates paradigmatically, at the level of overall 'content'. Negations of specific elements in the text's repertoire (i.e. social conventions) act to prestructure the reader's comprehension of the socio-historical issues raised by the text and point to ways of reassessing them. Iser claims that negation characterises 'good' literature, which has the function of calling into question 'familiar' norms and conventions. Given the cross-cultural nature of ethnographic films and the pedagogical intentions of their authors, these films characteristically 'negate' the spectators' own cultural assumptions, asking them to re-position themselves so as to understand the 'logic' and validity of different cultural schemata. By taking this expectation for granted, however, and by failing to challenge specific assumptions, some films may actually reinforce ethnocentric interpretations, for example, that the Yanomamo shamanistic use of drugs is 'irrational', 'unsustainable' or even 'immoral', as some students suggest in response to *Magical Death*; that the healing dance in *N/um Tchai* or the trance session in *A Balinese Trance Seance* express little more than a blind and 'ridiculous' subjugation to superstition; that conflict of sex roles in *Maasai Woman* is a prime example of 'primitive sexist backwardness'; or that the New Guinean highlanders in *First Contact* were almost sub-human and savage cannibals that needed colonialism in order to 'understand the world'.

Iser also proposes the concept of 'secondary negation', a more complex invalidation of the 'familiar' which is common in modernist literature (prime examples are Joyce's and Beckett's novels). This entails the negation of conventional interpretive strategies and expected modes of reading orientation, as in the disappearance and/or problematising of the narrator's perspective and constant switching of frames of reference through multiple and fragmentary narrativity. Recent anthropological documentaries and ethnographic films (e.g. *Cannibal Tours, Number Our Days, Kenya Boran*) have also increasingly incorporated the use of 'secondary negation' through experimental and self-reflexive qualities that bring about consciousness of the very activity of communication and representation, putting interpretation and meaning in brackets, 'laying bare the historicity of our concept of meaning' (Iser 1978, p. 223). Although in part merely attracted by 'innovative' forms of representation and/or responding to their need for the author's reflexive mediation to help bridge the cross-cultural gap, spectators manifest more than facile engagement in these films; students seem to accept the 'invitation' to participate actively in discerning the diverse layers of representation.

Consideration of the basic textual strategies of openness and closure and of the structure of the blanks, elucidates the reader-text relation and the complexity underlying student 'symptomatic' readings. Firstly, even when powerfully guided by textual schemata, viewers' opportunities to fill in the large number of 'blanks' in ethnographic film, including the author's intentions, seem to be potentially endless. Secondly, my findings show that students' (mis)readings – and their construction of meaning via the 'attribution' of pre-assumptions (Worth 1981) – are linked more to ethnocentric and hegemonic stereotyping than to relativistic or critical interpretations. While these findings have crucial implications for teaching practices (which I discuss at the end of this chapter), they also point to the need for further theoretical consideration of students' reading predispositions and, more specifically, to the mechanisms by which they constitute meanings in the course of the reading act.

## The reading act

We never look at just one thing; we are always looking at the relation between things and ourselves. (Berger 1972, p. 9)

Theories to explain how viewers make sense of ethnographic films can be drawn from cognitive and phenomenological approaches to readership and from psychoanalytic film studies. While emerging from different epistemological paradigms, these two orientations converge in some important respects. For instance, while Iser (1978) sees the reading act as a complex of experiential phenomena and a series of cognitive acts (e.g. consistency-building, image-making, ideation) leading to 'gestalt-formation', film theory defines it as a dialectic of symbolic-imaginary operations (e.g. gazing, interpellation, suturing, subject-positioning) resulting in 'subject-construction' (Metz 1977; Mulvey 1975; Heath 1981). Both approaches share the notion that reading activities ultimately define the production of meaning as well as the reconstitution of readers.

A basic condition of reception is that a text (literary or filmic) cannot be perceived in all its aspects at once. As Iser suggests, we can experience a text *as a whole* only when we have finished experiencing it. To some extent, the reader is transcended by the temporal dimension of texts, which can only be grasped after consecutive phases of reading. This makes the reader a 'moving viewpoint which travels along inside that which is to be apprehended' (Iser 1978, p. 109). The 'wandering viewpoint' is a continuous positioning and re-positioning that allows readers to uncover, distinguish and connect the multiplicity of elements and perspectives in the text.

In this constant adjusting of our picture to fit with new information we reconstruct the text and ourselves as a meaningful 'totality' (gestalt): we are 'conformed' by the very object we are producing. Although readers constantly search for 'consistency', the process of gestalt-formation is, for Iser, characterised by both 'unity' and 'transition'. This is partly because, in the process of assimilating and appropriating the 'object' and the 'unknown' experiences emphasised in the text, readers must at some point hinder their own previous experience: 'The division, then, is not between subject and object, but between subject and himself' (Iser 1978, p. 155). Iser argues that this dividing impact can help further readers' consciousness. Thus, 'good' reading is a 'therapeutic experience'; it helps the reader to gain access to hidden or non-manifest subjective dimensions (e.g. conventions, prejudices, stereotypes) and to reshape them into new forms of gestalt. In this light, ethnographic film has the potential to expand students' cross-cultural understanding and thus trigger new forms of consciousness. But the presentation of a world too alien, and even threatening, to the spectator may also create a subject-position that is too divisive. In this case, one can expect 'uninformed' viewers to resort to stereotyping or even to reject the text as a whole as, for example, some students do with *Magical Death* or *Anasternaria*.

While useful, Iser's framework remains at an individual level. It does not account for the social and historical forces that affect reading practices. Iser proposes that the social function of literature is to 'negate' conventions (e.g. prejudice) in order to help us lead 'better' and more 'productive' lives – similar to the anthropological aim of promoting cultural relativism. This utopian goal, however, idealises a particular version of 'educated' textuality and individualised readership. The construction of a model reader embodying the paradigm of 'liberalism' is naive because it does not consider the intentions of authors and assumes that a 'liberal' reader can be free of particular 'biases' and determinants.

In contrast, Lacanian film theory conceives of the subject/spectator as an already multiple and decentred entity. For Lacan (1977), the human 'subject' is constituted in the intersection of two co-existing and complementary orders: the imaginary (the register of images, phantasy, identification, duality) and the symbolic (the register of language, cultural order, law and discourse). At an early age (seven to eighteen months old), when we gain access to the symbolic via repression (i.e. castration) of imaginary identification with the mother, we enter the discursive complex of culture (the field of the Other). In this process, we, as subjects, become signifiers within a network of signification, becoming 'subjects' of the enunciated, that is, we are 'spoken' by ideological and discursive formations. Yet in this process of creation of meaning and identity, we are also alienated from our own drives ('aphanisis' or the 'fading' of the subject) and constituted as 'lack', which signals the formation of the unconscious and the inauguration of desire (desire of the Other).

In Lacanian terms, human signification constantly reproduces alienation and desire; for instance, the articulation of a statement in language gains meaning through *negativity*, that is, by eliminating other alternative meanings that remain in the field of the Other. The unconscious also speaks, through constant openings and closures, the codes and signifiers of cultural discourses ('the unconscious is the discourse of the Other'). This perspective offers a key for analysing Western representations of, and unconscious desire for, the 'primitive' as a cross-cultural signifier. As Said (1979), Todorov (1984) and Kuper (1988) have argued, the 'primitive' has been culturally constructed as 'other'[5] by negating racial and cultural identities in order to construct, by opposition, an identity of 'self'. Throughout the history of Western colonialism, these representations of otherness have been loaded with a dualistic and fetishised image of the 'primitive' as both 'original presence' and 'lack' of 'civilisation' (White 1978; Jameson 1981). More specifically, these forms of signification can be observed in ethnographic film tropes as well as in students' preconceptions of the 'primitive', as I will discuss below; similarly, students' unconscious signifying practices (e.g. dreams) seem to reproduce the dualistic representation of the 'other'.[6]

In film-viewing we also find a constant division of the subject-in-language: mediated by unconscious discursive practices, the film 'subject' (i.e. the position to be occupied by the actual spectator) is an entity 'constantly missing and moving along the flow of images' (Heath 1981, p. 88). Yet, as with all discursive situations, spectators are also repeatedly united or *sutured* into the text at the level of a common ideology. Initially conceptualised as a 'pseudo-identification' or as the 'junction of the imaginary and the symbolic' (Lacan 1977; Miller 1977), the notion of suture has been extensively applied in film theory in ways that parallel Iser's model of 'filling in'.[7] At a micro level, typical mechanisms of suturing are the techniques of shot/reverse shot, by which the missing field of the single shot is filled with the 'presence' of the reverse shot (Dayan 1976; Oudart 1977), and point-of-view editing, i.e. gazing character/gazed image/gazing character (Rothman 1976). At a more macro level, Heath (1981) sees suture as a 'multiple function' that entails larger mechanisms of 'joining' the subject/spectator to the chain of textual discourse ('no discourse without suture') and suggests focusing on the level of textual narrativity: 'narrative makes the join of symbolic and imaginary, process and reflection . . . the spectator is placed as subject for the narrative relations and constituted in their reflection' (1981 p. 122). Through the suturing of subjects into its narrative, film discourse interpellates spectators – via recognition and identification – and forces them to participate in its ideology.

From this perspective, we can analyse the various ways in which student/ spectators are 'bound into' ethnographic film textuality. One fundamental suturing mechanism is that of the spectator's cultural identification with the 'normalising' gaze (Foucault 1977) of the camera, with the editorial perspective and with its scientific narrative about the 'primitive other'. More strongly than with films on or about Western culture ('us'), cross-cultural representations of the 'other' trigger a massive identification with the textual discursivity itself, and thus a more powerful form of ideological interpellation. As Trinh T. Minh-ha suggests, 'the privilege to sit at table with "us" ... proves both uplifting and demeaning. It impels "them" to partake in the reduction of itself and the appropriation of its otherness by a detached "us" discourse. The presence of a (grateful) witness serves to legalise such discourse, allowing it to mimic, when-ever necessary, the voice of truth' (1989 p. 67). Given this larger suturing into culture, students strongly identify with the surveillance function of the voyeuristic camera and are powerfully interpellated by its politics of differentiating, classifying, qualifying, rewarding or punishing of the 'primitive' – most evident in their responses to conventional and strictly observational ethno-graphic films.

At the level of narrative in the strict sense (i.e. story telling), I have observed students' suturing primarily via identification with the 'plot' (which explains their preference for films employing personal narratives, e.g. *Dead Birds, The Kawelka: Ongka's Big Moka*) yet not necessarily with the 'characters', as would be common in Hollywood narratives. In general, students have difficulties in identifying with the peoples represented as 'subjects' (determined by race and culture), yet they do seem capable of 'relating' to particular aspects of them (determined by sex, age, forms of gestalt or subject-positions). For instance, identification by gender can be found among female students in response to films such as *N!ai, The Story of a !Kung Woman, 1952–78* and *The Women's Olamal* and among males in response to *Meat Fight* and some of the Yanomamo films; identification by age and gender is also common, among males, in response to *Naim and Jabar* and *A Rite of Passage*. On a more micro level, the multiplicity of gazes represented in ethnographic films also serves continually to (re)structure spectators' identifications and power relations with specific textual perspectives (e.g. those of the anthropologist and peoples represented). Given that the observed/observing gaze of the 'primitive' is seldom returned in most conventional ethnographic films, students are all too often unconsciously positioned in the voyeuristic, omnipotent role of the film-maker. When there is a returned gaze, it is usually a non-threatening one, again satisfying the viewers' power-reinstantiating preference for the gaze of those perceived as receptive and amenable, as sub-ordinate or even 'weak' males, or for the gaze of women or children.[8]

The tendencies described here indicate the interpellatory power of ethno-graphic film, which all too often results in unconscious domination of the spectator, a domination rooted in the Western 'political unconscious' (Jameson 1981). Within this perspective, we need to study further how students construct meanings through their multiple forms of alienation, identification, pleasure and power relations with the film subjects. At the same time, we must not forget the role of student/subjects as active gap-fillers; as recent critiques (Linker 1984; Smith, 1988) have emphasised, even though signifying practices – both conscious and unconscious – cannot operate outside cultural discourses, the mechanisms of suturing do not always translate into monolithic or transcendental processes of domination. The fragmentation of textual discourse and the multiple forms of interpellation necessarily create contradictory subject-positions that allow space for spectators' agency and resistance. In order to analyse the various informing discourses that affect the construction of spectators' subjectivity and their correspondent construction of meaning, we need to consider the mediatory role of socio-historic processes in spectatorship.

## Interpretive strategies

[The unconscious] represents nothing, but it produces. It means nothing, but it works. Desire makes its entry with the general collapse of the question 'What does it mean?' (Deleuze/Guatarri 1983, p. 109)

Like all spectators, students 'read' films guided by their own conventionalised knowledge of what is 'good', 'believable', 'interesting' or 'boring'. Whereas it is difficult to assess how introductory courses affect students' subjectivity and interpretive conventions in the long run, by analysing viewers' sets of expectations, preferences and affective valuations of films and represented subjects we can add to our understanding of the interpretive strategies students use to construct anthropological knowledge.

The need to consider the role of interpretive mediation leads us to the field of contemporary hermeneutics and its critique of 'essentialism', the belief in the existence of an ultimate meaning. As Gadamer (1975) and others (e.g. Geertz 1973) have proposed, interpretation can only be understood in the context of cultural and historical mediation. More radically, and similar to Lacanian theory, Jameson (1981) claims that we have access to the 'real' only through texts and interpretive paradigms ('ideologemes'). Fish (1980) argues that there is no such thing as 'pure' perception since 'reality' is always mediated by social interpretive conventions: readers do not 'read' texts; they 'write' them.

Unlike Iser's individualised reader, Fish proposes that our interpretations are shaped by communal patterns and that all texts are only constituted as such by 'interpretive communities' which 'are made up of those who share interpretive strategies not for reading (in the conventional sense) but for *writing* texts, for constituting their properties and assigning their intentions' (1980 p. 171, emphasis added). Working on the basis of common understandings and strategies, different communities (e.g. anthropologists, film-makers, students) define their own understanding of what 'true' or 'good' texts are, and how to read (i.e. 'write') them. In addition, readers generally belong to several communities and thus participate in different strategies, thereby also partaking in inter-communal interpretive struggles for 'writing' texts. As we shall see below, students' membership in or access to different types of interpretive communities (e.g. student fraternities, religious and political associations, special interest groups) powerfully affects the ways they interpret and value films.

While Fish's radical emphasis on the powerful reader proves useful for deconstructing the hegemony of the text, it fails to account for the guiding and interpellatory force of the textual schemata and for the power relations which determine the dominance of certain interpretive communities. It may be more accurate to conceive of interpretation as a 'secondary revision', as 'an essentially allegorical act, which consists in *rewriting* a given text in terms of a particular interpretive master code' (Jameson 1981, p. 10, emphasis added). This suggests the need for analytical categories to account for readers' 'master codes', which can be identified and studied in terms of both their 'form' (e.g. aesthetic conventions of genre, tropes, style) and 'content' (e.g. historical paradigms, ideologies and meta-narratives of the 'primitive').

Jauss's aesthetics of reception (1982b) is particularly instructive with regard to 'form'. He proposes that readers can be isolated neither from the 'horizon of expectations' of a given time nor from the horizon of previous readings of a given text. 'Horizon of expectations', a constitutive and mediatory mechanism, refers to intersubjective structures of historico-aesthetic knowledge, the 'system of references' of a group expressed in textual and aesthetic conventions of genre, form and style (e.g. novel, poetry, documentary, ethnographic film). Our historico-aesthetic horizon is largely unconscious and thus elusive and hard to understand fully or transcend, yet in the reception process we project, fuse and change our horizons by means of transforming our expectations into conventionalised knowledge (i.e. master codes) until a 'new' text defamiliarises these conventions and expands them into a new horizon.

A more specific way of studying anthropology students' horizons is by analysing their 'film literacy' (Amelio 1971; Worth 1981). In my observations, most students come to class with a relatively high knowledge of, and preference for, the technology of television or film language and styles yet with a limited knowledge of documentary and ethnographic film and little critical competence to analyse them. While seeing conventional ethnographic film as the 'raw' or 'amateur' version of non-fiction texts, most students prefer the professionalism of made-for-TV documentaries addressed to a more 'general viewer' and encompassing a broader contextualisation and general overview of cultures. Students' overall preference for personal narratives combining humour and drama indicated a deep-seated desire for entertainment in the form of grati-ficatory and hedonistic 'plaisir' (Barthes 1973) characteristic of consumer societies. While this does not necessarily provoke critical or elaborated interpre-tation, students with higher levels of interpretive competence do engage in more elaborated forms of creative, productive or 'poietic' pleasure (Jauss 1982a) and tend to generate more 'surplus meaning' (Morley 1980). In general students are open to 'innovative' forms of textuality that challenge their conventions, but only to some extent. They prefer dramatic, ironic or technically sophisticated and stylised films and may even reject texts that radically challenge the very nature of representation (e.g. *Reassemblage, Films Are Dreams*).

Thus there is a need to expand students' film literacy, thereby also expanding their horizons of expectations. Jauss (1982b) suggests that this last process operates as an endless play of 'question and answer' wherein the text is primarily an answer, but not necessarily a formulated or explicit one; at the same time, texts question readers about their respective horizons. Constantly shifting over time, texts also act as mediators between different historical horizons. Jauss proposes an historical reading, or 'application', as the most advanced and comprehensive interpretive activity, one where readers supposedly can find the 'answer' of the text by distinguishing and reconstructing past horizons of expectation and then 'applying' their new aesthetic understanding – thus broadening the 'horizon of one's own experience vis-à-vis the experience of the other' (1982b p. 146). This reconstruction of horizons has important implications for the use of ethnographic film in teaching: despite the fact that many instructors show films which have been produced in various contexts over the last sixty years, the historical con-textualisation of these texts is not undertaken in most introductory courses. Historical readings are fundamental in ethnographic film reception. Their neg-lect not only limits students' understanding of the films but, even worse, also tends to perpetuate the notion that the peoples represented are 'societies without history' (Wolf 1982).

Jauss's theory of aesthetic reception offers valuable insights for the analysis of spectatorship. It is, however, relatively indifferent to political and ideological discourses and practices and, like Iser's, it idealises the utopian and innovative function of 'high' literature. In particular, Jauss privileges the aesthetic dimension of the 'horizon', referring to literary conventions (form, style, genre) as nearly exclusive determinants of textual 'influence'. As empirical reception researchers (Morley 1980; McRobbie 1982; Radway 1984) have shown, how-ever, readers' responses to a given text are largely guided by 'extra-aesthetic' conventions, which leads us to consider the domain of readers' affects, values and attitudes and values toward the text's 'content'.

Williams' notion of 'structure of feeling' (1977) is particularly useful here because it combines historico-aesthetic assumptions and expectations with lived social practice within a context of power relations.[9] Conceptualised as a mediating category between social, experiential and representational practices, 'structure of feeling' accounts for the 'feel' of a social group – 'the characteristic elements of impulse, restraint, and tone; specifically affective elements of con-sciousness and relationships' (1977 p. 132). Structures of feeling cannot be reduced to the ideologies of social groups or to class relations but are manifest as their ethos, the 'idiosyncratic' and common-sensical conventions and attitudes that articulate a group's 'presence'. From an anthropological perspective, students' structure of feeling demand to be analysed as part of a cultural formation, which suggests, in addition to an aesthetic of reception, the need for an ethnography of reception (Hall and Jefferson 1976; Radway 1984). From a more restricted perspective on spectatorship, students' 'feel' for ethnographic films and for the 'primitive' can be analysed in relation to interpretive patterns and strategies of identification and pleasure, issues which need to be further investigated.

In addition, as Williams suggests, we need to analyse students' structures of feeling – as well as their horizons of expectations – within the dynamics of social struggle, power and hegemony. A fundamental way in which dominant groups exert power over 'residual' and 'emergent' groups is by seeking to impose and naturalise their sets of feelings, values and interpretive strategies, and, by extension, their own representations of the 'real'. The recent history of this hegemony in the United States can be seen in the 'master codes' formed during the 'Age of Reaganism' and its 'brutal Darwinian picture of self-help and self-promotion' (Said 1983, p. 136), which have naturalised the power of 'First World' techno-cultural, economic and military hegemony over 'other' worlds. Among students/ spectators, this discourse is quite evident in their more distant and 'negative' feelings toward a radically 'different' other and in more conservative (i.e. ethnocentric) values and attitudes toward notions of 'primitiveness'. We can expect to see a radicalisation of these tendencies as a result of the Gulf war: the 'triumph of civilisation' and its 'smart technology' over what US General Schwarzkopf described as those who 'are not part of the same human race . . . as the rest of us are.'

## Ideology and discourse

Although the history of Europe as Subject is narrativised by the law, political economy, and ideology of the West, this concealed Subject pretends it has no 'geo-political determinations'. (Spivak 1988, p. 271).

A conversation of 'us' with 'us' about 'them' is a conversation in which 'them' is silenced. 'Them' always stand on the other side of the hill, naked and speechless, barely present in its absence. (Trinh T. Minh-ha 1989, p. 67)

At the level of the 'content' of interpretive 'master codes' we need to consider (a) viewers' knowledge and preconceptions about the 'primitive' and how these frame student responses to ethnographic film; (b) the constitution of 'preferred meanings' and identities of the 'primitive' by ethnographic films and how their specific forms of power and knowledge may affect spectators; and (c) the process of negotiating meanings and representations and the ideological struggle for signification that characterises the construction of anthropological knowledge.

My analysis of students' assumptions about the 'primitive' before taking the course[10] showed that most of them conceptualised 'primitiveness' as both an essentialist *presence* – an 'original' and 'basic' form of life characterised by instinct and survival – and as a 'lack' or regressive *absence*, signalled by a lack of culture, of development and of intelligence. They see the 'primitive' either as 'simple', 'pure' and 'naive', thus emphasising 'positive' attitudes associated with the romanticised image of the 'Noble Savage'; or as 'wild', 'backward' and 'lacking' education, language, morals, thus emphasising a 'negative' valuation, corresponding to the dehumanised image of the 'Barbarian' (White 1978). A minority of students (six per cent) came to the classroom with a relativistic understanding of the term 'primitive' and with some level of awareness of its hegemonic connotation.

Students largely speak for, and are spoken by, the popular mythologies and stereotypes of the 'primitive' perpetuated and disseminated through an increasingly sophisticated 'culture industry'. As a free-floating signifier, constantly reinterpreted through intertextual media representations, the 'primitive' is now positioned and consumed in all kinds of contexts: on other planets, in the future, in 'postmodern MTV'. Nevertheless, the popular notion of the 'primitive' retains much of its colonialist and racist signification, as subaltern 'other' to the West. While idealising the most remote 'other', students also see the more proximate 'other', such as 'Third World' people and ethnic 'minorities' in the United States as approximations to the 'primitive', emphasising their differences rather than similarities, seeing their non-mainstream lifestyles as technologically and intellectually 'inferior' and characterised by cultural 'backwardness'.

While the content of these preconceptions may not be surprising, their significance as social constructs requires consideration from at least two perspectives. On the one hand, preconceptions have to be understood as formations of our historical horizons and as the 'spontaneous' ways in which we know the world, while on the other, preconceptions (as forms of knowledge) and stereotypes (as 'fixations of difference' (Bhabha 1983)) are inevitably rooted in historico-cultural structures that need to be analysed in terms of both social interests and power relations (Foucault 1980). Thus, a fundamental pedagogical task is that of criticising the politics of representation by which our preconceptions are naturalised and reproduced through different forms of intertextuality.

Critical anthropology has made it more evident than ever that ethnographic films are inevitably inscribed within hegemonic discursive formations (MacDougall 1975; Nichols 1980; Marcus and Fischer 1986; Tomaselli, *et. al.*, 1986; Tyler 1986; Clifford 1988; Lansing 1990). To pursue this critique, I would propose that an ideological and historical analysis of tropes (Burke 1969; White 1978) in ethnographic film be developed as a very useful tool for understanding their specific construction of knowledge and identities of the 'primitive other', and for reconstructing their 'answers' to Western horizons of expectation. We can see, for example, that early films (e.g. *Nanook of the North*, *The Hunters*, *Dead Birds*) exercised their rhetorical power through the trope of romantic metaphor, poeticising anthropological knowledge and constructing a mythical, essentialised and universalised 'primitive' (A variant of this trope can also be seen in contemporary films such as *The Nuer, Forest of Bliss*). Indicating a different political agenda, metonymy and realism have figured prominently in conventional ethnographic films (e.g. *Trance and Dance in Bali*, the Yanomamo films) which have aimed to 'explain' the 'primitive' through 'factual' scientific accounts that inevitably confound experience with narrative (Brodkey 1987): the use of a strictly observational and omniscient camera gaze, a discourse of detached 'neutrality', and a metonymic fragmentation of cultures (e.g., focus on single events) all result in authoritative objectification and the dissection of film subjects as mere 'data' and 'evidence' (Tyler 1986).

The subsequent synecdochic move to 'integrate' represented cultures includes: (1) the more recent anthropological documentaries (e.g. series like *Odyssey, Disappearing World*) that employ both the narrative of 'pre-cooked' anthropological information and a form of domesticated exoticism to inform and entertain large TV audiences; and (2) the incorporation of the film-maker/ author in the text, initiated by Jean Rouch and continued by 'participatory cinema' and 'self-reflexive' styles (e.g. *Kenya Boran, Number Our Days*). The increasing use of irony in contemporary ethnographic film can be seen to express a more critical and comprehensive 'secondary negation' (Iser 1978), which attempts radically to question and deconstruct its own narrativity and to reflect critically on the insufficiency and inadequacy of our cultural master codes to account for the 'other' (e.g. *Cannibal Tours, Reassemblage, Films Are Dreams, Cannibal Tours*). Although neither self-reflexive nor ironic films are completely free from ideologies of exploitation, that is, via cultural manipulation, self-indulgent or narcissistic figuration of the other,[11] they do invite more complex forms of reading than conventional ethnographic films and explicitly challenge stereotypical representations.

While some of these films are still seen as 'avant garde' and are rarely shown in introductory courses, 'factual' films continue to be considered more 'ethnographic' because they are seen to provide more detailed, analytical, theoretically grounded, 'holistic' and 'truthful' information (Heider 1976). Given these assumptions, they, together with documentaries and early narratives, are the most widely used in introductory education. As a result, student/spectators are primarily confronted with films that construct idealised, objectified, exoticised, primitivised peoples, identities that correspond with the Western fascination with and condescension toward the 'primitive other'.

This ideological correspondence, however, is not a simple 'reflection' of class and intercultural power relations, or of the authors' conscious intentions. Even after the reception of their texts, author/film-makers themselves are not necessarily aware of their historical horizons of expectation, of how they are 'spoken' by their own tropes, or of the potential ideological impact of their films. As Williams (1977) proposes with regard to mass media, producers implicitly communicate hegemonic 'structures of feeling', ideologies and capital interests in the course of arranging social experience, the 'raw' material of cultural texts, according to forms of naturalised 'common sense'. Thus, even when texts are not communicating social structures of domination directly, they do so indirectly, primarily via connoted or unconscious meanings. This process operates similarly in conventional ethnographic film, where the interests of scientific 'truth' as a form of cultural capital (Bourdieu, 1977) often represent hegemonic ideologies and discourses of power over and knowledge of the 'other' (although this varies depending on how much the constructed knowledge is negotiated with film subjects and on the degree of cultural criticism and self-reflexivity of authorial messages).

Hall (1980) has observed that, in order to perform their 'ideological work', media producers encode texts by selecting and negotiating 'preferred meanings' which aim to predetermine the process of decoding, that is, to obtain particular 'preferred readings'. This does not, however, translate into perfectly 'transparent' communication: as texts and readers embody multiple and fragmentary experiences, ideologies, and discourses, there is a relation of 'no necessary correspondence' between encoding and decoding activities. Hall proposes that readers 'appropriate' the meanings that best fit as 'imaginary' solutions to their own socially experienced contradictions, 'answers' that confirm their sense of self, truth, rightfulness, and oppose or negate those that challenge their ideological formations and identities. Reading is thus a *struggle* for signification within hegemonic structures. This politics of signification, encompassing differential types of interpellation and subject positioning, results in observable patterns of response or 'preferred reading' (i.e. 'hegemonic', 'negotiated', 'oppositional').

Hegemonic readings were found in students' responses to most tropes of ethnographic film (Martinez 1990a); even the most 'personal' narratives can trigger readings that legitimise the authorial discourse by implicitly disempowering the film subjects or encapsulating them within dominant interpretive paradigms, cross-cultural labels or stereotypes (e.g., 'they basically have no culture . . . they only live for fighting'). As discussed above, however, hegemonic readings (commonly linked to aberration) were more often observed in response to the conventional format of 'closed', factual, single-event films and distanced/ objectifying representations of the 'primitive'. In these cases, students seemed to retreat more readily to their preconceptions in reaction to the limited space allowed for a dialogic viewership, the minimum cultural contextualisation internal to the film, and the 'lack' of identificatory communication. A wider range of negotiated readings were found in response to texts using more 'open' strategies, personal portrayals, and films with greater internal contextualisation. Socialised into the discourse of liberal pluralism, (e.g. 'everyone is different', 'primitive peoples are somewhat similar to us'), many students do privilege the 'exception to the rule' and 'individual free will' and can thus appear relatively open to negotiating texts. Yet, as seen above, negotiated readings were limited by the 'fit' (i.e. suture) into dominant cultural identities and discourses, and by preconceptions of the 'primitive', resulting in many cases in paternalistic views of the film subjects (e.g. 'they dont know any better'). Different forms of oppositional (i.e. counter-hegemonic) readings were found mainly in response to relatively 'open' films which convey a critical and self-critical message, seeming to trigger a re-evaluation of students' preconceptions. Responses challenging textual authority or actively deconstructing hegemonic messages (e.g. colonialism, cultural domination) in order to reconstruct alternative forms of knowledge (e.g. political expressions of cultural relativism) were almost non-existent. Often, students' political and cultural alignment, if any, with the 'primitive' resulted in romanticised idealisation (e.g. 'we should leave them alone'). Evoking alternative subject-positions and/or particular forms of 'otherness', oppositional readings were more frequent among students marginal to or outside mainstream culture (e.g. among African-Americans and 'Third World' students).

These responses need to be analysed critically to avoid rigid generalisations. Critics of the notion of hegemony and of Hall's typology of preferred readings have argued that the latter overlooks and reduces the 'universality' of negotiated readings (Newcomb 1984), polarising the reading activity in terms of dominance and opposition (Fiske 1986; Condit, 1989), and that its formulation seeks a necessary correspondence between experience and textuality (Grossberg 1984). These critics regard the range of ideological responses as a continuum rather than a discrete categorisation and the dynamics of response as a multiple and variable positioning within discursive formations. In particular, Marxist discourse theory has expanded Hall's model by emphasising the notion of *difference* at the levels of meaning (i.e. polysemy, openness), subjectivity (i.e. fragmentation, overdetermination, subject positions) and social formation (i.e. cultural diversity).

Drawing primarily on Lacan, Althusser and Foucault, discursive models in cultural studies (Kuhn 1982; McRobbie 1982; Hall 1983; Grossberg 1984) reject the separation between 'society' (class interests, economic forces) and 'culture' (symbolic forms of representation), and between experience and textuality. Discourse theory claims that the struggle for signification should not be directed towards developing anti-hegemonic strategies but against all moments of power and domination. As power constantly slips within all forms of textuality, without ever condensing in any given form, the relation between reader and text then becomes one of continuous domination and resistance, of suture and 'rupture'. Feminist media researchers (Kuhn 1982; McRobbie 1982) have argued that mass media cannot convey only patriarchal ideologies. There are always moments (e.g. blanks, silences, counter discourses) in those texts which cannot be coded within hegemonic rhetoric; all texts carry resistant and oppositional readings already coded within their structure. Similarly, Fiske (1987) has elaborated on the 'semiotic excess' of TV messages which cannot be exhausted by dominant codes, thus allowing viewers space for oppositional decodings resulting in 'play' and deconstructivist pleasure.

By the same token, in every ethnographic film-viewing 'event', there is encoded contradiction and available space where students can actualise their own set of discursive positions and reconstitute their interpretive technologies. Even closed films may generate resistance to the exoticised, objectified and/or disempowering representation of peoples. Some students, for example, are critical of the power relations between the anthropologist and the Yanomamo subjects in *A Man Called Bee*; others notice and identify with the Yanomamo reluctance to be filmed in *The Ax Fight*. However, with the exception of the rare viewer who rejects the whole representation as authoritative, closed texts are generally read from an aberrant/hegemonic perspective.

In response to more open or 'negotiated' films, which actively voice the represented subjects' perspective, students find numerous opportunities to oppose disempowering representations. As in the case of mass media viewers' resistance to patriarchy, female students tend to negotiate and even oppose patriarchal discourses in ethnographic film (for example, in response to *N!ai, Story of a !Kung Woman, Andean Women, Maasai Women*). Although this critique is generally directed against the 'backwardness' of represented cultures, it also triggers students' resistance against their own culture's forms of sexual hegemony. Reacting to political domination, students have come to criticise the intentions of the film-makers', even in 'balanced' or 'sympathetic' films like *First Contact* as 'concealing' colonial exploitation. In response to *Maids and Madams*, some students oppose the representation of black women as racist, 'degrading' and 'offensive'. Yet there are some limits to resistance: many students also feel threatened by socio-cultural criticism and thus read it as 'negative' (i.e., as a negation of their own discursive position). In response to *Cannibal Tours*, for example, some students react defensively, arguing that the film-maker has exaggerated and that the tourists are portrayed in 'unrealistic' ways.

When oppositional readings do occur they are generally motivated by the spectators' predisposition to respond in such a manner. As Condit (1989) has argued in her analysis of college students' responses to TV programmes, access to and participation in an organised 'counter-rhetoric' may prove to be more relevant than personal competence for generating critical and oppositional readings. I have also noticed (1990b) that students who are active in particular special interest groups (e.g., homeless support organisations, anti-Apartheid movement) read films in predominantly oppositional ways, questioning the disempowering representation and stereotyping of film subjects, while those who belong to more conservative organisations (e.g. fraternities and sororities) place themselves in a hegemonic position and allow themselves less space to negotiate texts and their own preconceptions. Such constraints on the openess of students to 'difference' point to the need for analysing the boundaries of 'difference' in terms of its articulation with hegemonic power.

In this respect, Hall (1985) argues that post-structuralism has privileged the principle of 'difference' (i.e. discursive fragmentation) over 'unity' (i.e. discursive hegemony) and proposes to bridge this binary opposition. Reconsidering hegemony as the expression of 'pluricentered' and 'multidimensional' power, Hall proposes to rethink 'unity' and 'difference' in terms of 'articulation', which refers to

a connection or link [between representation and practice, text and reader] which is not necessarily given in all cases, as a law or fact of life, but which requires particular conditions of existence to appear at all, which has to be positively sustained by specific processes, which is not 'eternal' but has constantly to be renewed. (1985, p. 113)

Thus, the relation between 'writing' and 'reading' cannot be seen as monolithically or unilaterally determined either by textual meanings or the reader's activity. Rather, the relation text-reader produces correspondences of ideologies and master codes that are articulated within specific socio-historical conditions of reception.

From this perspective, we can attempt a conclusive evaluation of the tendencies described above as 'symptomatic' responses. Firstly, the interpretive 'gap' documented by my research indicates a lack of articulation between spectators and particular films (e.g. 'factual' films) mainly because students do not completely match the text's implied/model reader and because films and/or represented subjects do not fit students' aesthetic expectations and ways of feeling. While such lack of articulation can also entail critical readings, students' (mis)interpretations generally result in the reconstitution of fixed forms of knowledge (i.e. stereotypes). Secondly, despite the 'aberration' observed in student response, at a broader level, viewers' readings are generally articulated with – and largely sutured into – films' ideologies. As seen before, most critical interpretations correspond to films that question cultural domination or challenge stereotypical representations. Similarly, students' hegemonic readings somehow correspond to films' disempowering representations and hegemonic meanings – mostly manifest through connoted and/or unconscious messages. Most negotiated readings, generally corresponding to students' expected forms of representation (e.g. 'good' documentaries), indicate a broader articulation with spectators' preferred subject positioning as 'general viewers' and with 'consensual' knowledge of the 'other'. Thirdly, while all students are potential 'critical readers', only a few are able to 'disarticulate' (i.e. deconstruct) textual discourses. As mentioned before, oppositional responses are found mostly among non-mainstream students who are already predisposed to react critically and/or among those who do the additional interpretive work, moving beyond negotiating to reconstructing alternative forms of knowledge of the 'other'.

Finally, these considerations strongly suggest that the forms of 'articulation' of ethnographic film spectatorship need to be studied both in the larger frame of cultural textuality of the 'primitive other' and in concrete situations of reception. At the broader level, recognising that 'writing' and 'reading' about the 'primitive' are necessarily articulated by shared cultural master codes, we need to analyse the specific ways in which films and spectators participate in, interact with and even subvert their own meta-narratives of the 'other'. At the same time, we need to focus on the multiple and changing forms of articulation between text and reader in specific contexts of reception. The results of my research show significant variability depending on the specific teaching approaches employed; these results have to be correlated with studies of spectatorship in different contexts (e.g. public and private colleges and universities, high schools, adult spectatorship) and with comparative analyses of responses in different historical settings. This dual approach to articulation will not only provide insights into the ways in which spectators 'read' ethnographic films and film-makers and instructors 'write' cultures; it will also help us to understand how, as 'overdetermined' and active subjects, we all construct anthropological knowledge.

### Spectatorship and pedagogical practice

My emphasis on the complex role of the spectator in the construction of anthropological knowledge not only raises new questions for study but also challenges current pedagogical practices. It leads me to propose a 'negation' (Iser, 1978) of conventional uses of film in introductory courses and to call for teaching strategies that can help students learn about other cultures by, at the same time, deconstructing authoritative and univocal representations. As critical anthropologists (Simon and Dippo 1986; Brodkey 1987) have proposed, such alternative approaches require a 'negative critique', that is, 'any systematic, verbal protest against cultural hegemony' (Brodkey 1987, p. 67), entailing reflexive awareness of students' signifying practices about others and the political implications of those practices. While acknowledging that this overall agenda and details of the relation between spectatorship, textuality and pedagogy need to be examined more extensively in future works, I will reflect briefly in this final section on the implications that using film has for our teaching practice and suggest some alternative strategies. In doing so I shall draw on my research experience of an introductory anthropology course focused on the use of film (see footnote 2) but the analysis applies to the use of films in general. The pedagogical implications of this research may be summarised in the following observations.

1. The old but often overlooked adage that images speak louder than words, that they communicate more strongly than books at the emotional, subliminal and ideological levels, radically challenges the naive use of films as mere 'illustrations' of written texts and theoretical paradigms. Although the role of films in creating an 'illusion of reality' and 'immediacy' has been acknowledged before (Heider, 1976) the issue needs to be reassessed. As discussed above, the mimetic and rhetorical power of visual figuration not only recreates 'illusions' of the 'real' but also *constructs* our sense of 'reality' and subjective identity, thus powerfully 'telescoping' (Baudrillard 1988) viewers into the simulacra of textual representation of the 'primitive'. Even more, the suturing power of ethnographic images activates unconscious signifying practices and a complex and powerful process of ideological interpellation that far exceeds the impact of written texts and poses commensurate risks of engendering viewer's alienation, revulsion, condescension and/or unreflexive stereotyping. The recognition of these

dangers calls for a much more self-conscious use of films and a re-examination of our pedagogic task within the present moment of 'crisis' and experimentation in anthropology.

2. The evidence of 'aberrant' readings, not only at the level of texts' syntagmatic structure (i.e. text elements, themes and horizon) but at the paradigmatic level (i.e. negation) as well, points to the seriousness of the interpretive 'gap' between particular films (especially the more 'closed' ones) and undergraduates. Moreover, this evidence also suggests that aberrant readings may be inevitable in most ethnographic visual representations. While it may be impossible to reconstruct the implied meanings of any text, all texts being the sum of their own 'misreadings' (Bloom 1976), this understanding has even stronger implications with respect to cross-cultural representation of the 'primitive', where 'misinterpretations' are more loaded with prejudices, stereotypes and hegemonic notions of otherness.

While recognising that instructors cannot completely avoid aberrant readings, there are alternatives that may help lessen them and their automatic re-triggering of stereotypes. We need to identify and study what kind of misreadings particular films generate, instead of ignoring or overlooking them. We may then be able to help students become aware of, and reflect on, the preconceptions that inform viewers' (mis)interpretations. Probably a more circumspect option is to evaluate carefully the levels of correspondence between reader and text (that is, between 'implied reader' and actual viewer) before screening films and to design teaching strategies that build from a common understanding.[12]

3. Although helpful, such strategies for lessening misinterpretation provide only partial solutions; we must look at teaching methods and approaches which may serve unwittingly to perpetuate cultural hegemony. My own study suggests that teaching approaches which combine evolutionary theory (and a similar sequencing of films), the use of films as illustrations of 'factual' knowledge, and a selection of 'closed' texts, are more likely to reinforce students' role as 'blind' believers in univocal and authoritative representations. The positivist notion that the more 'objective' and distant accounts of culture are more 'truthful' and 'neutral', and therefore better entrées into 'authentic' instruction, may prove false and naive because it overlooks the mediating role of interpretation before, during and after the construction of 'factual' knowledge, and thus also conceals the ideological impact of visual media.

In preference to the 'closed' univocal texts which imply a passive, uncritical receiver, material could be selected from films that convey at least the 'openness' to engage spectators as worthy contributors to the active co-construction of knowledge. Teaching approaches that combine interpretive and reflexive anthropology with contemporary post-colonial history, incorporating critical theory and a more diverse selection of films (including reflexive, critical and experimental films) are more likely to result in open, elaborated and reflexive readings. Such openness tends to be both situated in and evocative of self-empowering, identificatory and pleasurable viewing experiences. Recognising that pleasure can be either a teaching resource (as a productive and interpretive activity) or detrimental to learning (as self-gratification and escapism), instructors might do well to capitalise on the openness of more pleasurable representations, especially in introductory courses and early in the semester, and work toward transforming passive and escapist pleasure into creative or 'poietic' (Jauss 1982a), reflexive and critical pleasure.

4. The crisis of representation in the pedagogical practice of ethnographic film is, at least in part, a 'crisis of contextualisation'. Although the importance of contextualisation has been widely recognised within the field (Asch 1975; Heider 1976), my study suggests a need to reframe our understanding of it. We need to broaden our perspective and to recognise that it is not only the 'other' that needs to be contextualised but also, and equally important, the *self*. Films need to be framed as *texts* within their respective theoretical underpinnings and filmic strategies, both as informational sources and as representational means; students need to be contextualised as *spectators* in their viewing experience, horizons of expectation and interpretive strategies; and, finally, *instructors* and their own theoretical perspectives need to be contextualised within the diverse communities of academic discourse.

Conventional practices for surrounding a film with 'ample' contextualisation of the represented subjects, although of crucial importance, may not be enough. In their research, Hearne and DeVore (1973) provided extensive contextualisation of Yanomamo culture through study guides, books, the complete film series, and extensive lecture presentations, yet their students still reacted by resorting to hegemonic stereotyping of the Yanomamo. By the same token, cross-cultural comparative approaches can help contextualise students' understanding of other cultures, but they may also prove to be insufficient. After showing *The Ax Fight*, for example, it is not enough to say 'we are also violent . . . they are not the only ones', and so on because the visual pragmatics of textual messages overpower any attempt to draw a 'fair' comparison.

This evidence points to the importance of framing films as representational means: we need to inform students about the specific textual strategies that ethnographic films use to communicate and the power they have to prestructure interpretations. Like all readers, students can better understand films if they are equipped with the reading skills – and the kind of film literacy – necessary to analyse and criticise anthropological messages. Historical readings of film are fundamental to spectators' reconstructing of their horizon of expectations about texts and about the 'other'. In addition, the analysis of film tropes can greatly contribute to relativising authoritative representations and make evident their rhetorical power to construct knowledge and the identities of film subjects. On a micro scale, study of film techniques (e.g. use of interviews, narration, camera approach) can also help viewers to understand how texts construct their 'message'. In sum, students need to know about the multiple texts and subtexts films communicate and how they are conveyed, including the analysis of denoted and connoted messages.

Students also need to see themselves as spectators and to analyse how they construct textual meanings. Beyond the learning of 'factual' information, the use of film requires that viewers express their immediate and visceral reactions (to both the film and to the 'primitive') and that they elaborate and discuss their viewing experience and interpretations in the classroom. By encouraging this, instructors can contribute to students' self-awareness of their own 'structure of feelings' about the 'primitive', helping them to expand their 'reading' skills and competence and making them more aware of their own conventions and identification with particular interpretive communities. Teaching students about their spectrum of 'preferred' ideological readings of ethnographic films can contribute to helping them re-examine their own preconceptions of the 'primitive' and thus increase their ideological range. Like most spectators, students tend to take their own interpretations as natural. Thus, an important goal would be to incorporate into introductory courses a study of 'socially motivated deconstructive critical' thinking (Fiske 1986). Such training, which would include both textual and ideological criticism, can provide students with the necessary tools to analyse and criticise film tropes and to deconstruct the hegemonic messages inevitably inscribed in ethnographic films.

As members of specific teaching communities, we have the task of expanding our self-reflexive teaching methods and contextualising our own academic communities, their respective epistemological frameworks and representational practices in ethnographic film. As Simon and Dippo (1986) have proposed, we need to recognise how our involvement in the production of knowledge affects the ways we participate in cultural hegemony and in the legitimation of particular interests. This form of contextualisation may help students and teachers to relativise and criticise authoritative forms of textuality that all too often confound experience with narrative and facilitate their own participation as active constructors of anthropological knowledge.

5. The use of film in teaching thus demands an expanded instructional role from professors: the employment of a complex and powerful medium requires a more sophisticated 'translator' of cultures. Such an expanded role would entail understanding the language of visual representation and its rhetorical and interpellatory power, as well as knowledge and application of film criticism. Although most anthropology professors are generally not trained for assuming the tasks of film critique, the experimental use of films and open discussion of student interpretations in the classroom offers many possibilities for self-training in this area. Inter-departmental collaboration with other fields (e.g. film studies, literary criticism, communications) can also prove to be of special value for a multidisciplinary analysis of films. In addition, periodic workshops and colloquia on the use of film in teaching should be further promoted; efforts in this direction carried out by the Society for Visual Anthropology have been valuable for exchanging experiences and training instructors.

Although the expanded instructional role outlined above may appear over ambitious and even idealistic, it is a logical consequence of the complexity of ethnographic film spectatorship. It also represents an urgently needed response to the crisis of representation in anthropology, a crisis which requires that we enhance our self-reflexive and self-critical practices in order to identify the limits of our knowledge claims as well as their potential impact on the social construction of anthropological knowledge.

## Notes

I am extremely grateful to Carolyn Taylor for reading earlier versions of this paper and for her invaluable contributions to it. I also warmly thank Lucien Taylor, Claudia South, Diana Lee, Paul Gelles and Nancy Lutkehaus for their helpful comments and suggestions.
  1  While respecting the particular 'language' of each medium and its form of communication, I use the term 'text' to refer to both written and filmic media. Drawing on theories of the text (Barthes 1977), I stress the term to underline the similarities of written and visual media as forms of discourse and communication, as both products and producers of meaning and knowledge. Correspondingly, the terms 'reader', 'viewer', 'spectator' and 'reading subject' are used interchangeably to emphasise the idea of active agency in the decoding and interpretive process and in the co-construction of meaning and textuality.
  2  This ongoing study has been conducted since spring 1987 under the supervision of Dr Nancy Lutkehaus. Partial funding has been provided by the Spencer Foundation, the Fulbright Commission and the Center for Visual Anthropology at USC. Data have been collected in ten sections (five different professors) of an introductory anthropology course entitled 'Exploring Culture Through Film' where I work as a teaching assistant. The course, which is geared to meet general education requirements, uses from 15 to 25 films per semester and meets in sections of roughly 100 students each. Approximately 90% of the students are upper middle class, Caucasian, non-majors. Qualitative methods of analysis included direct classroom observation, comprehensive interviews with students and professors, student case studies, and content analysis of student assignments and reported student dreams (related to the films and to the 'primitive'). Quantitative methods were applied to attitude scale tests, student profile questionnaires and film preference rankings. Preliminary reports have been presented in the form of papers at the American Anthropological Association meetings from 1987 to 1990 and as a research report to the Spencer Foundation.
  3  MacDougall cites such films as *Nanook of the North*, *The Ax Fight*, *Chronicle of a Summer* and *Kenya Boran* as exemplary of participatory and open-ended texts primarily on the grounds that they voice more than the author's perspective. However, while this claim of openness may be valid for reflexive films that do incorporate the film subject's point of view, which seems essential to any truly 'open' text, this does not apply to *The Ax Fight*, where 'indigenous commentary' is completely absent.
  4  Eco also proposes to see the 'author' as a textual strategy, inserted in the text as an 'actantial role' or 'sujet de l'énoncé' and whose function is that of 'establishing semantic connections and activating the Model reader' (1979, p. 11). From here on, when I refer to 'text', I will also mean to imply this sense of the author as a textual strategy.
  5  In many applications of Lacanian theory in anthropology, the Other (field of the

symbolic) has been equated with the 'primitive other'. However, in Lacan's own terms, the Other (with capital 'O') refers to the ultimate signifier (the phallus) while the 'other' is a mere fetishised substitute of the Other.

6  In an exploratory analysis of dreams that students reported with reference to films shown in class and to the 'primitive', I have found that they seem to reproduce the archetypical notion of the 'primitive' as both the threatening barbarian linked to unconscious fears of castration, death and alienation and the idealised savage linked to pleasurable experiences of protection, participation and spiritual communion.

7  Oudart distinguishes three stages in the process of suturing: (1) the spectator's pure pleasure of seeing prior to the articulation of cinema; (2) the breaking of the illusion or the loss of 'total vision' and the recognition of an 'absent field' outside the image, a transition which marks the movement from cinema to cinematic discourse; (3) the suturing of discourse or the reappropriation of the 'absent-one' by substituting it with a perspective in the film (e.g. camera, character).

8  See the excellent study by C. Lutz and J. Collins (1991) of the multiple gazes in *National Geographic* photographs.

9  Williams uses as examples the contradictory structures of feeling of the defeated Puritans and the restored court in England between 1660 and 1690, and the rise of the new British bourgeoisie during the period of 1700–1760. Other studies have incorporated the category to analyse the postmodern subject's relation to selfhood and language in popular and avant garde texts (see Pfeil 1988).

10  Data were collected in the form of written essays on the first day of class during the spring semester of 1988. Students were to write about the notion of 'primitiveness', personal experience with 'primitive' societies, information about them learned from media, their knowledge of 'primitive' peoples' daily lives, appearance, beliefs, values and relation to 'modern' societies.

11  Tyler (1986) has sharply criticised the subjacent hegemonic meaning of these more recent tropes: 'Now ... she [the other] has become the instrument of the ethnographer's "experience", the ethnographer having become the focus of "difference" in a perverse version of the romanticism that has always been in ethnography, no matter how desperately repressed and marginalised by the objective impulses of seekers of pure data ... the other is the means of the author's alienation from his own sick culture, but the savage of the twentieth century is sick too; neutered, like the rest of us, by the dark forces of the "world system", IT has lost the healing art.' (p. 128)

12  These strategies may include familiarising students with the film format, showing documentaries before the more specialised ethnographic films or even including a film sequence on the historical development of ethnographic film; starting with films on more assimilable topics (e.g. daily life, socialisation, marriage) rather than those about the most 'distant' topics (e.g. warfare, witchcraft); beginning with films on more familiar cultures (including the students' own) and progressively moving to the most 'exotic' ones.

### References

*Books and articles*

Adorno, T. and Horkheimer, M. (1977), 'The culture industry: enlightenment as mass deception', *Mass Communication and Society*, Sage Publications, Beverly Hills, pp. 349–83.

Althusser, L. (1971), 'Ideology and the ideological state apparatuses', *Lenin and Philosophy and Other Essays*, Brewster, B. (trans.), Monthly Review Press, New York, pp. 127–86.

Amelio, R. (1971), *Films in the Classroom*, Standard Publishing, Cincinnati.

Asch, T. (1975), 'Using film in teaching anthropology: one pedagogical approach' in P. Hockings (ed.), *Principles of Visual Anthropology*, Mouton Publishers, Chicago, pp. 385–420.

Banks, M. (1990), 'The seductive veracity of ethnographic film', *Society for Visual Anthropology Review*, VI, 1, pp. 16–21.

Barthes, R. (1973), *The Pleasure of the Text*, The Noonday Press, New York.

Barthes, R. (1977), *Image-Music-Text*, Hill & Wang, New York.

Baudrillard, J. (1988), *Jean Baudrillard: Selected Writings*, Poster, M. (ed.) Polity Press and Stanford University Press, Cambridge and Palo Alto.

Bhabha, H. (1983), 'The other question', *Screen*, XXIV, 6, pp. 18–36.

Berger, J. (1972), *Ways of Seeing*, British Broadcasting Corporation and Penguin Books, London.

Bloom, H. (1973), *The Anxiety of Influence: A Theory of Poetry*, Oxford University Press, Oxford.

Bourdieu, P. (1977), *Outline of a Theory of Practice*, Cambridge University Press, Cambridge.

Brodkey, L. (1987), 'Writing critical ethnographic narratives', *Anthropology and Education Quarterly*, XVIII, 2, pp. 67–76.

Burke, K. (1969), *A Rhetoric of Motives*, University of California Press, Berkeley.

Clifford, J. and Marcus, G., (eds.) (1986), *Writing Culture*, University of California Press, Berkeley.

Clifford, J. (1988), *The Predicament of Culture*, Harvard University Press, Cambridge.

Condit, C. (1989), 'The rhetorical limits of polysemy', *Critical Studies in Mass Communication*, VI, 2, pp. 103–22.

Crapanzano, V. (1980), *Tuhami: Portrait of a Moroccan*, University of Chicago Press, Chicago.

Dayan, D. (1976), 'The tutor code of classical cinema' in B. Nichols (ed.), *Movies and Methods*, University of California Press, Berkeley, I, pp. 438–51.

Deleuze, G. and Guatarri, F. (1983), *Anti-Oedipus: Capitalism and Schizophrenia*, University of Minnesota Press, Minneapolis.

Eco, U. (1979), *The Role of the Reader*, Indiana University Press, Bloomington.

Fish, S. (1980), *Is There a Text in this Class?*, Harvard University Press, Cambridge.

Fiske, J. (1986), 'Television: polysemy and popularity', *Critical Studies in Mass Communication*, III, pp. 391–408.

Fiske, J. (1987), *Television Culture*, Methuen & Co, New York.

Foucault, M. (1980), *Power/Knowledge: Selected Interviews and Other Writings*, Pantheon Books, New York.

Foucault, M. (1977), *Discipline and Punishment*, Vintage Books, New York.

Gadamer, H. (1975), *Truth and Method*, Continuum, New York.

Geertz, C. (1973), *The Interpretation of Cultures*, Basic Books, New York.

Gitlin, T. (1978), 'Media sociology: the dominant paradigm' in T. Gitlin (ed.), *Theory and Society*, VI, pp. 205–53.

Gouldner, A. (1976), *The Dialectic of Ideology and Technology*, Oxford University Press, New York.

Grossberg, L. (1984), 'Strategies of Marxist cultural interpretation', *Critical Studies in*

*Mass Communication*, I, pp. 392–421.

Hall, S. (1985), 'Signification, representation, ideology: Althusser and the post-structuralist debate', *Critical Studies in Mass Communication* , II, 2, pp. 91–114.

Hall, S. (1980), 'Encoding/decoding' in Hall, S., Hobson, D., Lowe, A. & Willis, P. (eds.) *Culture, Media and Language*, Hutchinson, London pp. 128–138.

Hearne, T. & DeVore, P. (1973), 'The Yanomamo on paper and on film', paper prepared for the Anthropological Film Conference, Smithsonian Institute, Washington DC, May 12, 1973.

Heath, S. (1981), *Questions of Cinema*, Indiana University Press, Bloomington.

Heider, K. (1976), *Ethnographic Film*, University of Texas Press, Austin.

Holland, N. (1968), *5 Readers Reading*, Yale University Press, New Haven.

Holub, R. (1984), *Reception Theory: A Critical Introduction*, Methuen, New York.

Iser, W. (1978), *The Act of Reading: A Theory of Aesthetic Response*, Johns Hopkins University Press, Baltimore.

Iser, W. (1974), *The Implied Reader: Patterns of Communication in Prose Fiction from Bunyan to Beckett*, Johns Hopkins University Press, Baltimore.

Jauss, H. (1982a), *Aesthetic Experience and Literary Hermeneutics*, University of Minnesota Press, Minneapolis.

Jauss, H. (1982b), *Toward an Aesthetic of Reception*, University of Minnesota Press, Minneapolis.

Jameson, F. (1981), *The Political Unconscious*, Cornell University Press, New York.

Kuehnast, K. (1990), 'Gender representation in visual ethnographies: an interpretivist perspective', *Commission on Visual Anthropology Review*, Spring 1990, pp. 21–9.

Kuhn, A. (1982), *Women's Pictures: Feminism and Cinema*, Routledge and Kegan Paul, Boston.

Kuper, A. (1988), *The Invention of Primitive Society: Transformations of an Illusion*, Routledge, New York.

Lacan, J. (1977), *Ecrits: A Selection*, W. W. Norton & Co., New York.

Lacan, J. (1977), *The Four Fundamental Concepts of Psycho-Analysis*, W. W. Norton & Co., New York.

Lansing, S. (1990), 'The decolonisation of ethnographic film', *Society for Visual Anthropology Review*, VI, 1, pp. 13–15.

Lévi-Strauss, C. (1966), *The Savage Mind*, University of Chicago Press, Chicago.

Linker, K. (1984), 'Representation and sexuality' in B. Wallis, (ed.) *Art After Modernism: Rethinking Representation*, David R. Godine, Publisher, Inc., New York, pp. 391–415.

Lutz, C. and J. Collins (1991), The Photograph as an intersection of gazes: the example of the *National Geographic, Visual Anthropology Review*, 7, 1, pp. 134–49.

MacDougall, D. (1975), 'Beyond observational cinema', P. Hockings, (ed.), *Principles of Visual Anthropology*, Mouton Publishers, Chicago, pp. 109–24.

MacDougall, D. (1978), 'Ethnographic film: failure and promise', *Annual Review of Anthropology*, VII, pp. 405–26.

Marcus, G. and Fischer, M. (1986), *Anthropology as Cultural Critique*, University of Chicago Press, Chicago.

Martinez, W. (1990a), 'Critical studies and visual anthropology: aberrant versus anticipated readings of ethnographic film', *Commission for Visual Anthropology Review*, Spring 1990, pp. 34–47.

Martinez, W. (1990b), 'The ethnographic film spectator and the crisis of representation in visual anthropology', M. A. thesis, University of Southern California.

McRobbie, A. (1982), 'Jackie: an ideology of adolescent femininity' in B. Waites, T. Bennett, and G. Martin, (eds.), *Popular Culture: Past and Present*, Croom Helm, London, pp. 263–83.

Metz, C. (1977), *The Imaginary Signifier*, Indiana University Press, Bloomington.

Miller, J. (1977), 'Suture', *Screen*, XVIII, 4, pp. 24–34.

Morley, D. (1980), *The 'Nationwide' Audience: Structure and Decoding*, British Film Institute, London.

Mulvey, L. (1975), 'Visual pleasure and narrative cinema', *Screen*, XVI, 3, pp. 6–18.

Nelson, C. & Grossberg, L. (eds.) (1988), *Marxism and the Interpretation of Culture*, University of Illinois Press, Chicago.

Nichols, B. (1981), *Ideology and the Image*, Indiana University Press, Bloomington.

Oudart, J. (1977), 'Cinema and suture', *Screen*, XVIII, 4, pp. 35–47.

Pfeil, F. (1988), 'Postmodernism as a "structure of feeling" ', L. Grossberg and C. Nelson (eds.), *Marxism and the Interpretation of Culture*, University of Illinois Press, Chicago, pp. 381–403.

Pinney, C. (1989), 'Appearing worlds', *Anthropology Today*, V, 3, pp. 26–8.

Radway, J. (1984), *Reading the Romance: Women, Patriarchy and Popular Literature*, University of North Carolina Press, Chapel Hill.

Rothman, W. (1976), 'Against the system of the suture', B. Nichols (ed.), *Movies and Methods*, University of California Press, Berkeley, I, pp. 451–59,.

Said, E. (1979), *Orientalism*, Vintage Books, New York.

Said, E. (1983), 'Opponents, audiences, constituencies and community', H. Foster, (ed.), *The Anti-Aesthetic: Essays on Postmodern Culture*, Bay Press, Seattle, pp. 135–59.

Silverman, K. (1983), *The Subject of Semiotics*, Oxford University Press, Oxford.

Simon, R. and Dippo, D. (1986), 'On critical ethnographic work', *Anthropology and Education Quarterly*, XVII, 4, pp. 195–202.

Smith, P. (1988), *Discerning the Subject*, University of Minnesota Press, Minneapolis.

Spivak, G. (1988), *In Other Worlds: Essays in Cultural Politics*, Routledge, New York.

Taussig, M. (1987), *Shamanism, Colonialism and the Wild Man*, University of Chicago Press, Chicago.

Todorov, T. (1984), *The Conquest of America*, Harper & Row Publishers, Inc., New York.

Tomaselli, K., Williams A., Steenveld, L. and Tomaselli, R. (1986), *Myth, Race and Power: South Africans Imaged on Film and TV*, Anthropos Publishers, Bellville.

Tompkins, J. (ed.) (1980), *Reader-Response Criticism: From Formalism to Post-Structuralism*, Johns Hopkins University Press, Baltimore.

Trinh T. M. (1989), *Woman, Native, Other*, Indiana University Press, Bloomington.

Tyler, S. (1986), 'Post-modern ethnography: From document of the occult to occult document' in J. Clifford and G. Marcus, (eds.), *Writing Culture*, University of California Press, Berkeley, pp. 122–40.

White, H. (1978), *Tropics of Discourse*, The Johns Hopkins University Press, Baltimore.

Williams, R. (1977), *Marxism and Literature*, Oxford University Press, Oxford.

Wolf, E. (1982), *Europe and the People Without History*, University of California Press, Berkeley.

Worth, S. (1981), *Studying Visual Communication*, Gross, L. (ed.) University of Pennsylvania Press, Philadelphia.

Worth, S. and Gross, L. (1974), 'Symbolic strategies' in L. Gross, (ed.) *Studying Visual Communication*, University of Pennsylvania Press, Philadelphia, pp. 134–47.

*Films*

Asch, T. and N. Chagnon (1975), *The Ax Fight*, Documentary Educational Resources (DER), Watertown, Mass. Colour, 30 mins.

—— (1975, *A Man Called Bee*, DER, Watertown, Mass. Colour, 40 mins.

Asch, T. and L. Connor (1979), *A Balinese Trance Seance*, DER, Watertown, Mass. Colour, 30 mins.

Bateson, G. and M. Mead (1952), *Trance and Dance in Bali*, New York University Film Library, New York. Black and white, 20 mins.

Chagnon, N. (1970), *Magical Death*, DER, Watertown, Mass. Colour, 29 mins.

Connolly, B. and R. Anderson (1984), *First Contact*, DER, Watertown, Mass. Colour, 54 mins.

Curling, C. (1974), *Masai Women*, ISHI Films, Philadelphia. Colour, 52 mins. (Granada Television), (Anthropologist: M. Llewellyn-Davies)

Flaherty, R. (1922), *Nanook of the North*, Philadelphia: Pennsylvania State University Audiovisual Services, 16mm. Black and white, 55 mins.

Gardner, R. (1965), *Dead Birds*, Film Study Center, Harvard: McGraw-Hill Films Inc., 16mm. Colour, 83 mins.

—— (1985), *Forest of Bliss*, Del Mar, California: McGraw-Hill Films Inc., 16mm. Colour, 56 mins.

Hamermesh, M. (1985), *Maids and Madams*, New York: Filmmaker's Library, 16mm. Colour, 52 mins.

Haramis, P. (1969), *Anastenaria*, Berkeley: University of California Extension Media Center, 16mm. Black and white, 17 mins.

Harris, H. (1970), *The Nuer*, Del Mar, California: McGraw-Hill Films Inc., 16mm. Colour, 75 mins.

Llewellyn-Davies, M. (1984), *The Women's Olamal: The Organization of a Maasai Fertility Ceremony*, BBC Television. Colour, 110 mins.

Littman, L. (1976), *Number Our Days*, Direct Cinema Ltd., Los Angeles. Colour, 29 mins.

MacDougall, D. and J. Blue (1974), *Kenya Boran*, American Universities Field Staff, Hanover. Colour, 66 mins.

Marshall, J. (1958), *The Hunters*, Colour, 73 mins.

—— (1969), *N!um Tchai*, Black and white, 20 mins.

—— (1972), *A Rite of Passage*, Colour, 14 mins.

—— (1974), *Meat Fight*, Colour, 14 mins.

—— (1980), *N!ai, The Story of a !Kung Woman, 1952–78*, Colour, 59 mins.

Miller, N. (1976), *Naim and Jabar*, Wheelock Educational Resources, Hanover. Colour, 50 mins.

—— (1976), *Andean Women*, Wheelock Educational Resources, Hanover. Colour, 17 mins.

Minh-ha, Trinh T. (1982), *Reassemblage*, Women Make Movies, New York. Colour, 40 mins.

Nairn, C. (1974), *The Kawelka – Ongka's Big Moka*, Granada Television, 'Disappearing World' series. Colour, 52 mins. (Anthropologist: Andrew Strathern)

O'Rourke, D. (1987), *Cannibal Tours*, Direct Cinema Ltd., Los Angeles. Colour, 77 mins.

Rouch, J. (1955), *Les Maîtres Fous*, DER, Watertown, Mass. Colour, 35 mins.

Rouch, J. and E. Morin (1961), *Chronicle of a Summer*, New York: Contemporary/McGraw-Hill Films Inc., 16mm. Black and white, 90 mins.

Spensiper, S. (1989), *Films are Dreams that Wander in the Light of Day*, UCLA Dept. of Urban Planning, Los Angeles. U-Matic, 20 mins.

**Part Three**

Politics, ethics and indigenous imagery

# Introduction

The first three chapters in this part deal with the politics and ethics of ethnographic film-making. They are addressed, like most of the preceding chapters in the book, to those visual anthropologists who see themselves as creating 'film ethnographies' and for whom visual anthropology is, principally, about the use of film and video to communicate ethnographic knowledge. This is visual anthropology because it is anthropology done in the visual mode. The remaining three chapters deal not with *film*, as an anthropological strategy or technique, but with *films* (in principle any films) as cultural products. This is visual anthropology because it is the anthropological study of visual media.

Faris (Chapter 9) comes first for the same reason that Hastrup comes first in Part One: his objective is to puncture the more inflated claims and aspirations of those who champion the advantages of film as a way of transmitting ethnographic knowledge. He hopes thereby to encourage serious consideration of the famous question posed by a Navajo elder to Worth and Adair: 'Why make movies?' (1972, p.5). The claimed advantage of film he is especially concerned to challenge is that the medium itself offers an escape from the dilemmas of power, objectification and 'conceptual imposition' which are being wrestled with by postmodern ethnography.

We delude ourselves, argues Faris, if we imagine that, merely by presenting on film what we consider to be oppressive or exploitative social relations we can, *ipso facto*, reveal the nature of these relations to viewers, let alone stir them to 'ameliorative action'. Nor is it an answer simply to let 'them' do the filming. What matters is not who is holding the camera but who is doing the viewing: whose 'desire' is being satisfied. Ethnographic film, even when the camera is 'in their hands', is a Western 'project' – something *we* do to *them*.

The Kayapo . . . do not join the global village as equal participants, as just more folks with their video cameras. They enter it already situated by the West, which gives them little room to be anything more than what the West will allow. (p. 176)

The subject of ethnographic film will always be object, no matter who does the filming, so long as *we* are the viewers. The West is now everywhere, within the West and outside, in structures, minds and technologies. (p. 178)

Put like this, of course, *the* dilemma for ethnographic film, how, as Faris eloquently puts it, to 'obliterate otherness while preserving difference' (p. 174), is equally *the* dilemma for ethnographic writing. Indeed ethnographic writing played an important part in creating the dilemma in the first place, it being one of the means by which the West has objectified non-Western peoples. If film offers no easy escape from the dilemma, ethnographic film-makers may console themselves with the thought that Faris's polemic (as he himself calls it) suggests another question, logically prior to (and therefore more troubling than) 'Why make [ethnographic] movies?', and which many an anthropologist must have been asked, in one way or another, by his or her puzzled informants: 'Why do anthropology?'.

Kuehnast (Chapter 10) invites ethnographic film-makers to consider the role of visual media (and therefore of their own productions) in bringing about precisely that 'colonisation of the world mind' (p. 184) to which Faris refers with the remark that, 'The West is now everywhere'. Coining the phrase 'visual imperialism' she asks how those who produce 'visual ethnographies' can 'avoid exporting cultural biases about gender, class or race . . .' (p. 182). The answer must be that they cannot, since it is in the nature of cultural biases to be unrecognised. But they can make themselves aware of the danger and it is the chief purpose of this chapter to encourage such self-awareness.

'Visual imperialism' is a form of ideological domination which has both dominant and dominated groups in its thrall. It is not a matter of the monopolistic control by an elite of the visual media but of the subtle, subliminal communication of a certain view of the world; not a matter of coercion but of consent; not a matter of class exploitation but of cultural domination. The export of visual media by the United States, Kuehnast tells us, is second only in importance to the export of aeroplanes. We might add here that Granada Television's *Disappearing World* series was placed fourth in a league table of 'British Television's All-Time Best Sellers' which appeared in *The Observer Colour Supplement* in 1988. Programmes from the series (which began in 1970) had by then been sold to ninety-three countries.

This must give serious pause for thought to visual anthropologists, especially those who collaborate with television companies, since all would now recognise that our 'visual ethnographies' are not simply records of other cultures, but interpretations of them, unconsciously suffused with our own cultural biases. Kuehnast gives a number of examples of cultural bias in some well-known ethnographic films – the stereotyping of women as marginal, for example, in *The Sons of Haji Omar* (Asch and Balikci 1978) and the editing out of 'foreign' influences (such as cars and radios) both in this film and in *N!ai: The Story of a !Kung Woman 1952–78* (Marshall 1980). Such film-makers are not, of course, 'malicious' but 'just unaware in terms of the set of biases underlying the era in which the film was produced' (p. 187).

The problem with cultural bias, whether it belongs to a whole generation or to an individual at a certain stage in his or her career, is that it is only recognised after the event. We can become aware of our biases but we cannot eliminate them completely. The way to deal with this problem, then, is to focus not only on the producers but also on the receivers of messages and here Kuehnast returns us to a theme which runs throughout the book: the need to 'empower' the viewer (see especially Martinez, Chapter 8). This can be done, firstly, by helping viewers - especially students of anthropology – to adopt an informed and critical attitude to the films they see; and, secondly, by following what Martinez calls a more 'open' or 'negotiated' film-making style which allows scope for the viewer to 'construct' the film's message. One way of doing this, suggests Kuehnast, is to make the ethnographer visible, as in *A Weave of Time* (Adair *et al.*, 1986) and *Thinking is Useless* (Boonzajer-Flaes 1988). The 'unpretentious approach' of these films 'transforms the information exchange from a myth-making process *about* the subject into a dialogue *with* the subject' (p. 190, emphasis in the original).

Asch (Chapter 11) moves us from politics to ethics: from broad issues of power and cultural bias to what Nichols (1981 p. 239) calls a 'central dilemma' of ethnographic film: 'what to do with people', a choice of words which reflects the power of the film-maker to manipulate the people filmed and to take advantage of their gullibility. Based on thirty years' experience of making films in collaboration with anthropologists, and honestly illustrated with the occasional cautionary tale drawn from that experience, this chapter is a kind of personal testimony: the product of one film-maker's attempt to overcome the tendency of ethnographic film to objectify and de-personalise its subjects. It consists, essentially, of a number of rules of thumb designed to guide the ethnographic film-maker in the discharge of his or her responsibilities to the people filmed, the anthropological community and future generations. Similar ethical considerations arise, of course, in ethnographic writing but, because of the relatively small and specialised audience for written ethnography and the ability writing gives to camouflage people and places, they can be more easily managed, circumvented or simply ignored.

Faris, Kuehnast and Asch deal with the political and ethical implications of using film as a strategy for the transmission of ethnographic knowledge. Their comments are directed at those visual anthropologists who are interested in film mainly as a way of producing alternative ethnographic texts. Another area of interest within the general field of visual anthropology is the study of 'visual communication' (Worth 1981) or 'pictorial aspects of culture' (Ruby 1989, p. 11). This involves asking 'what we [can] learn about a culture by studying what the members of a society [make] pictures of, how they [make] them, and in what contexts they [make] and [look] at them' (Worth *op cit.*, p. 92). The next three chapters are examples of this second interest applied to film, video and television: instead of treating the products of these media as ethnographic *texts* they treat them as ethnographic *data*.

One advantage of this approach is that it immediately liberates us from the interminable debate about what makes a film ethnographic: as cultural products, all films are grist to the ethnographer's mill. Tomaselli (Chapter 12) considers various films that have been made about the San of Namibia and Botswana, including a feature film (and major box-office success), *The Gods Must be Crazy* (Uys 1980), a television documentary, *People of the Great Sandface* (Myburgh 1985) and a film now regarded as a classic of the ethnographic cinema, *The Hunters* (Marshall 1958).

The first has been criticised by anthropologists within the Anti-Apartheid Movement for perpetuating 'the myth of the Bushmen living in splendid isolation, uncontaminated purity and primitive affluence' (p. 208) and for playing, thereby, into the hand of government planners, bent on creating a game park where the Bushmen could live in their 'original' state. *Sandface* has been criticised for ignoring the links, going back over hundreds of years, between the San and their black and white neighbours, a criticism that has also been levelled at *The Hunters*.

While not denying the ethnographic validity of these criticisms, Tomaselli argues for a broader and more complex reading of the films in terms of the particular historical conditions of their production, including the motives and biographies of their makers and the different responses of different audiences. We should not dismiss them out of hand as flawed ethnographic texts (which they certainly are) but take them seriously as data for ethnographic analysis. One consequence of treating the Uys and Myburgh films in this way is to realise that the view of the San they portray – remnants of 'stone age' hunters, living in 'original affluence' – was lifted ready-made from anthropological textbooks of the 1950s and 1960s. As for playing into the hands of apartheid planners, therefore, the damage had already been done by anthropologists, long before these particular film-makers arrived on the scene. This prompts Tomaselli to ask whether the attack on Uys is 'an indication of guilt atonement' on the part of Anglo-Saxon anthropologists, for whom the origins of their discipline 'in colonialism and racism remain a sore point' (p. 210).

Turning briefly, at the end of this chapter, to consider the strategies whereby film-makers can help the survival rather than hasten the demise of groups like the Bushmen, Tomaselli focuses, like Faris and Kuehnast, not on getting the ethnographic 'facts' right but on issues of power and accountability. Rather than making 'ever more mass distributed movies about their plight' film-makers should attempt to loosen their own control, both over the subjects of their films (so that they may become truly 'subjects') and over audiences.

If anthropologists are to guide constructive processes resulting from their encounter with communities, they need to theorise the nature of that encounter and to acknowledge the power structures and relationships that develop . . . The lack of epistemological writing on methods of production alerts us to the fundamental issue: who initiates videos or films and why? (p. 216)

For both film-makers and anthropologists, in other words, the first step to a solution of the problem is to recognise that they are part of it.

Chalfen (Chapter 13) and Hughes-Freeland (Chapter 14) also treat visual media as ethnographic data rather than as techniques for communicating ethnographic knowledge, but they are less concerned with politics and power relations than with the more neutral concept of culture. By showing how the technology of image production and transmission is appropriated differently in different cultural settings they are, in effect, making a case for, and demonstrating the potential of, a specifically anthropological analysis of media, in opposition to those who might echo Carpenter's claim (quoted by Chalfen, p. 237) that 'These media swallow culture'.

Chalfen, who has become a leading figure in the 'anthropology of visual communication' in the United States over the past twenty years, describes a number of research projects he has initiated over that time, all of them aimed at understanding the relationship between 'image-making', whether by means of film, still photography of video-recording, and culture. The result of this research, it seems, has been to show that 'culture' is too vague and broad a concept to shed much light on the 'dynamic process that constitutes visual communication' (p. 238). One must go further and investigate the specific interests and identities that differentiate people within an apparently homogeneous cultural setting. He found, for example, that working-class teenagers, when given cameras and told to make films on any subject they liked, made films about themselves and their immediate environment while middle-class teenagers from the same North American city made films about 'unfamiliar things and unknown people found in areas away from their familiar environment' (p. 229); in other words, about the 'Other'.

While it may be easy to accept the complexity, and plurality of modes of expression, within what we otherwise think of as 'our' culture, we are perhaps less ready to accept the same for 'other' cultures. Chalfen points out that 'It is not enough to think of the generalised Navajo, Kayapo ... Tongan or Indian videographer, and so on. Image makers are people embedded in personal and public histories and in particular socio-cultural contexts' (p. 224).

Hughes-Freeland's chapter is an early outcome of an innovative research project, still in progress, which is aimed at understanding 'how television contributes to the way in which particular Balinese people perceive cultural identity, social change and the role of the state' (p. 253). She proceeds in the traditional manner of the anthropologist by analyzing a particular case: a drama-documentary about a masked dance, *Arja*, made by Indonesian State Television in accordance with government policy to 'develop' certain cultural traditions judged beneficial to the fostering of a sense of Balinese identity. This enables her to show that, notwithstanding the electronic medium employed and the conscious motive of nation-building, the programme conforms to certain conventions of traditional Balinese narrative. 'This indicates a cultural specificity in media where many have predicted the end of cultural plurality' (p. 254).

This is an important finding which accords with Chalfen's conclusion, on the basis of his research on 'indigenous imagemaking' within the United States, that 'media do not swallow cultures'. But this is only half the story: the other half concerns 'cultural specificity' in the response of viewers. In common with several other contributors to the book (e.g. Martinez, Vaughan, MacDougall and Kuehnast) Hughes-Freeland stresses the active role of the viewer who does not just 'receive' but 'interacts with' a film or television programme.

What matters is how the 140 million or so people 'able to watch television programmes' are watching . . .; which people, maybe, and what kind of eyes and minds they are bringing to their viewing. TV sets are receivers, but people are viewers. (p. 000)

Her research is at too early a stage to provide answers to these questions but, like those asked by Chalfen, they mark out a distinctive field and set out a challenging agenda for the anthropological study of visual media.

### References

*Books and articles*
Ruby, J. (1989) 'The teaching of visual anthropology', in P. Chiozzi (ed.), *Teaching Visual Anthropology*, Editrice 'Il Sedicesimo', Florence.
Worth, S. (1981) 'Margaret Mead and the shift from "visual anthropology" to the "anthropology of visual communication" ' in L. Gross (ed.) *Studying Visual Communication*, University of Pennsylvania Press.
Worth, S. and J. Adair (1972) *Through Navajo Eyes: An Exploration in Film Communication and Anthropology*, Indiana University Press, Bloomington, Indiana.

*Films*
Adair, J., S. Fanshel and D. Gordon (1986), *A Weave of Time*, Navajo Film Project, New York Colour, 60 mins.
Asch, T. and A. Balikci (1978), *The Sons of Haji Omar*, National Film Board of Canada/ National Anthropological Film Center of the Smithsonian Institution. Colour, 58 mins.
Boonzajer-Flaes, R. (1988), *Thinking is Useless*, University of Amsterdam. Colour, 30 mins.
Marshall, J. (1957), *The Hunters*, Film Study Center, Harvard. Colour, 74 mins.
Marshall, J. (1980), *N!ai: The Story of a !Kung Woman, 1952–78*, Documentary Educational Resources, Watertown, Mass. Colour, 59 mins.
Myburgh, P. (1985), *People of the Great Sandface*, Anglia Television, 'Survival' series. Colour, 120 mins.
Uys, J. (1980), *The Gods Must be Crazy*, Mimosa Films. Colour, 109 mins.

# Anthropological transparency: film, representation and politics

There is in anthropology and in ethnographic film-making today a curious, but rather distinct optimism, an aura of explicit excitement, essentially a confidence, even a notion of progress – almost joy. The recent establishment of the Granada Centre for Visual Anthropology, at a time when anthropology in Britain is, at least quantitatively, in dramatic and precipitous decline is one indication, as is the appearance of various new books on the subject (e.g. Rollwagen 1988; Edwards, 1992). Even more strangely, this optimism seems fully cognizant of the representational crises of anthropology and proceeds as if film were somehow immune to them; or somehow addresses, solves or has ways round them and is thus able to secure for the West what today orthodox ethnography is no longer able to (cf. Tagg 1988, pp. 8ff).

I am much less sanguine about the future of either ethnographic film or ethnography and I think the enthusiasm is particularly misplaced with regard to ethnographic film (video). Let me outline why, citing three areas of concern; areas which, paradoxically, seem to be the focus of greatest optimism. These are, of course, those of most interest in contemporary ethnography. First, there is the tract of reflexivity, which seems essentially to boil down always to some form of 'they talk/we listen', and to the idea that this somehow solves the problem of power and conceptual imposition. Secondly, there is the enthusiastic concern for self-photography – the idea that if they film (or videotape) themselves, this will somehow solve the West's representational dilemmas; and thirdly, there is the issue of transparency – the idea that filmed power relations are readily apparent and transmitted directly to viewers. This is essentially the idea that, if victims are filmed, this will sooner or later lead to an alteration of their status. Whatever else may be said, it seems to me that there are particular delusions, illusions, and hoaxes associated with these projects. Yet they are projects which today seem to receive particular attention.[1]

## Consumption

None of these areas would be problematic if it were not for an inevitable contingency of ethnographic film, or film which purports to document one or another aspect of the lives of subalterns. While the status of film as document is no longer really persuasive, its status as representation, as a form of negotiation, is still under consideration.[2]

But the contingency of which I wish to speak is best expressed as the issue of want, of desire, of consumption of the subaltern – an old Western notion. That is, we are filming them; or we want films of them by them; or this is the medium in which we prefer to see (or only can see) them expressed or presented or represented. This is most commonly expressed today in the tropes of humanism: a sympathy for, and a celebration or revelation of the integrity of local expressions; or a critique of the exploitation commonly dictating the lives of such peoples. This nevertheless turns the representation into fetish (and the fetish into representation).

Now there is certainly nothing wrong (in and of itself) with arguing against exploitation, or with attempting to bring about appreciation of the logic or wisdom of another discourse of some merit. But it is the structural space and intellectual historical force of an anthropology or of a documentary cinema engaged in such activity that now seems to me problematic. It conflates horizons of dominance and of rationalism with objectivity and politics. It is rather, as Gayatri Spivak (1990, p. 60) has expressed it, 'an ignorance [we have been] allowed to possess.'

Desire and consumption motivations in the West have well-known implications. If we have learnt nothing else from the feminist critique, we have learnt that want has some very shady aspects. Its potential narcissism in film is particularly suspect. This can be seen in everything from the specific register in which the ethnography or the ethnophotography is set (the script), to the analytical closure which has been required since the development of the novel (on which all film narratives are today modelled) and the positivism which structured our classical anthropological totalising categories, such as 'culture' and 'society' (Gross 1990). This is a longing for both the pre-linguistic (Tagg 1988, p. 4), the transcendent as well as (contrarily) for direct verbal and textual access.

As there cannot be an unfocused film, intention has to be potential, with all the latent possibility this holds for voyeurism. To call photographic attention to something is to make it available to the gaze – statically (in still photography) as recipient or moving (in film) as aggressor (Mulvey 1989, p. 16ff) and this is not made less problematic because it is filled with good intentions.

This critique does not deny pleasure or desire as a subjective enterprise, indeed, it liberates pleasure and emancipates it from the fetish that results from empirical and ahistorical consumption and the maintenance of standards of authenticity, objectivity and truth. But I do not think film, or at least ethnographic film as heretofore practiced, restores the subject – it always situates the object, and thus the desire, the want and the consumption that I here critique. As far as I know, the possibility of a liberated desire, an elimination of object and a restored subject, is unknown in ethnographic film-making.

## Politics

Politically, at least two different sorts of difficulties have beset ethnographic film. First, film is often used by the well-intentioned to 'document' what is, in the minds of the film-makers, oppression or exploitation; or to call attention to a situation about which they want to stimulate audiences to ameliorative action. This may be in a rather naive, direct manner (in the mode of transparency noted above) on the assumption that the very appearance of victims will, in some unarticulated fashion, stimulate movement on the part of viewers. This, of course, may not happen.

But there are, possibly, other problems. To denounce is perhaps to participate in a dangerously programmatic sort of politics. If today our politics are not seamless, are not free from method, are not free from will and from the will to truth, we run the same risk as all the intellectual political currents of the past – a sort of received orthodoxy of measurement, of party schemes, of knowledge, of the unfolding (with help) of a right, a truth, a good; more corrections to the Fall of Man. This is certainly the fate of much social protest film. Putting the facts directly (or vicariously) is as poor as politics as it is, frequently, as film. I shall elaborate on this below.

This raises a second political question for ethnographic film. Is the critique political (about exploitative social relations) or cultural (for example, about the arrival of the West's television or religion)? These may not always be clearly separated, but every attempt must be made to distinguish them, for a film cannot make this discrimination. The eliding of the two has resulted in a type of determinism, a conflation of culture and politics, of content and form, which can generate, for example, such unfortunate concatenations as 'fascist (or bourgeois) aesthetics', as if this assignment could be axiomatically made on appearance. This was one of the outcomes of the ill-fated ethnographic film, *Southeast Nuba* (1982). (See also Faris 1988).

My position is that anthropologists, as human beings, have every right to posit *political* objections to specific social relations, and to argue for others on the basis of a better way to relate to one another. But this is not (or should not be) a critical statement about culture, about the *means* by which the social relations are presented and inscribed and by which content and form seem irrevocably or naturally linked. We are in no position to judge critically their cultural aberrations from the Western norm; it must be a political objection to social relations. It may not always be easy to separate these but, if we are to be critics, we must make the attempt. We can only really be *cultural* critics of the *culture* of our own systems, for these are the only social forms of which we have a sufficiently intimate know-ledge. Although most of us, perhaps, cannot recognise our demons because we live comfortably with them.

There is in ethnographic film never an 'unfocus'; all possible politics in such a register are bound to be programmatic. A seamless politics may be impossible, for since viewers, readers and observers are always agents, how can such motion not be Western? The perpetual ratio (Foucault 1973, p. 378), the distancing that is anthropology's project, could be said to have its metaphorical corollary in the focal distance, the constant holding at length necessary to photography.[3] This, it seems to me, makes it a very difficult means by which to mount a critique of alternative social relations. Fiction film, of course, is an excellent means to do so.

## Self-photography and the community of trust

There have been experiments to allow other voices, other distance, other space and other focus. But from what I know of these efforts, they mostly reveal what a limited and Western modality ethnographic film thus far really is. It is one more form of arrogation developed by an expansionist capital (while not, of course, reducible to it). We simply have, insofar as I am aware, few alternative practices with the available technology. Cameras (or camcorders) in the hands of others do not necessarily privilege their voices any more than reflexivity, as the naive view has it, obliterates the inherent power differentials of the ethnographic encounter. The subjective voice of the object is a figment of the same dialogical imagination that thinks reflexivity is a facile possibility in ethnographic research. But focus there must be and, if staging and authenticity become problematic in the hands of non-Westerners, the privileged view of the camera cannot.

Yet time and time again reference is made to the potentiality of video or film 'in their hands'.

The camera . . . can also allow others to tell their stories in their own voice, with their own views. It is then we will know 'the other' has returned the gaze. (Kuehnast 1990, p. 26)

Let me be very clear. There is perhaps nothing wrong with 'the camera in their hands'. It is the 'we' of this quotation that disturbs me – the constancy of the 'Other'. We distance or we assimilate; but surely the task is to obliterate otherness while preserving difference. Agency in such self-photography is still left to the intention of viewers and, unless one is to credulously fetishize the film-maker, it is not the camera's gaze that is the problem but that of the viewer. Local intellectuals and film-makers only exist in concert with Western intellectuals and film-makers so long as we watch. This is not (simply) a technical issue, although it is that too; the entire evolution of photographic technology has been grotesquely Western. It is also an issue of representation to viewers, to consumers. There has never been, to my knowledge, a film of them by them (or by us) *for* them. There is certainly no *popular* demand, however much there may be collaboration from an elite, an entrepreneur, an 'informant', or 'agents of change'. Local people present themselves to each other – that is what we call culture – and this may be decried or celebrated, depending on whether you are a believer or a critic. But it has not, up to now needed film or anthropology (although there are some pitifully poignant examples of anthropological texts becoming *their* cultural canon).

But representations to other, Western subjects, is another issue. Film, however didactic, pedantic, instructional, is only observational. It cannot be made to listen. Intention and design are unavoidable. The Navajo (Worth and Adair 1972) or the Kayapo 'representing themselves' (Turner 1990, p. 11) are not unproblematic – there must be cognizance of tropes of authenticity and our judgements of what 'them' is to appear. I have seen no non-Western gestures, undoubtedly because Westerners are primary viewers (but then I may not be informed of some). The nexes of power and history can make such gestures seem pathetic in their hands. Are we listening to *their* film?

Many of the conceits of anthropological practice – authority, authorship in ethnographic writing, claims to translation, and the opaque vanities of observation – are now fully exposed in current literature. And this is also true of ethnographic film-making, but with certain displacements that are significant. Yet the celebration of video projects, of the Other as 'representing themselves' is still greeted with certainty, even fervour. There is something about this which I find disturbing – an attitude almost of amorality. Let me quote from Turner (1990, p. 12) on the Kayapo.

When these reflexive dimensions (the Kayapo video-taping and the Western film-makers filming the Kayapo video-taping) of audio-visual documentation of a contemporary cultural reality, like that of the Kayapo, are considered together with the ways . . . that the Kayapo have begun to incorporate audio-visual media, and the material activity of audio-visual recording (e.g. the presence of Kayapo video-camera-persons and non-Kayapo film crews) into their own collective acts of political confrontation and cultural self-definition, it becomes apparent that the use of audio-visual media has taken on dimensions of meaning without close parallels in traditional anthropological methods of fieldwork. The quantitative shift certainly approaches, if it has not already reached, the point of qualitative transformation. For the anthropological film-maker, the change has had the character of a shift from participant observation to observant participation. . . . The nature of 'culture' itself is changing together with the techniques we employ to study it.

Apart from some revealing nineteenth century atavisms in his expression (quantity/quality), as well as the unfortunate use of old anthropological cliché ('participant observation' was always a sinister fiction), Turner's observation is probably very much conventional wisdom to many now involved with such work. But the Kayapo are at best filming, principally, themselves: those with whom they share culture, friendships and perhaps kinship. The family album or the home movie audience, however, is not the end result. The Kayapo are hardly the primary recipients and, consequently, techniques (framing, sequence, etc.), are, if nothing else, subject to an external agency.

The insistence that ' "culture" itself is changing' is frequently linked to another gesture by which it is held to be justified – a postmodernist gesture in anthropological theory which celebrates the obliteration of time and space and stresses focus on the new concatenations and social relations that encompass the world (cf. Marcus and Fischer 1986; Marcus 1990). This is the global village, a type of shopping-mall approach or celebration of pastiche which in my view is not only dangerously and depressingly apolitical (while claiming to be a cultural critique), but also theoretically dubious with its latent macro-functionalism and its retreat into a sort of positivist 'apprehension' of 'new' reality. What or who determines the parameters of such pastiche? The world is now complex. There are new cultures and new cultural processes in motion, and communication makes these often tandem, linked and syncretic. What else is new? The new ways in which this works and fits together should be the subject-matter of anthropology, but, except for the most static and dull of projects, have we not always been doing this? Like the new photographic dialogic – having them undertake their own filming and video taping – this strikes me as an attempt to keep our hands on, to secure access, to keep the old ties that bind, although now ostensibly on their terms. Beware the white man celebrating something you do.

It is not, of course, a matter of people having cameras for the first time. Nor is it a matter of defining culture or of new and changing self-definitions of culture. People have been doing that for ages; they have always represented themselves to themselves. And that is what they do with home movies and home video where editorial prerogative is irrelevant, and people are bound by ties other than observation, perhaps even ties of love and trust. This is commonly what studio photographers in other cultures do.[4]

Video has not, however, been used before by subalterns and marginals to the West, and using it to address the West may be derived from the classical motivation of subjects: that of want, of consumption. There is, as noted, obviously nothing wrong with Kayapo, or any other people, videotaping whatever they may like. But as I have tried to stress, the means of realizing both the power of the technology *and* its influence are not available to the Kayapo, nor are the motivations of cultural presentation for non-Kayapo consumption. I find their use of video, as described by Turner, rather forlorn. It is almost as if, now, they are equal partners with news photographers and photojournalists. The Kayapo and others of the Third World do not join the global village as equal participants, as just more folks with their video cameras. They enter it already situated by the West, which gives them little room to be anything more than what the West will allow. Technology not withstanding, they will enter only on our terms, unless they forcibly exclude us, prohibit our entry into their lives, eliminate our visits, our technologies and our help, refuse to allow us to view their videotapes, and show them only to themselves. That, after all, is what their cultures have been doing all along. Perhaps we may help best by leaving them alone. What, after all, are you doing here?

Let me be clear. This is not some sentimental, nostalgic notion; not some attempt to preserve, to establish reserves, nor to halt the global expansion of the West (would that it were possible!). It is an acknowledgement, firstly, that change is not necessarily something to be celebrated. We have every reason to be depressed by some change. 'Partial truths' (Clifford 1988) can also mean partial lies; and, secondly, that they just may not need us at all to represent them in photographs, with our sympathy, our understanding, our technology nor any other of our morally dubious enterprises. The problem is not the ciné camera or camcorder (this is not a Luddite objection and I have already noted the limitations imposed by the device). It is that we of power are the subjects, the viewers, the wanters, the covetous.

## Film examples

I should like to illustrate the above polemic with reference to films many have probably seen. I am sure the illustrations could apply to others. There is a scene in *Southeast Nuba* (1982), for example, in which we are interviewing a young elder (and an old friend of mine) about Leni Riefenstahl's visit and those who came to the area after the publication of her book *The People of Kau* (1976). (This, of course, was after she had seen and followed the maps in Faris (1972).) Poba responds, saying that the people were mostly Germans and of the 'worst' sort, who photographed mostly blood (from the bracelet fights and the age organisation-based female cicatrization). But if you watch carefully when I asked him what those tourists were about, he looks very uncomfortable and hesitates, before finally responding, 'they wanted pictures.' For here we were, (I was), ostensibly a friend, with a film crew and camera in his face, 'wanting pictures'. He immediately realised the embarrassment of contradiction, even if I, at least at the time, did not so acknowledge it.[5]

Regarding the issue of power, there is something of the same displacement going on in Dennis O'Rourke's *Cannibal Tours* (1987). We become progressively aware that O'Rourke is also a camera, also has desires (like the tourists), and is also presenting a particular sort of 'document' (of the tourists). We begin to see that the tourists also have little choice in the way in which they are photographed, or edited, nor about whether they are included, mocked or exposed. And these are people who are, ostensibly, fully aware of the power of the camera. Yet they may never see the film, nor O'Rourke's presentation of them and had no option but to be served up to critical audiences who will condemn them. Everyone is a victim of the camera, certainly the documentary camera. You may remember that very painful scene in which a young Papuan man is caught between the tourists' cameras and the film-maker's camera. Of course we see only him and the tourists, but the tourists see him and the film-maker, and he sees cameras everywhere. One is not easily sympathetic to the tourists – who are indeed grotesquely Western – but are they not also victims? What do the Papuans do for a living if the tourists no longer come? The only people who are not victimized in this very interesting film are the film-makers, though O'Rourke's method certainly allows another sort of subtle 'exposure'.

Both of these films introduce us to perhaps the most damning projects of all, projects not, however, confined to film, but latent in the critical anthropological project. That is, the degree to which only Westerners are agents, critics and victims, the degree to which the most advocating of films commonly boil down to nothing more than arguments Westerners are having with each other – even if they are arguing about the Other.

A very traditional film which I have always thought succeeded in giving some voice to indigenous differences is Elizabeth Fernea's *The Veiled Revolution* (1982), which considered re-veiling in Cairo and which allows a series of local views of veiling to be presented. As we watch women discuss regaining control over how their bodies are to appear to men and redefine their own sexuality, we begin to see (if we want to) how shallow are the ordinary views of Westerners, especially feminists, on women in Islam. They discuss commanding new attitudes from men, insist on new places in the mosque, save money on clothes, reduce competition based on appearance, and reject the West. We listen to a tired old Egyptian suffragette criticise re-veiling. She speaks to the interviewer in French, while sitting on Louis XIV furniture, and talks about the old days of emancipation, which actually meant surrender to the West (but is she not, from this perspective, a victim?). The structure of film-making, as received by us, leaves no other space. Of course, what is most clear in this film (having now shown it to large undergraduate classes several times) is that a political critique *must be brought to it*, and the success of the film is in having the materials available so that is possible. Undergraduates do not commonly have such a political critique, but they can appreciate it, can apply it ('see' it) in the film once they are guided to do so.

Much of the same situation occurs in the old, quite traditional film, *Maasai Women* (1974), in which, by the end of a long interview with an extraordinary elder woman, we begin almost to feel sorry for the Western interviewer (Melissa Llewellyn-Davies) because she has no co-wives and has not been circumcised.

The representational project (of them to us by us) is a Western project, and thus filmic versions of this, irrespective of who's filming, are going to be inevitably Western projects so long as *we* consume them. The subject of ethnographic film will always be object, no matter who does the filming, so long as *we* are the viewers. The West is now everywhere, within the West and outside, in structures, minds and technologies. The epistemic privilege – what has been called the 'cunning' of (our) reason – permeates and dramatically influences most possible projects of others' presentation of themselves to us. They are not co-constructions, they are one-way filters. A genuine (not to be confused with a true, real or authentic) voice of difference is not appropriable. Perhaps we can sometimes experience it but, thus far, we have been unable to transmit it very well.

That does not mean that there cannot be some very interesting film projects. Indeed, I think there are very many didactic possibilities but I am not well informed. It is difficult, at least for me thus far, to gauge the potential in this area of postmodernist anthropology, as practiced by someone like Stephen Tyler

(1987a). The destruction and deconstruction of received concepts, the retreat behind, or advance beyond metaphorical meaning undoubtedly sounds promising. What Tyler means, however, what kind of journey he anticipates, is not clear; and certainly not clear in visualist modalities where he has otherwise been an articulate critic (1984). But the gestures represented by, say George Marcus and Michael Fischer (1986), are positively depressing in their celebration of pastiche, their aggressive enthusiasm for anthropology's central role in mediating the new and emergent social relations apparent today, their delight at the mall and their dismissal of the security of place and the comforts of historical continuity. This is rather like staking out new territory that had been previously overlooked or was not previously important, a form of anthropological secondary strip-mining. Our diets (not withstanding our appetites) are not always healthy so long as we objectively consume representations of subalterns.

Now this leaves open, of course, representations as entertainment, like filmed operas, or the bizarre filmic or video presentations of concerts and huge professional sporting events; or even films designed for poetic and subjective reasons; or ethnographic film *as* (not of) performance and/or fiction. This makes explicit our own cultural inscriptions, contributions and authority. To leave authenticity to local presentation is an exciting possibility, for focus may change dramatically. But it certainly threatens the veracity of Western representation, exposes its fragile contingency and plays havoc with the West's notions of truth and authenticity, the anthropological saw that has been our discipline's commodity fetish. If we lose that, if we cannot claim some form of *privileged* representation, are we needed at all?[6]

## Conclusion

I have argued that the concatenation of ethnography with indigenous cinematographic enterprises confounds an already problematical, undertheorized and obstinate set of endeavours. There must be not only the suspension (or the explicit and deliberate specification) of disbelief, of irony, but also the elimination (or the making candid) of desire, of avidity. For these projects were founded in Western objective space. Neither anthropological reflexivity nor photographic transparency nor indigenous participation, evacuate or challenge the politico-intellectual foundations of these projects and their expansion in and of themselves.

The discouraged might respond, 'So what'? But, with full awareness of the dramatic historicity and classic power relation of the anthropological enterprise, the now-maturing critique of the West's visual privilege, the irrevocable exteriority of the photographic image and the motions of desire in all film productions, I would argue that, with intelligent creativity, humility, and above all, listening (a modality largely deposed with the triumph of the camera), we have every reason to proceed optimistically. And there may well be many other experiments which establish new relationships in the use of photographic images of which I am unaware. I hope so. Some of the historical critiques of studio traditions are very interesting (cf. Pinney 1992). One of the great advantages of still photos (over film or video) is precisely that other modalities may be more easily admitted and they are open to the addition of assigned discourses. They are not 'saturated' with the aggressive semiotic limitations of moving pictures.

Let me close with the conversation Sol Worth and John Adair had with Sam Yazzie, a Navajo elder, prior to their experiments in Navajos making films in the 1960s. Many readers will know it, and I do not mean to be pessimistic in quoting it, only that we try to consider the question.

Although Sam was old, tired, and still coughing a great deal, there was no mistaking the authority in his manner. Finally Adair felt that it was the time to bring up the subject of our visit. Adair explained that we wanted to teach some Navajo to make movies and mentioned Worth's part in the process several times. By the time Adair had finished, Yazzie (Sam) was looking at Worth frequently, seeming for the first time to acknowledge his presence as legitimate. When Adair finished, Sam thought for a while, and then turned to Worth and asked a lengthy question which was interpreted as, 'Will making movies do the sheep any harm?'

Worth was happy to explain that as far as he knew, there was no chance that making movies would harm the sheep.

Sam thought this over and then asked, 'Will making movies do the sheep good?' Worth was forced to reply that as far as he knew making movies wouldn't do the sheep any good.

Sam thought this over, then, looking around at us, said, 'Then why make movies?'

Worth and Adair honestly respond, 'Sam's question keeps haunting us. We did not answer it then, and it is not directly answered in this book' (1972, p. 5).

## Notes

1    In an interesting paper which appeared after this one was first written, Ginsburg (1991) addresses well a specific case in Australia. While her conclusions are somewhat more optimistic (and differently focused) than mine, this is an important critical source on 'indigenous' (a more appropriate label for local production than the equivocal 'participatory') media.

2    Make no mistake, representation it must be, since the camera is always to inscribe and cannot thus but distance. It will always be an 'othering' device. Photography cannot be insulated from its exteriority. This compulsory and essential restriction certainly requires qualification and there is no attempt here to dismiss film mandatorily. Indeed, I would argue that this limitation precisely opens up new avenues – perhaps, for example, of critical aesthetic relevance, – completely free of the 'burden of representation' (Tagg, 1988).

3    Chris Pinney, (1992) has traced other parallels in the histories of anthropology and photography, related to 'seeing'.

4    Of course there are conventions in all this that bear scrutiny: the implications of 'home' in home video; the distinctly monumental posing styles of studio photographers, etc. But these considerations are beyond the concerns of this paper and discussions are to be found in some recent feminist literature and photographic criticism.

5 I was uncomfortable not only with the dramatic intrusiveness of film-making, but also with the (to me) surprising new resistance to cameras and Europeans. I have recorded something of this discomfort in Faris (1988). There are many pertinent issues in *Southeast Nuba* (1982) which are not developed at all. Indeed, the film shares much of the imagery that it criticises in Riefenstahl's work (Riefenstahl 1976; Ryle 1982). While authenticity *vs.* cultural debasement may seem like a single issue, it actually boils down to the following: (1) a debate between Europeans (Faris vs. Riefenstahl); (2) a sort of tired invective against Islam (for objections to this, see Faris 1988, pp. 118–20); and (3) a weak tirade against the local Government's development plans (a rather stock-in-trade cynicism of the *Disappearing World* series and many BBC productions). However grotesque Riefenstahl's local social relations, the Southeast Nuba did not care whether she was a fascist. The inserted stills of Riefenstahl with Adolph Hitler thus strike me as violent, unpleasant in the extreme and, given the critique here, ultimately irrelevant. The new social relations of the Nuba – body painting and dancing by the hour for European tourists – require a new cultural definition, a pastiche. Objections to this have to be political, not cultural. *I* cannot represent them in cultural terms.

6 There is reported an incident in a Performance Group experimental re-enactment of Ndembu ethnography. One woman, an actor in the production, queried the sexism of a 'ritual' scene, and suggested changing the performance to eliminate it. Turner denied this. Here, the opening of ethnography to performance closed down to the 'real' character of Ndembu life (Turner 1982, p. 93), even though everything else had changed quite 'dramatically' in the staging of the activity. The West might rule, but not women.

## References

*Books and articles*

Biesele, M. (1990), 'Reclaiming a cultural legacy: The Ju/'hoansi of Namibia', *Aperture*, 119, pp. 50–7.

Clifford, J. (1988), *The Predicament of Culture. Twentieth-Century Ethnography, Literature, and Art*, Harvard University Press, Cambridge.

Edwards, E. (ed.) (1992), *Anthropology Photographed*, Yale University Press, New Haven.

Faris, J. (1972), *Nuba Personal Art*, Duckworth, London.

Faris, J. (1988), 'Southeast Nuba: A biographical statement', in J. Rollwagen (ed.), *Anthropological Film-making*, Harwood Academic Publishers, London, pp. 111–22.

Foucault, M. (1973), *The Order of Things. An Archaeology of the Human Sciences*, Vintage Books, London.

Ginsburg, F. (1991), 'Indigenous media: Faustian contract or global village', *Cultural Anthropology* VI, 1, p. 92–112.

Gross, C. (1990), 'Report of conference, "Anthropology and the end of society"', *Anthropology Today*, VI, 3, pp. 18–19.

Kuehnast, K. (1990), 'Gender representation in visual ethnographies: an interpretivist perspective', *Commission on Visual Anthropology Review*, Spring, 1990, pp. 21–30.

Marcus, G. (1990), 'Imagining the whole', *Critique of Anthropology* XI, 3, pp. 7–30.

Marcus, G., and Fischer, M. (1986), *Anthropology as Cultural Critique: An Experimental Moment in the Human Sciences*, University of Chicago Press, Chicago.

Mulvey, L. (1989), *Visual and Other Pleasures*, Indiana University Press, Bloomington.

Pinney, C. (1992), 'The parallel histories of anthropology and photography: or, the impossibility of photography' in E. Edwards (ed.), *Anthropology Photographed*, Yale University Press, New Haven.

Riefenstahl, L. (1976), *The People of Kau*, Harper and Row, New York.

Rollwagen, J. (ed.) (1988), *Anthropological Film-making*, Harwood Academic Publishers, New York.

Ryle, J. (1982), 'Invasion of the body snatchers', *New Society* (30 September 1982), pp. 549–51.

Spivak, G. (1990), *The Post-Colonial Critic*, Routledge, New York.

Tagg, J. (1988), *The Burden of Representation*, University of Massachusetts Press, Amherst.

Turner, T. (1990), 'Visual media, cultural politics, and anthropological practice. Some implications of recent uses of film and video among the Kayapo of Brazil', *Commission on Visual Anthropology Review*, Spring, pp. 8–13.

Turner, V. (1982), 'Dramatic ritual/ritual drama: Performance and reflexive anthropology' in J. Ruby (ed.), *A Crack in the Mirror*. University of Pennsylvania Press, Philadelphia, pp. 83–98.

Tyler, S. (1984), 'The vision quest in the west, or what the mind's eye sees', *Journal of Anthropological Research*, XL, 1, pp. 23–40.

Tyler, S. (1987a), *The Unspeakable. Discourse, Dialogue, and Rhetoric in the Post-Modern World*, University of Wisconsin Press, Madison.

Tyler, S. (1987b), 'Still rayting. Response to Scholte', *Critique of Anthropology* VII, 1, p. 49–51.

Worth, S. and Adair, J. (1972), *Through Navajo Eyes. An Exploration in Film Communication and Anthropology*, Indiana University Press, Bloomington.

*Films*

Curling, C. (1974) *Maasai Women*, Granada Television, 'Disappearing World' series, London. Colour, 52 mins. (Anthropologist: M. Llewellyn-Davies)

—— (1982), *Southeast Nuba*, BBC, Bristol. Colour, 58 mins. (Anthropologist: J. Faris)

Fernea, E. (1982), *The Veiled Revolution*, Icarus Films, New York. Colour, 38 mins.

O'Rourke, D. (1987), *Cannibal Tours*, Direct Cinema, Los Angeles. Colour, 77 mins.

# Visual imperialism and the export of prejudice: an exploration of ethnographic film

The Corcoran Gallery of Art in Washington, DC housed an exhibit in the winter of 1990 entitled 'Black Photographers Bear Witness'. The black artists in this show dramatically expressed through their art how it feels to be a commodity. One artist, Carrie Mae Weene, described her experience in this way:

Each of us carries around little packages of consumer racism in the form of neat . . . characteristics and qualities reserved for specific groups unlike ourselves. The unfortunate part of the business is that these stereotypes are not harmless expressions but have real . . . effects on the material well-being of those singled out as objects of these expressions.[1]

Weene's political art raises important questions: who has the power to represent whom and what are the effects of these represented images in shaping our attitudes and our memories about other groups? Such questions are paramount in a world where visual representations perpetuate dominant ideologies and operate as an economic currency. In particular, these questions are relevant to visual anthropologists who are hired to direct or produce ethnographic films for corporate or governmental entities. How do visual anthropologists avoid exporting cultural biases about gender, class, or race, especially when we consider Worth's argument (1974) that our films reflect more about ourselves than they do another culture?

My intention in this paper, not unlike the concerns of interpretivists who critique written ethnographies (Marcus and Fischer 1986; Clifford 1988), is to explore our visual interpretations of culture. The interpretive discourse may assist us in examining our inscriptions of the cultural 'other'. In this manner, reflexivity can be seen not as a negative force that strives to eradicate meaning, but as a positive force that provides new energy by challenging uncontested concepts, 'reflexivity is the burden that we can neither carry nor throw off' (Lawson 1985, p. 8).

I propose that visual anthropologists create an ongoing dialogue with one another as a means to explore critically ethnographic film and to uncover the ways we unintentionally encode 'the other' with dominant ideological inscriptions of gender, race, or class, or what I call 'visual imperialism'. I suggest a set of criteria for analyzing the degree to which our interpretations reproduce hegemonic discourse and result in the perpetuation of myths, prejudices, or limited understandings about other peoples. The result of our critical analysis, furthermore, finds its way into educational institutions where there is a great need to educate audiences about the critical viewing of ethnographic films.

## Visual imperialism

Visual imperialism is the colonisation of the world mind through the use of selective imagery that acts as a representation of a dominant ideology or, as in many instances, a representation of the truth. Discussion about dominant ideology in the mass media is an important contemporary concern where war, poverty, violence, and other gender, class and race struggles have become an economic currency. Visual imperialism examines what Mina Davis Caulfield aptly noted twenty years ago, that 'the underlying form of exploitation under imperialism is not that of class over class, but rather culture over culture' (1969, p. 193).

America may be considered one of the visual imperialists of the world. It has been estimated that, in terms of total income from sales, visual media are the United States' second-largest export, surpassed only by aeroplanes. Experts in many fields are aware of how this export product is shaping the economy of the entire world. Some have asserted that American visual entertainment is the most powerful force in shaping the global culture.

Its appeal is so seductive that broadcasting regulators around the world are restricting the number of American programs on their airwaves. This practice is in part a simple show of protectionism, but it also reflects the attitude that a country dominated by US television has been invaded as surely as if by military imperialists. (Gilder 1990, pp. 18–19)

Many have examined the role of visual media in perpetuating dominant ideologies (Althusser 1971; Hall 1972; Heidegger 1977; Foucault 1979; Nichols 1981; Lauretis 1987; Eco 1986; Tomaselli *et al.* 1986; Gunn 1987; Horkheimer and Adorno 1988). Seldom, though, have visual anthropologists applied this type of reflexivity to their own films. The problem that confronts the reflexive visual anthropologist is similar to the historian's conundrum as Hayden White identified it in *Tropics of Discourse* (1978). What makes for easily understood cultural experiences are those that are predicated upon making the strange familiar. This is accomplished by offering examples or comparisons often encoded with cultural biases. How to avoid the ethnocentric or visual imperialistic tendencies are problems not easily solved in ethnographic film. The literature is full of contradictions about how to control the visual medium so that it does not perpetuate dominant ideologies.

Cultural and visual imperialism was a major theme in Horkheimer and Adorno's 'Culture Industry' thesis, according to which the capacity for representation is positively correlated with the degree of domination (1988, p. 34). In their schema, the factory not only duplicated products but also duplicated the worker's consciousness. They implicated the mass media as a static cultural filter through which everything offered for mass consumption must pass.

Horkheimer and Adorno's work advanced the dominant ideology thesis which held that the hegemonic class was the controller of material and mental production. Visual imperialism, by contrast, is not set up on the same formula whereby dominant ideology equals conformist behaviour. Instead, visual imperialism operates in a complex, interactive arena where dominant ideologies compete for the attention of dominant and subordinate groups alike, where the use of the visual medium as a cultural apparatus is coded with cultural biases. Visual imperialism is the subliminal message of cultural hierarchy where the condition of one culture over another culture is communicated by presenting what is natural, normal, and desired in culture through the dominant culture's set of racial or gender stereotypes, and what is unnatural, abnormal and undesired through the subordinate culture's set.

Visual imperialism, according to Eco's arguments, reveals that the mass media are a totalitarian device with no totalitarian dictator. Monitoring and controlling the production of the visual medium is thus not possible. 'There exists an extremely powerful instrument that none of us will ever manage to regulate . . . in confronting it, we are all the proletariat' (1986, p. 141). Eco contends that the only way to control the effect of the visual image is at the point where the image is received – the audience. Suggesting that this must be approached more like guerrilla warfare than strategic warfare (1986, p. 143), Eco focuses less on the dominant ideology issue and more on affecting the audience and awakening them from their hypnotic state. He sees this as the only effective way to deal with visual imperialism.

Teresa de Lauretis (1987), a feminist theorist and semiotician, takes a position similar to Eco's on the ways women are objectified for consumptive ends. She does not believe that the elimination of the hegemonic control over visual media is a solution to visual imperialism. Instead, she challenges us to rethink issues about the production of 'positive' and 'negative' images of women. She asserts that to remain fixated on a morally dualistic model leads us to the assumption that the audience is naive and purely receptive. She shifts the nature of the problem of dominant ideology from one of coercion to one of consent. Dominant ideology does not dictate meaning; rather, meaning is a negotiation between the receiver and the visual medium.

In this way, visual imperialism acts less as a mono-formula and more as a disruption. It inhibits the ability of subordinate classes to propose or promote a counter-ideology. It is not just, therefore, the monopolistic control of the visual medium by a dominant group. Visual imperialism concerns the effects of a dominant ideology on both dominant and non-dominant groups alike. Compliance and consent form an ambiguous arena in which this interaction takes place.

We can see this interaction in popular media, where the visual export is often a constructed commodity of 'the Other' that is then packaged in the form of entertainment or as a ploy in an advertisement. The effect is so powerful that Eco believes that TV advertising can function as a revolutionary message in depressed countries (1986, p. 141). But this impact is more than Horkheimer and Adorno's suggestion that a capitalistic society controls its people through a specialized visual diet of carefully selected images. Instead, it is a complex and interactive market, where the players, the rules, and the stakes are constantly shifting; where, as Althusser argued, economy and ideology are interwoven, they are inseparable (1971). It is within this context that visual anthropologists must consider their role. The visual image no longer acts only as a scientific proof of culture. The constructed visual image is a powerful material artefact that has acquired economic and political value in a global culture.

What roles do visual anthropologists play in the marketplace of cultural transformation? While we may have many roles, one that cannot be overlooked is our tendency to become cultural brokers for other worlds in the economic exchange of global images. We know that before anthropology was academically established, explorers, adventurers and merchants sold images of exotic, non-western peoples to Westerners. MacDougall argued that the visual ethnographer 'reaffirms the colonial origins of anthropology. It was once the European who decided what was worth knowing about "primitive" peoples and what they in turn should be taught' (1975, p. 118). It is evident today that those who have access to capital are the 'new Europeans', are more likely to be able to tell their story, and thus to become the gatekeepers of cultural memories.

Ethnographic film can be examined through the Horkheimer and Adorno model where the cultural apparatus of film is seen as the transmitter of dominant ideology, or it can be examined from the perspective of Eco and Lauretis, where the focus is on intervening at the level of the audience. Both approaches address the insidious effects of visual imperialism in ethnographic film. Since most ethnographic films find their way into educational institutions, we need to assist students in assessing the interactions between dominant ideologies, dominant or subordinate class responses, and the ethnographer's roles. Martinez (1990, p. 39) offers important information towards a better understanding of audience response. But more is needed than the gauging of audience's emotional response. Audiences are in need of critical thinking and viewing skills that can be applied to the film, a cultural apparatus that has offered us few instructions on how to interpret it (Abercrombie *et al.* 1980, p. 2).

### Towards a dialogue in ethnographic film-making

Ethnographic film-making is a complex undertaking. The production of visual images about 'the Other' is more than mere objective representation. We make choices; we interpret not only what information will be recorded by light on celluloid but we also choose what memories will remain about a culture. Throughout this century, anthropologists' use of the camera as an aid to scientific documentation has provided a way to distance the observer from the ethnographic other, to quantify our perceptions and to increase our precision. But the effect of the camera's product, whether the images were still photographs or moving pictures, was more than just 'a minute time sample' (Collier 1962, p. 6). The visual image was, in fact, not only a representation of reality but also a construction and an interpretation of another culture based on codes from the film-maker's own culture (Worth and Adair 1972; Ruby 1980).

Since our visual ethnographies are expensive undertakings that usually require collaboration with non-anthropological institutions, those of us in this field may be more susceptible than our ethnographic-writing counterparts to compromising our research standards as an unconscious acquiescence to the demands of the communication industries. Over the eighty years of ethnographic film production, examples of such acquiescence can be found in many films that include strong tones of racism, classism, and sexism. These productions were not necessarily malicious, just unaware in terms of the set of biases underlying the era in which the film was produced. 'The great enemy of truth is very often not the lie – deliberate, contrived and dishonest', said John F. Kennedy, 'but the myth, persistent, persuasive and realistic' (cited in Shaheen 1990).

Parallels exist between the production of a museum exhibit and the production of a film, since biases can be communicated to an audience by a free-standing exhibit as well as by a motion picture.[2] Recently, some museums have begun to develop criteria to assess their exhibits as a means of reducing ethnocentric biases. Visual ethnographers may benefit from a similar assessment aimed at fostering the creation of more conscious, less biased films.[3] I shall apply similar standards to those that museums use in their exhibits to examine a variety of ethnographic films and their treatment of gender, race, and class. The following critiques serve to illustrate the ways in which stereotypical images or prejudices are perpetuated about other cultures.

To initiate the dialogue, I shall examine how gender is represented in ethnographic films (Kuehnast 1989; 1990). The criteria include:

1. Does the film assign traditional or rigid roles to women (and other subgroups) that deny the viewer information about cultural diversity?
2. Are women consistently presented as nurturers and men presented as cultural/economic brokers?
3. Are opportunities taken to give examples of both men and women in significant roles that do not contradict historical fact?

Many feminist scholars argue that an androcentric bias exists in most ethnographic scholarship (Rosaldo 1980; Scott 1986; Moore 1988). This can be explained 'as the male perspective taken to be representative of the culture, whereas the female view is typically portrayed as peripheral to the norm or somehow exceptional or idiosyncratic' (Conkey and Spector 1984, p. 4). In many contemporary ethnographic films there are numerous examples of how women are filmed in a peripheral cultural role. We see this in the film *The Sons of Haji Omar* (Asch and Balikci, 1978) where the role of women among the Pashtoon people of Afghanistan is mentioned less than their herds of sheep.[4]

In reviewing some 30 hours of the uncut footage of the *Sons of Haji Omar* and reading the field notes of the sound recordist, Patsy Asch, I was left wondering why the women were portrayed as marginal to the seasonal herding practices, when the significance of their role is clearly outlined in her film notes. As an example of this discrepancy, Asch comments on the exhaustive work schedule that women have on these yearly journeys: '. . . she was usually at work from 5 a.m. to 9:30 p.m. . . .' (Roll 38). 'The only way a wife can get help (in setting up a tent) is from a co-wife, mother or daughter . . . As soon as the tents were up the men and often children, spread out a carpet and relaxed while the women . . . dug a fire pit . . .' (Roll 122).

Throughout the filming process, Asch reveals the fragility of the film crew's situation in terms of completing the project. 'We didn't want to film Anvar's caravan in Narin because we thought (and then they said) it would embarrass them and put further hostile pressure on them for allowing us to travel with them.' Asch continues 'many times during the journey it became clear that they didn't want us associated with them and would try to put distance between us and the caravan' (Roll 100). Asch's notes bring out an aspect of ethnographic film-making with which few have dealt: how do the subjects feel about being filmed? 'Durani said we shouldn't film any more, that it was evil and that we would all suffer later because it was against God's will' (Roll 36). Or 'Throughout, it was the teenage girls who were the most difficult to film because they had a reputation to preserve' (Roll 41). Asch's notes uncover important considerations that need further discussion among visual ethnographers. When do we quit filming in order to preserve the integrity of the relationships with the people we film?

While the stereotyping of gender behaviour is one area where constant reflexivity is required on the part of the ethnographer, the stereotyping of indigenous groups occurs just as often, sometimes blatantly and sometimes subtly. At a recent symposium, *The Politics of Portraiture*,[5] the issue of indigenous stereotyping was addressed in terms of visual representations of America's multi-cultural groups. Some of the examples given of stereotypes were found in ethnographic film and photographs, others were found in advertising. In any case, the ideological construction of an 'other' can be equally damaging, whether it is the romantic stereotype of the Native American's 'harmony with nature' (Archambault 1990) or the racist portrayal of a 'lazy Mexican-American' on the popular children's show *Sesame Street* (Lopez 1990). Selling culture as a commodity can be found in many advertisements, from those of the Italian clothier Benetton, where the promotion 'United Colors' is a euphemism for everybody's beautiful, to the 'sun dried raisins' that shuffle across the stage singing Afro-American Marvin Gaye's 'Heard it through the Grapevine' as a sales pitch for California raisins. I do not wish to imply by these examples that visual anthropologists construct images for a similar end; only that these same stereotypical images can sometimes be unwittingly emulated in ethnographic film.

We find evidence of racial stereotyping in the early ethnographic documentaries produced by the Pathé Science Series from Harvard University in the the late 1920s.[6] The film *The Masai* (1929) is a striking illustration of the evolutionary bias that still dominated anthropology at that time. The narrative emphasizes the evolutionary characteristics of the Maasai, such as skin colour, nose size, and the amount of 'white blood' in the descent system. This series, though clearly antiquated, is part of our visual ethnographic roots, where visual images produced by the camera were accepted in the social sciences as a credible source of objectivity. Films from this early genre carry with them the cultural belief system that 'the eye does not lie'. The implication was that the camera represented objectivity, especially when a scientist stood behind the lens. Although 'seeing is believing' was a central assumption in early ethnographic films, the overall acceptance of most ethnographic films as fact and data goes largely uncontested even today (Kuehnast 1990).

A contemporary film on the Maasai offers an excellent illustration of how gender and racial biases can permeate ethnographic film narrative. *Masai Women* (1974), a Granada Television collaboration with anthropologist Melissa Llewelyn-Davies, uses cultural comparisons between the British and Maasai cultures. This relativity technique reduces gender to a simplistic model: 'Unlike European women and children, who are considered to be an expense to men, Maasai women and children are considered to be a man's wealth'. Llewelyn-Davies ignores the possibility that a woman's power may lie outside the control of material wealth – that power may be defined through another category. Annette Weiner distinguished a non-western definition of power in 'the cosmic sphere' (1976, p. 120), where a woman is the gatekeeper of ritual passages between age groups. Defining gender or race only by a Western standard of power creates an image with a shadow, the shadow usually representing the subordinate group. This degree of 'invisibility' is what Ardener had in mind when he called attention to the lack of representation of muted groups (1975, pp. 221–3). He argued that the omission of groups in the description of a cultural whole implies that these groups are of less value in a given society.

Invisibility also occurs in the way many non-western groups have been depicted in ethnographic film. The invisible, in this case, is the effect of outside Western influences. Hardly a culture exists today that is not coping with the implications of technology, television, and environmental disruption. To drop these issues from the film creates a product of the exotic. Examining the uncut film footage for Marshall's *N!ai, The Story of a !Kung Woman, 1952–78* (1980) and Asch and Balikci's *Sons of Haji Omar* (1978), one can see the degree to which automobiles, radios, and other technology have been edited out, giving the appearance that these groups are still pristine, unaltered by the colonial world. Though both films discuss the effect of cultural change on their respective groups, neither film-maker utilises the footage available that demonstrates the infiltration of western artefacts in the day-to-day life of these groups.

Jean Rouch's classic and controversial *Les Maîtres Fous* (1954) offers a poignant example of what it means to break with the romantic traditions of the big screen, full of images of a pristine people, and instead confront the world now dominated by colonial and imperial forces. The film documents the possession ceremony performed by members of the Hauka cult who act out caricatures of British colonialists. This bizarre and, at times, incomprehensible ceremony of trance is contrasted with footage of the cult members' normal, day-to-day life as ditch diggers, bus drivers and other such labourers. The irony of the title, 'the masters of madness', is that it refers both to the Hauka cult members and to the British colonialists. Rouch's controversial style should be reconsidered, especially in the midst of the many pristine film images of cultural change (Stoller 1992).

Other more recent films convey a less dramatic view of the effect of cultural change but are still effective. Adair's *A Weave of Time* (1986) integrates cultural change through the lives of four generations. Having studied Navajo culture earlier in his career, he returns forty years later to his original informants. The film begins around a picnic table where Adair and his informant's children, who are now adults, gather to celebrate this reunion. Eschewing sentimentality, Adair's narrative presents the day-to-day decisions of a Navajo family that live simultaneously in the world of their ancestors and the world of the dominant American culture. Adair's presence throughout the film, first in photographic retrospectives and then as narrator, not only deals with culture change of the Navajo world, but also includes himself as a part of the change. He becomes visible in the film-making process. This visibility of the ethnographer in his or her film adds a dimension that is often lacking.

In an ethnographic film, the camera represents the ethnographer in most instances and portrays the sensibility that 'you are there because I was there' (Clifford 1988, p. 22). But just as the Wizard of Oz tries to remain out of sight when Toto pulls back the curtain, ethnographers try to remain invisible behind their camera, as if to protect the illusion of their authority by saying 'Pay no attention to that man behind the curtain'. The films of Robert Boonzajer Flaes, such as *Thinking is Useless* (1988), offer a good example of the Wizard coming out from behind the curtain. He includes himself in the visual text. In doing so, Boonzajer Flaes reveals himself and empowers the viewer. This visibility is an encouraging trend because it removes the distant, observational gaze. Such an unpretentious approach transforms the information exchange from a myth-making process *about* the subject into a dialogue *with* the subject.

## Conclusion

*Memory makes us human. Without it people are turned into a formless mass that can be shaped into anything.* (Heller and Nekrich 1986, p. 3)

Visual anthropology is a complex interaction between people who have a story to share and the visual medium for recording that story. As a tool, the camera has been used for the documentation of cultures. The modern invention of this instrument has given all of us an extraordinary new means of travelling through time and space without ever leaving our armchairs. As we reach deeper into the visual consciousness of a global culture where we watch each other through one another's eyes, we must ask ourselves about our role in this economic arena, where we have the ability to etch indelible memories or to airbrush them out of existence. The visual images we create about others can easily diminish or accentuate certain aspects of their lives, sometimes so extremely that a given quality of experience is erased while another is exaggerated to absurdity.

Historically, anthropology has been a process of memory-making so that we might not forget the quickly-disappearing 'traditional' peoples of the world. When we make ethnographic films, we utilise the most powerfully pervasive memory-making device in the history of human culture. Our challenge then, as translators between two worlds, is consciously to understand the inherent pitfalls of a visually imperialistic economy. With this awareness, we can advance 'the struggle of memory against forgetting'.[7]

## Notes

I would like to express my appreciation to my colleagues at the Human Studies Film Archives: Jake Homiak, Ph.D., Wendy Shay, Pam Wentle, and Mark White who were helpful in their critiques of my work while at the Smithsonian.

In addition, the challenging and thoughtful comments offered by Paul Stoller, Professor of Anthropology, West Chester University and Resident Fellow at the Smithsonian Institution, have been invaluable to my research.

As a graduate student, my work in visual anthropology has been significantly influenced by the informative and helpful critiques of Professor George Lipsitz, Ethnic Studies, University of California-San Diego; Dona Schwartz, Journalism, University of Minnesota; and Professor Mischa Penn, Anthropology, University of Minnesota. In addition, the support of my committee advisers Frank C. Miller and Gloria Goodwin Raheja, University of Minnesota has been significant.

1   Exhibit label from an artwork of Carrie May Weene from the exhibition 'Black Photographers Bear Witness', the Corcoran Gallery of Art, Washington DC, Winter, 1990.
2   *Gender Perspectives: the Impact of Women on Museums.* Symposium sponsored by the Smithsonian Institution, Washington, DC, 8–10 March, 1990.
3   Robert Sullivan (1990) offers a framework in which to ask ourselves many pertinent questions. Sullivan was the Director of Exhibits Interpretation at the New York State Museum, Albany, New York.
4   Although Balikci's film falls short of offering a holistic perspective on the Pashtoon

people, it offers visual ethnographers an excellent resource for understanding the difficulties underlying ethnographic film-making. It presents an exhaustive documentation of the ethnographic film-making process. The 100,000 feet of colour film with sync sound is housed at the Smithsonian's Human Studies Film Archives. All Pashtoon dialogue on the sound track is translated into English on a separate tape. In addition, a second parallel-recorded tape has detailed ethnographic commentary covering almost all the visual sequences. Finally, a comprehensive written account of the Pashtoon people's reactions, many of which are negative, was provided by the sound recordist, Patsy Asch. Another film produced from this extensive archival project could be entitled *The Making of the 'Sons of Haji Omar'*. This film could show the difficulties and the ethical conflicts that arise in filming other cultures. I am convinced that a film such as this would be immensely more valuable to visual anthropologists than one more ethnographic film about a non-hegemonic group.

5  *The Politics of Portraiture: Icons, Stereotypes and Other Approaches to Multi-Cultural Imaging.* Symposium sponsored by the National Portrait Gallery, Smithsonian Institution, 24–25 January, 1990.

6  The Maasai footage is located in the Human Studies Film Archives, Museum of Natural History, Smithsonian Institution, Washington, DC.

7  See Milan Kundera (1981, p. 3) '. . .the struggle of man against power is the struggle of memory against forgetting.'

## References

*Books and articles*

Abercrombie, N., S. Hill and B. S. Turner (1980), *The Dominant Ideology Thesis*, George Allen & Unwin, Boston.

Aitmatov, C. (1988), *The Day Lasts More than a Hundred Years*, Indiana University Press, Bloomington, Indiana.

Aitmatov, C. (1989), *Time to Speak*, International Publishers, New York.

Althusser, L. (1971), 'Ideology and the Ideological State apparatuses', *Lenin and Philosophy*, Monthly Review Press, New York.

Archambault, J. (1990), 'The use of Indian imagery to promote tourism', a paper presented at the conference, *The Politics of Portraiture*, Smithsonian Institution, Washington, DC.

Ardener, E. (1975), 'Belief and the problem of women' in S. Ardener (ed.), *Perceiving Women*, C. Hurst & Co., London, pp. 1–17.

Balikci, A. (1975), 'Reconstructing cultures on film' in P. Hockings (ed.), *Principles of Visual Anthropology*, Mouton Publishers, Paris.

Becker, H. S. (1974), 'Photography and sociology', *Studies in the Anthropology of Visual Communication*, 1, pp. 3–84.

Becker, H. S. (1980), 'Aesthetics, aestheticians, and critics', *Studies in Visual Communication*, 6, pp. 58–68.

Becker, H. S. (1981), *Exploring Society Photographically*, University of Chicago Press, Chicago.

Caulfield, M. D. (1969), 'Culture and imperialism: proposing a new dialectic' in D. Hymes (ed.), *Reinventing Anthropology*, Pantheon Books, New York, pp. 182–212.

Clifford, J. (1988), *The Predicament of Culture: Twentieth-Century Ethnography, Literature, and Art*, Harvard University Press.

Collier, J. (1962), *Visual Anthropology: Photography as a Research Method*, Holt, Rinehart and Winston, New York.

Conkey, M. W. and J. D. Spector (1984), 'Archaeology and the study of gender', *Advances in Archaeological Method and Theory*, 7, pp. 1–37.

Eco, U. (1986), *Travels in Hyper-reality*, Picador, London.

Eco, U. (1990), *The Limits of Interpretation*, Indiana University Press, Bloomington.

Fabian, J. (1983), *Time and the Other: How Anthropology Makes its Object*, Columbia University Press, New York.

Foucault, M. (1979), *Discipline and Punish: The Birth of the Prison*, Random House, New York.

Gilder, G. (1990), *Life After Television*, Whittle Direct Books, Chicago.

Goffman, E. (1976), *Gender Advertisements*, Harper and Row, New York.

Gross, L. (1980), 'Sol Worth and the Study of Visual Communications', *Visual Communication*, 6, pp. 2–20.

Gunn, G. (1987), *The Culture of Criticism and the Criticism of Culture*, Oxford University Press, New York.

Hall, S. (1982), 'The rediscovery of 'Ideology': return of the repressed in media studies' in M. Gurevitch, T. Bennett, J. Curran and J. Woollacott (eds.), *Culture, Society and the Media*, Methuen, London, pp. 56–90.

Heidegger, M. (1977), 'The Age of the World Picture', *The Question Concerning Technology*, Harper Torchbooks, New York.

Heller, M. and A. M. Nekrich (1986), *Utopia in Power: The History of the Soviet Union from 1917 to the Present*, Summit Books, New York.

Hockings, P. (ed.) (1975), *Principles of Visual Anthropology*, Mouton Publishers, Paris.

Horkheimer, M. and T. W. Adorno (1988), *Dialectic of Enlightenment*, Continuum, New York.

Jameson, F. (1983), 'Postmodernism and Consumer Society', in H. Foster (ed.), *The Anti-Aesthetic*, Bay Press, Washington, pp. 111–125.

Kuehnast, K. (1989), 'Visual anthropology and the study of gender', a paper presented at the conference *Eyes Across the Water: An International Conference On the Future of Visual Sociology and Anthropology*, University of Amsterdam, Department of Anthropology, Amsterdam.

Kuehnast, K. (1989), 'Mediating the construction of gender in ethnographic visual images: problems of representation and interpretation', a paper presented to the American Anthropological Association Annual Meetings, 15–19 November, 1989, Washington, DC.

Kuehnast, K. (1990), 'Gender representation in visual ethnographies: an interpretivist perspective', *CVA Review*, Montreal, Spring, pp. 21–30.

Kundera, M. (1981), *The Book of Laughter and Forgetting*, Penguin Books, New York.

Lauretis, T. de (1987), *Alice Doesn't: Feminism, Semiotics, Cinema*, Indiana University Press, Bloomington.

Lawson, H. (1985), *Reflexivity: The Postmodern Predicament*, Open Court, Illinois.

Lipsitz, G. (1986), 'The Meaning of Memory: Family, Class, and Ethnicity in Early Network Television Programs', *Cultural Anthropology*, 1, pp. 355–87.

Lopez, Y. M. (1990), 'Use of Mexican and Chicano Images in Print Advertising', paper presented at Smithsonian sponsored conference, *The Politics of Portraiture*, (see note 5).

MacDougall, D. (1975), 'Beyond observation cinema' in P. Hockings (ed.), *Principles of Visual Anthropology*, Mouton Publishers, Paris.

Marcus, G. and M. Fischer (1986), *Anthropology as Cultural Critique*, University of Chicago Press, Chicago.

Martinez, W. (1990), 'Critical studies and visual anthropology: aberrant vs. anticipated readings of ethnographic film', *CVA Review*, Montreal, Spring, pp. 34–47.

Mead, M. (1975), 'Visual anthropology in a discipline of words' in P. Hockings (ed.), *Principles of Visual Anthropology*, Mouton Publishers, Paris, pp. 3–12.

Moore, H. L. (1988), *Feminism and Anthropology*, University of Minnesota Press, Minneapolis.

Nader, L. (1974), 'Up the anthropologist' in D. Hymes (ed.), *Reinventing Anthropology*, Random House, New York, pp. 284–311.

Nichols, B. (1981), *Ideology and the Image: Social Representation in the Cinema and Other Media*, Indiana University Press, Bloomington.

Ong, W. J. (1967), *The Presence of the Word*, University of Minnesota Press, Minneapolis.

Orwell, G. (1948), *1984*, Penguin Press, New York.

Rosaldo, M. A. (1980), 'The use and abuse of anthropology: reflections on feminism and cross-cultural understanding', *Signs*, 5, pp. 389–417.

Ruby, J. (1980), 'Exposing yourself: reflexivity, anthropology and film', *Semiotica*, 3, pp. 153–79.

Scott, J. (1986), 'Gender: a useful category of historical analysis', *The American Historical Review*, 191, pp. 1053–1075.

Shaheen, J. G. (1990), 'Our cultural demon – "the ugly arab": ignorance, economics create an unshakeable stereotype', *The Washington Post*, 18 August, 1990.

Stoller, P. (1992), *Cinematic Griot: The Ethrography of Jean Rouch*, University of Chicago Press, Chicago.

Sullivan, R. (1990), 'The Museum as Moral Educator', paper presented at the conference *Gender perspectives: the impact of women on museums*, Smithsonian Institution, Washington, DC, 8–10 March.

Tomaselli, K., A. Williams, L. Steenveld and R. Tomaselli (1986), *Myth, Race and Power: South Africans Imaged on Film and TV*, Anthropos Publishers, Bellville.

Weiner, A. B. (1976), *Women of Value, Men of Renown*, Texas Press.

White, H. (1978), *Tropics of Discourse: Essays in Cultural Criticism*, The Johns Hopkins University Press, Baltimore and London.

Worth, S. (1974), 'Symbolic Strategies', *Journal of Communication*, XXIV, pp. 27–39.

Worth, S. and J. Adair (1972), *Through Navajo Eyes*, Indiana University Press, Bloomington.

*Films*

Adair, J., S. Fanshel and D. Gordon (1986), *A Weave of Time*, Navajo Film Project, New York. Colour, 60 mins.

Asch, T. & A. Balikci (1978), *The Sons of Haji Omar*, National Film Board of Canada, National Anthropological Film Center of the Smithsonian Institution. Colour, 58 mins.

Boonzajer Flaes, R. (1988), *Thinking is Useless*, University of Amsterdam. Colour, 30 mins.

Curling, C. (1974), *Masai Women*, Disappearing World series, Granada Television, Manchester. Colour, 52 mins. Anthropologist: M. Llewellyn-Davies.

Harvard University (1929), *The Masai*, Pathé Science Series. 400ft, Black and white (silent).

Marshall, J. (1980), *N!ai, The Story of a !Kung Woman*, Documentary Educational

Resources, Watertown, Mass. Colour, 59 mins. (Anthropologist: Patricia Draper)

Rouch, J. (1954), *Les Maîtres Fous*, Documentary Educational Resources, Watertown, Mass. Colour, 35 mins.

# The ethics of ethnographic film-making

Anthropologists continually seek better ways to record and translate the beliefs and traditions of human cultures. The emergence of ethnographic film-making in this century has given humankind unprecedented opportunities to experience vicariously the details of life in unfamiliar, often distant and isolated places.

Unlike feature film-makers, ethnographic film-makers record events as they happen – no scripts, no actors, no sets, no retakes. But a good film-maker knows that detached scientific observation is not enough. The film must also capture the essence of the people, their passions, their fears, their motivations.

The development of trust between the ethnographer or anthropologist and the people he or she is studying is vital to success. That trust constitutes an unwritten contract, which brings certain obligations and ethical considerations into play that might never have occurred to anthropologists even two or three decades ago.

In 1960, when I began making ethnographic films through the Peabody Museum at Harvard University, our models were Robert Flaherty's *Nanook of the North* (1922), Merian Cooper and Ernest Schoedsack's *Grass* (1925) and Basil Wright's *Song of Ceylon* (1937).

*Song of Ceylon*, produced by the British Empire Marketing Board, is an exquisitely shot documentary narrated with excerpts from the diary of a seventeenth-century traveller. *Grass* documents the staggering migration of 50,000 people over the Zagros Mountains in Iraq and Persia in search of grass for their herds, and *Nanook of the North* depicts an Eskimo family's struggle for survival in the frozen North.

Flaherty's *Nanook* was the exception in documentary films in that it focused on individual lives and provided a sympathetic, personal view of Eskimo life. But the film was scripted. Flaherty used Eskimos as actors playing their own roles and in that sense created a prototype for feature narrative films rather than documentary films.

*Grass* and *Song of Ceylon* inspired generations of ethnographic film-makers with their stunning, often heroic approach to image-making. Views from mountain tops and valleys were breathtaking but permitted no intimacy with individual subjects. The people in these documentaries remained strangers to the viewer. The film-makers dealt with cultures in broad terms and with people from a distance. This distance tended to turn people into objects.

Early film-makers went into the field with the most advanced equipment available to them and filmed whatever they wanted with little regard for the sensibilities of their subjects. Their sole objective was to collect images and make a film that would be both scientifically objective and interesting to anthropologists and audiences at home. Although the subjects of the films were generally co-operative, they were powerless to influence the process of making the film or the final product resulting from their collaboration.

Starting as early as 1946, French ethnographer Jean Rouch paved the way to a more personal approach to ethnographic film-making. He learned the language of his subjects and spent a great deal of time in the field getting to know them and letting them know what he was trying to accomplish.

In the context of the times in which they lived, I am sure Rouch's predecessors and others who followed the models of early ethnographic film-makers felt no ethical twinges about their approach, but today things are different. The world is changing and threatening indigenous societies at an ever-quickening rate. Exposure to the outside world can occasionally pose grave dangers to the people and societies we study. With this in mind, we can no longer view our subjects as objects. It is no longer enough to film wherever and however we want for the simple sake of scientific inquiry. Our social contract with our subjects demands that we ask ourselves whether we are working with them for legitimate reasons or simply for personal gain; whether we can get the footage we need without doing injury to people who have so generously allowed us to live with them and see and understand their most closely-held beliefs and customs.

Having wrestled with these questions for the past thirty years, I have developed a methodology for ethnographic film-making that I believe responds to important ethical issues facing film-makers and anthropologists today. Taking the following steps encourages not only ethical conduct on the part of film-makers but also better long-term relationships with subjects and ultimately better, more personal film documentation.

## Know your subjects

If you have not done extensive field-work in a community, work with an anthropologist who knows the language and the society well and who is interested in focusing in depth on one specific issue or area of study. Spending at least two or three months in the field before filming begins will give you an opportunity to become familiar with your subjects and their routines, develop trust and let the people know what you are attempting to accomplish. With the solid language skills of the anthropologist and an understanding of the culture, you and the anthropologist with whom you work will become more sensitive to the subtleties essential to making a good representative film.

### Avoid misleading biases

No matter how objective the ethnographer tries to be, personal, conceptual and theoretical biases inherent in his or her training and interests will find their way into the film. Ethnographers are constantly in the way of their own observations.

One way to counteract this tendency is to be aware of your biases and seek diverse points of view when you put your team together. Having both men and women involved, for example, will give you perspective on the activities of all members of the society you are studying, women and children as well as men. Some societies isolate male ethnographers from women's activities and female ethnographers from certain male activities, so collaboration is essential to getting a film that will be useful to future generations.

Another way to confront the problem of bias is to use a reflexive approach. In a traditional *documentary* about the Yanomami Indians of southern Venezuela, for example, the film-maker would shoot film as an anonymous outsider, an objective observer of how the Yanomami live. Viewers of the film would have no idea who the film-maker was or how he or she was reacting to the events being filmed. In a *reflexive film*, the film-maker and anthropologist step forward and become part of the film, openly interacting with the Yanomami, letting the viewer see how questions are phrased and conclusions drawn from events. The film-makers do not become the subject of the film, but are included as other elements of the Yanomami environment are included when they are influencing what is recorded.

Several years ago I made a film about an axe fight among the Yanomami (*The Ax Fight*, 1975). The fight broke out spontaneously between members of two factions in the village. I filmed the event from one point of view, as I observed it. But because there was some confusion about the causes of the fight, simple observation could not fully explain the event. We included a diagram with arrows to show how the event developed, a kinship chart to show how family relationships contributed to the tension that preceded the fight, and a filmed discussion among the anthropologist, sound man and myself, as we tried to make sense out of the chaos that surrounded the fight. The film audience sees who the film-makers are and how they are reacting to the events they have observed. This reflexivity permits the audience to observe and, if they wish, challenge the subjectivity film-makers bring to their work.

Making a reflexive film may not always be appropriate or possible. In 1978 I showed students at the University of Adelaide, *A Balinese Trance Seance*, the first of four films I had made with Patsy Asch and Linda Connor on Jero Tapakan, a Balinese trance healer. Several students criticized the film because it contained no reflexive elements, even though other films in the series which we were still editing were reflexive. Sensitive to the possibility of inadvertent bias, we took the film back to Jero and filmed her comments as she viewed the footage. The result was a new film: *Jero on Jero: A Balinese Trance Seance Observed*. Of course this film reflects a bias toward privileged discussions between anthropologists and the people they study and Jero's comments are edited to reflect the concerns of Western students, but this is clear in the film.

## Shoot whole events

Long takes of whole events or at least complete sequences within an event permit the subjects' actions to influence the structure of the final film.

Most ethnographic film-makers depend on grants to finance their films and many granting agencies require applicants to submit a script with their grant application. Unfortunately, the existence of the script encourages the film-maker to shoot bits and pieces of film to fill in the script. With artful editing, the results can be dramatic, as they were in Sergei Eisenstein's *Battleship Potemkin* (1925). Eisenstein showed the Russian tsar's elite guards firing on peaceful demonstrators at the steps of the palace. The viewer sees a woman's glasses shot out, a woman collapsing, a baby carriage bouncing unattended down the steps. But the montage the audience sees is controlled by the editor and need not depict the event in a way that is recognisable to the participants.

Film-makers who shoot long takes of an entire event or, at least, of entire sequences within an event provide a more complete and objective view of indigenous relationships than can be achieved through edited and spliced short takes. What is more, the participants in the event rather than the film editor, provide the chronology and action of the event.

## Support your film with good written documentation

If at all possible, transcribe and translate all audio tapes while you are still in the field, particularly all tapes related to synchronous recording for the film. Graduate students are more likely to make the extra effort to get the transcriptions and translations of tapes related to a filmed case study because they need the information for their theses. But few established professionals find the time for this extra step, which provides vital detail and context for present and future students of anthropology who are likely to use your film.

If the film-maker fails to give the audience adequate background and a context for viewing certain activities or events, the film may unwittingly support common prejudices about primitive or isolated cultures, the very misunderstandings anthropologists are striving to dispel.

## Make and archive an uncut version of your work for scholarly research

Film-makers may expose 15 to 100 feet of film for every foot used in the final edited version of a film. The unused footage is usually thrown away and lost forever to future scholars. Just consider the cost, time, effort and expertise that went into your fieldwork that could be preserved for the benefit of others.

To avoid this waste, you can file a copy of your uncut, unedited work, along with copies of all transcriptions and translations of your audio tapes in the Human Studies Film Archives at the Smithsonian Institute in Washington, DC This research film leaves a more complete view of a culture than is possible in an edited version. Once you have earned the trust of a society and imposed on them to film the most intimate and vital aspects of their lives, it makes ethical sense to leave a complete and permanent record of your work for the benefit of future generations of students and scholars and the heirs of the culture you filmed.

Today one can even work with people like Gary Seaman at the University of Southern California's ethnographics laboratory and archive to store a video tape or laser disk version of all your visual material, field notes and articles and have all this material integrated by and instantly accessible on his hypercard programme (see Chapter 18 by Seaman and Williams in this book). Granting agencies have supported the making of uncut research films but the practice is not yet widespread among ethnographic film-makers.

### Seek feedback from the subjects of your film

The notion of showing a finished cut to the subjects of the film before general distribution was unheard of in my experience before Columbia University ethnomusicologist Alan Lomax raised the issue in 1968 at Colin Young's Ethnographic Film Conference at the University of California, Los Angeles.

The decline of colonialism in the 1950s and 1960s and the emergence of women's and minority rights movements fostered more sensitivity among some ethnographic film-makers to the rights of their subjects to control, at least to some extent, the final version of the film.

Seeking feedback from the subjects has two distinct advantages for the film-maker as well. It serves as an accuracy check and it solicits additional information from your subjects that might not come out in any other situation. With this feedback you can make final revisions that often result in a better film.

The benefits of seeking feedback from subjects apply just as much during the process of filming. In 1978, Doug Lewis, Patsy Asch and I used video feedback while filming the Ata Tani Ai, a small isolated society on the Island of Flores in eastern Indonesia. We were preparing to record an extremely complex society-wide purification ritual. After viewing the videotapes, our subjects understood what we were trying to accomplish and why. They helped us through five months of filming, even though originally they had been apprehensive about being filmed.

### Get feedback from sample audiences

A film-maker or anthropologist who knows much more about the subject of the film than the audience can easily misjudge what the audience will understand from the film. Lecturing with the edited film before representative audiences of students, colleagues or the general public gives you an opportunity to see if the film is communicating with the audience as you intended.

Jean Rouch toured France with the edited version of his *Les Maîtres Fous* (1954) about the religious ceremony of the West African religious sect, Hauka. During the ceremony the Hauka entered a trance and were possessed by spirits associated with Western colonial powers, such as the governor general, an engineer, the doctor's wife, and so on. The film contains powerful images of possessed men rolling their eyes and foaming at the mouth, eating a sacrificed dog and burning their bodies with flaming torches.

These disturbing images shocked French audiences, who recoiled from the film because it left ambiguous the important relationship between the Hauka movement and the colonial experience of its members. Rouch suggests that the ritual provided a psychological release that enabled the Hauka to endure the power and humiliation of colonial authority with more dignity. In fact, the Hauka cult disappeared as colonial authority declined in the 1950s and 1960s. The feedback Rouch received from people in his own culture during his tour with *Les Maîtres Fous* not only led him to revise the film before general distribution, but also permanently changed the way he made films. He realised that people viewing aspects of life in an unfamiliar culture need a context for interpreting what they see.

## See that the film is properly distributed

Subjects the world over are more sophisticated today and want to know how footage will be used before they allow you to film them. Reluctant subjects are often willing to be filmed to preserve the culture for the education and benefit of future generations. The film-maker has an obligation to see that the films are used as promised in ways that do not jeopardise the dignity or the well-being of the subjects. The more control you can exercise over distribution the better your chances of fulfilling the unwritten contracts you have drawn with the people you film which, to the ethical film-maker, are as binding as any legal contract.

For me this was a lesson hard-learned. In 1975 Patsy Asch and I worked in Afghanistan with a Canadian anthropologist, Asen Balikci. Our objective was to film a pastoral migration but, when the Moslem nomads saw our camera gear, they refused to be filmed. Eventually we convinced them that the film was being made for educational purposes and would be valuable to students in other cultures interested in their traditional way of life, which even they knew was changing rapidly. When we returned to the United States, the Smithsonian Institute gave the National Film Board of Canada, co-sponsor of the project, rights to edit the film. We were told we would have to wait at least five years before we could edit our educational films. We had been naive in accepting a verbal agreement for a contract that was never signed.

The educational films we had promised our subjects were never made. The National Film Board edited the footage for a television programme that was transmitted in Canada and the United States a year later. After the Soviet Army had invaded Afghanistan, the BBC bought the film and re-edited it to 'bring it up to date'. In essence the BBC added an introduction and conclusion. The introduction included news-reel footage of the Soviet invasion and some fighting. Then the narration implied that the people we had filmed, people named and located in the film, were part of the fiercest of Afghanistan resistance forces. Whether this was true or not, the new version of the film placed our subjects in grave danger of being tracked down by Soviet intelligence officers and killed.

Many people and circumstances contributed to the abrogation of our contract with our Afghan subjects, but I learned a difficult personal lesson. As film-makers we must not enter into agreements with our subjects if we are not sure we can keep our promises. Without legal control over how our footage would be used, I should not have made promises to my subjects and, in most circumstances, I should not have filmed.

The Afghan experience is an extreme example but I think there are more subtle ethical issues to consider in how footage is used. Once we have gained the trust and taken the time of the people we film, is it fair to do nothing with the film? Or, at the opposite extreme, is it right to make a film for television that reaches a wider audience but may be so superficial that, rather than informing the audience it reinforces existing stereotypes of our subjects?

### Make a royalty arrangement with the people filmed and see that they receive money

Sarah Elder and Lenny Kamerling decided to have the Inuit people they were studying not only help make *At the Time of Whaling* (1975) and *On the Spring Ice* (1976) but also share in the copyright and royalties. The notion of sharing royalties was unusual at the time, but once it came up, it seemed like a practice that should have been in place long before.

Royalties, however, must be handled carefully to assure benefit rather than detriment to the people filmed. Even 200 US$ can be a windfall to a person in a remote village and can permanently change that person's position in the community. Sometimes the process of transferring royalties through banks or money orders can be so cumbersome and costly that the subject of your film may actually owe money before papers are in order and payment received. Ousmane Sembene portrayed this situation beautifully in his film, *Mandabi* (The Money Order) (1964).

The ideal way to get money to isolated subjects is to take it directly or send it with a trusted friend. The anthropologist, who is familiar with the culture, is probably the most qualified person to decide how royalties should be distributed to best serve the individuals and societies featured in the films.

We gave Jero Tapakan, the Balinese trance healer, a percentage of the royalties for films we made of her and will give a percentage to the Balinese village we worked with on a film of a village cremation ritual. When we finish our film about the purification ritual in the eastern Flores, a percentage of the royalties, as requested by the community elders, will go into an education fund.

## Publish a study guide or monograph to be distributed with the film

In 1969 Karl Heider made an impassioned plea for written background material to accompany films. The films, he said, particularly those used in teaching, are incomplete without solid, written background material and deeper interpretation of the culture or events portrayed in the film. Jointly publishing written material and film, however, goes against the traditions of current book and film distributors. In general, book distributors don't distribute films, and film distributors don't distribute books.

In 1971 John Marshall and I, with the help of Frank Galvin, Laurence and Lorna Marshall and Marilyn Wood, founded Documentary Educational Resources (DER), a non-profit distribution corporation. DER has produced study guides for the Bushman and Yanomamo films. The Smithsonian Institute has written excellent film monographs, and Linda Connor, Patsy Asch and I recently produced a book, *Jero Tapakan: Balinese Healer* (1986), which is available in a box with four videotapes on Balinese possession, magic and healing.

So the combined distribution of printed material and film is possible and promises to gain momentum in the decade ahead as new technologies develop. Before the year 2000 we may be distributing three hours of high-definition video on a 2-inch square computer diskette held on the inside flap of an accompanying paperback book. Students will be able to read about a subject while viewing the film using freeze frame and fast forward or reverse for closer study.

## Ongoing commitments

One more ethical question relates indirectly to ethnographic film-making. What role can and should the film-maker and anthropologist play in the future of the societies they study, particularly with regard to development?

Ethnographers gain a great deal from their interaction with indigenous populations; if not fame and fortune, at least knowledge and a comfortable university faculty position. We owe it to our subjects to do what we can for them in return. Ethnographers are often in the best position to know how to help the people they study integrate into contemporary life. The modern world is encroaching so rapidly on small-scale isolated societies that their survival will ultimately depend on their ability to adapt.

Ideally, development is managed by citizens of your subjects' native country but local policy-makers often have little knowledge or interest in indigenous cultures. You can speak to the needs of your subjects and share your knowledge with local social scientists and policy-makers. Information you provide may enable the policy-makers to make better choices for their people.

We are all products of our times. We cannot really fault early ethnographic film-makers for their distance and apparent indifference to their subjects. Ethical truths are relative to a particular culture and a particular moment in history. As film-makers we should, at least, be aware of and take seriously the ethical concerns of the time in which we live.

Cultures are now under ferocious pressure to change and change quickly. Many will disappear. That is why anthropology and ethnographic film-making are so important. We have learned over time that anthropological studies are not a one-way street but an exchange that involves a contract between ethnographer and the people being studied, a contract which implies that in exchange for an intimate understanding of a culture and the privilege of recording it, the ethnographer will do nothing to exploit or misrepresent his or her subjects, now or in the future.

**References**

*Book*

Connor, L., P. Asch and T. Asch (1986), *Jero Tapaken: Balinese Healer*, Cambridge University Press, Cambridge.

*Films*

Asch, T. and N. Chagnon (1975), *The Ax Fight*, Documentary Educational Resources (DER),Watertown, Mass. Colour 30 mins.

Asch, T. and L. Connor (1979), *A Balinese Trance Seance*, DER, Watertown, Mass. Colour, 30 mins.

Asch, T., L. Connor and P. Asch (1981), *Jero on Jero: A Balinese Trance Seance Observed*, DER, Watertown, Mass. Colour, 16 mins.

Cooper, M. C. and E. B. Schoedsack 1925, *Grass*. University of California Extension Media Center. Black and white, 66 mins.

Eisenstein, S. (1925), *Battleship Potemkin*, First Studio Goskine, USSR. Black and white, 75 min. (silent)

Elder, S. and L. Kamerling (1975), *At the Time of Whaling* DER, Watertown, Mass. Colour, 38 mins.

Elder, S. and L. Kamerling (1976), *On the Spring Ice*, DER, Watertown, Mass. Colour, 45 mins.

Flaherty, R. (1922), *Nanook of the North*. Révillon Frères. Black and white, 70 mins.

Rouch, J. (1954), *Les Maîtres Fous*, DER, Watertown, Mass. Colour, 35 mins.

Sembene, O. (1968), *Mandabi*, New Yorker Films. Colour, 90 mins.

Wright, B. (1937), *Song of Ceylon*. Ceylon Tea Propaganda Board, London. Black and white, 45 mins.

# Myths, racism and opportunism: film and TV representations of the San

The central dynamic between film-makers and subject-communities is one of power. Questions of accountability with regard to production and distribution practices are rarely dealt with in ethnographic films, or in publications about them.[1] In this chapter I will examine the origins and effects of critical responses to films and television programmes about the San, specifically those films which some American academics within the Anti-Apartheid Movement argue are part of the problem leading to their destruction.

### What's in a name?

The San of Namibia and Botswana have been labelled with a variety of 'scientifically-derived' names, most being external impositions which sooner or later take on pejorative connotations. Wiley *et al.* (1982, p. xix) in commenting on John Marshall's *The Hunters* (1958), objected to the label, 'Bushman', as 'a racist, pejorative term used by those who sought to dehumanize them as a prelude to their removal from the land and slaughter'. In defying Edwin Wilmsen's (1989, pp. 26–32) critique, Rob Gordon insists that Paul Myburgh's use of 'Bushmen' in *People of the Great Sandface* (1985) is correct since 'San' is derived from 'Sab', meaning robber. 'Bushmen' stems from Dutch, meaning bandit or outlaw. Gordon (1990a, p.30) argues that 'San' is mystificatory, and that 'Bushmen' is a 'lumpen-category' once used by colonial authorities for resisters to colonial rule. He concludes: 'perhaps it is time to make Bushmen (and banditry) respectable again'.

While none of the films discussed in this chapter make banditry or begging respectable, the squabbles amongst anthropologists and historians about naming have serious political consequences. One is to foreground the apparent 'scientific' nature of anthropology and, in so doing, to suppress the unspoken subjectivities of anthropologists and/or film-makers. More immediately, however, the debate opened a space for political opportunism on the part of the South African authorities. The South West African Department of Tourism and Conservation, the South African Defence Force and other state departments played certain paradigms against others in film and other media in their abortive attempts to establish a 'Bushmen' reserve in Namibia, and to dispossess the !Kung, and other groups of their previously inhabited territories and waterholes. The disagreement over 'naming' thus empowers 'scientific' discourse over the everyday collective nouns used by people to describe themselves. 'Science', certainly positivist science, is ahistorical and easily mobilised for ideological and political purposes. The 'Bushmen' have never considered themselves a single entity or society (Marshall and Ritchie 1984); this has been the prerogative of anthropologists, film-makers and state authorities whose misleading scientific categories told them otherwise. Most films about the San have thus been located within this incorrect assumption, one that coincides with the direction the South African government tried to impose vis-à-vis a 'Bushmen homeland'. Jamie Uys's *The Gods Must be Crazy* (1980) is the most well-known example, having earned more than 100 million US$ worldwide.

### Cinema, social science and the San

The unprecedented international success of *The Gods Must be Crazy* (hereafter *Gods I*) cracked open a debate within American social science and media studies on the way white South Africans have represented 'Bushmen' on film and television (Volkman 1988; Gordon 1990a, 1990b; Tomaselli 1990; Blythe 1986; Lee 1985). In *Gods I* a coke bottle thrown from a plane disrupts the harmony of an isolated band of 'Bushmen' as they begin to fight over it. Xi's quest in the film, set in the Kalahari Desert, is to return the bottle to the Gods. Xi's trek takes him through the lives of a clumsy white botanist and the woman he is trying to impress, a 'coloured' jack-of-all-trades, and marauding black terrorists. He is imprisoned by the strange white society for killing and eating a goat. As in Jaques Tati's *Monseur Hulot's Holiday* (1953), Xi's relationship to the people around him hardly impinges on his consciousness, and he returns to his band unchanged in the face of his novel and traumatic experiences.

Critiques of *Gods I*, and Uys's earlier *Beautiful People* (1974), a Disneyfied comedy about animals in the Kalahari which includes a vignette of 'Bushmen' imitating them (see Blythe 1986), range from historically sensitive explanations of the Afrikaner psyche (Davis 1985) to reductive equations of Uys's films with official apartheid propaganda (Gilliam 1984; Lee 1985) which single-mindedly seize their viewers in vice-like racist pronouncements. The argument that directors 'position' their viewers in an uncritical relation to their films arose from British Screen Theory which dominated critical media studies during the 1970s and early 1980s. In this now discredited paradigm, scholars assumed that their decoding of a film's dominant messages coincided with the way all viewers understood – or should have understood – them. This assumption underlies the dominant academic response to Uys's films, and makes no distinction between documentary and other film genres, or the way audiences, in fact, make sense of films.

Critics foregrounded certain elements of Uys's films but simultaneously suppressed the broader historically and culturally discursive contexts from which Uys and his films emerged. Richard Lee (1985), for example, mistakenly classified *Gods I* alongside two earlier, supposedly South African-produced, racist films, which although shot on location in South Africa, were produced by foreigners. These were the British-made *The Wild Geese* (1977), about mercenaries rescuing an old and sick black African leader from tribal conflict somewhere in Central Africa, and the American-produced *Zulu* (1966), on their defeat by the British at Rorke's Drift in Natal in 1879. Having reminded readers of white South African racism on the basis of these foreign-made films, he concluded that *Gods I* was part of this 'official' apartheid conspiracy, notwithstanding its much more disarming style. All this conclusion shows is that British and American perceptions of black Africans are part of an international discourse on race and racism, to which *Gods I* is connected.

The preferred North American analytical frameworks lack four necessary dimensions in their application to films made in South Africa. Firstly, the complex relations between film-makers and the production of ideology tend to be reduced to vulgar analyses of the mechanistic relations assumed to exist between film-makers and the apartheid state. Secondly, the technological, ideological and subjective processes which shape discursive cinematic practices in particular historical conjunctures in different societies need elaboration. The third dimension relates to how and why different audiences interpret the same films differently. As will become clear, the application of solely ethnographic criteria to an analysis of the two *Gods* films and *People of the Great Sandface*, suppresses crucial autobiographical, psychoanalytic and symbolic information residing in the texts of these films. And, fourth, as Alan Rosenthal (1989/90, p. 59) cautions with regard to Toby Volkman's (1988) critique of *Gods I*, audiences approach comedy and fantasy differently to documentary. They do not necessarily interpret everything they see literally.

Uys is portrayed by his critics as a cynical and ruthless opportunist who deliberately and maliciously distorts the image of 'Bushmen' for the political purposes of the South African government. Fundamental ideological questions are lost in the welter of accusations made against him by an incensed anthropological community as they bore witness to the destruction of the San in Namibia, which was under South African control until 1989. A seemingly bewildered Uys, however, continues to play out his innocence and anti-academic rhetoric in media interviews and press releases. His remarks about the *Gods* films constantly invoke white myths about the 'Bushmen' as a happy, culturally innocent and isolated group of hunter-gatherers, whose social equilibrium can only remain in balance with nature when alien influences like the coke bottle are purged. These myths, however, remain at their most destructive in his publicity kits, as they are presented as anthropological facts. In his publicity for *The Gods Must Be Crazy II* (1989) for example, Uys reasserted that the 'Bushmen' still live in their pure, pristine condition of remote primitive affluence, in exactly the way that he fictionalised their existence in the two *Gods* films.

Uys's slapstick comedies, through drawing on ethnographic and documentary codes, are very different to Paul Myburgh's documentary, *People of the Great Sandface* (1985). Myburgh (1989) claims to have lived with the Gwikwe and other bands in the Kalahari Desert on and off for ten years. His inspiration for this film was catalysed, he states, by his studies of anthropology, and the films of explorer Robert Flaherty and British documentarist John Grierson, both of whom made their respective contributions during the 1930s. *Sandface* resembles the Flaherty films in its 'man-against-environment' theme, the struggle of Myburgh's 'last band' of 'wild Bushmen' being against thirst and the temptation of a water tap in a Botswanan government settlement. The film also recalls Grierson's intent of dignifying working and marginalised people. *Sandface* similarly tries to redress the image of a group so often made fun of in comedic narrative cinema and tourist images. In *Sandface*, the lives of the isolated remnants of a Gwikwe band are documented through four metaphorical seasons, not unlike the time-scales used by Flaherty in his films. The desert substitutes for Flaherty's Arctic wastes (*Nanook of the North*, 1922), or the rocks and sea of the Isle of Aran (*Man of Aran*, 1934).

Despite its fundamental differences to the *Gods* films, *Sandface* too, has been labelled a 'fraud' and argued to perpetuate the 'killer-myth' of 'the wild Bushman' (Gordon 1990, p. 30a). In Namibia, the San are dying faster than they are reproducing themselves in squatter settlements (Volkman 1986, p. 27) and, in Botswana, where Myburgh made his film, they have suffered similar pressures of dispossession, resettlement and the negative effects of tourism (Hitchcock and Brandenburgh 1990).

### History denied

Wiley *et al.* charge that *The Hunters* is a denial of history, as does Gordon (1990a, p. 31) of *Sandface*. Neither film referred to the social linkages between the San and their hostile white and black neighbours who chased them into the Kalahari over many hundreds of years. But, then, neither did many of the social anthropologists who originally studied them (eg., Lee and DeVore 1968; Thomas 1959; Silberbauer 1981). The dominant anthropological paradigm until the late 1970s was that the San were remnants of the stone age living in a state of 'pristine primitiveness'. As Gordon (1990b, pp. 3–5) argues, *Gods I* (though to a lesser extent, *Sandface*), rode to box-office success both in South Africa and the United States as 'part of a larger current in contemporary scholarly discourse' which ignored modern influences and tried to reinforce the myth of Bushmen living in splendid isolation, uncontaminated purity and primitive affluence (see Wilmsen and Denbow 1990). Jacqueline Solway and Richard Lee (1990) mention *Gods I* in this paradigmatic context, borrowing an image from the film in formulating the 'Coke Bottle in the Kalahari Syndrome' whereby:

> modernity falls mysteriously from the sky, setting in motion an inevitable spiral of cultural disintegration that can only be checked by the removal of the foreign element. This is clearly a caricature, but it reveals the common and unstated perception of foraging societies as so delicately balanced and fragile that they cannot accommodate innovation and change . . . The 'Coke Bottle in the Kalahari' imagery also bears a subtext, the rueful recognition of the unlimited capacity of 'advanced societies' to consume everything in their path. (p. 109–10)

Treating *Gods I* as ethnographic data of the dominant 'consuming' society which re-presents the San in media, as do Solway and Lee, offers more constructive leads than simply dismissing it as 'propaganda' or 'Kalahari . . . caricature' (Wilmsen and Denbow 1990, p. 493). The latter part of Solway and Lee's statement accounts for Gordon's recurringly published lament that the 'Bushmen' have become the most highly scientifically (and commercially) commodified 'disappearing' group anywhere in the world, and is a reference to the myth so effectively commercialised by Uys in his two *Gods* films. Any society under the extraordinary gaze of international lenses is going to experience stress as their very 'disappearance' becomes consommé for television and film audiences elsewhere. Where whole societies once fell under the gaze of a few European explorers, their disorganised and tatty remnants are now 'authentically' redressed and packaged between TV advertising slots, which themselves, in South Africa for example, use myths about the Bushmen to 'demonstrate' that a Japanese four-wheel drive vehicle can go 'where the Bushmen go', perhaps even outperforming them in the desert. In this vein, Renato Rosaldo (1989, p. 17) links *Gods I* to the idea of 'imperialism with nostalgia', a trajectory incorporating films like *Heat and Dust*, *A Passage to India* and *Out of Africa*, as well as *Zulu* and *Wild Geese*. The colonial societies seen in these films appear decorous and orderly, as if constructed in accordance with the norms of classic ethnography. The narratives of these films, however, barely hint at these societies' impending collapse.

## Expeditionary discourse

Western fascination with exploring the 'unknown' has long focused on expeditions to exotic places inhabited by people seen to be primitive neolithic relics: the peoples of Papua New Guinea, the Amazon Basin, Pygmies in Central Africa and the Inuit peoples of North America, have all been part of the popular Western imagination from at least Victorian times.

Early accounts of how whites searched the Kalahari for glimpses of 'wild Bushmen' form the bulk of many filmic and written accounts from the 1890s, continuing almost to the close of the twentieth century. This expeditionary metaphor was first articulated in *The Denver African Expedition* (1926), made by the Universities of Denver and Cape Town. It encoded a 'zoo ethos' and a method of luring 'the elusive little yellow men' into the open. Time and shifting academic perceptions about societies and ways of studying them humanised the expeditionary discourse into 'endearing' diminutive metaphors rather than overtly racist themes. Elizabeth Marshall Thomas (1959, p. 7), for example, wrote about how the San would hide 'like foxes in the grass' to avoid 'strangers', notably the Marshall expeditions of 1950–53. Other studies reflected the 'expeditionary' social discourse of exotic tribes with regard to the ways of the 'First' and/or 'harmless people': for example, Lourens Van der Post's *Lost World of the Kalahari* (1954) and its literary sequel, *The Heart of the Hunter* (1961), and his TV series *Testament to the Bushmen* (1982). John Marshall's *The Hunters* (1956) and National Geographic's *Bushmen of the Kalahari* (1974), also fall into this discourse. To paraphrase James Clifford (1988, p. 167), these journeys make sense as a 'coming to consciousness', of encountering and coming to know the 'Other'. Uys, for example, especially talks about, *and* images, the San in four of his films in this way. In *Gods I*, the clumsy girl-shy botanist comes to understand Xi, though Xi is traumatized in his encounter with modernity with its incomprehensible white laws and punitive institutions.

Marshall only admitted setting up scenes, especially the 'kills', in *The Hunters* (1956), almost 38 years after the film's release. This was done to perpetuate the myth of 'wild Bushmen' (Gordon 1990a, p.32). An irony, then, is that the arch-villain, Jamie Uys, in his naivete, cut through academically legitimised myths, by offering a perverse allegory in *Gods I* of the disruptive effects of Western civilisation and modernity on a fictional Bushmen clan. But this was interpreted as 'racist' by American commentators whose own analyses and edited films until the late 1970s had, paradoxically, eliminated most traces of alien contamination, and who themselves contributed to the myth of modernity versus the traditional (see Volkman 1988, p.242; Howell 1988, p.7; Gordon 1990a; and Wilmsen 1989).

To what extent, then, is the attack on Uys an indication of guilt atonement by those who contributed to the unilinear model of human material development? The roots of Anglo-Saxon anthropology in colonialism and racism remain a sore point in the discipline. While some schools of modern anthropology would seem to have finally divested themselves of these taints, certain residual insecurities remain. These, I believe, are to be found firstly, in the nature of embarrassment with early racism in American cinema and its unique tradition of blackface actors, and of the *Amos and Andy* genre; secondly, in questions of 'objectivity' claimed by social science and the essentially positivistic nature of much of the anthropological enterprise; and thirdly, in the supportive relationship of certain early schools of anthropology to the theory of apartheid itself.

Social science has often proved itself incapable of preventing historical processes destructive of particular groups of people. Often, the best it could do was to publish and make films on 'vanishing' and 'disappearing' peoples. Indeed, social science has often held itself outside history and process altogether, basking in its seeming ideological innocence and claims of neutrality. Alternatively, it was harnessed by governments for their political ends, as was the case with Afrikaner *volkekunde* (ethnology – see Sharp 1979) and conservative cultural theory (Muller and Tomaselli 1990), which unconsciously underlies Uys's isolate model and purist ethnic representation of the San. In his terms, the San are indeed 'a kind of narrow and opaque window to the Pleistocene' (Yellen 1984, p. 54), a perspective which was of use to apartheid planners.

*Sandface* is not concerned with *finding* wild Bushmen, although Myburgh (1989, p. 27) claims that the Gwikwe *was* the last nomadic clan to exist in Botswana. This is another myth, asserts Gordon, on which entrepreneurs throughout the twentieth century have made money. *Sandface*, in fact, does not operate within the paternalistic discourse of the 'expedition', although Myburgh's interview gives the impression of his 'coming to consciousness' while making the film. He claims to have so thoroughly immersed himself into Gwikwe culture that he believed himself 'beyond the point where (his) subjectivity could have been a limitation to the truth' (Myburgh 1989, p.29). The 'expeditionary' metaphor in *Sandface* works at a different level, concealed in Myburgh's mostly third person narration. *Sandface* is really Myburgh's own self-exploration, an ethno-biography in attempting to re-discover a coherent unity and culture so thoroughly evacuated by postmodern societies (Tomaselli *et al.* 1991). As such, it is Myburgh rather than the Gwikwe who may be unable, like Monsieur Hulot, to 'come to consciousness'.

When Myburgh talks about 'wild Bushmen', however, he is articulating the anthropological paradigm of his student days, irrespective of his rejection of textbook commentaries on the San. This contradiction is evidenced all through *People of the Great Sandface* through his dependence on largely conventional Western documentary film codes, a sense of progression and closure, and direct address narration which speaks 'for' the Gwikwe seen in the film.

## Crew–subject relations

While desperately seeking a 'connectedness' (even if mythological), anthropologists and film-makers tend to create discourses about 'their' subject-communities which have more to do with their own positions in dominant societies than with actual situations on the ground. Self-validations of 'closed discourses' are often derived from taken-for-granted assumptions about class and social science. Uys, Myburgh, Van der Post and Marshall exhibit four different kinds of connectedness, each premised on particular ideologies, assumptions, myths and practices.

Van der Post's motivations for filming and writing about the San were basically two-fold: first was 'atonement' for the massacre of the last Bushman rock artist and his clan perpetrated by his grandfather, and the influence of his part-Bushman nanny, Klara, on his childhood (Van der Post 1986). Van der Post (1961, p. xv-xvi) hoped his books would 'incite a campaign' to benefit the

'Bushmen'. It is not clear, however, how he expected this to happen. Second, Van der Post was searching for origins. The 'First People' provided a vehicle for this recuperation of Southern Africa's original culture and its social harmony. In *A Mantis Carol*, for example, Hans Taaibosch is a bridge between the Western and San cultures, between the pre-modern and the modern: 'Hans Taaibosch was not only himself but also a mirror in which there was also a reflection of ourselves' (Van der Post 1975, p. 154).

Myburgh (1989, p.26) was drawn by the 'wind' in his head (see also Marshall Thomas, p.24), a desire to interpellate himself as a 'Bushman'. Myburgh felt that he had 'to become a Bushman, a Gwikwe in order to speak for the Gwikwe'. This attempt at taking on another identity resulted in Myburgh smudging his inter-pellation with a thesaurus of white myths which overdetermined his attempts at fully integrating himself into a San subjectivity – at least in the way he presented his film. As such, the film is really an auto-biography which often connects and empathizes with what Myburgh perceived as 'Bushman' culture, but which just as often also dismisses it (Tomaselli *et al.*, 1991). Like Van der Post, Myburgh was searching for his origins, a sense of self, a First Culture. Myburgh's *Sandface*, however, cannot be so dismissively retitled 'People of the Great White Lie' just because his historically naive narration repeats some of the numerous white myths about the 'Bushmen' excavated by Gordon (1990a). Myburgh has more in common with Van der Post than he realizes as both sought to discover the 'mind' of the San, and not necessarily offer data-filled 'scientific' ethnographies, although *Sandface* does tend to meander between the two forms of encounter.

Van der Post's Jungian analysis stresses the 'collective unconscious': the 'Bushman' as 'our dreaming selves' (Barnard 1989, p. 110). This unconscious 'longing' is perhaps analogous to Myburgh's (1989, p. 26) more earthy metaphor of 'wind': 'when I first went into the Kalahari the feeling of the "wind" inside my head was the same feeling as the "wind" outside my head. I felt like I had come home. Home is an intangible qualitative place, that feeling of familiarity within'. Although Myburgh is physically absent from the visual track, his subjectivity percolates through every frame; but the interpellation – 'wind' – of a 'bridging' Hans Taaibosch – largely eludes him. Myburgh's empathy with his 'band' is evident, but the mysticism of the 'Bushman mind' and the joining of the pre-modern and modernist 'winds' is under-developed in the film.

Marshall's initial intention might have been expeditionary in intent. The hundreds of reels of film shot by himself and his family between 1950 and 1953[2] suggest an expeditionary atmosphere as the white 'bwanas' dressed in safari suits and pith helmets traverse an inhospitable terrain in their Dodge Power Wagons to direct filming proceedings. The film documentation of this phase and *The Hunters*, cut from the Marshall Expedition footage of the early 1950s, locates the young John Marshall as an adventurer and an explorer of the exotic. An epi-stemological rupture, however, occurred after Marshall returned to the United States where he then studied anthropology. Anthropology through film followed, with the !Kung San series, filmed during his adventurer phase of the early 1950s.

This footage was edited very differently to that used in *The Hunters*, and was accompanied by anthropological study guides. But with the demise of the San in the 1970s under apartheid, he interpellated himself as a family member, a rescuer. Marshall was the only film-maker to address materially the plight of the !Kung groups with which he worked. He established the Ju/Wa Bushman Foundation in 1981 to facilitate the survival of the Ju/Wasi through agriculture. He published ethnographies of the San, concentrating on how to improve their material conditions, rather than concerning himself with 'mind', or a search for origins and self. *The Hunter's* narration does, however, encode a respect and poetic tone and something of the mysticism of a Van der Post. The narration is in the third person, but Marshall nevertheless shows an intimacy with his subjects, interpreting their behaviour and what they are thinking, doing and saying. Apart from this film, and *N!ai: Story of a !Kung Woman* (1980), Marshall has made very few films on the San, the 800,000 feet of 16mm shot on the various Marshall Expeditions since 1950 notwithstanding.

For Uys, a basic narrative structure of repetition with difference, used successfully as the core of most of his twenty-five feature films, mobilised the mythical discourse about Bushmen to which both explorers and anthropologists had contributed. These mostly made fun of Boer-Briton taboos and the humorous way these played out in the white South African Afrikaner-English inter-cultural context. Metaphorically, then, *Gods I* may *not* be about Bushmen or Uys's idealist projection of bantustans as claimed by his American critics, but about the Eden myth and the way Afrikaners imagine an ideal state for themselves separate from alien influences (Tomaselli 1990). Only Uys seems to have no sense of further responsibility, whether financial or moral, towards the 'Bushmen'. His payment of a meagre R2,000 to his star actor, N!Xau, for *Gods I* and R5,000 for *Gods II* plus R200 a month (*Vrye Weekblad*, 17 November 1989) underscores an exploitative streak of the worst kind. This is, no doubt, rationalised in his discredited claim that the 'Bushmen' are still hunter-gatherers living the life described by anthropologists of the 1950s – too much money might 'spoil' this exemplar of primeval life.

## Ethnographic motives

Contemporary academic interest in the San has been sustained partly because of their accessibility to observation even while 'disappearing'. However, the prominence given to the San in the late 1980s is a direct product of the world's antipathy towards apartheid, as well as a major, often traumatic, introspection, caused by Wilmsen's (1989; Wilmsen and Denbow 1990) savage critiques of scholars like Lee and DeVore. This interest heightened as the San were caught up in the South African military onslaught against Angola. While the emphasis is well placed, it runs the risk of focusing on apartheid as the single factor threatening the survival of the San, while neglecting other causes.

While anthropologists like Gordon, Volkman, Lee and Wilmsen and film-makers like Marshall have done everything they can to discredit myths and stereotypes about the San, they should not be surprised at the way the myths motor on, given their original anthropological stimulus. Paradigms might 'shift' in science, but they don't always evacuate popular discourses or genres of representation. Given the noise of accusation and counter-accusation in *Current Anthropology* (1990) and *CVA Review*(1990–1), the student might be forgiven for wondering just what it is that separates myth from fact.

Even if Gordon's sarcastically dismissive account of Myburgh and his film is valid, there are other ways of reading and making sense of *Sandface*. This is through nomadic aesthetics offered by Teshome Gabriel (1988), where the overriding quest is for water. If Myburgh's (1989, p. 27) claim that he 'lived with the Bushmen according to their own ancient manner', is correct, then unlike anthropologists and film-makers who brought trucks stocked with food, water and other comforts of modernity, Myburgh thirsted and hungered along with his adoptive clan. Whether or not he deliberately constituted his band and reconstructed a nomadic existence is not, then, the main issue in terms of cinematic ethno-biography (though the criticism remains in terms of his ethnographic claims). The 'thirst' that Myburgh speaks of must then, in terms of this analysis, also be a metaphorical one. It is a thirst for deep memories of the past which are thought to offer a key to opening the meanings of the present. Or, as Van der Post's biographer expresses it, 'past experiences interact with present circumstances, until the exploration of the interior wilderness of Africa becomes also the exploration of the interior wilderness of the heart of man' (Carpenter 1969, p. 82). In terms of Gabriel's (1988, p. 75) theory of nomadic aesthetics, what Myburgh presents are images belonging to the past. Though representing remembrances, 'they carry simultaneously possibilities and promises, because they also belong to the future'. This intent, however, was partially subverted through Myburgh's reliance on closure, emphasis on individuals rather than collective relations, and acceptance of official history ('Time and history have taken a heavy toll on their numbers'), which undermine the openness of nomadic aesthetics.

### Film and TV: archetypal windows

Media theorists have battled against the perception by most film and video makers that their cameras are windows looking on 'real life'. Anthropologists charged that *Sandface* and the *Gods* movies did not offer accurate representations of the way things are – that they were lies. This visual positivism collapses the distinction between two forms of coded reality: the representations of everyday life, and their *re- representation* on screen. The problem for the film viewer is how to distinguish between the mental text elicited by the re-presentation on screen, the representation as it occurred or was enacted, and the pro-filmic event itself (what actually existed prior to the making of the film). Failure to see these distinctions will result in the film being read in terms of a single criterion –

ethnographic – thus missing other levels of encoding (e.g. psychoanalytical) in which the key to interpretation exists.

Since both Myburgh and Van der Post (in *Testament to the Bushmen*) are searching for origins, for the 'mind' of the Bushmen, for 'original (South African) culture' they 'speak for' their subjects, telling us what they are doing, thinking and saying. Their objective is not ethnography, even San survival, as both imply that this 'people' had already disappeared. Van der Post tells us that this occurred before he even started to write about the Bushmen; while Myburgh states that his was the last 'wild' band to exist, moving to a settlement during the filming itself. Van der Post and Myburgh are searching for universal subjectivities, a way to the future, an essential South Africanism that first colonialism, and then apartheid, destroyed. They are less concerned with providing ethnographic detail and validity. Neither are they addressing the material needs of the San as does Marshall in his fund-raising film, *Pull Ourselves Up or Die Out* (1984), which complements an appeal pamphlet distributed through Cultural Survival.

No film, however, is neutral when threatened people are its subjects. Uys's *Gods I*, for example, was considered a dangerous film by anti-apartheid anthropologists for two main reasons. Firstly, there was Uys's perpetuation of stereotypes about the San, which exonerated the brutality of European colonialism and apartheid from complicity in their demise. Secondly, the film was *used* by apartheid planners to argue the case for a game park in which international safari tourists could view and live with 'Bushmen' in their 'original' state. This park would freeze the San in terms of the apartheid mythical construct so effectively popularised by *Gods I*.

The game park idea had its roots in *volkekunde* (ethnology) as developed by Afrikaner Nationalist ethnologists. *Volkekunde* offers a static, genetically determined sense of 'ethnos' which locates particular 'races' in specific 'homelands'. The interrelation of place and inherited social identity also has another origin. This source can be traced back to the proposition that eighteeth- and nineteenth-century discoverers/explorers/expeditionary enterprises mapped out the unknown world, both physically and cognitively. The same people who discovered and named lakes and mountains also discovered and named 'tribes' and peoples and decided that where they were found is where and how they had always lived. It is not surprising, then, that journals like *National Geographic* see their province as exploring both geography and anthropology, since studying environments and peoples are seen as two sides of the same project.

It is in this vein that the idea of a national park for the Bushmen in Namibia should be seen. It was envisaged that the San could not survive outside 'their' environment. Prevention of the 'biological crime' of permitting 'such a peculiar race to die out' (Reitz 1948, p. 17), required that their habitat be protected. This line of thinking underscores the notion that a symbiotic relationship exists between people and their environment, and to destroy the one means to destroy the other. The problem arises when the idea is opportunistically used to promote sectarian political ends and reinforce the notion of tribalism in other contexts.

Gordon (1984) charged that this plan would 'conserve (the Bushmen) to extinction'. Referring to the effect of *Gods I* on apartheid thinking and the game reserve idea with regard to the San in Namibia, he concludes that 'Some films can kill' (Gordon 1990c, p.1). The game reserve plan, however, was shelved in 1989 following a world outcry and lobbying by Marshall.

## Theorising crew–community encounters

If cinema has contributed to the demise of the Bushmen, then new strategies should have been developed to counter this. Instead of making ever more mass-distributed movies about their plight, one response could have facilitated the techniques developed by anthropologists more attuned to the politics of survival. Great strides have been made in providing video channels for disadvantaged and repressed communities, even transforming the relations of production, as facilitated by Eric Michaels with Aboriginals in Australia. See, for example, O'Regan (1990), Terence Turner (1990) with the Kayapo in Brazil, and Marshall's fund-raising interventionist films like *Pull Ourselves Up or Die Out*.

When the camera and technical processes remain in the hands of the anthropologists, problems occur concerning the nature of the relationships that develop, crew assumptions about the composition, cohesion and nature of the 'community', issues of form, and questions of power. If anthropologists are to guide constructive processes resulting from their encounter with communities, they need to theorise the nature of that encounter and to acknowledge the power structures and relationships that develop. This is done by Marshall in *N!ai: Story of a !Kung Woman* (1980) with his vignette on Uys's concluding shots of *Gods 1*. But this reflexivity about another film is lacking from his own films, although a Documentary Educational Resources (DER) catalogue states: 'Ironically, some of N!ai's problems stem from the wealth she has acquired through her work with the Marshall film crew, as well as work from numerous other white photographers and film-makers who have found her beautiful' (Marshall Cabezas and Nierenberg 1990, p. 14). N!ai's photogenic demeanour has become the community's nemesis: they are just as dependent upon her as is she on white film crews.

The Study Guides produced by DER make no mention of how any of Marshall's films were made nor of the nature of the crews' encounters with the Ju/wasi and other bands filmed. The films are presented as though they were innocent: the archetypal windows to the San, although Timothy and Patsy Asch have helpfully written on how to use the Marshall films to teach anthropology. The lack of epistemological writing on methods of production alerts us to a fundamental issue: who initiates videos or films and why?

Films about people are specific discourses embedded in broader, constantly changing social processes and ways of encountering others, whether or not these are acknowledged in the films themselves. Marketing success is intertwined with dominant discourses which determine what kind of representations are most vulnerable to commercial exploitation. *The Hunters*, for example, cinematically anchored the evolutionary theory of isolate human material development that was the accepted teaching model within social science in the 1950s. Though superseded in contemporary anthropology, this model is now an accessory to contemporary popular Western belief in the superiority of modern over pre-modern societies. This is basic to the success of the *Gods* films for, even though Uys makes fun of runaway technology through the use of comedic devices first developed by Buster Keaton, the technology can be made to save the day. *Testament to the Bushmen*, like *Sandface*, straddles the pre-modern/modern trajectory in an initially anthropologically convincing way. These productions recall the more pristine times, but herald 'disappearance'. They empathize with, rather than make fun of, the San's encounters with others.

*Sandface* tells us something about Myburgh and his search for self, but does not explain much anthropologically. Perhaps this is the problem with most films about the San. By not writing about their filming experiences, film-makers exclude a whole level of ethnographic detail that needs to be known in order to make sense of particular films and the relationships that develop between crews and their subjects during particular conjunctures. In the interview in *CVA Review*, Myburgh exposes himself in a way that few have had the courage to do. This interview provides additional data from which to make sense of *Sandface*, of Myburgh himself, and ultimately of Western perceptions of and encounters with, and attempts to merge with, or bridge between, or mirror, the Other.

## Conclusion: the nomadic lens

What I have tried to offer is an argument which explains the subjectivities of four film-makers and how these identities hailed them in different directions, though all remain adamant on the ethnographic accuracy of their respective statements about the San. To recast the 'Coke Bottle in the Kalahari Syndrome', perhaps it is academia which suffers from the syndrome as a result of problems within social science itself. Let us not forget that anthropologists had themselves ignored evidence of modernising influences amongst the San. They objected to Uys raising questions of modernity in *Gods I* partly because he embedded his narrative in a paradigm which denied these influences and which they had earlier legitimised. The ultimate comment may be that Marshall's *N!ai: Story of a !Kung Woman* (1980), the first edited ethnographic film to admit modernity amongst the San, was made at the same time and place as *Gods I*, and includes a scene on the making of Uys's film. The two films intersected each other, each a comment on different paradigmatic moments and ways of representing the San. These films may well articulate two sides of the same coin, the one side now legitimated at the expense of the other.

Film-makers either impose inappropriate aesthetics on 'their' nomads, or they can try to reveal an aesthetic intrinsic to the people being filmed. The cinematic apparatus imposes an aesthetic permitted by the technical properties built into the recording technology. But this aesthetic can be adapted in the course of its travels into stories and places beyond the conceptual boundaries and ideological frames imposed by the dominant media. And herein lies the contradiction:

A travelling aesthetic requires travelling theory and criticism; yet theory and criticism are canonized, and thus become a way of fixing rather than liberating their objects. Nomadic practice thus creates havoc for such an orientation. Intrinsic to the nomadic mode of expression is an ever-constant shifting of form and content and the relationship among them and audience. (Gabriel 1988, p. 74–5)

Myburgh's film has traces of a nomadic aesthetic but he fails to draw it out. *Testament to the Bushmen* suppresses the visuality of the nomadic aesthetic under conventional documentary conventions. The *Gods* films encode the nomadic as a psychic wilderness which exists in the Afrikaner mind only. Only in *The Hunters* does Marshall have any sense of the nomadic – the problem for him thereafter is a question of material San survival.

## Notes

I am greatly indebted to Ruth Tomaselli, Ken Harrow and Patrick Dionne for their critical comments and help in the preparation of this chapter, and to the Human Sciences Research Council, Fulbright, the Smithsonian Institution and the African Studies Center, Michigan State University, for resources to undertake the research.
1    Exceptions are O'Regan (1990) on Eric Michaels; Michaels (1986, 1987); *Media Development* ('Video for the People') 36(4) 1989 and Turner (1990). Most published commentators on questions of accountability would not, however, regard themselves as anthropologists, but as communication scholars.
2    Held in the Human Studies Film Archive, Smithsonian Institution, Washington DC.

## References

*Books and articles*
Asch, T. and Asch, P. (nd), 'Images that Represent Ideas: The Use of Films on the !Kung to Teach Anthropology' in Biesele, M., Gordon, R. and Lee, R. (eds.), *The Past and Future of !Kung Ethnography*, Helmust Buske Verlag, Hamburg.
Barnard, A. (1989), 'The lost world of Laurens van der Post', *Current Anthropology*, XXX, pp. 104–13.
Blythe, M. (1986), 'A Review: *The Gods Must be Crazy*', *UCLA African Studies Center Newsletter*, Spring, pp. 17–21.
Carpenter, F. (1969), *Laurens van der Post*, Twayne, New York.
Clifford, J. (1988), *Predicament of Culture*, Harvard University Press, Cambridge.
Davis, P. (1985), 'The Gods Must be Crazy', *Cineaste*, XIV, pp. 51–3. Also published as 'The Missionary Position: An Analysis of Jamie Uys' *The Gods Must be Crazy*', *Pacific Coast Africanist Newsletter*, IX, (1985), pp, 7–11; and Tomaselli, K.G. and Hennebelle, G. (eds.) (1986), *Le cinéma sud-africaine est-il tombé sur la tête?*, CinemAction, Paris. Literally translated, this title is a pun on *The Gods Must be Crazy*: 'Has South African Cinema Fallen on its Head?'

Gilliam, A. (1984), 'The Gods Must be Crazy', *Interracial Books for Children*, XV, p. 34.

Gabriel, T. (1988), 'Thoughts on Nomadic Aesthetics and the Black Independent Cinema: Traces of a Journey' in Cham, M. and Watkins, C.A. (eds.), *Blackframes: Critical Perspectives on Black Independent Cinema*, MIT, pp. 62–79.

Gordon, R. (1984), 'Conserving Bushmen to extinction'. Paper presented at First World Conference on Culture Parks. Published as 'Conserving Bushmen to extinction: the metaphysics of bushmen hating and empire building', *Survival International Review* (1985), XLIV, pp. 22–42.

Gordon, R. (1990a), 'People of the Great Sandface: People of the Great white Lie', *CVA Review* (Spring), pp. 30–4.

Gordon, R. (1990b), *The Bushman Myth and The Making of the Namibian Underclass*, Mimeo (forthcoming in Westview Press).

Gordon, R. (1990c), 'The prospects for anthropological tourism in Bushmanland', *Cultural Survival Quarterly*, XIV, pp. 1–3.

Hitchcock, R. and Brandenburgh, R. (1990), 'Tourism, Conservation, and Culture in the Kalahari Desert, Botswana', *Cultural Survival Quarterly*, XIV, pp. 20–4.

Howell, N. (1988), 'The Tasaday and the !Kung: reassessing isolated hunter-gatherers', Paper delivered at 53rd Meeting of the Society for American Archaeology, Phoenix Arizona, April.

Lee, R.B. (1985), '*The Gods Must Be Crazy* – but the producers know exactly what they are doing', *Southern Africa Report*, June, pp. 19–20.

Lee, R. and DeVore, I. (1968), *Man the Hunter*, Aldine, Chicago.

Marshall, J. and Ritchie, C. (1984), *Where are the Ju/wasi of Nyae Nyae? Changes in Bushmen Society 1958–1981*, Centre for African Studies, University of Cape Town.

Marshall Cabezas, S. and Nierenberg, J.(1990), *Films and Videos From DER*, DER (Documentary Educational Resources) Watertown, Mass.

Michaels, E. (1987), *For a Cultural Future: Frances Jupurrurla Makes TV*, Artspace, Art and Criticism Series, Sydney.

Michaels, E. (1986), 'The impact of television, videos, and satellites in Aboriginal communities' in Foran, B. and Walker, B. (eds.), *Science and Technology for Aboriginal Development*, Project report No 3 (Canberra, CSIRO).

Muller, J. and Tomaselli, K.G. (1990), 'Becoming appropriately modern: towards a genealogy of cultural studies in South Africa' in Mouton, J. (ed.), *Knowledge and Method in the Social Sciences*, Human Sciences Research Council, Pretoria, pp. 287–305.

Myburgh, J.P. (1989), 'Paul Myburgh talks on People of the Great Sandface: An interview with Keyan Tomaselli', *CVA Review*, (Fall), pp. 26–31.

O'Regan, T. (ed.) (1990), 'Communication and tradition: Essays after Eric Michaels', *Continuum: An Australian Journal of Media Theory*, III.

Reitz, D. quoted in Boydell, T. (1948), *My Luck's Still In*, Stewart, Cape Town.

Rosaldo, R. (1989), 'Imperialist nostalgia', *Representations*, XXVI, pp. 107–21.

Rosenthal, A. (1989/90), 'Review of *Image Ethics*', *Film Quarterly*, XLIII, p. 59.

Rosenthal, A. (1988), *New Challenges for Documentary*, California University Press, Berkeley.

Silberbauer, G. (1981), *Hunter and Habitat in the Central Kalahari Desert*, Cambridge University Press, Cambridge.

Sharp, J.S. (1979), 'Two separate developments: anthropology in South Africa,' *RAIN*, XXXV, pp. 4–5.

Solway, J.S and Lee, R.B. (1990), 'Foragers, genuine or spurious? Situating the Kalahari

San in history', *Current Anthropology*, XXXI.

Thomas Marshall, E. (1959), *The Harmless People*, Vintage, New York.

Tomaselli, K.G. (1990) 'Annoying anthropologists: Jamie Uys's films on 'Bushmen' and animals', *SVA Review* (Spring), pp. 75–80.

Tomaselli, K.G., Gabriel, T., Masilela, N. and Williams, A. (1991), 'A dialogue on autobiography in *People of the Great Sandface.*' Mimeo.

Turner, T. (1990), 'Visual media, cultural politics, and anthropological practice: some implications of recent uses of film and video among the Kayapo of Brazil', *CVA Review* (Spring), pp. 8–12.

Van der Post L. (With Pottiez, J-M) (1986), *A Walk With a White Bushman*, Hogarth Press, London.

Van der Post, L. (1975), *A Mantis Carol*, Island Press, Covelo, Calif.

Van der Post, L. (1961), *The Heart of the Hunter*, Penguin, Harmondsworth.

Volkman, T.A. (1986), 'The hunter-gatherer myth in Southern Africa: preserving nature or culture?', *Cultural Survival Quarterly*, X, pp. 25–32.

Volkman, T.A. (1988), 'Out of Africa: *The Gods Must Be Crazy*' in Gross, L., Katz, J.S. and Ruby, J. (eds.), *Image Ethics: The Moral Rights of Subjects in Photographs, Film and TV*, Oxford, New York, pp. 237–47.

Wilmsen, E.N. (1989), *Land Filled With Flies: A Political Economy of the Kalahari*, Chicago University Press, Chicago.

Wilmsen, E.N. and Denbow, J.R. (1990), 'Paradigmatic history of San-speaking peoples and current attempts at revision', *Current Anthropology*, XXXI, pp. 489–524.

Wiley, D., Cancel, R., Pflugrad, D., Elkiss, T. H. and Campbell, A. (1982), *Africa on Film and Videotape 1960–1981: A Compendium of Reviews*, African Studies Center, Michigan State University, East Lansing.

Yellen, J. (1984), 'The integration of herding into prehistoric hunting and gathering economies' in Hall, M. and Avery, G. (eds.), *Frontiers: Southern African Archaeology Today*. Cambridge University Press, Cambridge.

*Films*

Asch, T. and N. Chagnon (1975), *The Ax Fight*, Documentary Educational Rescources, Watertown, Mass. Colour, 30 mins.

Cradle, E. and J. Grant (1926), *Denver African Expedition*, Universities of Denver and Cape Town, and the South African Museum. Black and white, *c.* 5 hours.

Enfield, C. (1966), *Zulu*, JE Levine Films New York. Colour, 135 mins.

Flaherty, R. (1922), *Nanook of the North*, Révillon Frères, Paris. Black and white, 70 mins.

—— (1934), *Man of Aran*, Gainsborough Pictures. Black and white, 76 mins.

Ivory, J. (1982), *Heat and Dust*, Merchant Ivory Productions UK. Colour, 130 mins.

Lean, D. (1984), *A Passage to India*. EMI, UK. Colour, 163 mins.

Marshall, J. (1956), *The Hunters*. Harvard Film Study Center. Colour, 73 mins.

—— (1980), *N!Ai, the Story of a !Kung Woman*. Documentary Educational Resources, Watertown, Mass. Colour, 59 mins.

—— (1984), *Pull Ourselves Up or Die Out*, Documentary Educational Resources, Watertown, U-Matic, colour, 20 mins.

—— (1986), *!Kung San: Traditional Life*, Documentary Educational Resources, Watertown, Mass. Video, colour, 26 mins.

McGlaglan, A. (1977), *The Wild Geese*, Euon Lloyd Productions, London. Colour, 134 mins.

Myburgh, P. (1985), *People of the Great Sandface*. Anglia Television, 'Survival' Series. Colour, 120 mins.

Pollack, S. (1986), *Out of Africa*, Technovision. Colour, 150 mins.

Tati, J. (1953), *Monsieur Hulot's Holiday*, Cady. Black and white, 91 mins.

Uys, J. (1974), *Beautiful People*, Mimosa Films, Bloemfontein. Colour, 90 mins..

—— (1980), *The Gods Must Be Crazy*, Mimosa Films, Botswana. Colour, 109 mins.

—— (1989), *The Gods Must Be Crazy II*, Mimosa Films, Botswana. Colour.

Van der Post, L. (1959), *Lost World of the Kalahari*, South Africa. Black and white.

—— (1982), *Testament to the Bushmen*. Bellinger-Bermeister, South Africa. 6 x 30 mins.

Wolper, D. (1974), *Bushmen of the Kalahari*. National Geographic Society, Washington, DC. Colour, 52 mins.

# Picturing culture through indigenous imagery: a telling story

From a recent flurry of publications, we can clearly see a growing interest in indigenous image production. Innovative uses of native-generated imagery and the political uses of image communication in general are attracting new areas of research and commentary in visual anthropology. In this paper, I shall take a very broad approach to the existence and understanding of indigenous image-making, perhaps more inclusive than previous discussions but several central themes unite the growing variety of projects. Firstly, where is culture in these forms of camera-generated human representation? Or, where is indigenous culture in indigenous film communication? Several important points of orientation are embedded in this wording. When I comment on indigenous production, for example, I am directing attention to a *process* of image communication, one that includes the dynamic interaction of image-makers, image products, and image audiences. Also, when I refer to film, I try to generalize to include other image forms, including still photography as well as celluloid/filmic (a chemical process), and videotape (an electronic process) models of motion pictures.

   Going one step further, the question becomes, secondly, how is indigenous culture manifest in, or responsible for, the image products that are part of a process of visual communication? As a general question, this is easily asked but too expansive to work through here. I shall limit myself to asking how pictorial texts or certain audiovisual narratives are embedded in cultural contexts.

## Alternative motivations and models of activity

It is now possible to discern several categories of indigenous image production (Chalfen 1989). In some cases, we have examples of what might be called coerced image production – when social scientists have offered cameras to native members of communities for 'pure' research objectives (if such may be said to exist). In still photography we can cite the studies of Robert Ziller *et al.* (1977, 1981) and, in film, the studies of Worth and Adair (1972), Bellman and Jules-Rosette (1977), Carpenter (1972) as well as my own work with teenagers living in Philadelphia (1981).

In other instances, the focus of study has been on what native peoples are doing with their new methods of image communication, including new uses of videotape technology. Here I would include observations of the practices of neighbourhood still photographers in Yoruba made by Stephen Sprague (1978), as well as more recent articles on indigenous videographers by Joyce Hammond, who studied Tongans living in Utah (1988), by Jayasinhji Jhala who focused his studies in the Surendranager District in India (1989), and my study of home videotapes made in Philadelphia (1988).

In yet another growing collection of activity, we find attention being given to action-oriented projects with more overt political implications. This work often focuses on how locally made films and videotapes are being used by indigenous community members, primarily groups of Brazilian Indians, Inuits, and Australian Aborigines. Examples are found in the publications of Kennedy (1982), Carelli (1988), Michaels (1985a, 1985b), Ginsburg (1989), Turner (1990) and Gray (1988), among others. Faye Ginsburg summarises:

almost always, the first activities with the camera are both assertive and conservative of identity: documenting injustices and claiming reparations, making records of the lives and knowledge of elders who witnessed the often violent destruction of life as they had known it – from recording food gathering and hunting techniques, to dramatizing dream time stories, to recreating historically traumatic events for the camera. (1989, p. 19)

In one of the better accounts of research in this category, Terence Turner reports on his work in Brazil:

The Kayapo have used their own capacity for video in a variety of ways: The documentation of their own traditional culture, above all ceremonial performances; secondly, the recording of important events and actions such as the Altamira demonstration, or the capture of the gold mines of Maria Bonita and transactions with Brazilians, so as to have the equivalent of a legally binding transcript of business contracts or political agreements (for example, the negotiations of contracts with air taxi pilots for the supply of the captured gold mines); and fourthly, as an organizing tool. An example of the latter was the appeal of the assembled Kayapo chiefs for attendance at the Altamira demonstration, which was videotaped at the close of their planning meeting at Gorotire to be sent around to other Kayapo and non Kayapo native communities. (1990, p. 9)

This particular model of work could go in several important and far-reaching directions. One logical extension would be to study relationships between communications technologies and cultural transformations. Here we would be reading the work of Jack Goody (1977) and Benedict Anderson (1983) for print literacy, as well as that of Raymond Williams (1975) and Todd Gitlin (1986) for the implications of innovated televisual communication. In discussing indigenous media production among the Kayapo, Turner states:

If the Kayapo are any indication, the processes of cultural and ethnic self-conscientization that have been catalyzed by the new media and their use in world-wide networks of communication are becoming far more important as a component of 'culture' (or, by the same token, 'ethnicity') both in the sense of becoming more complex and rapidly developing and in that of becoming more central to basic social and political processes. The nature of 'culture' itself is changing together with the techniques we employ to study and document it. This is a phenomenon that calls for more study and documentation by anthropologists than it has thus far received. (1990, p. 13)

Relationships of indigenous imagery and systems of mass communication are clearly attracting the most enthusiasm at the present time. Anthropologists and communication scholars are being drawn to a relatively new area of visual anthropology, a collection of theory, observation, and practice that can lead in several directions.

## The need to know the cultural context

This paper is a kind of cautionary tale. It will make a simple point in a straight-forward manner. While we are fascinated by the fact that it is not 'us' making these films, should we not go further to gain knowledge of specifically *who* is behind the camera, *what* is being said, and *how* ideas are being expressed? It is not enough to think of the generalised Navajo, Kayapo, American teenage movie-maker, American home movie-maker, Tongan or Indian videographer, and so on. Image makers are people embedded in personal and public histories and in particular socio-cultural contexts.

How do we really know what has been done or what we have in an audio-visual message form without adequate knowledge of potentially different kinds of expression and reports from different socio-political-cultural sectors of a community? Is it possible that different people, located in different socio-cultural sectors of the community, see and report the world in different ways? This would lead us to ask how the subculture, ethnicity or socio-political position of the person(s) behind the camera is related to, or influences and maybe determines, the version of life we get to see in the film/videotape. In a related context, we might examine the ways people express ideas in an audio-visual medium and, in turn, how these 'ways' are tied to socio-cultural features surrounding the pro-duction and use of the image product. Admittedly, these concerns overtly focus less on empowerment and political issues; in this perspective, more attention is given to a semiotics of representation, or what I have called 'correlational sociovidistics'(1981).

## From image culture to narrative

During the past fifteen years, I have been most concerned with the structure of the pictorial renditions of life produced by ordinary people with cameras. I have been studying *audio-visual narratives* as a relationship of what Nelson Goodman would see as ways the world 'is given' and ways it is taken (1972, pp. 25–27). I have been observing what happens when people use their camera-voices instead of, or in addition to, their pencils and paper or tape recorders.

My ethnographic research on indigenous image production falls within the general area of the anthropology of visual communication (Worth, 1976) and, more specifically, within the realm of what Margaret Blackman has recently called 'the culture of imaging.' In her introduction to Banta and Hinsley's *From Site to Sight – Anthropology, Photography, and the Power of Imagery* (1986), Blackman calls attention to the changing patterns of belief and behaviour brought to making, viewing and understanding photographic images within the context of anthropology (1986, p. 11). I have stepped out of the confines of anthropological image-making into the real lives of ordinary people and have offered notions of 'Kodak culture and Polaroid people.' Later, I shall attempt to integrate these terms more fully.

## Picturing culture

I am also following some leads and ideas suggested by such titles as *Writing Culture*, edited by Clifford and Marcus (1986), *Talking Culture* (1988) by Michael Moreman and, as suggested most recently, *Picturing Cultures* by Joanna Scherer (1990). Interestingly, in his introduction to *Writing Culture*, James Clifford acknowledges that it is easy to overlook photography, film, performance theory, documentary art, the non-fiction novel, 'the new journalism' and oral history, among others (1986, p. 19). In a sense, this paper is picking up on one component of this neglect and I anticipate hopefully that much more will be said in the next few years.

In addition, psychologist Halla Beloff has even titled her 1985 book *Camera Culture*, though she offers little explicit clarification of this term. Upon some reflection, we realize that there are many subcultures of imaging and that we know relatively little about them as a collective. With regard to still images, for instance, I am calling attention to the variety of pictorial forms represented by such examples as photojournalism, fine art photography and wedding photography; and commercial forms (e.g. advertising photography) as well as amateur forms such as 'photo-club' photography and snapshots, to mention just a few.

More to the point, I have been studying the construction of native-generated pictorial forms *as an ethnographic problem*. How are certain constructions of photographic imagery related to the social and cultural contexts in which they originated and are used? What in life helps to structure the native's construction of audio-visual texts and audio-visual narrative forms?

Before going further, a word about the term 'audio-visual' might be helpful. This is an awkward term because of technological connotations, usually anti-intellectual, as in 'audio-visual aides', the 'A-V department', or, as one of my undergraduate anthropology advisers once said, 'Oh, yes, Chalfen, you're the one who went on into A-V'. The fact remains that when we speak of images, in virtually all cases we are simultaneously referencing some form of verbal accompaniment, be it written or spoken. A second orienting principle is that we are seldom, if ever, asked to deal with single images. We seem 'to take' our pictures in groups, most commonly in sequences, and always in social contexts of encoding and decoding. All of this has important implications for literal understandings of how image communication is related to storytelling, narrative and even discourse.

Given this background information, we may now turn to explicit and implicit demands of camera technologies and of image genres, and to how they contribute to the pictures people create and the statements they make about themselves through their own pictures. What goes into the structuring of these narrative forms? People use cameras and, in a sense, cameras use people. I have decided to adopt an autobiographical orientation for the telling of this story, describing some of my personal experiences and the examples that I have gathered in past and current research.

### Student documentary film laboratory

One of the first examples comes from my participation as a graduate student in a documentary film-making laboratory directed by Sol Worth in 1965. This year-long course was given at the Annenberg School of Communications at the University of Pennsylvania. Students worked in pairs as they wrote, directed, filmed and edited a 16mm black and white film, usually for the first time (Worth 1963). After a few semesters, Professor Worth began to sense patterns in the ways this group of white, middle and upper-middle class male and female graduate students organised their film communication and selected subject-matter for their films. Students could select any theme and topic, as long as they stayed within their budgets and the one year time restriction.

More importantly, he began studying what this group of people wanted to communicate and, in turn, what they were simultaneously saying and revealing about themselves, both intentionally and unintentionally. In the early 1960s Worth developed a notion of 'bio-documentary film' which he described as:

a film made by a person to show how he (or she) feels about himself (or herself) and his (or her) world. It is a subjective way of showing what the objective world that a person sees is really like. . . . In addition . . . it often captures feelings and reveals values and attitudes that lie beyond the conscious control of the maker.

The bio-documentary is a film made by a person who is not a professional film-maker; by someone who has never made a film before. It is a film that can be made by anyone; by a person . . . who has been taught in a specific way to make a film that helps him [or her] to communicate to us the world as he (or she) sees it. (1964, pp. 3–4)

Worth added a comment especially relevant to narrative studies: '. . .In part, this kind of film bears the same relation to documentary film that a self-portrait has to a portrait or a biography to an autobiography' (1972, p. 25). He felt that, if looked at in the right way, one could see how these students were communicating as much information about themselves (in what he called 'feeling concerns') as about the specific topics of their films.

Interestingly, Worth's students took a very indirect route to speaking about themselves, possibly disguised in unconscious ways. Worth noted that when making their first films, these students structured their filmic narratives in elliptical or ambiguous ways (1965, p. 4). In a related strategy of being indirect, most of them chose unfamiliar people and places for their films, subjects that were not themselves but rather collections of 'others.' They sought representatives of unfamiliar exotic subcultures within or just outside the city of Philadelphia, including gospel preachers, tugboat captains, mentally-ill children, semi-professional boxers, etc.; not too unlike, by the way, what social scientists and anthropological film-makers working in American culture might select. In short, they exhibited something like an ethnographic impulse to say something about others and, in turn, themselves. We should recognise here that these students chose *not* to turn their cameras on their own living conditions, their families, or on their physical selves in any direct manner. They maintained their presence behind the camera's viewfinder, holding the tape recorder's microphone, and at the editing table. Clearly, making a movie meant *constructing a film*, not becoming a 'star' on the silver screen.

### The Navajo film-making project

The next chapter of this story takes place during the summer of 1966 when Sol Worth and John Adair introduced bio-documentary film-making procedures into the Navajo community of Pine Springs, Arizona. As a second-year graduate student, I was fortunate enough to serve as a research assistant throughout the project. Here the agenda was marked by an explicit attempt to examine potential links between Navajo cognition, culture and films made by Navajos for the first time (Worth and Adair 1972). As part of a participant-innovation-observation process, film instruction was done in a non-direct manner. We deliberately avoided making statements about what these films should be about, who and what should be filmed and how their footage should be structured and/or edited. While we offered to drive them to any location of their own choosing, each of the six Navajo film-makers decided to make their films in the community. They selected processes and products that were immediately familiar, including rug weaving, silversmithing, giving a curing ceremony and making a shallow well. We found that all of the Navajo films shared a pattern of narrative characteristics unlike that found in first films made by Anglo-Americans. They certainly were *not*, as one professor of documentary film tried to persuade me, 'just like anyone else's home movies.'

This project offered a unique opportunity to contrast and compare what anthropologists had written about Navajos and what the Navajo film-makers elected to show us about themselves through their own films. Of particular interest, we had a chance to study the literature on narrative styles that characterized Navajo myths, folktales and storytelling in general, and to compare these statements to the structure of narratives developed in their films. In one particular case, available materials let us compare narratives underlying both an anthropologist's and a Navajo's telling of a silversmith at work. In the Navajo-made film, for instance, Johnny Nelson included activities and scenes that were totally absent from John Adair's 1938 film on silversmithing. The most obvious example is the attention that silversmith John Baloo gives to searching for materials to be used in the process – silver nuggets, sandstone for the cast – and the amount of walking required to do this. Patterns of searching and looking are different, patterns of showing and telling are different. When John Adair asked Johnny Nelson: 'Why did you have a silver mine [in the film] when the Navajo never mined silver?' Johnny replied, 'That's the way to tell the story' (1972, pp. 152, 206).

Much has been said about the unusual amounts of Navajo footage given to scenes of walking – unusual, that is, to Western eyes, expectations, and conventions of documentary film narrative. Scenes of Navajos walking emphasised an event or act in itself, rather than as more common to Anglo films, a bridge between activities. Worth and Adair do a good job of explaining this finding by relating it to the Navajo 'extreme sense of motion' (1972, p. 204), of 'eventing' as explained by Harry Hoijer (1951) and to a narrative style characteristic of many myths, tales and stories that emphasise travel and where the 'long journey' is a central theme (1972, p. 205). Worth and Adair state:

What we are suggesting here is that people within the context of their culture have different codes for 'saying' different things, that one's cognitive system might well employ a meta-code or program that would relate the rules for one mode of communication to rules for the other. . . . [W]e seem to have some evidence that the *rules of Navajo myth and storytelling* are more relevant to showing events like . . . making silver jewelry . . . than are the 'real' events that occur when these activities are actually performed. (1972, p. 152; emphasis in original)

So, here, the structure of the filmic telling is developed in part through the organisation of other codes and narratives embedded within the culture. This finding is particularly appealing and indicates, in my view, that more attention should be focused on how cross-code relationships operate in culturally structured ways.

### The Philadelphia teenage film-making project

In 1967, directly after the Navajo project, I initiated research about a similar set of questions within the city of Philadelphia. My sense at that time was that one did not need to travel 2000 miles to a non-Western, Fourth World context to discover additional information on relationships between filmic expression and culture. The heterogeneity of subcultures within a complex society provided ample opportunities, especially within the fourth largest city in the United States.

In the Philadelphia work, I asked a series of groups of teenagers to make 16mm black and white films on subjects of their own choosing. Here I wanted to see *if* and *how* such variables as gender, ethnicity and social class played roles in the ways these young people told about themselves. I was specifically interested both in the content and form of their filmic narratives and in the ways different groups of people decided to organise themselves to complete this communicative task. I borrowed and applied Worth's non-directive teaching methods, associated with the bio-documentary, to work with small five-member groups of teenagers. Since I was working with groups of people and since I intuitively believed that ideas for films were derived more from the social rather than the idiosyncratic – that authorship was a social affair – I took the liberty of transforming the bio-documentary into the 'socio-documentary' (Chalfen 1981, p. 4).

One logical expectation was that all the films would look nearly the same – after all, the teenagers were all the same ages (between 13 and 16), they were all taught film-making by the same person using the same instructions with identical types of equipment (also identical, by the way, to the equipment used in Worth's documentary film workshop and in the Navajo Project). At the other extreme, thinking that film was such a personal medium of expression and the possibilities were infinite, one might have predicted all films to be distinctly different.

However, neither of these extreme alternatives emerged. It appears that subcultural factors played crucial roles in the structuring of these filmic narratives, where the teenagers put themselves in the communications process and the kinds of stories they preferred to tell about themselves in relation to their lives and surroundings.

Perhaps one of the more provocative findings of the Philadelphia work was the emergence of two distinctly different structures of filmic narrative in conjunction with two different statements about the film-makers or, if you prefer, different models of discourse. Young people from two dissimilar subcultures produced two dissimilar but internally consistent patterns of film communication. Specifically, film-making subjects from black and lower socioeconomic backgrounds preferred *to use and manipulate themselves and familiar aspects of their immediate environment*. In contrast, the white and more affluent subjects preferred *to use and manipulate images of unfamiliar things and unknown people found in areas away from their familiar environment.* This latter pattern had a lot in common with the results provided by the graduate students in Worth's film-making laboratory. Might we speculate on a dominant pattern in film narrativity in middle-class America?

To summarise from the overall project, I found the social class variable to be more significant than either ethnicity or gender. The films and production styles of males and females and of blacks and whites *within the same social class* were closer to one another than the patterns that emerged for the middle-class vs. lower-class groups. These findings reveal several important relationships to research on class and ethnic variables. For instance, one is a direct connection between a preference for manipulating symbolic events – as in film-making – and a feeling for control over one's environment. A desire and ability actually to explore and manipulate an environment of natural events may correlate with a preference for exploring and manipulating symbolic events. Thus, a behind-camera orientation would be more natural for people in more dominant or powerful positions in the social order. Clearly the teenagers from white middle-class backgrounds assumed this position in the implicitly realised politics of film-making as a symbolic form of communicative activity. They came from families who are in the business of 'calling the shots', meaning doing the hiring and firing, or working independently in white-collar professions. As often noted, the power positions in film production lie in behind-camera activities and editing but not in on-camera appearances. In short, narrative styles and cultural messages proved to be linked to social factors. The meta-messages of films made by these two socio-culturally different groups are very different. Members of the lower-class group were saying 'Look at Me' while the higher-class group preferred to say 'Look at Me See'.

Might additional evidence of this difference in narrative stance be found in verbal renderings? What has been said about other communicative codes that might be co-ordinated with these findings? In a 1955 article on social class and modes of communication, sociologists Leonard Schatzman and Anselm Strauss compared the ways that middle-class and working-class interviewees structured descriptions of a tornado. Using a metaphor compatible with this paper, the authors say:

In short, the middle class respondent . . . figuratively . . . stands between his own images and the hearer and says, 'Let me introduce you to what I saw and know.' *It is as though he were directing a movie, having at his command several cameras focused at different perspectives, shooting and carefully controlling the effect.* By contrast, the lower-class respondent seems himself *more like a single camera which unreels the scene to the audience.* In the very telling of the story he is more apt to lose himself in his imagery. The middle class person . . . stands more outside his experience. He does not so much tell you what he saw as fashion a story about what he saw. (1966, p. 446; emphasis added)

All such statements must be evaluated very carefully. But this code-class alignment, as described by Schatzman and Strauss, was seen in a literal sense in the filmic narratives made by different groups of teenagers in Philadelphia.

The authors of another sociolinguistic study found similar relationships between social class, 'stance' and narrative style. In 1989 Dennie Wolf and Deborah Hicks compared the verbal narratives of two seven-year-old girls. One girl, Malka, came from a white upper middle-class social milieu and attended a private school, both of which emphasised literacy-related activities; the second girl, Rene, came from a black working-class background and attended a public school. When both girls were asked to re-tell the story contained in a film they had both seen, their storytelling narratives differed in ways consistent with previous examples. Malka, the middle-class respondent, 'assumed the outside voice (perspective) of the narrator and maintains this particular stance through-out . . . In sum, it seems that Malka takes the stance of a *spectator* as she narrates the events from the film' (Wolf and Hicks 1989, pp. 345, 347).

In comparison, Rene, the working-class girl, demonstrated less of a report of events and more of a *participatory* stance towards events in her narrative, making extensive use of dialogue strands (1989, p. 348). In their summary, Wolf and Hicks state:

Malka assumes greater distance from events occurring in her replica play, narrating actions in a voice of a narrator . . . – in short, the *when* and *why* of what happened. Rene takes a somewhat different stance, narrating events in part from the perspective of a narrator but in part from the perspective of the characters involved in the action. Some of the important events on the story are recounted through the eyes of the characters involved. (1989, p. 349)

These findings sound suspiciously like the alternative perspectives mentioned by Schatzman and Strauss and similar to the narrative patterns demonstrated by the Philadelphia film-makers. Wolf and Hicks conclude that their findings are 'like many other aspects of narrative competence, highly sensitive to sociocultural variation in terms of how separate voices are used to encode events' (1989, p. 349). I continue to search for studies that will better illustrate these comparisons and explain certain variations, studies that will also offer collaborative evidence both for correlations across verbal and visual codes and ties between social class and narrative forms.

## Home mode pictorial communication

So far I have been reviewing examples of indigenous image-making generated in experimental contexts, where audio-visual texts have been coerced into existence. This approach is subject to the occasional criticism that one cannot teach the technology of image production in a manner that is free of culture or ideology. We might, therefore, turn to instances of picture-taking which are culturally so well embedded and institutionalized that data are produced as part of everyday life.

If we remain film-centric, this brings us to the symbolic world of home movies, family films and 'cinema naivete' (Chalfen 1975). But the larger context of this image-making activity includes materials that fit into what I have elsewhere called 'home mode communication.' Examples of home mode *verbal* communication would include such personal forms as diary and journal writing, personal letter and postcard writing and taped-letter communication, among others. In *pictorial* forms I would include snapshots (including print and slide formats), family albums, home movies and, most recently, home videotapes. The drawback here is that we do not have the opportunity to observe the actual ('natural' or otherwise) production of the texts, so new attention must be given to reconstructing the origins of the materials.

Perhaps my most serious efforts to develop notions of picturing culture and the culture of imaging are found in a book entitled *Snapshot Versions of Life* (1987). This title was a compromise – my original choice was 'Kodak Culture and Polaroid People.' Aside from the playful aspects of this phrase and its euphonically pleasing qualities, I had in mind something rather serious, a point that lends itself to the themes of this chapter. By Kodak culture I meant

whatever it is that one has to learn, know, or do in order to participate appropriately in what has been outlined as the home mode of pictorial communication . . . By studying Kodak culture, we want to learn how people have *organized themselves* socially to produce personalized versions of their own life experiences. In turn we want to consider how ordinary people have *organized their thinking* about personal pictures in order to understand certain pictorial messages and make meaningful interpretations in appropriate ways . . . (and) how Kodak culture provides a structured and patterned way of looking (and showing) the world in terms of reality construction and interpretation. (1987, p. 10; emphasis in original)

Within this area of amateur photography, most people seem to believe that technology somehow promotes unified and standardised ways of 'speaking about' or showing the world – in short, that 'people don't take pictures, cameras do'. This is an unfortunate twist on a frequently quoted title originally provided by anthropologist Paul Byers when he insisted 'Cameras Don't Take Pictures' (1966). The thinking is that once you've seen one snapshot or home movie, you've seen them all, implying that social differences between people using these mass consumer cameras do *not* make a difference. I am reminded here that Kodak advertises itself as 'America's Storyteller.'

In one study I examined consumer-oriented guidebooks and manuals for advice on how to structure home movies, that is, how to create correct and proper narratives in this genre. Specifically I noted prescriptions for planning, shooting, appearing in and exhibiting home movies. Comparing this advice to what is found in 'authentic' home movies, I discovered a reciprocal non-overlapping pattern of emphasis. The guides stressed attention to planning and scripting home movies, camera work and even editing techniques. In dramatic contrast, from the films I saw and the home movie-makers I spoke with, emphases were put on appearing *in* these movies and in *being seen* during the screening of the movies. In short the prescribed paradigm did *not* describe the norms for actual behaviour (Chalfen 1987, p. 57).

In a related finding, the manuals promoted a narrative structure that emphasied *the manipulation of real-life everyday reality*. Home movie-makers on the other hand seem to emphasise the use of their cameras *to record, document, and reproduce a preferred reality*, a telling of it 'like it is.' Here it is interesting to note that the 'naive' home movie-maker embraces the view of film-making often promulgated by social scientists of certain schools, namely that editing is 'bad', planning the subjects' activity is taboo, objectivity is destroyed by heavy-handed editing, and so on. And yet few of us would be willing to say that anthropological film-makers should take their lessons on narrative structure from 'unsophisticated' home movie-makers.

It thus appears that home movie-makers have their own ways of telling stories of home and family-relevant life. Conventions of this narrative form did *not* imitate conventions of established documentary film practice; *home movies imitated home movies* with great consistency.

## Snapshots and family albums

Still photographic examples of home mode communication have been examined much more than home movies by scholars in social history, art history, folklore, sociology, American studies, photographic criticism and communication. But virtually no one has analyzed snapshot collections or family albums as *stories we tell to ourselves about ourselves.* What do ordinary people use this medium to say? How is the narrative organised, and how is the communication fashioned?

Collections of snapshots, made and used within white middle-class America – the group I have studied the most – are remarkably well-structured in terms of content and form. When groups of snapshot images are ordered into family albums, photograph custodians usually let time tell the tale. A natural chronology provides the answer to problems of sequence and ordering. Yet the dimensions of these pictorial narratives are amazingly restricted and constrained, given the infinite possibilities of topics and settings that people *could* select and that cameras *can* record. This symbolically realised world favours, for example, events and activities that occur in the first years of life but not the last years; it favours being young but not getting old, getting married but not divorced, new possessions rather than old and damaged ones, first times rather than last times. Pictorial life stories and narratives are characterised by such clichés as putting one's best foot forward, showing the sunny not the seamy side of life, illustrating life's thrills of victory without any agonies of defeat. They reflect the maxim used by Ronald Reagan in his TV ads for General Electric in the 1950s, 'Progress is our most important product'.

Some of the earliest social science commentary on amateur photography is found in Pierre Bourdieu's relatively little known book, *Un Art Moyen* (1965). This contains results of research on amateur photographic practice in the early 1960s done in several areas surrounding Paris. Bourdieu suggested that 'amateur photography only existed most of the time because of its function within the family' and that 'one of the principal functions of amateur photography was to solemnize and eternalize the great moments of family life, to reinforce the integration of the family group by celebrating itself in pictures' (Grace *et al.* 1977, p. 44). Family-oriented photographic ritual was, he wrote, common to all social classes.

But are all social classes telling the same stories in this pictorial genre? Are narratives and texts from different social classes structured in similar ways? My impression is that differences *do* exist with regard to choice of subject-matter (people, places, events, activities), relationships between people participating on-camera and behind-camera, and what is regarded as an appropriate 'presentation of self' on-camera. The great majority of working-class snapshots, for example, focus on people who are usually members of nuclear or extended families. Humans dominate these narratives, both in terms of the view and the show. Most of the people in these pictures, furthermore, are looking directly at the camera and are smiling most of the time.

Middle-class snapshots and albums contain more variety. They, too, feature family members but they also include such non-human topics as landscape, objects of nature, animals (even animals other than the family pet), buildings and the like. It also appears that middle-class family photographers and their subjects do *not* insist on smiling faces; a variety of facial expressions and moods can be appropriately included in this view. In short, these two groups may be telling relatively the same kinds of stories about themselves in terms of general themes, but they are doing it in different ways. Is it fair to say that different narratives – including voices, registers, tones, repertoires of expressions – are apparent? In a sense, the environmental topography of these two gazes *differed* across the two symbolic worlds produced by these two social classes.

These tentative findings seem to be corroborated by some of Bourdieu's work in France in the 1960s:

That the working class happily confined themselves to photographing their families on family occasions indicated the limited range of aspirations that constituted working 'class-ness.' And that the predisposition to explore only the most immediate possibilities was determined by the limited objective economic and social conditions of the working class. Their photographic practice was fed back into the reproduction of the objectively subordinate economic and social position.

Middle class practice, in comparison, was far more ambitious insofar as it attempted to expand the range of subject matter that could be photographed. This was a practical realization of those aspirations and dispositions which characterized the middle class. (Grace *et al.* 1977, pp. 46–7)

In this way, Bourdieu speculates on how amateur photographic practice both reflects and constitutes different class characteristics and reproduces social relations. I am not prepared to go that far at the moment. A close reading of Bourdieu's *Distinction* (1984) may, however, turn this around; here he examines relationships between the structure of social class and systems of classifications which structure perception of the social world and designate the objects of aesthetic enjoyment: 'Taste classifies, and it classifies the classifier' (1984, p. 6). More work is clearly needed.

Alan Thomas, an historian, noted another correlation between social class and photographic representation in a sample of Victorian family photograph albums (1977):

From the selection and arrangement [of photographs] emerges a tone which suggests the personality of the album's owner (just as the personality of an author can be sensed behind a prose narrative), and because the images we see are actual, located in time, space and social class, a sense of that particular world – a social statement, in short – also emerges. (p. 43)

Thomas examines, among others, 'the Waterloo album' from the world of middle-class trade and commerce, the album of Emma Mary Hoyle, representing the landed gentry, and 'the Wimpole album' of the Countess of Hardwicke, representing the aristocratic layer of Victorian society. In his summary overview, he states:

These albums run true to type: the conventional ideas associated with these three distinct social classes of the Victorian period emerge clearly and, one might almost write, predictably: aristocratic assurance, the narrow, rather unimaginative range of vision of the landed gentry, the drive of the rising bourgeois family. To what extent, one wonders, are the owners of these albums responding to a prevailing idea or image of themselves? It is virtually impossible to answer such a question. But obviously, the family photograph album encourages self-perception and a certain degree of objectification of self and family; the figures in its pages play out, as it were, roles and stories to an audience of family and friends. Naturally it is possible for the owners to shape these stories, in conformity, of course, with the date, and guided by prevailing ideas of what the facts mean. (1977, p. 57)

These are studies of still photography, but why might we not expect similar findings for motion pictures? In any event, research along these lines definitely illustrates a sub-culturally sensitive set of factors which has previously been overlooked.

### Japanese American family photography

What happens when we leave Anglo-American examples and examine home mode narratives generated in other cultural contexts? Herein lies the next part of my story. In 1983 Lynne Horiuchi asked me to join a National Endowment for the Humanities sponsored project that resulted in a travelling exhibition entitled *Turning Leaves: The Photograph Collections of Two Japanese American Families*. (The Results of this project will appear in a monograph of the same title, to be published by the University of New Mexico Press, April 1991.) One objective was to see how first (*Issei*) and second (*Nisei*) generation Japanese Americans used their cameras and their own family photographs to see and retain their immigration experiences and periods of early citizenship in the United States.

We discovered that both collections of family photographers shared an attention to six topics. Specifically, both the Nagano and the Uyeda/Miyamura photograph collections contained significant numbers of photographs devoted to family relationships, school, church, sports, work and death, including shots of funerals and trips to the cemetery (Chalfen 1988b, p. 13). Some of these topics, such as attention to family, are not surprising at all. However, other topics presented us with marked contrasts to Anglo-American picture collections, as in their pictures of church, work, death and, to some extent, school. In this medium of home mode expression, narrative that includes the importance of a family member's classroom, work and/or a funeral, including subsequent care of the gravesite, were totally appropriate and maybe even expected. We also discovered that the photographers in our study showed a preference for recording last moments – such as farewell gatherings, last times together – rather than first ones. Japanese American family photographers therefore told several different stories in slightly different ways. Across cultures, then, these pictorial narratives may *not* be all the same.

### Home video versions of life

Within the past decade, the home mode has been given 'new life'. The celluloid model of home movies has virtually disappeared, even after synchronized sound was added to Super-8 equipment and after Polaroid floundered with their seriously flawed Polavision (an instant home movie system). Now, however, the videotape model of home moviemaking has emerged, in some cases, with a vengeance. We are currently witnessing a rapid and accelerating penetration of this technology into consumer culture and the rituals of everyday life. Attention must now be given to 'Sony Society'.

Few have paused to consider the cultural significance and potential consequences of this audio-visual capability. Never before have we been able to record and retain as much audio-visual detail about ourselves. This, in turn, may re-focus a line of questioning relevant to all instances of indigenous image-making. What stories do ordinary people now tell about themselves and what kinds of information can they preserve with this relatively new recording technology? What versions of life can we hold on to, and pass on to future generations that we could not or did not want to retain previously? Or is contemporary home videotaping just a case of old wine in new bottles?

Not having conducted any structured study of these questions, I can only offer a few random observations and some preliminary thoughts. In 1987, I solicited examples of home videomaking from Philadelphia residents as part of the 'First Philadelphia Home Video Festival' (Chalfen 1988a). Several examples of work relevant to themes of this chapter were contributed for screening. I recall such scenes as children and parents seated around a Christmas tree, telling stories and recounting past holidays, family members doing the week's laundry, a child's room by room tour of the family's three-floor house, among others. I have seen examples of grandchildren making videotaped interviews of grandparents, concentrating on earliest memories of immigration. Some of these tapes even used family photographs for purposes of elicitation. In one case, a 101-year-old woman was driven around the neighbourhood where she was born and pointed out personally significant landmarks and described details of change. I have also seen people initiate examples of cultural revival and revitalisation because a family member purchased a camcorder. Activity is occurring at both ends of life – more moment/process-of-birth tapes appear as well as life-after-life tapes. One elderly man, for example, made a videotaped message to be shown to family members after his death. My general impression is that people are finding this mass-consumer video technology well suited to autobiographic and biographic impulses. It appears that new chapters will have to be added to books like *Lives: An Anthropological Approach to Biography* (Langness and Frank 1981).

The question remains: Can this new technology provoke new narrative forms in which we construct and reconstruct knowledge and, in turn, create and recreate ourselves?

### An alternative view

Some comments made by Edmund Carpenter (1972), a sensitive observer, are at odds with what I have written above. He describes many experiences in New Guinea, where he had been employed to find more effective uses for electronic media. He says that government administrators 'viewed media as neutral tools and they viewed themselves as men who could be trusted to use them humanely' (1972, pp. 190–191). Carpenter introduced a variety of new media including still and motion picture cameras, and asked members of several communities to make their own films:

I've recorded life histories extracted from informants. I've encouraged those who were literate to write their own. Since around 1960, I've put cameras in a variety of hands. The results generally *tell more about the medium employed than about the cultural background of the author or cameraman.*

In each case I had hoped the informant would present his own culture in a fresh way & perhaps even use the medium itself in a new way. I was wrong. What I saw was literacy and film. *These media swallow culture.* The old culture was there all right, but no more than residue at the bottom of a barrel. (1972, p. 182, emphasis added)

The first part of this quotation takes us back to Blackman's comment presented at the beginning of this paper – we are always dealing with a relationship of 'what's happening' in front of the camera and 'what's going on' behind the camera, in both literal and metaphoric terms. But here we get a sense of media determinacy and a tie to the previously mentioned notion of camera culture, but, in my opinion, in too strong a dose.

Examples of research presented in this paper offer another perspective on Carpenter's 'residue', if, indeed, 'the old culture' can be credited with no more status than that of residue. I am certainly not arguing that media equipment is neutral: there are biases built into camera equipment and film stock (Potts 1979). People and culture must, however, be put back into the photographic process to counteract the idea that cameras foster or even force a sense of homogeneous narrative into existence. The message that 'cameras don't take pictures' must be maintained.

## Conclusion

I have suggested, as has been recognised before, that film practice is indeed influenced by culture. But while it is easy enough to say that indigenous media and native models of image communication are culturally 'related', it is another matter to demonstrate how culture plays a significant role at virtually all points in the dynamic process that constitutes visual communication. I have also speculated that relating film practice to culture is a lot more complex than a taken-for-granted dismissal of the issue would allow. I have suggested that we must resist the idea of cultural homogeneity and accept that any culture will be internally pluralistic. This in turn suggests a complexity of representational styles and models.

The task of relating film to culture requires that we think less in terms of media production and more in terms of media *communication.* We need more case studies that focus on how, often within the same culture, people organise themselves and their thinking to participate in visual communication, how communicative products are put together and how examples of mediated communication are shown and seen. This redirects our attention to other themes, to patterns and relationships of codes, conventions, and contexts that render indigenous imagery meaningful.

The second purpose of my paper has been to focus on cross-code relationships. The examples that I have cited offer an overview of how an integrated culture and communication approach may be applied. The contrasts and comparisons illustrated above begin to clarify the role narrative structure plays in this behaviour and how pictorial channels of communication are tied to non-pictorial ones.

I have also suggested that much important work remains to be done on how codes of narrative expression are linked to one another. Indigenous ways of telling find expression through alternative channels and codes which are not isolated from one another but connected in culturally structured ways. According to this thinking, it is easier to conclude that media *do not* swallow cultures, especially mediated versions of life and narratives produced in personal, non-professional contexts. We may need to work harder, learning to see how, in fact, this does not happen. Later in his article, Carpenter repeats the point cited above: 'I think media are so powerful they swallow cultures. I think of them as invisible environments which surround and destroy old environments . . . media play no favorites: they conquer all cultures' (1972, p. 191). This is too simple. The examples in this paper indicate a heterogeneity of indigenous film expression rather than an amalgamated homogeneous one. One reason is that storytelling, in the broad sense used throughout this paper, comes in many shapes and forms. I am finding that socio-cultural diversity plays itself out in a diversity of 'tellings', whether in the literal sense of 'stories' or the more general sense of narrative performance and communication behaviour.

In this effort, it is helpful to think of film-making less in terms of film with a capital F and more in the contexts of representation, expression, and narrative. Preoccupation with professional practice, broadcast standards, and models of mass communication is very distracting. The type of analysis suggested in this paper requires a keen awareness of the pushes and pulls of dominant media practice, which potentially influence indigenous narrative structure. Here I am reminded of a recent example from contemporary American culture. Home videographers have reported a tendency to shape their tapes of family life in ways that they hope might win $100,000 if the tape were selected for broadcast on *America's Funniest Home Videos*. This may be an apt example of swallowing, in more ways than one.

The examples in this chapter illustrate the potential complexity of the relationship between culture, media, and narrative. My comments have addressed the presumed transparency of the medium: it is only transparent if viewers endorse a belief system that treats it that way. This research on indigenous image-making barely scratches the surface of understanding relationships between culturally structured lenses, socially developed pictorial narratives and a situationally sensitive process of audio-visual communication. We still have much to learn about how narrative articulates with communicative codes and mediated representation, and whether anthropologists are an important part of the communication process or not.

## References

Anderson, B. (1983), *Imagined Communities*, Verso, London.

Bellman, B. and Jules-Rosette, B. (1977), *A Paradigm for Looking: Cross-Cultural Research with Visual Media*, Ablex, Norwood, New Jersey.

Beloff, H. (1985), *Camera Culture*, Basil Blackwell, New York.

Blackman, M. L.(1986), 'Introduction', *From Site to Sight – Anthropology, Photography, and the Power of Imagery*, Peabody Museum Press, Cambridge, Mass., pp. 11–16.

Bourdieu, P. et al (1965), *Un Art moyen: essai sur les usages sociaux de la photographie*, Les Editions de Minuit, Paris.

Bourdieu, P. (1984), *Distinction: A Social Critique of the Judgement of Taste*, Harvard University Press, Cambridge, Mass.

Bourdieu, P. (1990), *Photography: A Middle-Brow Art*, Stanford University Press, Stanford, California.

Byers, P. (1966), 'Cameras don't take pictures', *Columbia University Forum*, IX, 1, pp. 27–31.

Carelli, V. (1988), 'Video in the villages: utilization of video-tapes as an instrument of ethnic affirmation among Brazilian Indian groups' *CVA Newsletter*, May, pp. 10–15.

Carpenter, E. (1972), *Oh, What a Blow That Phantom Gave Me!*, Holt, Rinehart and Winston, New York.

Chalfen, R. (1975), 'Cinema naivete: a study of home moviemaking as visual communication', *Studies in the Anthropology of Visual Communication*, II, 2, pp. 87–103.

Chalfen, R. (1981), 'A sociovidistic approach to children's film-making: the Philadelphia project', *Studies in Visual Communication*, VII, 1, pp. 2–33.

Chalfen, R. (1987), *Snapshot Versions of Life*, Popular Press, Bowling Green, Ohio.

Chalfen, R. (1988a), 'Home video versions of life – Anything new?', *Society for Visual Anthropology Newsletter* IV, 1, pp. 1–5.

Chalfen, R. (1988b), 'Japanese American family photography: a brief report of research on home mode communication in cross-cultural contexts', *Visual Sociology Review* III, 2, pp. 12–16.

Chalfen, R. (1989), 'Native participation in visual studies: from Pine Springs to Philadelphia' in R. Boonzajer Flaes (ed.), *Eyes Across the Water*, Het Spinhuis, Amsterdam.

Clifford, J. (1986), 'Introduction: Partial Truths', *Writing Culture – The Poetics and Politics of Ethnography*, University of California Press, Berkeley, pp. 1–26.

Ginsburg, F. (1989), 'In whose image? Indigenous media from Aboriginal central Australia', *CVA Review*, Fall, pp. 16–20.

Gitlin, T. (ed.), (1986), *Watching Television*, Pantheon Books New York.

Goodman, N. (1972), 'The way the world is', *Problems and Projects*, Bobbs-Merrill, New York, pp. 24–32.

Goody, J. (1977), *The Domestication of the Savage Mind*, Cambridge University Press, Cambridge.

Grace, H., Merewether, C., Schofield, T., Smith, T. (1977), 'Mods and decos: Notes on critical practices of photography' in M. Nickson and E. McGillivray (eds.), *Working Papers on Photography*, Victoria, Australia, pp. 36–47.

Gray, A. (1988), 'Indigenous peoples and video', *CVA Newsletter* May, pp. 22–4.

Hammond, J. (1988), 'Visualizing themselves: Tongan videography in Utah', *Visual Anthropology* 1, pp. 379–400.

Hoijer, H. (1951), 'Cultural implications of some Navajo linguistic categories', *Language* 27, pp. 111–120.

Jhala, J. (1989), 'Videography as indigenous text and local commodity', *CVA Review*, Fall, pp. 8–16.

Kennedy, T. (1982), 'Beyond advocacy: A facilitative approach to public participation', *Journal of the University Film and Video Association* XXXIV, 3, pp. 33–46.

Langness, L.L. and Frank, G. (1981), *Lives – An Anthropological Approach to Biography*, Chandler and Sharp, Novato, California.

Michaels, E. (1985a), 'Constraints on knowledge in an economy of oral information', *Current Anthropology*, XXVI, 4, pp. 505–10.

Michaels, E. (1985b), 'How video had helped a group of Aborigines in Australia', *Media Development* 1, pp. 16–18.

Moreman, M. (1988), *Talking Culture--Ethnography and Conversational Analysis*, University of Pennsylvania Press, Philadelphia.

Potts, J. (1979), 'Is there an international film language?', *Sight and Sound*, 48, pp. 74–81.

Schatzman, L. and Strauss, A. (1955), 'Social class and modes of communication' in A. G. Smith (ed.), *Communication and Culture*, Holt, Rinehart and Winston, New York, pp. 442–55. (Reprinted from *The American Journal of Sociology*, 60, pp. 329–38.)

Scherer, J. (1990), 'Picturing culture: historical photographs in anthropological inquiry', *Visual Anthropology*, 3, 2–3 (Special Issue).

Sprague, S. (1978), 'How I see the Yomba see themselves', *Studies in the Anthropology of Visual Commication*, 5, 1, pp. 9–28 (Special Issue).

Thomas, A. (1977), *Time in a Frame – Photography and the Nineteenth-Century Mind*, Schocken Books, New York.

Turner, T. (1990), 'Visual media, cultural politics, and anthropological practice: some implications of recent uses of film and video among the Kayapo of Brazil', *CVA Review*, Spring, pp. 8–13.

Williams, R. (1975), *Television: Technology and Cultural Form*, Schocken Books, New York.

Wolf, D. and Hicks, D. (1989), 'The voices within narratives: the development of intertextuality in young children's stories', *Discourse Processes* 12, pp. 329–51.

Worth, S. (1980), 'Margaret Mead and the shift from 'Visual Anthropology' to the 'Anthropology of Visual Communication'', *Studies in Visual Communication* VI, 1, pp. 15–22.

Worth, S. (1965), 'Film communication: an examination of reactions to a group of student films', *Screen Education*, July/August, pp. 3–19.

Worth, S. (1964), 'Film-making as an aid to action research', Unpublished paper presented at the Society for Applied Anthropology Meetings, San Juan, Puerto Rico.

Worth, S. (1963), 'Student film workshop', *Film Comment* I, 5, pp. 54–8.

Worth, S. and Adair, J. (1972), *Through Navajo Eyes: An Exploration in Film Communication and Anthropology*, Indiana University Press, Bloomington.

Ziller, R. C. and Smith, D. E. (1977), 'A phenomenological utilization of photographs', *Journal of Phenomenological Psychology* VII, 2. pp. 172–82.

Ziller, R. C. and Lewis, D. (1981), 'Orientations: self, social and environmental percepts through auto-photography', *Personality and Social Psychology Bulletin*, VII, 2. pp. 338–43.

# Representation by the Other: Indonesian cultural documentation

This paper started off as a means to draw attention to certain kinds of video production which I encountered during field work in Java in 1989. Until recently, discussion of 'ethnographic film' and 'visual anthropology' concentrated on film produced by us, for our own consumption. I wanted to remind colleagues that there are filmic resources other than our own productions which may be of relevance to social anthropology.

I am going to address a particular sphere of cultural documentation, that of Indonesian State Television broadcasting. My discussion draws on a research project I am involved in about television and culture change in Bali.[1] The project has a number of objectives, one of which is the video-recording of cultural programmes broadcast by the Balinese state television channel in order to provide an archival resource for analysis. We are also studying local responses to these programmes, particularly those responses which relate to the standardisation of performance aesthetics and norms. We are interested in how much homogenisation arises from filmed representations on television and aim to make analytical statements about the effect of these televised representations on performance practice in Bali.

This research is not 'about' ethnographic film. Rather it is an anthropological enquiry into the power of films broadcast on television to transform social and cultural practice. Here I address two general and related questions. Firstly, which elements need to be taken into account when we are analysing representations produced by other cultures? Secondly, how can we make valid anthropological and context-specific inputs into arguments about technological expansion and the resulting homogeneity or 'globalisation'?

The issue of globalisation in the context of image-making technology has increasingly concerned a number of social theorists. It is time that anthropologists in general, not only 'visual' anthropologists, started to take on the implications of the arguments raised by Jonathan Friedman and others concerning cultural variation in the appropriation of technology (1988). This is a massive field, and I will presently illustrate one particular form of this appropriation in an analysis of a television documentary broadcast in Bali, which shows that it is a specifically Balinese narrative style which structures the television film in question. The technological medium may come from Japan, but the images it reproduces and disseminates are locally produced. This raises specific problems about the usefulness of the term 'documentary' in this particular cultural context, as well as pointing to one kind of thing we might investigate, namely the culturally variable use of technologies.

The need for urgent attention to this issue was endorsed by a trend which emerged during the *Film as Ethnography* conference. Before going into the Indonesian material, I shall say something about this trend because it indicates one way in which we might be constructing our own representations of how 'the Other' represents itself.

### Whose camera is it anyway?

The eyes of the anthropological community and the viewers of television series such as *Disappearing World* (Granada) and *Under the Sun* (BBC 2) have been turning of late to images of documentaries made by the Other. These are often so-called community projects in which the video camera is wielded by members of the group (e.g. American Indians and Australian Aboriginals and, most recently, Amazonian peoples[2]) rather than the outsider. In the past few years numerous films about the plight of the rain forest shown on British television have made us accustomed to the sight of Chief Ropni and Payakan of the Kayapo tribe being filmed by the visiting crews filming their own documentation of the events in process.

While it is encouraging to note a greater recognition that it is not only we who control picture production, such images have resulted in generalised ideas about the control of the camera by the Other. It is Chief Ropni and Payakan specifically who are actively involved in a campaign to protect their territories and resources. They have received funding from a number of sources for their campaign, which includes video documentation of their political struggle. Despite the specific conditions under which these leaders have come to have the video camera, the image of the be-plumed, half-naked Ropni shouldering a camera both bemuses and amuses the television audience, bringing together as it does strongly contrastive icons of primitivism and modernity and generating a stereotype of 'the Kayapo' making movies.

A second, more worrying, effect of this kind of representation in a film made for television is that it endorses the image of the Noble Savage. Images of this kind, if anything, hinder understanding of what is going on when film or video technology is in the hands of 'the natives' because they suggest that the monopoly grip on film technology, with its attendant privileges and prerogatives, has been loosened. We appropriate the image to explain ourselves to ourselves. Indeed, so strong is the image that some theoreticians might feel that the act of classifying it as a symptomatic postmodern icon is explanation enough and stop there. Meanwhile, the process which started before the production of those film images, and continues after them, is left out, ignored by the self-reflexive formulation of postmodernist chic and carelessness, where fragment and image are prioritised over history and experience. 'The' Kayapo implies a distance and uniformity which blocks the proper recognition by anthropologists and others of the phenomenon behind the tribal tag. Despite the transfer of technology, *we* remain in control of the production of images of the Other, through 'our' funding and our reception of them.

Apart from problems of ethics and images, it is clear that the Kayapo project is a particular political campaign, supported, among other things, by Western guilt. Chief Ropni and his tribe are making their own *Disappearing World* movie, but is this the kind of image we should have in mind when we think of others representing themselves? Or is it simply that Western image-makers are not interested in more routine forms of image-making in underdeveloped countries which are less exotic and less politically poignant in the short term, less interesting for peak viewing and less packageable?

It is necessary, then, to know who is wielding the camera, on whose authority and to what end. My material comes not from the extreme case of hunters and gatherers caught up in the high-profile rain forest scenario, but from Indonesia, where video technology rapidly took hold in urban communities through the entrepreneurial response of (mainly) Chinese families to the availability of state-of-the-art Japanese technology. In 1982, households headed by professional middle-class Indonesians had video recorders and the filming of weddings and ceremonies has been normal among this class for the past ten years. Thus, the access to technology described here is not the result of intercession by outside agencies, but an established urban trend.

Furthermore, the Ministry of Information is responsible for all media, broadcast and print, and defines policies for both production and censorship. The Indonesian use of documentation is symptomatic of its use in a number of developing countries in which there is a marked state control of information. This control is justified on the grounds that it is a necessary prerequisite for the political stability which will allow economic development to proceed according to plan and keep the foreign investors happy. It is unimaginable that films like those we have seen on television about the Kayapo would be broadcast in Indonesia. Firstly, the threatened tribes such as the Asmat and Dani of Indonesian New Guinea (Irian Jaya) would never be allowed to have projects of the kind set up in Brazil and, secondly, foreign film crews would not be allowed in to film any kind of tribal situation which reflected badly on state policy.

## Film and TV in Indonesia

Indonesian State Television came into full operation in August 1962. Information from the *Indonesia Handbook* (1990, pp. 214–217) states that by 1989 there were ten broadcasting stations in the republic: Medan, Palembang, Jakarta, Yogya, Surabaya, Denpasar, Balikpapan, Ujungpandang, Manado and Bandung. Ten mobile production units are available to eleven provinces: Aceh, West Sumatra, West Kalimantan, Irian Jaya, Maluku, East Nusatenggara, Central Java, West Java, and a further unit for East Java and Bali. In 1990 there were nearly nine million registered television sets and over 140 million people 'able to watch tv' out of a population numbering around 185 million. Between 54,000 and 55,000 public television sets have been made available to local communities by the state. Recently, two privately owned cable facilities have been set up: one in the capital, Jakarta, run by President Suharto's son and a second in Surabaya, East Java, which opened in mid-1990. More recently, the *Guardian* (24 January 1991) reported the opening of an educational station, which is to be run by Siti Hardiyanti Rukmana, daughter of Suharto. These 'private' facilities are not state controlled as such but they are not far from the centre of power.

The Indonesian mass media is concerned with the promotion of nationhood and the definition of cultural orthodoxy, albeit within a plural setting, and there is a strict control of the published media. Research into Indonesian radio broadcasting, however, indicates that there is less centralised control in this branch of the media, this being an exception to the regulation associated with repressive and authoritarian states. In 1986 there were 32.8 million radio receivers in Indonesia tuning in to 560 radio stations. Of these, fifty belonged to the state-run Radio Republic Indonesia and another 150 to local government authorities; the rest were independently run, though not without some kind of monitoring by the officers of the Ministry of Information (Wild, n.d.).[3]

Indonesia has a thriving film industry, reaching a peak in 1977 with 134 films. In 1986, between seventy and ninety documentaries and 156 tv-episodes and some features were produced (Armes 1987; Lent 1990). Between 1988 and 1989, 116 informative films were produced: these are categorised in the *Indonesia Handbook* as 'seething development films' (*Gelora Pembangungan*), documentaries, animated films and the ever-popular puppet series for children *Si Unyil*. In 1988, eighty-eight feature films were produced. In the 'Fourth Development Programme Phase' (*Repelita IV*), between 1984–85 and 1988–89, the number of feature films produced was 332. Many of these features are exported for screening to Malaysian audiences.

There is little film-making done by Indonesians which we would readily recognise as ethnographic or anthropological; nor is it entirely clear what the documentaries referred to above consist of. They are probably television development programmes which give information about progress in the twenty-seven provinces or present new technologies and techniques. Like many of their British counterparts, anthropological departments in universities do not consider themselves ready or 'strong enough', either to develop such specialisations or to commit themselves to funding for visual projects.[4] The one Indonesian anthropological film-maker whose work has been shown internationally, Dea

Sudarman, works for the long-running anthropological film slot on Japanese television, *Our Wonderful World* (*Subarashii Sekai Ryoko*) (Ginsburg 1988, pp. 52–6; Ichioka 1988, p. 69). The Japanese represent an important market for Indonesian culture but Dea Sudarman's film, *The Asmat*, about a tribe living in Indonesian New Guinea, has also been used by the Indonesian Government to promote Asmat art overseas and to develop more extensive markets for Indonesian culture (Hughes-Freeland 1989). This is an important factor in the production of non-fiction films and programmes which I will term documentary, a problematic category which I shall return to below. Such films are never televised in Indonesia, so it was with great interest that I learnt from Geam Samanar Warakai, during the Manchester conference, that ethnographic films, such as Connolly and Anderson's *Joe Leahy's Neighbours*, are shown on television in Papua New Guinea.

Before moving on to the case of cultural documentation on Balinese television, it is helpful to signal two contemporary Indonesian cultural trends. Firstly, recent developments in Indonesia indicate that certain cultural traditions or practices are in the process of being earmarked as valuable cultural resources for contemporary Indonesian society.[5] Secondly, their value is seen to lie in their contribution to the development of national pride and to the tourist industry.

These two objectives are not mutually exclusive in the short term but some claim that, in the long term, they will undermine the values which they are claiming to enhance.


## TV in Bali

Of the programmes broadcast on Indonesian State Television, 80 per cent are nationally produced and 20 per cent are imported from overseas. The national productions break down as follows: news and information 37 per cent; education and religion 16 per cent; entertainment, art and culture 37 per cent, and other subjects, 10 per cent (*Indonesia Handbook 1990*, p. 217).

Within the education, art and culture category, Balinese television has a regular slot for traditional performance. Between September 1990 and the end of December 1990, there were twenty-one programmes of televised Balinese 'traditional' performance, including the following which were recorded for the research project:

— a classical drama in a single episode;
— a number of 'detached' dances, so called because they are not performed in a formal dramatic context which the Balinese would recognise, but rather serve to entertain visitors at secular or touristic functions;
— a drama by the Gong Duta Bon Bali group (to my knowledge one of three popular drama troupes working in the island) in four episodes;
— *Sendratari*, the newest theatrical genre in Bali which emphasises (what we think of as) dance rather than sung and other vocal elements, in two episodes;

this is a genre which has been developed by the Balinese Academy of Performing Arts (STSI) in the capital, Denpasar;
— *Arja*, a dance opera in five episodes;
— a drama-documentary about *Arja*;
— a new creation based on *Kecak*, the so-called monkey dance, which itself
evolved out of singing styles to accompany trance dancing, in one episode;
— a new creation mask dance drama by the staff of the Office of Culture and
Education, in two episodes; and
— Prembon, a mixture of *Arja* and masked dance, in two episodes, to be
finished in January 1991.

I now consider certain elements in Balinese cultural forms which have determined the way in which a particular television programme has been produced.
The programme in question is the drama-documentary about Arja listed above,
which is a good example of how local narrative styles are represented through the
medium of modern technology, in this case television broadcasting.

## Telling it like it is?

Adrian Vickers has noted that

In Bali there is no concept equivalent to Western notions of 'fiction', only degrees of
veracity related to the sacredness of form, language and narrative. Such veracity is not
necessarily the same as 'historicity', since its sense of causality and order is distinctly
Balinese. (1990, p. 163)

Vickers is here addressing the question of reliability in Balinese historical
narratives and asking whether they can be read as historical texts, according to a
Western idea of history. If they cannot, how might an understanding of history
and causality be constituted so as to read the Balinese texts in an appropriate
fashion?

The creative recounting of local histories in Bali is of double concern to us
here. Balinese histories may be etched into the leaves of the *lontar* palm, but they
are the stuff of story-telling. The telling may be verbal, it may be enacted by
humans or puppets and now it may be televised. The narratives in these contexts
display similar conventions of interpretive history and, within the frame of the
latest medium, new genres present themselves to convey representations of the
Balinese past.

Secondly, just as veracity and historicity in Bali do not share the kind of
congruence we might take for granted, so too there is a different set of assumptions about the place of naturalness in visual representations. Naturalness in
general is problematic and is not necessarily valued in all behavioural contexts,
despite British enthusiasm for conventional 'naturalness'. How much more,
then, should naturalness be avoided in visual representations in Bali. Characterisation in theatrical genres is highly conventional and genre-specific. Acting

skill resides in the way in which the conventions are fulfilled, in the unexpectedness of timing and in the wit of verbal and gestural devices.

We might pause here to consider the extent to which our analysis and understanding of such product(ion)s might diverge from Western-produced documentaries, ethnographic or otherwise. It appears that the distinction between fiction and non-fiction is not necessarily appropriate for the classification of Indonesian representational frameworks. But is the distinction cut-and-dried in its Western birthplace either?

In Western Europe and North America, what is called 'documentary' is not a stable genre. It is created by political alignments and ideas about power and access: it is negotiated according to the prevailing conditions obtaining during production. Within the field of specialist documentary production, there is little consensus about what documentary is, what its conventions and its intentions are and what its objective(s) (if any) might be.[6] Given the history of the documentary idea, it might be more expedient to regard it as a heuristic category than as an analytical concept with which to analyse particular representations by particular Others.

In the long term it will be important to ask whether it is useful to identify as documentaries a class of non-fictional productions made by the Other. This, of course, will have certain implications for how we regard 'ethnographic representations of the self' in such contexts: indeed, one of the difficulties of the Indonesian ethnographic film *The Asmat* was the lack of clarity about whether lapsed rituals were being staged especially for the purposes of the film.

The Arja programme uses what we in the West would call a drama documentary style. This genre is favoured by television producers and regarded with intense suspicion by documentary film-makers. Although documentary film itself is by no means a stabilised and unitary genre, most documentary film-makers acknowledge that documentary creates its own narrative forms, rather than merely reproducing an observed reality which is somehow 'natural' and 'out there'. Indeed, documentary has recently been characterised as a 'do-it-yourself reality kit' (Vaughan 1986, p. 175). There is, however, a sense that documentary has an ethical responsibility not to lie and not to exploit (overtly) the gullibility of the viewer or the documentary subject. Internal disputes between documentary film-makers are forgotten when the drama-documentary looms, and the fighting film-makers rally in opposition to this new foe, declaring that documentary conventions of narrative recounting (undefined as these are) are more 'authentic' and more 'ethical' than the drama-documentary which re-stages events and uses actors to depict incidents which happened in the distant or recent past.

Andrei Tarkovski has described the art of film-making as 'sculpting in time'. All films, whether fiction, documentary, or drama-documentary, are constructed narratives determined by subjectivity and selective framing. As such, they tend to be ranked lower in the scale of reliability than what is classed as an historical document. The reliability factor of a filmed documentary is not as generically stable as our idea of what an historically valid document is.

Since the historical narrative in Bali is a kind of qualified non-fiction, and given the negative attitude to transparently 'natural' behaviour, the use of the drama-documentary to present a history of a theatrical form might be seen as a peculiarly appropriate response to the potentials of the latest technology.

The programme about Arja reveals in its style and in its construction of a kind of historical discourse, features found in Indonesian narratives both in past kingdoms and the current nation. If film is 'sculpting in time', Balinese and Javanese historical chronicles have also represented a non-linear and non-naturalistic notion of time, which I would suggest bears on how we attempt to characterise these ostensibly 'non-fiction' events in visual media productions.

### Heading for development and preservation

Arja is often described as 'Balinese opera'. It is usually performed outside the temple during temple birthday ceremonies. It lasts through the night and is distinctive today in that it gives female performers the opportunity to take on significant roles, as we shall see. Arja has been earmarked by the local government as a tradition which is worthy of being developed and preserved. The government slogan is '*membina, mengembangkan, melestarikan*' meaning 'to build/cultivate/develop, to expand/develop, and to make everlasting and unchanging'. To this end, Indonesian State Television (TVRI) in Bali produced a documentary about Arja, entitled 'Arja heads for development and preservation in Bali' (*Arja di Bali menuju pelestarian*). There is no culturally perceived contradiction in the policy of developing and preserving a tradition. Extensive work has been done by Western scholars to show how, in the context of Javanese and Balinese chronicles, the creation of tradition is nothing new nor is it unique to modern state representations conveyed in the media of film or video.

The Arja documentary is a constructed narrative which selects specific features to construct a legitimate history of Arja's origins in order to justify present interpretations for a future end. If we agree with Vickers that appropriateness is a basic principle of causality in the Balinese web of relations which allow a narrative to emerge, then what is 'true' or 'reality' is what is most fitting, most appropriate (Vickers 1990, p. 169). This definition of reality may sound familiar to those who have spent months in the cutting room trying to make it 'feel right'. How then does this particular drama-documentary representation demonstrate the principles I have outlined?

The programme opens with an establishing shot of a well-known temple at sunset. We then see a man singing a song (described as a *pantun*) while a woman makes offerings, an action which is characteristic of Balinese everyday life. The front-woman, or narrator, of the documentary emerges from the household context, which seems to be presented as the original and authentic home of what we know as Arja. She describes the *pantun* as rare and as the oldest in Bali, dating from the rule of I Dewa Agung Gede Sakti (1775–1825) in the kingdom of Klungkung in East Bali, but she makes no connection with Arja. Instead she goes on to explain that Arja is a mixture of various 'arts' (*kesenian*, an Indonesian word), and that we will be seeing the three 'oldest forms'.

The first form presented is *Arja doyong* or *dhadhap*. As the explanatory commentary continues, we are shown images of an elderly and unidentified solo male performer in a modern village. This is described as the base or origin of Arja as we know it. According to one I Made Kerta, it was first seen in the village of Singapadu in 1900. No further explanation is given; and I Made Kerta remains a name invoked to announce an inscription of origin: once a source is named, it is legitimate. With a date of origin, it is doubly legitimate and thereby becomes inscribed in a 'real' and appropriate historical context. We learn that such performers would wander the villages and perform for money: this is enacted in the film.

The second form is processional theatre which accompanies the masked mythical beast, *Barong Pangkal*, on its purificatory rounds of the village on the *Hari Raya* (Holidays) of Galungan and Kuningan. The main characters are introduced by means of a split screen: Punta, the devoted servant of the king; his brother Wijil, also known as Kertala; Mantri Manis, the ruler; Condong or Inya the female attendant, and Galuh, the princess or queen. These last three are played by women.

A scene is then shown concerning the king of Jenggala's preparations to go hunting before a ceremony to celebrate the rituals for the third month of his child's life. We can see how the servant roles translate into low level Balinese the songs of the nobility which are in *kawi*, an old language, now used for literary and dramatic purposes and not comprehensible to everyone in the audience. Although this is cast as a historic form of Arja, it is the form of Arja familiar to scholars of performance today. It also includes dialogue which praises current developments: 'even in the mountain villages, everyone feels the benefits of development . . . it is a just and fertile kingdom, based on Pancasila'. Pancasila is the Indonesian State ideology.

Although the documentary positions this scene in historic, not contemporary time, the dialogue is contemporary. The 'explanation' creates no link with *Arja doyong*, nor does it discuss when and how women came to participate. The way in which the Barong Pangkal is explained and the characterisation of Galungan and Kuningan as national holidays creates a disconnection from the Balinese context of cultural knowledge. Galungan and Kuningan are explained in an Indonesian way, as there are ten days which make up the holy period for the Balinese; the two 'holidays' are national holidays. These features, and the sporadic subtitles in Indonesian suggest that the documentary is aimed at an Indonesian, not a Balinese audience: it is disconnected from the everyday experience of a Balinese person as a continuity. The narrative style is also one of disconnection.

This is emphasised in the third phase of the presentation, which is given no relational position with regard to the first two kinds of Arja. This scene shows farmers (portrayed by teachers from the Balinese Academy of Performing Arts (STSI, Denpasar) and other local performance acadamnies) resting after harvest and singing; they start to sing in Balinese and soon switch to Indonesian. Vocal noises and the slapping or tapping of tools completes the accompaniment.

This scene cuts to I Made Bandem, head of (STSI), with a caption giving his name and designating him as *budayawan* – cultural expert. He explains that this is *Arja pengangon* (herders' Arja) and that it consists of *macapat* songs (a traditional genre) sung by farmers after the harvest. He says that as tractors replace buffaloes, this kind of Arja is coming under pressure and needs to be preserved. This 'form' of Arja has not been dealt with by non-Indonesian researchers as far as I know.

Then follows a brief interlude of a dance teacher and pupils under some trees, during which the female narrator explains that local government is working together with artists in order to make Arja everlasting by performing it at *Pesta Kesenian*, an annual Arts Festival held in the Balinese capital Denpasar, to increase the appreciation of the public. This sentence is repeated twice, as the picture moves to a performance of Arja given at the 1990 Pesta Kesenian. The section shown is a comic interlude between three women discussing the best way to manage a copious embonpoint or, in the words of the dialogue, 'If your breasts are long, wrap 'em up tight in a scarf'.

The documentary reveals narrative features which are economically selected so as to use the story of Arja as a way of showing what the government is doing; the narrative is addressed to how the origins are being developed, although the disjunction here is barely concealed by the leap from the farmers singing to the joking of the three women on stage. No causal link between 'origin' or 'traditional form', in terms of similarity or generic evolution, is attempted. The different kinds of Arja are left in their own spheres, and the 'development and pre-servation' become causally valid thanks to the benevolent patronage of the local government and the participation of local artists, which gives legitimacy to Arja being made up of the components of 'the art of dance, drama, music and make up', sanctioned by the resulting appreciation of the public. The use of authoritative names and dates of origin, the appearance of a well-known cultural expert and the insertion of modern panegyrics addressed to the government are some of the selected features which create the fitting conditions for a 'real' history of Arja.

The documentary, then, appears to conform to the conventions of Balinese narratives in pre-electronic media days: what goes into the narrative is what is appropriate for the conditions of its production. In this case, the purpose is to present Arja as a form of theatre, with a many-faceted past which makes it a vehicle for Balinese identity in the modern era. This version of Arja's history is given the stamp of authority in the form of I Made Bandem's appearance as the 'cultural expert', a televisual equivalent to what, in a written text, might be a quotation from a prior source. This serves to make the drama-documentary an effective telling, a telling which ratifies actions being taken to develop Arja and, more broadly, to develop Bali-in-Indonesia. The Arja drama-documentary is a story for making sense of this development. Again, to quote Vickers,

Balinese do not narrate 'events' in chronological order for the purposes of writing history, but they tell stories about other things that we would call 'mythical' or 'legendary' in order to refer to 'events'. The texts which are produced are more than 'literature' in the narrow sense that we understand books; they are the way phenomena are made sense of. (1990, p. 178)

In this case, the event is Arja-in-development, represented in a number of different contexts. The contexts do not connect to form a narrative argument based on one stage leading to another. Rather, the different representations of Arja multiply to show how it is that Arja is being developed, or rather, to show the inevitability of such a policy.

The big difference between *lontar* leaf chronicles or traditional performances and television documentaries or drama-documentaries is the number of people who are given access to the particular features which have been deemed appropriate and 'reality' constituting. As our research project is still in its early stages, it would be premature to suggest to what extent the Balinese will receive the selected features as truth, or what kind of truth and reality there will be. It is also difficult to anticipate responses to, and transformations of, artistic standards and a possible homogenisation of performance through the workings of the mass media. The work of STSI in altering Balinese perceptions of performance in their own villages seems to have been considerable, before the televising of STSI dance-drama (*sendratari*), which inspires huge enthusiasm in viewers. It is difficult to know whether television programmes of a documentary order, either constructed histories or performances filmed in a studio, will create a new order of difference in the way in which the Balinese reproduce their culture from pre-tv days. The Arja documentary suggests that there is an appropriation of the technology to reproduce narratives in a fashion appropriate to Balinese historiography. One wonders if the scale of the broadcast will bring about any radical changes, or whether there will be a moment of cultural disjunction.

## Conclusion

Jean Rouch has invited us to watch an ethnographic film as 'observers of an observation of an event' (cited in Eaton, 1979, p. 49). This invitation can be repeated at one further remove and applied to the many aspects of representation in the visual media. We may consider the products, but the modes of reproduction of representations and their modes of reception, or audience response, are equally important. I would again urge that we try to resist making big generalisations or establishing icons of indigenous representation in video technology; and, following on from this, that we specify who is involved in production 'by the Other', and for what purposes: what rationales, what audience and so forth.

This also raises questions about practical and theoretical strategies for dealing with the production of films and programmes by a group which is itself questioning its identity and future (a questioning which arises from the 'feather and hi-tech' syndrome refered to above) and which is coming to terms with its entry into 'global culture'. This, of course, concerns how we generalise, imagine, and stereotype Others, an issue which it is the role of anthropology and regional studies to tackle.

The research project in Bali will document a particular set of representations of events designated as 'cultural'. The aim is to understand how television contributes to the way in which particular Balinese people perceive cultural identity, social change, and the role of the state, and to draw out the implications of this for the way in which ritual, tradition, and history are constituted within a culture. The research inevitably raises broader theoretical questions concerning issues of cultural boundaries and interlocking contexts, which are being widely debated by social scientists today.

I suggested at the beginning of this chapter that there is a place for anthropological case studies in dealing with the points raised by Friedman. He has recently argued (1988) that the constitution of cultural identity is determined by the ways in which different cultures appropriate modern technology. His aim is to refine the concept of globalisation and it is clear that this is an area of study which anthropologists are well suited to take up, regardless of whether they regard themselves as 'visual anthropologists'.

Parallel to the questions being asked about the inevitability of globalisation is a recent analytical emphasis, in social theory, on the character of the television audience in the West. De Certeau's analysis of everyday practices, for example, has implications for how we understand the impact of the visual media on cultural reproduction. His approach gives theoretical force to the integrity of the 'little person', to use an Indonesian idiom. By moving the spotlight away from strategies which are 'the games of the powerful', emphasis is given to the tactics of the common man, 'an art of the weak'. 'The space of the tactic', to paraphrase de Certeau, 'is the space of the other, of orality, of experience and cultural memory, of everyday life' (cited in Silverstone 1989, p. 81–4). Rather than thinking of the audience as a receiver, which will inevitably be controlled by the matter coming down the tube, it has been proposed that we think instead of the audience as viewer; that we move from a passive to a dynamic concept of a person who interacts with, rather than is constructed by, the broadcast media. This theorisation of modes of audience apprehension shares features with theories of reading in literary theory. Here there has been a shift in emphasis from the text as a dominating homogeneity, which creates cultural reality, to the text as something which is constituted by each act of reading. The restoration of active viewing to the audience does much to counter the 'dominance' theories of the media which are based on rather simplified accounts of the work of Foucault and Bourdieu in particular (see the chapter by Martinez in this book).

The theorisation of power in relation to practice is a perennial concern in the social sciences. In the fields of sociology and media studies, approaches such as that proposed by de Certeau have been enthusiastically recognised as providing crucial starting points for the analysis of television watching in the West:

watching television is the moment or space where the tactic counters the strategic.

While such approaches are long overdue in Western cultural analysis they might strike anthropologists as routine. Anthropologists are, after all, well aware that cultures tend to be plural and that such pluralities include cross-cultural interactions and emerging systems of dominance. Anthropologists have been analysing styles of attention among audiences for decades, although such concerns have become more central with an intensification of interests in performance. To return to the nine million or so Indonesian televisions, what matters is *how* the 140 million or so people 'able to watch television programmes' are watching those nine million televisions; *which* people, maybe, and what kind of eyes and minds they are bringing to their viewing. TV sets are receivers, but people are viewers. They do not see; they look, pay attention, get bored, ignore, select, disparage and praise.

The place of film and video in Indonesian society might be transforming the ways in which different Indonesians represent themselves to themselves and to other Indonesians but, as my discussion of the Arja drama-documentary has shown, new technologies do not necessarily dispense with old techniques and strategies. One wonders, however, what kinds of tactic might develop in response to the 'mass' dimension of the new technologies. The extent to which different elements and frames are creating change and at which level and in what terms any transformation may be grasped are matters which require further research.

I have been considering one instance of what I have called, perhaps somewhat cavalierly, documentary production in contemporary Indonesia. I have shown how a particular drama-documentary uses sparsely selected features to compile a historical background to contemporary policies of 'develop and preserve' in the case of Arja, which may also be seen to conform to one analysis of causality and narrative form in Balinese histories. This indicates a cultural specificity within media where many have predicted the end of cultural plurality. Such productions have come from the powerful and form part of strategic cultural programmes. The evidence to date suggests that representations need to be understood according to how they are constructed and read by their producers and their audiences. They should not be tested against ethnocentric generic classifications. Theoretical concerns in the social sciences indicate that specific studies of non-Western television production and apprehension would offer invaluable opportunities of arriving at a broader perspective. We should not assume that technology everywhere brings about the same relationships between power and practice.

## Notes

1   The project is entitled 'Television and the transformation of Balinese culture' and is designed to run for three years. Researchers on the project ar Dr M. Hobart (School of Oriental and African Studies, London University) and myself. The project is a

collaboration with the Balinese Academy of Performing Arts through its Director, Dr I Made Bandem. The project is funded by the British Academy and the School of Oriental and African Studies.

2 See Turner 1990. Such projects are of course not limited to 'primitives' or 'minorities' and it is important not to forget that 'modern' Westerners, who may be seasoned film and television viewers, also find it strange when they first find themselves controlling film production or 'seeing themselves' on the screen. See, for example, the discussion by Young (1988) of the *Challenge for Change* project in Canada, which encouraged the use of video as a means of inter-group communication and political protest.

3 World Radio Handbook 1986, cited in an unpublished paper presented to the 1987 meeting of the Association of Southeast Asian Scholars in the UK (ASEASUK) by Colin Wild, former head of the Indonesian section of the BBC World Service at Bush House. The 1990 *Indonesia Handbook* gives slightly different breakdowns: forty-nine state-run stations, with five co-ordinating stations and one in each of the twenty-seven provinces, with seventeen stations in the districts. In addition, there are 133 regional broadcasting stations managed by local administrations. The handbook makes no mention of the independent stations.

4 Dr Masri Singarimbun, anthropologist and director of the Population Centre, Gadjah Mada University, interviewed by Linus Suryadi (1988).

5 Hobsbawm's concept of 'the invention of tradition' (1983) is highly pertinent here. For an application of this idea to the Indonesian situation, see Hughes-Freeland (forthcoming).

6 See for example two articles on documentary by Nichols (1985) and MacDougall (1985), which show how the field can be fought over and defined.

## References

*Books and articles*

Armes, A. (1987), *Third World Film-making and the West*, University of California Press, London, pp. 147–54.

Eaton, M. (ed.) (1979), *Anthropology-Reality-Cinema*, British Film Institute, London.

Friedman, J. (1988), 'Cultural logics of the global system: a sketch', *Theory, Culture and Society*, V, pp. 447–60.

Ginsburg, F. (1988), 'Ethnographies on the airwaves: the presentation of anthropology on American, British and Japanese television' in P. Hockings and Y. Omori (eds.), *Cinematographic Theory and New Dimensions in Ethnographic Film*, Senri Ethnological Series no. 24, National Museum of Ethnology, Osaka.

Hobsbawm, E. and Ranger, T. (eds.) (1983), *The Invention of Tradition*, Cambridge University Press, Cambridge.

Hughes-Freeland, F. (1989), 'Indonesian image enhancement', *Anthropology Today*, V, pp. 3–5.

Hughes-Freeland, F. (forthcoming), 'Golek Menak and Tayuban: patronage and performance in two spheres of Central Javanese culture', in a collection of papers on the performing arts in Java and Bali edited by Bernard Arps.

Ichioka, Y. (1988), 'Ethnographic film-making for Japanese television' in P. Hockings and Y. Omori (eds.), *Cinematographic Theory and New Dimensions in Ethnographic Film*, Senri Ethnological Series no. 24, National Museum of Ethnology, Osaka.

Lent, J.A. (1990), *The Asian Film Industry*, Christopher Helm, London, pp. 201–12.

Macdougall, D. (1985), 'Beyond observational cinema' in B. Nichols (ed.), *Movies and Methods*, vol. II, University of California Press, Berkeley.

Nichols, B. (1985), 'The voice of documentary', B. Nichols (ed.), *Movies and Methods Vol. II*, University of California Press, Berkeley.

Silverstone, R. (1989), 'Let us then return to the murmuring of everyday practices: a note on Michel de Certeau, television and everyday life', *Theory, Culture and Society*, VI, pp. 77–94.

Suryadi, L. (1988), 'Masri Singarimbun : anthropologi: bagi Yogya, birokrasi dan pasar seni', *Citra Yogya*, March–April, pp. 16–28.

Turner, T. (1990), 'The Kayapo video project : a progress report', *Commission for Visual Anthropology Review*, Autumn, pp. 7–10.

Vaughan, D. (1986), 'Notes on the ascent of a fictitious mountain' in J. Corner (ed.), *Documentary and the Mass Media*, Edward Arnold, London.

Vickers, A. (1990), 'Balinese texts and historiography', *History and Theory*, XXIX, pp. 158–78.

Wild,C. (n.d.), 'Indonesia : a nation and its broadcasters', unpublished paper presented to the 1987 meeting of the Association of Southeast Asian Scholars in the United Kingdom.

Young, C. (1988), 'Documentary and fiction, distortion and belief' in P. Hockings and Y. Omori (eds.), *Cinematographic Theory and New Dimensions in Ethnographic Film*, Senri Ethnological Series no. 24, National Museum of Ethnology, Osaka.

*Films*

Connolly, B. and R. Anderson (1988), *Joe Leahy's Neighbours*, Documentary Educational Resources, Watertown,. Colour, 90 mins.

Sudarman, D. (1982), *The Asmat*. NVA, Japan, 'Our Wonderful World' series. Colour, 60 mins.

**Part Four**

# Television and new technologies

# Introduction

In order to read a book you are forced to touch it, take it down from the shelf and hold it in your hands or place it on the table in front of you. The same applies to still photographs. You take out the family photo album from the attic or the worn snapshot of your beloved from your wallet. Film is slightly different, unless you happen to be a projectionist. However, although the film is shown on a screen thirty yards away from you, you can see and 'touch' the beam connecting the projector to the screen and may even persuade the projectionist to let you see and handle the celluloid material neatly rolled onto a reel on the projector. You have a basic, even physical, feeling and knowledge of how these representational systems work. Most people do. Many people even know how to manipulate the semantic and syntactic potentials of writing, photography and film. In the brave new world of electronics, however, the art of manipulation belongs to the experts, to a limited pool of 'masters' highly dependent on an army of technicians to whom air waves and 'bits' are as natural as paper and celluloid. The final part of this book is about the brave new world.

It may be objected that television is hardly a medium unknown to the majority of the world's population, inhabiting what has appropriately (but simplistically) been described as the 'global village'. But, as noted by among others Ginsburg (1988), the fact that ethnographic film has increasingly become broadcasted anthropology, is a fairly recent phenomenon. Few countries can boast of long running ethnographic film series such as *Disappearing Wrold* in Britain and *Our Wonderful World* in Japan. Singer, Wright and Turton (Chapters 15–17) explore aspects of this fairly recent culture of 'broadcasting anthropology' from different, but overlapping, perspectives and approaches.

A particularity of broadcasting noted and emphasised by all three authors, is the particularity of its audience. Singer stresses the 'ephemeral' quality of the television image, constructed to be viewed once by a non-specialist public, which is in major contrast to ethnographic film in general (p. 265). Wright examines 'the constraints on visual anthropology to satisfy the demands of Western popular culture' and notes that moving into the realm of televised anthropology 'we move from the work of the individual anthropologist to that of industrial production' (p. 275). Finally, Turton underlines the paradoxical construction of the television audience in his concise description.

> A television programme is made to be seen by an audience which is not only numbered in millions but which is also uncommitted to the subject of the programme. It is not just that a certain number of the audience will have been 'hooked' while channel-hopping. Rather, it is precisely these 'floating' viewers whom the programme is aimed at in the first place. They are anonymous, unknown and unknowable except as a statistical aggregate. The television audience, then . . . has to be constructed, paradoxically, by the very institution which depends on it. (p. 288)

The main difference between a television audience and the 'normal' spectator of an ethnographic film thus appears to refer to differences in commitment and viewing contexts. The *gaze* of the spectator is different from the *glance* of the television viewer, as noted by Ellis (1982, p. 137). But, as noted by all three authors, and most emphatically by Turton, the concept of the television audience is an ideological construct employed by the executive producers of broadcasting companies on the basis of figures derived from viewer ratings. The problem for television programming in general and for the transmission of ethnographic films on television in particular, is that 'statistical aggregates' may serve as indicators of the commercial success of a particular programme or type of programme (after the event) but provide very little explanation of this success. This 'gap between production and consumption' (Young 1988), leaves very little space for experiments and new ideas, and the changes in programming patterns that this would stimulate. Changes occur only if viewer ratings force the executives to take action, which is why television, in a sense, is in competition with itself (Balikci 1988, p. 21). An illustration of this, which has been noted by several commentators on the relationship between ethnographic film and television (e.g. Loizos 1980; Henley 1985), is the rejection of *To Live With Herds* (MacDougall 1973), by executives of Granada Television, on the grounds that it lacked commentary, used subtitled interviews and was too slowly paced. It did not fit into the 'type' of ethnographic programmes shown on television. Today, of course, we know that broadcasting companies adopted many of the conventions employed in *To Live With Herds*, such as the subtitling of indigenous speech and interviews, which, fifteen years later, was so commonplace in television documentaries that it was almost becoming boring (Lydall 1992, p. 5).

Singer (Chapter 15) stresses not only the gap between television and its audience but also the 'ad hoc relationship' between broadcasting and anthropology, one result of which is that 'the greatest proportion of material shown on television in the 1970s and 1980s with anthropological content had little to do directly with anthropologists or the academic discipline' (p. 268). Quoting *Disappearing World* as an example, a series which is explicitly 'anthropological' in the sense that (almost) all programmes have made use of an anthropological consultant, Singer pertinently asks: 'how much is the material we identify as anthropology really aimed at affecting public attitudes and how much is it just another collage of raw material that happens to be anthropological in nature because that is where we have gained our access? (p. 269) Although the *anthropological* intentions became more evident at a later stage, when anthropologists (such as Singer) became directly involved in the series, the initial objectives, launched by Brian Moser and Denis Foreman, were 'to highlight the pressures that the West was putting on tribal society to change, and to record those societies before they were unrecognisable' (*loc. cit.*). One of the very first films of the series, *The Last of the Cuiva* (Moser 1971), exemplifies this point very well. Singer's main point, however, is that one of the most successful anthropological television series ever to be launched, was neither the direct result of a 'marriage' between anthropology and television nor the result of an anticipated audience demand: 'It was the result of broadcasting individuals . . . following a personal quest' (*loc. cit.*). Singer is probably right when he concludes that the future of anthropology in broadcasting relies heavily on 'the predilection of individuals in positions of power and influence' (p. 271) if it is to cope with the intrinsic constraints and problems of the culture of broadcasting.

In the following chapter Wright explores the use of narrative as one of the means by which television has been able to reach a mass audience. Drawing on both cinematographic and literary theory, Wright examines broadcasted anthropology as a story-telling activity where the 'narrative becomes a device for holding the attention of the audience' (p. 276). *Baka: People of the Rainforest* (Agland 1987) is used as an illustrative example of what Wright calls a 'poetic' use of montage in the construction of narrativity as opposed to the polemical use in Moser's *War of the Gods* (1971).

Story-telling is also a key factor in Turton's distinction between the worlds of broadcasting and anthropology. Referring to, among other aspects, the audience issue, he introduces a crucial distinction between anthropologists, programme-makers and film-makers. Anthropologists and programme-makers are communicators whereas film-makers are artists. Anthropologists share with programme-makers the 'compulsion to explain', film-makers, on the other hand, share with programme-makers the 'compulsion to entertain'. The introduction of the concept 'programme-maker' emphasises the specificities of the culture of broadcasting, a culture very different from both anthropology and film-making for several reasons, some of which have been discussed above and many aspects of which are dealt with in further detail in Turton's chapter, where he uses examples from his own experience working as an anthropological consultant for *Disappearing World* to illustrate his points. One of the main points, relating this chapter to those of Singer and Wright, is the character of the relationship between the anthropologist and the programme-maker. As Turton describes it, this relationship is characterised by 'the tension between telling a story and elucidating an issue, or problem', a tension which 'is a desirable ingredient in any collaboration between programme-maker and anthropologist' (p. 290).

The major part of this book has dealt specifically with 'film as ethnography' although many contributors have compared developments in visual anthropology with developments in writing anthropology and, in a sense, regarded these as two very different and separate forms of ethnographic representation. The two final chapters deal with examples of new technologies which enable the anthropologist to combine words, sounds and images in a multiplicity of complex ways.

Seaman and Williams (Chapter 18) focus on the potential of using computers in the production of 'hypermedia', a use which solves many of the problems involved in the storage of data, referencing and retrieval systems. Computer-based new technology opens new roads for integrating texts, images and sound which could have a profound impact on the development of new forms of ethnographic representation in research, teaching and presentation to wide audiences in, for example, museums. They assess the possible institutional impacts this may have as well as potential problems such as information overloading, the cost in both time and money and what may be referred to as problems concerning the relations of production in general.

One of the most successfully employed new technologies in multimedia presentation is the so-called videodisc. Macfarlane (Chapter 19) gives examples of the potential of the videodisc, focusing on the experience built up during the development of the BBC's Domesday Project and his own work with The Cambridge Experimental Videodisc Project. He argues that anthropology, due to the complexity of its subject-matter and its dependence on very different forms of data (images, notes, sound, objects etc.), could play an important role in the development of new technologies for research, teaching and the dissemination of information.

### References

*Books and articles*
Balikci, A. (1988), *Anthropology, Film and the Arctic Peoples*, (The Forman Lecture, 1988) *Anthropology Today*, 5, 2, pp. 4–11.
Ellis, J. (1982), *Visible Fictions. Cinema, Television, Video*, Routledge & Kegan Paul, London.
Ginsburg, F. (1988), 'Ethnographies on the airwaves: the presentation of anthropology on American, British and Japanese television' in P. Hockings and Y. Omori (eds.), *Cinematographic Theory and New Dimensions in Ethnographic Film*, Senri Ethnological Studies no. 24, Osaka, pp. 31–66.
Henley, P. (1985), 'British Ethnographic Film. Recent Developments', *Anthropology Today*, I (1), pp. 5–17.
Loizos, P. (1980), 'Granada Television's Disappearing World Series: An Appraisal', *American Anthropologist*, 82, pp. 573–93.
Lydall, J. (1992), 'Filming *The Women Who Smile*' in P. I. Crawford and J. K. Simonsen (eds.), *Ethnographic Film, Aesthetics and Narrative Traditions*, Proceedings from NAFA II, Intervention Press, Aarhus.

Young, C. (1988), 'Documentary and Fiction, Distortion and Belief', in P. Hockings and
    Y. Omori (eds.), *Cinematographic Theory and New Dimensions In Ethnographic Film*, Senri
    Ethnological Studies no. 24, Osaka, pp. 7–30.

*Films*

Agland, P. (1987), *Baka: People of the Rain Forest*, Channel 4 Television, UK. Colour, 104
    mins.
MacDougall, D. (1973), *To Live With Herds*, Film Images, New York. Black and white, 68
    mins.
Moser, B. (1971), *The Last of the Cuiva*, *Disappearing World* series, Granada Television,
    Manchester. Colour, 65 mins. (Anthropologist: B. Arcand)

# Anthropology in broadcasting

Let me begin by quoting from a giant. Grierson defined the documentary as the 'creative interpretation of actuality'. Since the inception of film, viewers and makers have been disputing the different ways actuality can be interpreted and, perhaps more importantly, have differed about the meaning of actuality itself. It is easy, for example, with the hindsight of cinema-verité, to be critical of Flaherty's manipulation of Nanook and the Samoans. Despite their striving to establish objectivity in the presentation of their material, by recognising that the film-maker and his paraphenalia are an integral part of the film-making process, the verité school, exemplified by Rouch, is also easily open to the charge of selectivity, manipulation and naivety. But then that is the inevitability of the film idiom. Film-makers have a distinct form of communication, in which a proportion of the viewer's interpretation is done for him or her, in the ordering and selection of the images; but a sizeable proportion is open to different interpretation. This is diametrically opposed to the ambitions of written ethnography and the one will never replace the other.

The relationship between anthropology and broadcasting is a whimsical one. It may at times reflect contemporary concern about 'the other' and current events certainly influence the quantity and direction of anthropological content on the screen. The Gulf War, for example, guaranteed programming about the Kurds, Arab life and Gulf political dynamics, while the interest in minorities in Central Asia has been awakened by the momentous political events unfolding there. But the process is arbitrary. This paper is aimed at trying to make sense of that arbitrariness.

In television, very little dialogue about how anthropology should be presented to a popular or even select audience is taking place or has ever taken place. It is a random process and it is quite clear that television fulfils a different role in our society to that of documentary film in visual anthropology. Since many discussions about visual anthropology seem to concentrate on presenting variations of a history of Flaherty through to contemporary works, I will here for a change concentrate on the presentation of anthropological and ethnographic ideas and material on television and not on film generally. 'Television?' questioned the writer and editor C. P. Scott in the 1950s, 'The word is half Greek and half Latin. No good will come of it.' But like it or not, television came, stayed and is expanding at a frightening rate. We may not appreciate its pervasive impact and influence on contemporary Western society or its growing influence elsewhere in the world but we cannot gainsay the extent of it.

The nature of the television image is ephemeral (and, in major contrast to ethnographic film, is not constructed to be viewed over and over again) nor can it fully be divorced from its major purpose – entertainment. Ethnographic film has an intended permanence often linked to literature and is not generally seen as entertainment. In contrast, the main importance of television is of transitory communication to a non-specialist public. Even with such caveats, I take as a starting premise that there *is* value in materials of an anthropological nature being presented to such an audience or, at least, I would not presume to deny such materials a public outlet. But in the same way as I would not expect many non-anthropologists to read and absorb *The Nuer*, nor would I expect them to include in their visual diet *Jaguar* or even *Dead Birds*. The material that most commonly finds a television outlet is packaged to appeal to different tastes and is only pedagogical by default. It is the present and future of this package on which I wish to comment.

There was recently an extraordinary and often vitriolic exchange in the *Society for Visual Anthropology Newsletter* (Autumn 1988 and Spring 1989) about Robert Gardner's film *Forest of Bliss* (1987). At the core of the debate was the question whether this film was anthropology, art, both or neither. The crucial area of contention was whether a film-maker tackling fundamentally human issues of importance to anthropologists but without having a grounding or even, necessarily, a specialised interest in the 'anthropological perspective' is likely so to disturb or confuse the images he or she is portraying as to do the discipline and its achievements a disservice. I raise this, not because I wish to get embroiled in the debate about *Forest of Bliss*, but because a high proportion of what broadcasters categorise as anthropology also presents ethnography from an academically ill-informed or ill-targeted perspective. This is not necessarily because of any intention deliberately to distort or misinterpret, but because the aims of television film-makers are different to those of anthropologists and the two only combine when the former needs the unique access or knowledge that can be provided by the latter.

Some part of any material given out on the small screen, whether anthropological in content or not, is received and digested by the viewer and creates or provokes some form of response. The extent of that response is difficult to determine and is likely, in any case, to be unconscious, but there is no doubt that it is there and increasing. Television viewing has, in recent decades, taken up a large proportion of time that was previously devoted to work, family interaction, play or other leisure activities. Simultaneously, it has created new stimuli – reading, music, plays, films etc. – and has also shown an ability to relay information about other societies with increasing accuracy. The difference between the popular natural history series of Armand and Michaela Denis, showing in the 1960s, and the most recent examples of television production shows a clear progression in ideas and presentation. The same may be said of the feature film world. Although *Emerald Forest* (Borman, 1985) or *The Mission* (Joffé, 1986) with their 'enactments' of tribal life, may ring alarm bells for contemporary anthropologists, the contrast between their attempts to present fictionalised anthropological data and those of, say, Cooper or Flaherty, is considerable.

It is mainly in communication studies that serious attempts to analyse the relationship between audiences and the impact of the message have been made. Visual anthropology has looked to film but not, to any great extent, television. This is extraordinary, in the light not only of the role television plays in our society but also of the role it is increasingly playing in the rest of the world. Already, most urban centres in the world have television, so do more and more rural regions. The use of satellite relays and solar powered sets is only years away – not even decades. We may shudder or, in certain instances, rejoice, but we have to try to understand what it will mean and what it has meant so far in our own backyard.

I am most concerned here with the relaying of material with an anthropological scope in Western society, in the belief that the television image exerts an extraordinary and insiduous influence on its Western viewers. Over twenty years ago, Marshall McLuhan wrote as follows:

Is it not strange that TV should have been as revolutionary a medium in America in the 1950s as radio in Europe in the 1930s? Radio, the medium that resuscitated the tribal and kinship webs of the European mind in the 1920s and 1930s had no such effect in England or America. There, the erosion of tribal bonds by means of literacy and its industrial extension had gone so far that our radio did not achieve any notable tribal reactions. Yet ten years of TV have Europeanised even the United States, as witness its changed feelings for space and personal relations. There is new sensitivity to the dance, plastic arts, and architecture, as well as the demand for the small car, the paperback, sculptural hairdos and molded dress effects – to say nothing of a new concern for complex effects in cuisine and in the use of wines . . . For good or ill, the TV image has exerted a unifying synesthetic force on the sense-life of these intensely literate populations, such as they have lacked for centuries. (1964)

The return wave of American influence on England and Europe as a result of television after the 1960s has been even greater. Surely no other medium could have, or has, exerted as pervasive an influence as television on public awareness?

Some communication theorists have suggested that this effectiveness is a result of television supplying certain social and pyshological needs of the viewing individual, such as escape from daily tensions and problems and the acquisition of knowledge and information to understand the world around them. But the goal of either quantifying or qualifying the influence of television on individuals or mass populations has been elusive. Communications sociologists, such as

McQuail, end up with intangibles: 'Communication effects are greatest where the message is in line with the existing opinions, beliefs and dispositions of the receiver'; or 'Communications can produce the most effective shifts on unfamiliar, light felt, peripheral issues; which do not lie in the centre of the recipient's value systems'; or yet again 'Communication is more likely to be effective where the source is believed to have expertise, high status, objectivity or likeability, but particularly where the source has power and can be identified with' (McQuail 1975, pp. 151–65).

In other words, viewers are happiest with the material they know, can identify with and which roughly conforms to their current ideology, which would appear to be a truism. We would not expect a conservative stockbroker to read the *Daily Star*, nor a Welsh miner the *Daily Telegraph*. Choice is an essential part of our democratic process. That choice is more limited when it comes via the airwaves. The three, and then four, channels of television that have been available to the British public over the past decades are not divided along lines of potential ideology like the press, nor into tabloids vs. quality, although there is a 'popular' versus more 'serious' division between the ITV network and BBC 1 on the one hand, and Channel Four and BBC 2 on the other. So choice is constrained and viewers have to move between channels to find programming most suited to their wants and needs. This has allowed minority taste programming to slip through the net. Other parts of the world swing towards different extremes of the choice spectrum, with up to 50 channel choices in parts of the US and single government controlled channels in many authoritarian nations.

Where does anthropology fit into this? In the past, like any other discipline that lends itself to visual representation, anthropology and broadcasting have had a totally *ad hoc* relationship. There have been films and programmes that have used images of societies outside the normal conceptual or geographic reach of viewers. But does Armand and Michaela Dennis looking at a Maasai dance during a safari constitute anthropology? To the extent that viewers either receive or reinforce their perception of the 'Other' from such material, the answer is yes.

Brian Street, in his *The Savage in Literature* (1975), highlighted the gap between the information and the knowledge known to anthropologists earlier this century and the popular portrayal of other societies by writers such as Haggard, Conrad and Buchan. The gap was enormous and it often took decades for the findings of anthropologists to be absorbed and relayed in popular representation. Where the lines of academia and popularisation are particularly weak, the convential wisdom of the past century is still finding itself perpetuated in print in the 1990s. This conforms to McQuail's finding that 'communication effects are greatest where the message is in line with the existing opinion, beliefs and disposition of the receiver'.

Television, however, is a more dramatic medium. The moving image is in a position to lend popular credence to activity, and insight into society, in a way that academic wisdom, literature or still photography has been unable to. A few line drawings or selected photographs were easily used to reinforce the evolutionary stereotypes of the popularizers of sixty years ago who called upon the intellectual rationalisation of anthropologists of decades earlier. Gilson, in a popular novel about West African pygmies was happily able to rely on Tylor and others to support his findings. 'The dwarfs were split into two distinct families, namely the Bushmen of the Kalahari Desert and the pygmies of the Upper Congo. Both these races are of a very primitive order of intelligence, in physical feature bearing a greater resemblance to monkeys than to men' (1919, p. 16). Gilson was by no means an exception in writing at that time. John Buchan thought of the 'Bushmen' as 'one of the lowest of created types still living in the Stone Age and prevented from advancing by the continual influx of superior races' while the 'Pygmies' had 'no social organisation' and their only skill was in following spoor and a rudimentary cave art (1909). Without denying the extent and entrenchment of contemporary bigotry and prejudice, I wonder whether Colin Turnbull and Philip Agland – popular ethnographer and television documentarist of the 'pygmies' respectively – reflected the attitudes of the 1980s or changed them? It is certainly remarkable that *Baka: People of the Rainforest* (Agland, 1987) should have been the most successful documentary of 1987 on Channel 4 and at the same time win the Royal Anthropological Institute's Biennial film prize in 1988. And whether the viewer liked or disliked the film and the structural devices that went into its making, the values it portrayed and its links to contemporary anthropological values were so different to the literary examples just given that we can only hope that they have been absorbed by an uncritical audience and recognised as part of his or her own contemporary value system.

This leads me to the most critical relationship in broadcasting – that between the communicator and his or her audience. The greatest proportion of anthropological material shown on television in the UK in the 1970s and 1980s had little to do directly with anthropologists or the academic discipline. It was overwhelmingly material produced by often talented amateur anthropologists; essentially, film-makers for whom anthropology was often incidental to the main subject matter. These were largely producers from current affairs, docu- mentaries and drama. Their programmes varied from travelogue, dance and music, thrillers, adventure, natural history and political reportage. Anthropology played a 'supporting role' and tended to reflect a loosely liberal conventional attitude towards other societies – a reflection, perhaps, of the attitudes held by the hierarchy in overall control of the broadcasting stations. If and when anthropologists were consulted to advise on the contents of such programmes, such consultation was brief and selective and they were rarely called upon to advise on the whole concept of the film or report. The producer remained the conduit for the ideas relayed to the main audience. Those ideas were, of course, shaped as much by the conventional wisdom of the age as by his own absorption of anthropological ideas through film and other media. There is often a desire to use the subject-matter to reinforce an idea or theme well outside the remit of anthropology: such as the wish to create danger or fear in a film about an adventure or political tension in a news story. The ethnography, therefore, will invariably be selective. It may reinforce stereotypes or gradually change them but, in any event, the process will be arbitrary.

Over the past two decades there have also been a number of broadcast programmes that consciously regard themselves as 'anthropology', a label that implies academic credibility, e.g. *Odyssey, Disappearing World, Worlds Apart, Under The Sun* and *Millenium*. These programmes generally give anthropologists a greater role in shaping the product: these are the programmes that are seen by our peers 'as anthropology on television'. Since I would estimate that at least ten times as much air time is given to natural history as to anthropology, perhaps the message that anthropology wants to relay to the public is one that they do not want to hear, or would be uncomfortable with. On one level that is what it should be, for if an understanding of a different society causes the individual to question his or her complacent attitudes, at least something is being achieved. But this touches an area that I suspect few of us in broadcasting have properly faced – how much is the material we identify as anthropology really aimed at affecting public attitudes and how much is it just another collage of raw material that happens to be anthropological in nature because that is how we have gained our access?

*Disappearing World*, of which I was once an unrepentant part, always proudly trumpeted its aims as 'recording other peoples' way of life before it was too late' (Moser 1988, p. 12), 'reaching an understanding of what the way of life portrayed was like to those who lived it' (Henley, 1985, p. 16), 'giving those for whom anthropology is literally a closed book a feeling of familiarity with the lives and preoccupation of the people of another and very different culture' (Turton 1985, p. 16) and so on. In reality, I believe that the early aims of Brian Moser and Denis Forman were the most achievable: to highlight the pressures that the West was putting on tribal society to change and to record those societies before they were unrecognisable. The embellishment of trying to understand, explain and elaborate on the complexities of social life were added later when Melissa Llewelyn-Davies, Chris Curling, Angela Burr and I joined the team and attempted to add what we then (in the early 1970s) thought were additional anthropological values.

I do not wish to debate the rights and wrongs of approaches towards *Disappearing World* here, nor of any subsequent series that took an anthropological label, but I do feel it important to emphasise one point. That series was not created as a means of filling an audience demand. It was the result of broadcasting individuals – in this case the Head of Programming at Granada Television and an enthusiastic idealistic film-maker, Brian Moser – following a personal quest. Forman's perception was that the material would have archival value and would contribute to our knowledge of the past (when the past came along). He had no real passion for 'understanding' other societies nor, in the Moser sense, a belief in righting society's wrongs. But the combination proved effective and, by using anthropologists as cultural guides, an academic authenticity and new dimension was added to the way other societies were portrayed on television.

To take the Foreman-Moser example a stage further, the essence of understanding the relationship between communicator and audience is to place it in its proper historical context. By this I am referring to a major gap in broadcast scheduling and an idiosyncratic wish to fill that gap in the 1960s. Until then the gap had happily been filled by a variety of materials bought or made in an *ad hoc* manner. After the *Disappearing World* series in the UK, or *Odyssey* in the US, had been established, the power play between broadcasters came into effect. Anthropology was 'seen' to have been catered for. In the UK, Anglia TV continued with its output of natural history programming and Granada took the tribes. Anthropology was left well alone by the others. Competition from the other major network, the BBC, was slow in coming for two reasons. Firstly, the regular and popular series *The World About Us* provided a diet of programming deemed by the controllers of the BBC to be sufficiently anthropological in nature. Secondly, Granada averaged between three to six hours per annum of television programming on the subject, a meagre diet that was thought to be sufficient. Only in certain academic circles was this small output seen as the Great Leap Forward. In the US the structure of the PBS network provided a comparable pattern; for a short period Ambrosini's *Odyssey* filled the network's needs and cable was still light years away from providing alternatives.

When competition was eventually organised in the UK, it took the form of *Face Values*. Prince Charles acted as 'the man in the street', asking the fundamental questions the man in the street was expected to want to ask of the field anthropologists. Although the series tackled themes that anthropologists believed their peers and interested film-makers would find important (such as ritual and economics), it was not regarded by anthropologist, nor audience, nor film critic to be a great success. Anthropology and broadcasting had not found a new rapprochement. Indeed, my assessment is that, during the 1980s the com-munication of anthropology through television made very little progress. The condescending fourteen programmes of *Human Jigsaw* made even *Face Values* shine and neither *Disappearing World* nor the BBC's *Worlds Apart* provide any radical new formula. My own and Bruce Dakowski's *Strangers Abroad*, attempted to bring the value of anthropological fieldwork and fieldworkers to the public eye but that hardly moved goal posts very far either.

In my earlier references to literature I was attempting to point out that the perculation of anthropological ideas to a popular audience using the written word is a slow process, partially because authors address a selective audience without the aim of changing the audience or pandering to its demands. Broadcasting is different and addresses different audiences on different levels. What a student audience might 'read' in an anthropological film made for a television audience is likely to be very different from what the public will 'read' in it. However much the television director may like to believe that he or she is satisfying his or her anthropological peers, he or she is tied into a communications system that makes a popular audience the prime target. Melissa Llewellyn-Davies' *Diary of a Maasai Village* (1984) was a courageous and rare attempt to sacrifice 'popularity' for experimentation (shorter would have been more acceptable to the BBC, and probably to most audiences, but would have affected both the anthropological and artistic creativity of the series). I mention this because I would like to end by outlining where the 1990s seem to be leading. The content of broadcasting will continue to depend upon the predilection of individuals in positions of power and influence. If they like flowers you will see more botany programmes.

Changes in the structure of the ITV network in the UK in 1991 have, however, allowed market forces a stronger leverage over individual choice than ever before. Factual programmes are relatively expensive; anthropological ones even more so. The pessimists would be justified in believing that anthropology in broadcasting is in serious jeopardy for the first time since the 1960s because of a new absence of obligation for the new franchise holders to produce a quota of 'serious' factual documentaries. The optimists must continue to rely on three other factors to counteract this opinion. Firstly, there is the public service remit of the BBC, which will continue to endorse the provision of programmes with an educational and instructive context, at least until 1996 when the license fee arrangement with the government will be under review. Secondly, there is pressure from individuals inside broadcasting with sufficient influence to override the current trend towards populism and profitability. The persistence of the BBC series *Under The Sun* and Granada's *Disappearing World* are two cases in point, with new, encouraging bursts of programming such as Channel Four's *The 'Savage' Strikes Back* and *Nomads* during 1991 and the ten-part series with David Maybury-Lewis, *Millennium*, in 1992. *Fine Cut*, my own new strand on BBC 2, will provide a further home for feature documentaries and is already in production with a film by Jean-Pierre Gorin and Daniel Marks on Samoan street gangs called *My Crazy Life* (1992), Jean Rouch's *Madame L'Eau* (1992) and Pavel Linguine's *A Small Russian Town* (1992); whilst an on-going dialogue should lead to productions with David MacDougall on Sicilian bandits, Melissa Llewelyn-Davies on a Maasai follow-up, Gil Gardinal on Canadian Indians, Nick Gifford on a Sudanese refugee family and a collaboration between Steve Lansing, Gary Seaman and myself in Tajikistan.

The third reason for optimism lies with public opinion over such issues as the environment. Environmental concern has become a major force in the 1990s. This is reflected in politics and subsequently, or consequently, in broadcast output. *Fragile Earth* on Channel Four and *Nature* on the BBC have become an essential core of programme planning in the UK, as have similar films on PBS and the Discovery Channel in the US. It is in this context that anthropology has already been given a new lease of visibility. The Kayapo and Brazilian rainforests (with or without Sting), the Baka and the Cameroons, and the Penan in Borneo have become the focus for world attention in a way that earlier ethnographers could never have envisaged. Anthropologists have always appreciated the relevance of knowledge about the working of human society. The public is now becoming belatedly aware of it also and, to my mind, in a far healthier manner: as a part of a new consciousness of global affairs, rather than as a form of escapism and voyeurism. May the optimists win the broadcast battle!

## References

*Books and articles*
Buchan, J. (1909), *The African Colony*, Blackwood, London.
Gilson, C. (1919), *In the Power of the Pygmies*, Milford.
Henley, P. (1985), 'British Ethnographic Film: Recent Developments', *Anthropology Today*, I, 1, pp. 5–17.
McQuail, D. (1975), *Communication*, Longmans, London.
Moser, B. (1988), foreword in A. Singer and L. Woodhead (eds.), *Disappearing World*, Boxtree (London) in association with Granada Television.
Street, B. (1975), *The Savage in Literature*, Routledge, London.
Turton, D. (1985), *In Search of Cool Ground: The Mursi Trilogy, 1974–85*, Granada Television, Manchester (brochure).

*Films*
Agland, P. (1987), *Baka: People of the Rainforest*, Dja River Films for Channel 4 Television, UK. Colour, 104 mins.
Borman, J. (1985), *Emerald Forest*. Embassy. Colour, 113 mins.
Gardner, R. (1963), *Dead Birds*. Film Study Center, Harvard. Colour, 83 mins.
—— (1987), *Forest of Bliss*, Jane Balfour Films. Colour, 90 mins.
Gorin, J. P. (1992), *My Crazy Life*, Allan Marks Productions. Colour, 90 mins.
Joffe, R. (1986), *The Mission*, Goldcrest. Colour, 128 mins.
Linguine, P. (1992), *Portrait of a Small Russian Town*, Le Monde. Colour, 90 mins.
Llewelyn-Davies, M. (1984), *Diary of a Maasai Village*, BBC Enterprises. Colour, series of four.
Rouch, J. (1965), *Jaguar*, Documentary Educational Resources, Watertown, Mass. Colour, 35 mins.
—— (1992), *Madame L'Eau*, Dutch Film Institute. Colour, 90 mins.

*Series*

| Series | Broadcaster | Series editor |
| --- | --- | --- |
| *Odyssey* | WGBH – Boston | M. Ambrosini |
| *Disappearing World* | Granada TV | B. Moser, A. Singer, D. Wason |
| *Worlds Apart* | BBC 2 | C. Curling |
| *Under The Sun* | BBC 2 | C. Curling, W. Hilary |
| *Millennium* | Global, KCET (LA), BBC 2, ABC (Australia) | A. Malone (Exec. Producer) |
| *World About Us/ Wideworld* | BBC 2 | A. Isaacs, T. Slessor |
| *Face Values* | BBC | D. Cordingley (Series Producer) |
| *Human Jigsaw* | Granada TV | A. Ross |
| *Strangers Abroad* | Central TV | A. Singer/K. Sabbagh |
| *The 'Savage' Strikes Back* | C4 | L. Holland (Series Producer) |

| | | |
|---|---|---|
| *Nomads* | C4 | P. Carmichael, C. Lukes |
| *Fine Cut* | BBC 2 | A. Singer |
| *Fragile Earth* | C4 | P. Moore |
| *Survival* | Anglia TV | G. Creelman/ |
| | | (Current Exec. Producer) |
| | | C. Wilcock |
| | | (Former Exec. Producer) |
| *Nature* | BBC 1 | J. Evans/ |
| | | A. Theunissen |

# Television narrative and ethnographic film

The extension of anthropology through public broadcast systems has defined new areas of enquiry. At one extreme, television has made available visual recordings of the world's disappearing cultures; at the other, it has both generated awareness and motivated responses to global ethnic and ecological issues. But, having granted these points, it has also had the effect of limiting the discipline. The broadcasters' understanding of 'good television' usually requires the moulding of ethnographic footage into familiar story-lines. The inevitable product of this demand is a very particular narrative style. An authoritative Western voice establishes the location of the film, introduces the cultural group (occasionally some individuals), and guides the viewer through some of their typical day-to-day routines. While this general organisational pattern is not dissimilar to the standard written ethnography (introduction to the geographical location, relation of man to environment, social organisation, kinship, exchange, religion, and so on), the televised ethnography differs in that there is little room for analysis, but a high dependence on 'self-evident' visual description. Indeed, the 'classic realist' ethnographic narrative often appears to be used as an excuse for screening a succession of 'interesting' or 'spectacular' images.

At its most elementary level, *narrative* can be considered the telling of a story; thus, the phrase 'narrative film' gives an important emphasis to the story-line. While we may question whether a 'story' is appropriate to the filmed ethnography, there are wider connotations to narrative. It therefore becomes necessary to expand our use of the term to account for the general conceptual scheme of the film: the film as a series of occurrences and the principles by which those occurrences are ordered. The crucial point, for the televised ethnographic film in particular, is that this sequencing of events can lead to misrepresentation. What is more, despite the film's 'real world' origins, it can be argued that the processes of selection and editing create a unique world that only really exists on the television screen. Thus, any inclinations the film-maker might have towards realism are undermined by the act of film-making itself. So, besides considering some of the narrative strategies used in ethnographic film, in this chapter I examine the constraints on visual anthropology to satisfy the demands of Western popular culture, but then question whether the point at issue is necessarily one of priorities.

## The central role of narrative

To the purist, 'true' ethnographic film appears to occupy a position far removed from the world of television. The 'serious' footage suitable for the small audience for anthropological study becomes opposed to the packaged production for a mass audience: on the one hand, the transparency of the medium, on the other, mediated edited highlights for public entertainment. In addition, it is a world in which we move from the work of the individual anthropologist to that of industrial production. It further implies the opposition of observation and narration. At one extreme there is the direct transferral of a scene to the viewer: the aim of the camera is to facilitate transparent access to the subject-matter. This is quite different to the telling of stories.

For anthropology, the raw material of film aims to shift authority to a viewer who is the already informed, offering a 'window on the world'. Taken literally, this observational standpoint is that of the philosopher Cratylus: because no true statement can be made about things that are always changing, nothing can be said – we can only indicate with the finger. For television, narration describes events or tells the story. Here the narrator stands in for the anthropologist as a neutral and unseen expert who contextualises and supplements the images. This role should be viewed with suspicion. Acting as a translator or buffer between the viewer and subject, the narrator witholds an essential ingredient of realist cinema by impeding the identification of the viewer's ego with the subject. This has the result of limiting our empathy and keeping the subject at a safe distance.

There is, of course, a distinction to be made between narrative and narration or, as Genette (1980) has indicated, between *mood* and *voice*. We should distinguish, that is, between the character whose point of view orients the narrative perspective and the narrator. A primary function of narrative in cinema, however, is 'to rein in the galloping connotations of images' (Andrew 1984, p. 76), which would otherwise make the film appear seamless and lacking in direction.

## The observational standpoint

In his biography of Robert Flaherty, Arthur Calder-Marshall (1963) outlines the essential problem for the ethnographic film-maker, namely that the subject is altered by the intrusion of the observer. 'The white explorer may wish to see a world as it was before the white man came; but he can only see it as it reacts to the coming of the first white man. He is looking for the rainbow's end, unless he can imaginatively reconstruct what things would have been like if he had not been there' (p. 252). But, in practice, film-makers tend to reflect the polarisation of the highly constructed fiction film and the 'found' situations of direct cinema. These stem from the respective positions established by Eisenstein and Bazin: the film that is 'made', its ordering of events controlled by the director, versus the film of which the final form is determined by the 'actual' course of events. This debate is also about the 'natural state' of the medium – subjective constructed meaning versus an objective 'transparent' recording. As Cratylus found, this distinction between *construction* and *finding* might also be true of everyday perception, as in Merleau-Ponty's belief that the world cannot be expressed except in 'stories' or 'pointed at' (1964, p. 28). But even in the act of pointing we cannot escape some degree of construction. We are limited to 'pointing at' landmarks on a type of map which charts 'the sedimentation of meaning'. And this map is drawn from our own life experiences.

The film-maker's problem of intrusion is shared by the anthropologist and taken a stage further by Said (1972): 'the observing ethnologist is a product of literate society, and because anthropology itself is subject to the enslaving laws of literacy, the zero state is a forbidden paradise to which literacy penetrates only at the same critical moment that the paradise is being obliterated' (p. 353). It appears that, however careful we are as 'observers', we remain bound by the 'laws of literacy'. Jean Mitry (1963) has described film as 'a world that organises itself in terms of a story' (p. 354). This may be a simple consequence of the fact that filmed events are sequential, for even in the days of silent cinema film narrative appears to have been based upon Western literary traditions. So, if narrative is unavoidable, this gives an important emphasis to the need to understand the terms in which narrative has been established. It cannot simply be regarded as the unfolding of events before the camera.

## The standard narrative patterns

Television documentary has tended towards a particular type of naturalism. It aims at authenticity and is generally opposed to 'artistic translation'. In this context, narrative implies making the subject comprehensible: the construction of a story for a specific audience. In the context of television, narrative becomes a device for holding the attention of the audience, as in *A Thousand and One Nights*, where Scheherezade's security depends upon her narrative ability. As long as she can entertain her audience and hold the Sultan's attention she will not be executed. Her survival, like that of the television producer, depends upon her capabilities as a storyteller. Strong characters, too, make 'good television'. Marcus Banks (1990) has rightly noted the attraction of Ongka's personality: 'Such people endear themselves to an audience' (p. 6). But the success of *The Kawelka – Ongka's Big Moka* (Nairn, 1974) might be due to another, equally attractive element: 'the contemporary Western perceiver does typically expect expository material at the outset, a state of affairs disturbed by a complication, and some character ready to function as a goal-oriented protagonist' (Bordwell

1985, p. 35). Although Bordwell is referring here to fiction film, his remark is equally applicable to the television documentary.

We find there are strong similarities in the ways documentaries are constructed. Although the subjects are different, the stories themselves – as with Propp's folktales – can be very repetitious. They run close to Umberto Eco's (1979) description of the 'closed texts' of *James Bond* or *Superman*: 'pulling the reader along a predetermined path, carefully displaying their effects so as to arouse pity or fear, excitement or depression at the due place at the right moment. Every step of the "story" elicits just the expectation that its further course will satisfy' (p. 8). These films imply a structure that must already be familiar to the assumed audience. So it is with ethnographic film. Before moving to the main part of the commentary, for example, we are given a description of the setting and the characters, a temporal summary (what has happened) and the narrator's report (what is happening now and what we are about to witness).

Looking further back, we found that while the caption cards in Flaherty's *Nanook* (1922) aim to tell a story, they also tend towards the poetic. The film opens with 'The mysterious Barren Lands – desolate, boulder strewn, windswept – illimitable spaces which top the world'. We are introduced to worlds of mystery whose secrets the film-makers promise to share. This is obviously a key to popularity that has not changed since the early days of ethnographic film.

A good contemporary example is provided by Agland's *Baka: People of the Rainforest* (1987). The scene is set with shots of the mist-shrouded forest, viewed from above. The introductory commentary tells us, in soft reverential tones usually reserved for church, library or museum, that 'This is the heart of Africa. Below the clouds lie the rainforests of South-East Cameroon. Home of the Baka pygmies.' We are clearly about to witness something special, perhaps sacred. A rare or exotic species, which we are privileged to view, but must be careful not to disturb. This narration establishes a definitive story-line: with its plots (and sub-plots) we follow a well-trodden path. Much of the entertainment value and wide popular appeal of *Baka* is due to its familiar narrative structure, which enables a TV audience to sit through what is, after all, a feature-film length documentary. On its first showing on British television (1 November 1987), the two-hour documentary drew an audience of 3¾ million.

In *Baka* we are introduced first to the location and then to personalities. As the plot unfolds, characters are developed and the seeds of disunity are sown. This necessitates the invocation of supernatural powers and order is restored. There is the minor problem of two-year-old Ali's rivalry with his sister, but this is 'only natural'. When all is finally resolved, there follows a hint of a new beginning. The main characters conform to the Western 'nuclear family' and join a long line of TV families. We find that the Baka, far from being remote and 'primitive', are as complex as any of us. The only 'serpent' that enters the Eden of the Baka, in the form of the dispute between Likano and Babu, is banished by two events – one cultural, the appearance of Jengi the forest spirit, and the other natural, the birth of a child. This bears an uncanny resemblance to stories from the Judeo-

Christian tradition.

Almost imperceptibly the narration glides from the Baka to the animals, the other inhabitants of the forest. While this may serve to show the total integration of the Baka with their environment, it may also suggest that they are just another species. If, in contrast, we listen to Likano's songs and animal impersonations they have an underlying theme: that of distinguishing the Baka from the animals.

The film has been edited to create scenes of some drama: the arguments between Likano and Babu and the cat which (supposedly) disturbed the women's fishing are the most obvious examples. Such devices of drama-documentary give ominous significance to the old silver-back gorilla. Rejected from the troupe and alone in the tree-tops during the storm, he becomes a portent for Likano's future state of affairs: later we find that Likano's increasingly unreasonable behaviour and concern to perpetuate the feud places him in danger of isolation and rejection from the Baka.

In one sequence a woman is shown building the wooden frame of a house. She prepares some leaves, then uses them to cover the frame. This procedure has not been filmed in 'real time': we see only what the film-maker considers to be the significant points of the construction. During this sequence, however, we are shown the men, in another part of the rainforest, smoking-out a termite mound, supposedly at the same time as the house is being built. Rather than show us what we would have seen had we been there at the time, then, the film resorts to artificiality to portray simultaneity. Nonetheless, there seems no reason why the simultaneity of events should not be considered an aspect of realism.

## Changing the patterns of narrative

Moving from the 'poetic' to the polemical use of montage, *War of the Gods* (Moser 1971) depends upon alternating sequences of images to establish the differences between two cultures: the Maku and the missionaries. Throughout these sequences the contrast between the two groups is heightened by sets of opposing images. Shamanism, exemplified by beliefs in animal spirits, versus Christianity, with its theology of original sin; sharing and exchange versus money for labour; Western goods (exemplified, for example, by carefully arranged and clean Tupperware) versus artefacts made from materials available in the environment; 'God's timetable' versus a life of timelessness; reliance on the aeroplane and radio versus close physical contact; and for a culture whose beliefs systems are integrated into all aspects of daily life, this becomes opposed to organised worship. The build-up of oppositions leads to an estrangement of the missionaries. They come to represent regimentation and permanence; providers of goods and questionable educational services; and, through their self-righteousness, the destroyers of the beliefs of others. This narrative style, in its use of montage, takes the viewer away from Bazinian contemplation towards Eisenstein's directed meaning.

The study of narrative in literature should obviously be of great value to the consideration of TV documentaries. Genette, for example, has aimed at a systematic organisation of the complex relations between the narrative and the story: *récit*, the order of events in the text, in contrast to *histoire*, the 'actual' sequence of events; and *narration*, the act of narrating itself (1980). There are yet wider implications, for Genette has to resort to other categories of narrative that are derived from the visual, with strong optical or photographic connotations. In this scheme of things, such terms as 'point of view' and 'focalisation' are featured. They are not, however, strictly limited to the visual domain, for they are intended to embrace the cognitive and the emotive, as well as the ideological. This is reminiscent of Eisenstein's claim that montage, dissolves, superimpositions and close-ups could be found even in the novels of Dickens (1949).

There is, in turn, a narrative tradition in the visual arts which again relies on familiarity and implies a literary element – in painting it is usually the representation of a moment in a story. It thus depends upon the viewer being already familiar with the story's wider temporal context. But television production has elevated the literary over the visual, which has led to this over-reliance on familiar narratives. I do not suggest that ethnographic films should necessarily be 'works of art', only that they should show greater respect for film and the wide range of possibilities the medium can offer. The 'visual qualities' of the medium are not limited to the exposition of temporal and spatial location or the precision of the image in its efficient conveyance of information and detail (that which can be conveyed in an expression). For Colin MacCabe, the camera's role in narrative is that it 'shows us what happens – it tells us the truth against which we can measure the discourses' (1974, p. 219). We might conclude that combining narration with the editing of the camera's points of view places the viewer in a privileged and unique position that is available neither to the subjects nor to those involved in making the film.

This is very evident in *The Eskimos of Pond Inlet* (Grigsby 1977). Grigsby's approach is one of constant movement from event to (non-)event, returning to previous scenes or continuing earlier interviews in a succession of viewings and re-visions. Rather than following a straightforward linear narrative the film proceeds in the manner in which the knight can be moved to gradually cover the chess board, and so builds up an overall impression of life in Pond Inlet. At one moment there is a travelling shot across the ice, accompanying the skidoos; then cut to a plane depositing a pick-up truck; then to the old people discussing the influence of the whites on their lives; then back to the skidoos where we overhear a discussion of the problems of travelling on wet ice. There is no commentary, except for the Igulingmuits' own sub-titled words and the occasional caption card. The plane's arrival has no explanation – it appears seemingly out of context – and while we might wonder why, the film has moved on. If we need an explantion for the plane it has to be found in Hugh Brody's book, *The People's Land* (1975), 'The arrival of an aircraft is always an important event for a small northern settlement; no sooner is the drone of engines heard in the sky than a buzz of rumour and speculation begins on the ground' (p.1).

In another part of the film an old man from Pond Inlet is at the site of his home before the government's resettlement programme. While this demands that we refer back to earlier sequences, we are unsure whether he is describing his old home to the audience, to the film crew, or to his son. But the theme of housing policy continues, despite the fact that the film then cuts to an earlier scene, where we find ourselves witnessing a free-wheeling discussion between the same old man and a woman, while the camera pans from one to the other.

In his desire to avoid explaining too much, the director has exercised caution with regard to the anthropologist's intrusion. The giving of importance to incidental events – the arrival of the plane, concern over a sick fish found in a pool, snippets of conversation, the children jumping across a hole in the ice – fits into the pattern of social documentation prescribed by the Mass-Observation Unit of the 1930s. It would be misleading to claim that Grigsby's style of narrative brings us, as viewers, any closer to the Igulingmuit by giving a clearer representation of them, for he draws attention to cinematic conventions as much as to the events we see on the screen. The film succeeds, however, by requiring the viewer to take on an active role that simultaneously questions the film's content and form: the events as we see them and the ways in which those events are presented. It is not the spectacular event or image which is avoided, but the convention of letting the sequence climax before cutting to another sequence.

## Conclusion

Perhaps we should not forget that the value of popular media resides in its popularity. The ability of TV to popularise is one of its assets and it can motivate viewers to develop their own interests in ethnography. While this may amount to televisual seduction, TV anthropology can be seen, not as opposing, but as complementary to written ethnographies. Not only does the recent RAI questionnaire (1990) suggest that 25 per cent of anthropology students have been recruited in this way, but surveys for the IBA of the effects of TV drama on the reading of novels found that 46 per cent of readers bought or borrowed a book as a direct result of seeing its TV serialisation (Wober 1985), and most of these people appeared to prefer the book.

In addition, because of its ability to offer an immediate representation of contemporary issues, television can give an up-date on a more recent turn of events. Some of the episodic possibilities of ethnographic film have been addressed in Leslie Woodhead's *The Mursi Trilogy*. A different example is provided by the relationship between Sandra Ott's ethnography *The Circle of Mountains* (1981) and the film *The Basques of Santazi* (Woodhead 1987). The book leaves us with only one road leading to the village. The film deals with the dilemmas of radical social change: the road has since collapsed, though a new road will soon be open to through traffic, including the *Tour de France* cycle race.

For Bertold Brecht, popular art and realism are natural allies. But 'Reality alters; to represent it the means of representation must alter too. Nothing arises from nothing; the new springs from the old, but that is just what makes it new . . . Methods wear out, stimuli fail. New problems loom up and demand new techniques' (1964), p. 110). Visual anthropology is now well established and increasing in its significance. But while many of the filmic aspects of the sub-discipline remain suppressed, few practitioners show an appropriate awareness of the medium's intrinsic properties. We might be forgiven for thinking that the film camera has been adopted simply as a technological convenience rather than as a visual recording device with its own scope and limitations. Film and television possess material and organisational qualities of their own and visual anthropologists should strive to achieve a critical and analytical sensitivity towards them, much as recent work on 'experimental ethnography' has offered a challenge to the conventions of ethnographic writing. Marcus and Fischer have suggested parallels between the 'new ethnography' and ethnographic film: 'contemporary practitioners of ethnographic film are well aware that it is as much a constructed text as are written works. Ethnographic film making thus poses challenges similar to that of ethnographic writing: problems of narrative and focus, of editing and reflexivity' (1986, p. 75).

While such analogies should not be pressed too far ('reading' film often implies a search for 'meaning' by way of attention to minute detail, usually at the expense of considering the film's overall composition), both forms of representation have been subject to a broader cultural trend towards reflexivity. Looking back, we find that a shift in emphasis from 'transparent' representation to the form of representation itself has increasingly characterised the intellectual concerns of the twentieth century. In visual anthropology, as in other academic disciplines, it is the issue of representation which is most frequently debated.

The televised ethnography stands at the convergence of two procedures which embody some of the dichotomies central to Western culture. At the same time, there is a real threat that the promise of a new approach from visual anthropology could be stifled by, or moulded into, the existing patterns of television. This is likely only as long as anthropology remains visually naive.

## References

*Books and articles*
Andrew, J. Dudley, (1984), *Concepts in Film Theory*, Oxford University Press, New York.
Banks, M. (1990), 'Talking Heads and moving pictures: David Byrne's *True Stories* and the anthropology of film', *Visual Anthropology*, 3, pp. 1–9.
Bordwell, D. (1985), *Narration in the Fiction Film*, Methuen, London.
Brecht, B. (1964), 'The popular and the realistic', J. Willett (ed. & trans.) *Brecht on Theatre*, Methuen, London, pp. 107–15
Brody, H. (1975), *The People's Land*, Penguin, Harmondsworth.
Calder-Marshall, A. (1963), *The Innocent Eye: the Life of Robert Flaherty*, Allen & Co., London.
Eco, U. (1979), *The Role of the Reader*, Indiana University Press, Bloomington.
Eisenstein, S. (1949), 'Dickens, Griffith and the film today', *Film Form*, Harcourt Brace,

New York, pp. 195–255

Genette, G. (1980), *Narrative Discourse*, Blackwell, Oxford.

MacCabe, C. (1974), 'Realism and the cinema: notes on some Brechtian theses', *Screen*, 15, Pt. 2, pp. 10–11.

Marcus, G. E. and Cushman, D. (1982), 'Ethnographies as texts', *Annual Review of Anthropology*, 11, pp. 25–69.

Marcus, G. E. and Fischer, M. M. J. (1986), *Anthropology as Cultural Critique*, University of Chicago Press, Chicago.

Marshall, A. Calder (1963), *The Innocent Eye: the Life of Robert Flaherty*, Allen & Co., London.

Merleau-Ponty, M. (1964), *Sense and Non-Sense*, Northwestern University Press, Evanston, Illinois.

Mitry, J. (1963), *Esthétique et Psychologie du Cinéma*, Editions Universitaires, Paris.

Ott, S. (1981), *The Circle of Mountains: A Basque Shepherding Community*, Clarendon Press, Oxford.

Royal Anthropological Institute (1990), 'Report on RAI Questionnaire', *Anthropology Today*, VI, 1, pp. 12–13.

Said, E. W. (1972), 'Abecedarium culturae: structuralism, absense, writing' in J. K. Simon (ed.), *Modern French Criticism*, University of Chicago Press, Chicago, pp. 341–85.

Wober, J. M. (1985), *Television and Reading*, IBA, London.

*Films*

Agland, P. (1987), *Baka: People of the Rainforest*, Dja River Films for Channel 4. Colour, 104 mins.

Flaherty, R. (1922), *Nanook of the North*, Révillon Frères, Paris. Black and white, 55 mins.

Grigsby, M. (1977), *The Eskimos of Pond Inlet*, *Disappearing World* series, Granada Television, Manchester. Colour, 52 mins. (Anthropologist: H. Brody.)

Moser, B. (1971), *War of the Gods*, *Disappearing World* series, Granada Television, Manchester. Colour, 66 mins. (Anthropologists: Peter Silverwood-Cope, Stephen and Christine Hugh-Jones)

Nairn, C. (1974), *The Kawelka: Ongka's Big Moka*, *Disappearing World* series, Granada Television, Manchester. Colour, 52 mins. (Anthropologist: Andrew Strathern)

Woodhead, L. (1985), *In Search of Cool Ground: The Mursi Trilogy* (*The Mursi*, 1974; *The Kwegu*, 1982; *The Migrants* (1985), *Disappearing World* series, Granada Television, Manchester. Colour, each 52 mins. (Anthropologist: David Turton)

Woodhead, L. (1987), *The Basques of Santazi*, *Disappearing World* series, Granada Television, Manchester. Colour, 52 mins. (Anthropologist: Sandra Ott)

# Anthropology on television: what next?

The importance of television in providing funds for making ethnographic films and opportunities for them to be shown to large audiences is obvious, especially in Britain where Granada Television and the BBC have been responsible for the overwhelming majority of such films made over the past twenty years or so. But those who travel the ever-widening circuit of ethnographic film festivals and visual anthropology conferences are usually highly critical of the television style of documentary film making – especially the didactic approach, the use of pictures merely to illustrate a spoken argument and the contrived narrative structures. These, of course, are the criticisms of film-makers, who may or may not be anthropologists, rather than of anthropologists who are not, and do not aspire to become film-makers.

I count myself in the latter category. My interest in television and ethnographic film arose from my experience of working as an anthropological consultant on an early programme in Granada's *Disappearing World* series, *The Mursi* (1974). The Mursi are a small group of cattle herders and cultivators living in the Lower Omo Valley of southwestern Ethiopa. The director of the programme was Leslie Woodhead, and it has largely been due to his enthusiasm and commitment to following the subsequent history of the Mursi that we have since made four more programmes about them and (in the case of the second programme) a neighbouring group, the Kwegu. I have also been anthropological adviser to the series since 1986.

Since this chapter is based entirely on my experience as a consultant for *Disappearing World* it might be objected that it should have been entitled 'Disappearing World: What Next?' My answer to such an objection would be that *Disappearing World* is the main reason why we in Britain can talk about 'anthropology on television' at all. This is not just because Granada was the first television company to make regular use of anthropologists as consultants and researchers and that it has remained loyal to this commitment to anthropology over the years, but also because of the influence the series has had on anthropological programme-making on British television in general. Scratch almost any programme, on any channel, which can be described as anthropological and you are very likely to find a *Disappearing World* connection of one kind or another.

In this chapter, then, I approach television as a means of communication for the anthropologist, rather than as a potential source of funds and distributional opportunities for the ethnographic film-maker. I offer some reflections on 'anthropological knowledge' and on the 'culture' of broadcasting and ask how should – or can – anthropology be presented on television in the 1990s. I shall argue that the way forward for anthropological programmes on television is that they should become more, not less, anthropological. By which I mean more responsive to the particular preoccupations and concerns of anthropology in the 1990s, which are, and are going to become, very different from what they were in the 1970s. Since our *subject* has changed radically, in other words, so should its presentation on television. This way forward offers the prospect of making programmes which not only appeal to a large audience *and* are anthropologically informed but which appeal to a large audience *because* they are anthropologically informed. This, I happen to think, was the secret of *Disappearing World*'s success in the 1970s.

Throughout my involvement with television I have seen it as a way of communicating anthropological knowledge to as wide and as large an audience as possible. But whereas twenty years ago 'anthropological knowledge' was treated as a fairly unproblematic category, the examination of it has now become a major – perhaps *the* major – preoccupation of anthropologists. Two characteristics of an anthropological account, which were thought little about in the early Seventies, have now come to be seen as existing in a rather uneasy tension with each other. Firstly, such an account embodies scientific, not commonsense knowledge. The information it contains is there because of its relevance to a broad agenda which sets out what questions are worth asking and how to go about answering them. What makes the account anthropological is not the particular nature of the information it contains but the general nature of the criteria according to which that information was selected. The most thorough-going attempt Leslie Woodhead and I made to present such an anthropological account on television was in our second programme, *The Kwegu*, which was transmitted in 1982.

In this we set out to describe the relationship between the Kwegu, a tiny group of about 250 individuals, and the Mursi, who themselves number no more than 5000. But despite the very particular nature of the case, the information presented in the programme was there because of its relevence to an ever widening range of problems or issues within anthropology: the nature of hunter/non-hunter relations in East Africa, the generation and maintenance of ethnic boundaries between economically interdependent groups and the legitimation, as part of the natural order, of exploitative social relations of all kinds. The very choice of Kwegu-Mursi relations as a suitable topic for the programme was a response to discussion and debate within anthropology about these issues. The result was a highly didactic programme in which virtually every scrap of usable footage was assembled to provide a visual counterpart (beautifully photographed by Mike Blakely) to a spoken argument.

The second characteristic of an anthropological account that is now seen to sit rather uneasily with the one I have just outlined is that what makes it convincing is the degree to which it is able to represent or 'translate' an indigenous viewpoint. The closer the account is able to get to this viewpoint, or perhaps one should say the more the reader or viewer is convinced that it has got close to this viewpoint, the more valid and therefore the more 'anthropological' it becomes. It follows that anthropology has the potential to raise awkward questions about our own taken-for-granted assumptions, including the assumption that we can, as outside observers, arrive at an objectively truthful account of the behaviour of people with very different cultural assumptions from our own, such as we attempted to present in *The Kwegu*. It is this last worry that has incrasingly come to preoccupy anthropologists in recent years.

There are two sides to it. Firstly, how can any anthropologist, particularly a Western anthropologist working in a non-Western context, reach an adequate, much less an authoritative, ethnographic understanding when the data he or she collects will be greatly affected by his or her cultural and disciplinary assumptions? Is not the claim to understand others *in their own terms* a *contradiction* in terms? Secondly, is not the very attempt itself to 'understand' another group of human beings – again especially a non-Western group – and then to represent them for the benefit of a Western audience, as we did in *The Kwegu*, an act of objectification and therefore one that diminishes the very humanity of the people who are thus 'understood' and represented?

One can go further. Is not this diminution of *their* humanity undertaken in the interests of bolstering or legitimising our own? I have in mind here the Western notion that to explore, control and understand the world is somehow to make ourselves more human, to extend the limits of our human nature. Thus, when Neil Armstrong stood on the moon in 1969 he was taking a 'giant leap for mankind', including, presumably, for the Kwegu and the Mursi, although the Mursi I took to see the event in an Addis Ababa cinema in 1974 did not quite see it like that. And when Dr Bronowski made a famous television series for the BBC on the history of science in 1973 he called it 'The Ascent of Man'. It is a striking indication of the way the world *we* live in has changed in the last twenty years that such statements now seem, at best, naively optimistic.

It is presumably the realisation that their discipline has been one of the means by which the West has objectified the non-Western world, thereby legitimising its claim to be the standard bearer of human progress and achievement, that has led anthropologists into their current soul-searching about the nature of anthropological knowledge. One direction this soul-searching has taken has been a concern with the parallels between anthropology and tourism; nobody, of course, dislikes a tourist more than another tourist. Is there a difference of kind between the anthropologist and the tourist, or simply one of degree? The anthropologist obviously spends longer in the field than would be usual for a tourist, and gains a more intimate and detailed knowledge of the people amongst whom he or she lives. But there *are* uncomfortable parallels, especially, perhaps, for an anthropologist who works with television programme-makers, thereby helping to satisfy the touristic urge of his or her compatriots by bringing foreign locations and 'exotic' peoples into their living rooms.

Tourists have become fairly commonplace in Mursiland in the last few years. This is partly because the traditional tourist route in northern Ethiopia – Axum, Gondar, the rock churches of Lalibela – has been closed because of military activity and partly because the Lower Omo Valley, in which there are two National Parks, has been made more accessible, by road, from Addis Ababa. During our last filming trip to the Mursi (January 1991) I interviewed three men, Aringatuin, Bio-iton-giga and Komorakora, whom I've known for over twenty years, about the tourists and about our own filming. Some of this interview was included in one of the two programmes that resulted from the trip, *The Land is Bad* (1991), but the following sequence is taken from unedited footage.

*DT*: When the tourists come up and down this road to the Omo and take photographs and when we come and film you like this – what do you say about it, privately?
*Aringatuin*: We say 'It's their thing. They're that sort of people – people who take photographs'. It's the whites' thing. What do we know about it? You are the ones who know. We just sit here and they take photos. There's one that, as you look at it, you can see your own body appearing. If it's bad, tell us.
*Komorakora*: *You* tell us: why do they shoot us?
*DT*: I'm trying to find out what *you* think, in your stomachs.
*Aringatuin*: In our stomachs we've no idea. They can't speak our language, so we can't ask them why they are doing it. We can talk to you because you speak Mursi. They come with Kuchumba [Ethiopian guides] who just sit in the cars. When the tourists have taken their photos, they drive off. We say, 'Is it just that they want to know who we are, or what?' We say, 'They must be people who don't know how to behave.' Even old women come and totter about taking photos. 'Is that how whites normally behave?' That's what we say.
*DT*: So that's what you say.
*Bio-iton-giga*: Goloinmeri – what are they doing? Do they want us to become their children, or what? What do they do with the photographs?
*DT*: They come because they see you as different and strange people. They go back home and tell their friends they've been on a long trip, to Mursiland. They say, 'Look, here are the people we saw'. They do it for entertainment.
*Komorakora*: Recently, the Administrator at Hana told us, 'Build a nice big house, with a fence – a big house, well built. The vets can use it when they innoculate the cattle and the tourists can photograph it. The tourists come to enjoy themselves. They can sleep in the house and go back the next day'. That's what the Administrator told us – what's his name?
*Bio-iton-giga*: Dawit Shumbulu.
*Komorakora*: Yes, Dawit Shumbulu. That's what he told us. We said to each other, 'Are we here just for their amusement?' Now you've said the same, so that must be it.
*Bio-iton-giga*: If they are going to take so many photographs, they should give us a lot of money, shouldn't they? But they don't.

*DT*: That's bad. Is that how they behave?

*Aringatuin*: Yes – we are always arguing with them. They cheat us deliberately.

*Bio-iton-giga*: They'll take a lot of photographs, give us a single note and then get in their cars and drive off.

*DT*: Don't you complain?

*Bio-iton-giga*: Of course – but they dive into their cars and escape.

*Aringatuin*: They're thieves aren't they? The whites are thieves.

*DT*: Yes, its bad. What about the Kuchumba [Ethiopians] – they're different from the whites, aren't they?

*Aringatuin*: Yes. They don't take photographs. They just ask for food. 'Give us a goat to eat' they say. So we just give them one. When a lot of them come it's for tax. Don't you have tax in your country?

*DT*: Yes, we do.

*Aringatuin*: There's none of this going around taking photographs with the Kuchumba – they're like us. This photography business comes from your country – where the necklace beads grow. You whites are the culprits. Give us a car and we'll go and take photographs of you.

The ironies come thick and fast in this extract and I shall only mention a few of them. Firstly, the anthropologist, who was kept out of the shot all the time, shows some reluctance to respond when he is asked a question: 'I'm trying to understand what *you* think' he says, as if to say 'after all, that's my job'.

Secondly, when he does succumb his explanation of the tourist's behaviour is very close to an explanation of what he and the film crew are doing – taking back pictures of the Mursi to entertain a Western audience. And this widespread dissemination of images of the exotic from the Lower Omo Valley has no doubt been one factor in attracting tourists. Indeed Darchu, who was the leading character in *The Kwegu*, told me during this trip that he had recently met an Austrian tourist who told him that he had seen him on television.

Thirdly, it is clear that the Mursi see their relationship to the tourists as highly unsatisfactory, essentially because they recognise it as one of unequal power. This I take to be the meaning of the question, 'Do they want us to become their children, or what?' By giving what the Mursi regard as only a paltry return, in cash, for the photographs they take, the tourists, who could clearly afford a lot more, demonstrate their unwillingness to enter into a more equal relationship with the Mursi – or perhaps any relationship at all. I have often been struck by the moral indignation that the tourists I have met seem to feel at being asked for money in return for photographs. It is almost as if they see such a transaction as lowering the quality of the experience they have come to enjoy: of making it more mundane, less exotic. This is sometimes presented as a concern that the people should not be 'corrupted' be Western influences of which tourism itself, of course, is a prime embodiment.

Fourthly, while it is true that anthropologists enter into more satisfactory, in the sense of closer and more equal, relationships with the people they study than tourists normally do, they generally take great pains, in what they write, to conceal the quality of that relationship. This is true also of our programmes, and is illustrated by the interview I have just quoted from. The anthropologist is represented as a disembodied voice, talking to people he has known for over twenty years as though they were anonymous representatives of a 'Mursi viewpoint'. This hiding of the relationship between anthropologist and people is done, ostensibly, in the interests of scientific objectivity but it may, rather, be a strategy for convincing ourselves – and others – that we are not tourists.

I shall come back to these points later but want to turn now from anthropological knowledge to the culture of broadcasting and to the matter of collaboration between programme-maker and anthropologist.

Terence Wright (p. 276 above) makes a striking analogy between the television programme-maker and Scheherezade, whose avoidance of execution depended on her ability to keep the Sultan entertained with her story. The analogy is striking, but it misses a crucial ingredient of the programme-maker's problem. For Scheherezade knew, at least, *who* her audience was: the programme-maker doesn't even have *that* advantage. A television programme is made to be seen by an audience which is not only numbered in millions but which is also uncommitted to the subject of the programme. It is not just that the programme-maker hopes that a certain number of viewers will be 'hooked' while channel-hopping. Rather, it is precisely these 'floating' viewers whom the programme is aimed at in the first place. They are anonymous and unknowable except as a statistical aggregate. The television audience, then, is not 'the innocent reflection of a given reality' (Ang 1991, p. 35) but has to be constructed, paradoxically, by the very institution that depends on it.

This commitment of television to an unknown and uncommitted audience is a fundamental feature of the culture of broadcasting and explains a lot about television programmes. This is why I have been speaking of 'programmes' rather than of 'films'. *Disappearing World* programmes can, of course, quite properly be called films, and it takes a special effort not to do so. But to understand their objectives and to judge their success, they should be seen as products of the culture of broadcasting rather than of the culture of film-making. Calling them programmes simply helps one to keep this in mind.

What drives the programme-maker – and I am exaggerating here to make a point – is the desire to hold the attention, on only one relatively brief occasion, of the 'floating' viewer. This is put with predictable bluntness by a CBS executive quoted by Ang: 'I'm not interested in culture. I'm not interested in pro-social values. I have only one interest. That's whether people watch the programme. That's my definition of good, that's my definition of bad' (1991, p. 27). What drives the film-maker is the desire to give permanent expression to his or her experience and, hopefully, to expand the experience of some others in the process. The programme-maker sees him- or herself more as a communicator than as an artist, the film-maker more as an artist than as a communicator. The acid test of the distinction I have in mind between a programme and a film, then, lies not in their form or content but in the objectives and motivations of their respective makers.

Put like this, it seems that the professional activity of the anthropologist has more in common with that of the programme-maker than with that of the film-maker. For the anthropologist also needs an audience, one made up of members of his or her own society and with whom, therefore, he or she shares some cultural understandings. The anthropologist's immediate audience, like that of any academic, is tiny, being made up of his or her professional colleagues and students. It is in front of and in communication with this audience that anthropological knowledge is 'made'. But the academic community does not exist in a social vacuum: it only appears to do so because of the considerable time it normally takes for academic knowledge to acquire the credentials of common sense.

Television offers the most powerful means yet invented of reducing this time lag – of turning yesterday's science more quickly into today's common sense (see also Singer, p. 267 above). It is not just the size and diversity of its audience that gives television this potential, nor the immediacy of the visual image nor even that the 'average person' spends a large and, apparently, increasing amount of time watching it. It is, rather, that for all these reasons (and no doubt others) television has come to play a key part in the way we represent and make sense of the world. I take it as self-evident that the anthropological profession should not turn its collective back on such a powerful means of communication. Indeed, one might even say that if anthropology does not exist on television it will not exist at all.

Programme-makers also see themselves as entertainers and in this they have more in common with film-makers than with anthropologists. Perhaps the most obvious way the programme-maker seeks to entertain, that is, hold the attention of, the viewer is by telling a story. The skill of the story-teller lies in giving us a new experience by taking us along a path we have followed many times before: we enjoy a story because we know what to expect. 'Frequently, the beginning is marked by a lack ... that motivates the course of events ... This form of beginning easily negotiates an ending in which this lack will be resolved in one way or another ... desire will be gratified, there will be a return, pleasure will be had' (Nichols 1981, pp. 74–5). But a story only works, whether as entertainment or explanation, because we are able to interpret the particular events and characters arranged within it by extrapolating from our pre-existing experience. The further these events and characters are removed from our everyday know-ledge, the more likely it is that the extrapolations we are called upon to make in order to follow and gain pleasure from the story will result in misrepresentation and misunderstanding. The problem with the presentation of anthropological knowledge in a narrative form lies in this process of extrapolation, as I shall now illustrate from our programme, *The Migrants* (1985).

While filming was in progress, it happened that the recently planted crops of some of the people we were living with were destroyed by an infestation of caterpillars, or 'army worms'. This was a dramatic event for the people and one that lent itself easily to visual representation in a narrative form. We filmed devastated cultivation areas and the army worms, in close-up, as they gnawed away at what remained of the sorghum. We filmed a debate at which ritual measures were called for to protect the remaining crops and we followed this up by filming both the ritual and, just before leaving, a conversation with the ritual 'expert' about the apparent success of his efforts. This footage was used to create, in the cutting room, a story which became an important sub-theme of the programme. It is true that a Western, predominantly urban, audience could not have been expected to appreciate the full significance, for the protagonists, of the events recorded in this story, but I am confident that it did not misrepresent their attitudes and motivations.

The programme contained another story, however, also built round the army worm problem, which did 'work' by relying on the extrapolation of inappropriate assumptions by the viewer. Towards the end of our stay, one of the men whom we already knew was going to be an important character in the programme – the 'Chairman' of the local 'Farmers' Association', Nyomaniali – asked if he could go with us as far as Jinka, the nearest administrative centre, in the helicopter that would be coming to take us back to Addis Ababa. He did not mention any particular reason why he wanted to go to Jinka, but I assumed he wanted to make some purchases in the market, using the money we had given him in return for his participation in filming. Leslie saw an opportunity here, not only to represent visually one of the main issues the programme was intended to cover – the development of closer links between the migrants and the local administration – but also to present this in the form of a story that would hold the attention of the viewers. We would take advantage of Nyomaniali's request by filming him reporting the army worm problem to the administrator in Jinka and requesting relief food.

The trouble with this story is that it worked, both as entertainment and explanation, only because it led the viewer to make inappropriate assumptions about the leadership role of Nyomaniali. He had certainly asked us to take him to Jinka and, once there, it was a perfectly 'natural' thing for him to talk to the administrator about the current problems of his community (although his own shorghum, incidently, had not been affected by the army worm). But by making it look as though he had gone to Jinka for the specific purpose of making a request for relief food we distorted and simplified his relationship to his fellow Mursi. We made his position seem more formal, his duties more onerous and his motivations more public spirited than I knew them actually to have been. The incident did represent visually Mursi dealings with the administration and it no doubt made good sense to the viewers. But it did so at the cost of hiding from them its meaning for the protagonists and, therefore, at the cost of denying them one small opportunity of seeing the world from a different cultural perspective.

The tension between telling a story and elucidating an issue or problem is a desirable ingredient in any collaboration between programme-maker and anthropologist. This is bound to be so with a *Disappearing World* programme, since these always start out (*pace* Marcus Banks, p. 118 above) with a proposal from a professional anthropologist, rather than from a programme-maker. Even though the proposal is likely to be much amended and adapted before it reaches the stage of acceptance, the fact that it arises from the particular research interests of an anthropologist, who has at least one eye on an audience of his or her own colleagues, is important for two reasons. Firstly, it is the only means of ensuring that a genuine anthropological issue, with comparative implications, is available to be explored by the programme. Secondly, it strengthens the position of the anthropologist in what is otherwise a very unequal power relationship: concern for one's professional reputation is a powerful incentive not to make too many compromises.

Another consequence of the programme-maker's overriding need to hold the attention of the viewer is what might be called a compulsion to explain, to make comprehensible. Anthropologists, being professionally committed to the view that culturally unfamiliar behaviour needs to be contextualised in order to be understood, will be sympathetic to this concern and therefore less critical than film-makers of the typical television documentary's heavy use of commentary. But since the amount of contextualisation that can be achieved within the space of a fifty-minute programme is severely limited, there is a strong temptation to take short cuts by appealing to values, attitudes and assumptions which a large cross-section of the audience can be expected to share. One such short cut is to 'domesticate' the unfamiliar by comparing it explicitly to the familiar (Jablonko 1988, p. 175).

I have been taken to task for doing this in our first programme, *The Mursi*, in which I compared the performance of Mursi orators to that of MPs at Westminster and the political role of their priest, or *komoru*, to that of a constitutional monarch. Peter Loizos, in his very useful review of the *Disappearing World* series, published in the *American Anthropologist* in 1980, points out that this comes rather oddly from an anthropologist 'for whom the comparison of traits from cultures of radically different orders is only occasionally enlightening' (p. 584).

I do not think, however, that Loizos hits the nail exactly on the head here. The most telling objection to my comparison of Mursi behaviour with that of the British is not that I was comparing traits 'from cultures of radically different orders' but that I was comparing *their* behaviour with *ours*. It is an excellent thing to demonstrate to the viewer that the subjects of the programme are not *that* different from ourselves, that we share with them a common humanity, and this indeed was one of the main factors guiding Leslie's choice of what to include in the commentary. But the trouble with this technique of 'domestication' is that it locates the focus and chief criterion of humanity in the *viewer's* cultural experience: *our* behaviour legitimates *theirs*. The problem we face in doing anthropology and, therefore, in putting it on television, is how to demonstrate the humanity we share with the people we study without privileging our own, or, as Faris puts it (p. 174 above), how to 'obliterate otherness while preserving difference'.

Another way of privileging our own humanity is by focusing on the impact of our culture and technology on the subjects of the programme. The dominance, centrality and richness of our way of life is then taken for granted, while the passivity, marginality and shallowness of theirs is (unintentionally) emphasised: they are interesting only to the extent that they react to us and our technology. An example of this is the use we made of 'the Mursi watching themselves on television' in *The Migrants* (1985).

We took a monitor and video play-back machine with us on this trip so that the Mursi could see our two earlier programmes, *The Mursi* (1974) and *The Kwegu* (1982). They responded, after some initial astonishment and amusement, with what can only be described as polite indifference but this did not prevent the image of 'television's newest audience' being given great prominence, both in the programme itself and in the acompanying publicity. This included a much-used photograph of Darchu, who had been the 'star' of *The Kwegu*, carrying the monitor on his shoulder, an image which can, of course, be 'read' in more than one way. The event was clearly much more significant for us, and especially for the film crew, than it was for the Mursi: it derived its significance from the culture of broadcasting.

During our last trip to the Mursi, Leslie and I had a disagreement about a similar issue, namely how the programme we were making should deal with the missionaries (tourists, perhaps, of another kind) who had recently established themselves in the Mago valley, at the spot where *The Migrants* had been made in 1985. I was concerned that we should preserve a Mursi view of the missionaries, which meant seeing them as distant and enigmatic figures, while Leslie, once he had been inside their Swedish prefabricated bungalow, was sorely tempted to take the camera inside to demonstrate, as he put it, the 'preposterous dissonance' between their lives and those of the Mursi. He decided not to in the end, but here is part of an argument we had on this subject, taken from a video recording made in the field.

*LW*: It's not about its amazement that would make me want to go through its door; it's about its preposterous dissonance with the world it's trying to attend to. Now of course that's a film-maker from England's judgement about its dissonance but those judgements are part of making this film. I'm not simply sticking, as it were, a glass wall in front of the Mursi and not in any way processing what comes through.

*DT*: You'll lose them, I'm sure you'll lose them. The minute you go into that bungalow and start . . .

*LW*: Well you may, for a few seconds, lose them. But that may be a legitimate part of the task. You may . . . We've done, for various valid reasons in my view, similar things in the past. But, by wanting to go through the door, I'm certainly not inviting people to say 'Gosh golly what a brilliant job these Western engineers have done in the middle of the Ethiopian bush'.

*DT*: Well of course you're not, I realise that. What you're inviting them to do is to respond in exactly the same way that *you* respond – and that's got nothing to do with the Mursi. It's your private response. It's my response, it was Pat's response, it's Charlie's response. We all respond that way but it's *our* response. It's got nothing to do with the Mursi. The Mursi have never stepped inside it; and, even if they did, they haven't got our cultural experience and background which would enable them to respond in the way you are responding. Now, if you want to make a film about us in the jungle coming upon missionaries living in a . . . in a wendy house, that's fine – that would be that kind of film. And even putting in three seconds of it, to my mind, is going to detract from what the film is really about – which is how the Mursi see the world. The significant thing about that mission for me is that they are marginal people on the edge of the Mursi's existance.

*LW*: That's right, they are. And for me, in trying to express that as strongly as I know how, one of the powerful ways of doing so is to see what it's actually like . . . But you see, the point is that the film after all, for better or worse, is not being made for a Mursi audience.

*DT*: It's not so much who our audience is, I suppose; it's a matter of how we want the film to affect the audience, what we want the film to do. Now that's where we probably differ. For my money, what we want the film to do is to give 'our audience' a taste of a different way of looking at the world.

*LW*: Well of course, and you know that over the years that's been my single strongest desire. We don't differ about that at all. But, I mean . . . for the life of me I can't understand why going down that route for a very brief space of time destroys that potential.

*DT*: It doesn't destroy it entirely. It detracts from it, even for three seconds . . .

*LW*: It won't be three second, it'll be twenty seconds.

*DT*: Well twenty seconds inside a wendy house, to my mind would . . . just as twenty seconds could make a film, I think – the right twenty seconds – twenty seconds could break it as well. I don't see why twenty seconds . . . I don't see why the length of time you spend on it is that important. Surely it's what it *is*.

*LW*: Yes, of course it is and I feel strongly that what it *is* is of interest and of relevance to a small part of the story we are here to relate.

*DT*: The story we're here to relate?

*LW*: The themes we are here to explore, if you want to put it that way.

*DT*: The theme then becomes what our world is doing to them?

*LW*: In part. That *is* part of what we're here to look at, yes. Is it not?

*DT*: I don't think so.

*LW*: You don't.

*DT*: I think that's what so many of these films do and that's a preoccupation with ourselves. Even there [at the mission] we're preoccupied with our world.

*LW*: How can it be otherwise?

*DT*: Well, we make the effort. What we do is we make the effort to try and see the world as the Mursi see it – from their point of view. And if 90% of the film is Mursi talking about what they think and then for 10% you have people in wendy houses – it seems to me that simply detracts from and renders that little bit less effective the other 90%.

*LW*: Yes, well we just don't agree about this.

What all this has been leading up to is the suggestion that the *Disappearing World* 'house style', which has had so much influence on the way anthropology has been presented on British television over the last twenty years, needs radical revision. The key characteristic of this style is the focus on a single and apparently clearly bounded rural community which is seen as representative of a total 'society' and in which the programme consultant has conducted intensive fieldwork. The anthropologist is expected to be able to shed sufficient light on the behaviour of the subjects of the programme to enable the programme-maker to present them to 'his audience' in as unproblematic and 'encompassed' a way as possible. When this proves difficult it tends to be seen as a failure of the anthropologist, who is regarded above all as an expert witness whose knowledge of the language and close relationship with the people is the main guarantee of the accuracy and authenticity of the information contained in the programme.

Since these characteristics reflect the 'distanced' empiricism of post-war British social anthropology, it is hardly surprising that some anthropologists are heard to complain that the series has an 'old fashioned' air about it; that it has become slavishly loyal to an outdated formula. Of course, there have been changes over the years which reflect anthropological sensibilities: we are now less likely to get titles like 'The Mursi', 'The Rendille', 'The Azande', 'The Sherpas' and 'The Pathan' and more likely to get titles like 'The Albanians of Rrogam' and 'The Cakchiquel Maya of San Antonio Polopó'. And, as those titles also indicate, we are more likely now to get programmes about peasants and even about European peasants, although I think there is still only one programme in the series which was made in an urban setting. This last point raises the difficulty – indeed the embarrassment – of the series title. But I shall pass quickly over that one since, as members of a profession whose most prestigious journal is still called *Man*, we do not have a leg to stand on when it comes to complaining about inappropriate titles.

In any case, these changes are, or would be, largely cosmetic. I want to argue for a more radical change that would reflect the more radical concerns of anthropology in the 1990s. The particular contemporary concern I have in mind, as is clear from what I said earlier about anthropological knowledge, is with the way this knowledge is produced. It is now part of current orthodoxy in the subject to recognise that an ethnographic account is a subjective construction – or perhaps one should say an 'inter-subjective' construction – rather than an objective description. It is the product of interaction between a particular fieldworker, with a particular cultural and biographical background, and the people with whom he or she has lived, rather than of detached observation.

This, of course, has always been true, but now it is both openly recognised and made a virtue of. The determination to treat the observer as implicated in what he or she is observing, indeed as part of what he or she is observing, has the methodological advantage of getting away from a spurious kind of objectivity and the political advantage of getting away from the objectification of others, particu-larly non-Western others, as 'understood', 'encompassed' and served up to a Western audience. I like the way Michael Jackson puts it when he writes:

given the ardous conditions of fieldwork, the ambiguities of conversations in a foreign tongue, differences of temperament, age and gender between ourselves and our informants, and the changing theoretical models we are heir to, it is likely that 'objectivity' serves more as a magical token, bolstering our sense of self in disorienting situations, than as a scientific method for describing those situations as they really are. (1989, p. 3)

For a television programme to reflect this understanding of how ethnographic knowledge is produced, the anthropological consultant would have to be treated less as a fount of expert knowledge and opinion and more as a means of initiating and carrying through a process of discovery unique to the situation of filming. He or she would not be expected merely to serve up, as so many facts, the accumulated understandings of previous research, but to use the experience of filming itself as a catalyst for *new* understandings. The information and insights contained in the programme would then derive, and be seen to derive, from that experience.

As a first step in this direction, one might begin by owning up to what the supposed expert does *not* understand about the people and events being filmed. *Disappearing World* programmes, like the books and articles written by their consultants, tend to look for 'certainties', based on intensive research and privileged access, and to explain away or ignore uncertainties. While we were filming *The Kwegu*, for example, I was busily trying to reach an understanding of the relationship between this small group of hunters and cultivators and the Mursi. At the end of the filming I had a very different understanding of this relationship than I had at the beginning, but we gave no hint in the programme of how this understanding was reached and, therefore, of its more or less tentative nature.

But this would only go part of the way. I am not suggesting, as I have heard it suggested by others, that a good 'story-line' for an anthropological programme would be the process by which the anthropologist 'works out' what is 'going on', solves the puzzle, cracks the code. This would simply be to change the anthropologist from expert witness to expert detective; it would not, by itself, avoid the problem of objectification and distancing.

To quote Michael Jackson again, we should explore the ways in which our experiences

connect us with others, rather than set us apart. In this process we put ourselves on the line; we run the risk of having our sense of ourselves as different and distanced from the people we study dissolve, and with it all our pretensions to a supraempirical position . . . As for our comparative method, it becomes less a matter of finding 'objective' similarities and differences between other cultures than of exploring similarities and differences between our own experiences and those of others. This, of course, demands the presence, not the absence, of the ethnographer. (1989, p. 4)

But the anthropologist should not be included as expert witness or detective, nor the film crew as intrepid explorers, since this kind of self-revelation only increases the distance between them and the subjects of the programme. What is required is self-revelation which exposes the quality of the social relationships through which and in which the programme was made. A good way, perhaps, of knowing one has achieved this is if one feels, as a result, uncomfortable, rather than heroic. An example of this comes towards the end of our most recent programme, *Nitha*, which is about the age set ceremony which took place in southern Mursiland in January 1991 and which had been last held in 1961.

This example relates to a criticism of our programmes to which Leslie and I have become increasingly sensitive over the years: namely, that they present an overwhelmingly male view of life in Mursiland. We attempted to deal with this criticism in *The Migrants*, by making a special effort to include interviews with women, as though their absence in the previous programmes had been nothing more than an unfortunate oversight. A chance occurrence during our filming of the age set ceremony enabled us to confront this criticism in a more honest if, for me personally, more uncomfortable way: by including in *Nitha* a sequence which gave a brief insight into the quality of my relationship with Mursi women and into the way it was affected by the situation of filming.

On the third and final day of the ceremony, just after it had reached its climax with the killing of three oxen, I noticed a group of women, standing as onlookers some distance from the enclosure which was the focus of events. They were mainly widows and members, through their husbands, of the age grade of senior elders (*bara*). It is members of this grade who have the responsibility of giving adulthood to the new age set and their wives are the only women who are permitted to attend the ceremony. The husbands of these women, then, had been age mates of Garana, the man who was taking the lead in organising the ceremony and who was to be the principal character in the programme.

Conscious of the need to include 'a women's point of view' of the events we had been filming, I walked over to this group, accompanied by the film crew, only to receive an indignant complaint from two of the women, Kirimye and another whose name I do not know. The following sequence is taken from the unedited footage.

*Kirimye*: Goloinmeri – you wanted to talk to us?
*DT*: Yes.
*Kirimye*: We won't talk.
*DT*: Why not?
*Kirimye*: When we say we're Garana's age mates, you just ignore us. When we say we've got a headache and ask for a pill, you just ignore us. Why should we talk?
*DT*: Listen to me. If we only talk to the men, my people are going to say, 'Are the Mursi all men, or what?' When we come here and only talk to the men, people at home say, 'Are they all men? Where are the women?' So that's why I wanted to talk to you.
*Kirimye*: O.K. Let's talk. You treated us badly yesterday. We are the wives of elders and these [indicating the older men, sitting near by] are our age mates. When we visit your camp you should treat us like the wives of elders – give us gifts; something to take for a headache. But you've completely ignored us. Why should we talk to you?
*DT*: You're mistaken. Haven't I distributed money to all of you – altogether 3000 Birr, to married women only, 10 Birr each?
*2nd Woman*: Is 10 Birr a lot?
*DT*: Are there only a few of you?
*2nd Woman*: There's a lot of us, that's true.
*DT*: Are you junior or senior elders?
*Kirimye*: That's our age mate, sitting over there. Now that the oxen are dead, it's all over. Let's stay here for a bit and then go to your camp . . .

*DT*: I don't want to talk about that [i.e., money] now. I only want to talk about the *nitha*. Why have you come to the ceremony?
*2nd Woman*: To see our children. We've come to see our children.
*Kirimye*: Oh, you talk to him then.

Some of this sequence was included in the programme but not the latter part, where I attempt to justify myself by talking about the money we had been giving out, specifically to married women. This was money provided by Granada in return for the right to film. Targeting the major part of it on married women was a practice I had started in 1985, during the filming of *The Migrants*. Grain stocks were then low and married women, as the chief providers of food for the family, were having to buy what food they could in highland markets. The principle was well established, then, and seemed to be accepted as equitable, both by men and women.

I was initially indignant at Kirimye's outburst, not only because married women had received most of Granada's money but also because I was spending a large part of every day giving out medicines, mainly to women and children. On reflection, however, it became clear to me that this was no defence against Kirimye's charge, the basis of which was precisely that I had treated her and her age mates simply as 'women': as part of an undifferentiated category. I had not treated them, as I had their male age mates, as worthy of individual respect and attention because of their status and role in the community. We had brought blankets, shoes and machetes for the twenty or so senior men in the southern part of the country where the ceremony was being held and had either given or promised larger amounts of money to certain key individuals amongs them.

This sequence, then, tells us, firstly, something about how Mursi women see themselves in relation to their male age mates. It is difficult to imagine such forceful characters playing the marginal role in Mursi life to which our previous programmes appeared to consign them. Secondly, it reveals something of how I have related to women, as compared to men, during my time with the Mursi and thus helps to explain why they have figured so marginally in our programmes. Thirdly, it taught me something – or, at least, enabled me to admit something – about the conduct of my own fieldwork, although I doubt whether it would have done this had it not been recorded on film. And that leads to my fourth point, which is that the incident that revealed all this was a product of the situation of filming and could hardly have been represented so vividly and yet so economically in any other medium.

Other relationships that would need to be revealed in a programme that treated the experiences of the observers as (to use Jackson's phrase) 'primary data' are those between film crew and people and between anthropologist and film crew. And, since all these relationships are liable to be fraught with some tension, it seems likely that their honest presentation would increase rather than decrease the interest of the audience.

I am certainly not asking, however, for the camera to be turned on ourselves as heroes who define and represent the subjects of the programme for the benefit of the viewer. The banishing of this kind of front-of-camera figure from television programmes about other cultures was one of the major services of *Disappearing World*. I *am* asking for such programmes to be presented more as encounters than as observations, more as dialogues *with* than as dialogues *about* people. This would require a willingness, on the part of both anthropologist and programme-maker, to dismantle the protective walls behind which they are used to hiding from the public gaze – and also from that of their colleagues. I have done just a bit of that dismantling in this chapter. More of it is needed. It might be uncomfortable, but it would make for good anthropology and, I believe, good television.

### Note

This chapter originated as a paper given at the *Film as Ethnography* Conference, entitled 'The Culture of Television and the Televising of Culture: Reflections of an Anthropological Consultant'. In its present form it is a slightly revised and expanded version of the fourth annual Forman Lecture, given at the University of Manchester on 10 December 1991. I am grateful to Paul Henley, Pat Turton and David Wason for their comments on the text and to Dennis Blackman, Edward Poole and Mark Woolstencroft of the Media Centre, University of Manchester, for their technical help with the lecture.

### References

*Books and articles*
Ang, I. (1991), *Desperately Seeking the Audience*, Routledge, London and New York.
Jablonko, A. (1988), 'New Guinea in Italy: an analysis of the making of a television series from research footage of the Maring people of Papua New Guinea', in J. R. Rollwagen (ed.), *Anthropological Filmmaking*, Harwood Academic Publishers, pp. 169–98.
Jackson, M. (1989), *Paths Toward a Clearing*, Indiana University Press, Bloomington.
Loizos, P. (1980), 'Granada Television's *Disappearing World* series: an appraisal', *American Anthropologist*, 82, pp. 573–94.
Nichols, B. (1981), *Ideology and the Image: Social Representation in the Cinema and Other Media*, Indiana University Press, Bloomington.

*Films*
Macdonald, B. (1991), *The Cakchiquel Maya of San Antonio Palopó*, *Disappearing World* series, Granada Television, Manchester. Colour, 52 mins. (Anthropologist: Tracy Bachrach Ehlers)
Wason D. (1991), *The Albanians of Rrogam*, *Disappearing World*, series, Granada Television. Colour, 52 mins. (Anthropologist: Berit Backer)
Woodhead, L. (1974), *The Mursi*, *Disappearing World* series, Granada Television, Manchester. Colour, 52 mins. (Anthropologist: David Turton)
—— (1982), *The Kwegu*, *Disappearing World* series, Granada Television, Manchester. Colour, 52 mins. (Anthropologist: David Turton)
—— (1985), *The Migrants*, *Disappearing World* series, Granada Television, Manchester. Colour, 52 mins. (Anthropologist: David Turton)
—— (1991), *The Land is Bad*, *Disappearing World* series, Granada Television, Manchester.

Colour, 52 mins. (Anthropologist: David Turton)

—— (1991), *Nitha, Disappearing World* series, Granada Television, Manchester. Colour, 52 mins. (Anthropologist: David Turton)

# Hypermedia in ethnography

The increasing availability of interactive multimedia and hypermedia database systems on personal computers will transform ethnographic methodologies. Gathering data in many different media has already been made possible by cheap, efficient technologies of electronic recording. Textual and audiovisual information made interactive will be able to provide the scholarly apparatus of referencing and contextualisation necessary to create new forms of academic publication and knowledge dissemination. Ethnographers must therefore learn not only how to collect information in the different media formats but how to process, analyze and integrate it into forms that convey meaningful understanding. Ultimately, the nature of the author/audience relationship will be greatly affected by a newly emerging 'hypermedia ethnography'.

In one of the few articles in the professional anthropological literature devoted to issues of hypermedia, Howard criticizes the written medium for its 'linear sequential mode' and states that: 'the writer of an ethnographic text is thus induced to seek prestige by selecting one path through the material and dramatizing its significance. . . . The reader is forced into a passive mode, dependent upon the writer's literary skills for a tour of this new territory' (1988, p. 305). What Howard says about written texts applies with even greater justification to ethnographic film. Film requires that its audience attend to a narrative delivered in a linear format. In contrast, hypermedia presentation has the potential of not only freeing us from some of the constraints of linear texts, it also allows the audience to extrapolate analyses on the corpus of evidence in a much more productive way than is possible with verbally encoded texts alone. A main issue in producing hypermedia ethnographies is how to structure the large mass of data inherent in the use of multimedia so that it can be made accessible to an audience. This is true even if the author is just providing 'raw data'.

Texts, pictures, graphics, film and electronic recordings, artefacts and other media have all been used historically as primary sources for research, yet they are gathered or constructed using different technologies and methodologies. They require different editorial approaches and are comprehended differently. The technological means of integrating these different media into a common interpretative format is now upon us but an appropriate methodology of representation has not yet emerged. Although the potential of hypermedia is clear to many observers, most of us have yet to realise the demands on both author and audience when different media are combined in new ethnographic genres.

## The ethnographic media

Given the nature of their task, and the difficulty of finding the right cognitive nuance in mere words, it is not surprising that ethnographers gathered 'field notes' in other 'media' formats as soon as appropriate technologies became available. For example, James Mooney, and his more famous contemporary Franz Boas, eagerly applied sound and picture recording technologies in their fieldwork (Jacknis 1990, pp. 205–06). As soon as these new technologies were available, they were also incorporated into multimedia presentations. Lantern slides, photographs, motion pictures, recorded sound, three-dimensional artefacts, maps and graphic abstractions, such as kinship diagrams, have all been important components of ethnographic presentation. The seamless integration of all the various media used in ethnographic interpretation has been incomplete to say the least. The most obvious reason for this lack of integration is that writing, recorded sound and pictures, especially moving pictures, call upon different sensory channels for their apprehension.

A written document relies upon visual perception of 'spoken' language and therefore exists as an encoded message. It is easy to reference, continuous and relatively easy to interpret. There are rules for interpretation and citation that derive from an elite cultural tradition and centuries of cultural experience. A written document may be approached in any number of ways and the information contained therein may be easily found over and over again. It may be read from start to finish, skimmed, jumped around in; backing up to re-read unclear sections is almost effortless; access through a table of contents or index is relatively straightforward; citation can be specific and precise. Training in interpretation begins in primary school. One drawback is that interpretation is restricted to those who know the language of inscription but, the fact that there exists a standardised transcription system increases the chances that the author's meaning and intent will be understood. Perhaps most important of all, written documents are easy and relatively inexpensive to produce. They are also durable, require little care during shipping, and can be used in almost any environment. Any literate person can pick up a document in their language and begin to use it right away. This relative utility, of course, comes at a high cost. Writing, or at least published writing, implies the communication of highly abstract representations.

Recorded speech shares many of the attributes of writing in that it consists of a linear stream of information, which is relatively easy to interpret. It also adds features, such as rhythm, tone, timbre and accent, which provide connotative subtleties but are difficult to reproduce in writing. Unfortunately, recorded speech is difficult to use as a referenced resource. Backtracking to repeat a section or sentence has traditionally been imprecise and tedious because recorded speech lacks cues equivalent to the page numbers and punctuation of writing. Skimming and jumping from point to point are both tedious. A recording may have a table of contents, but indexes are rare, if they exist at all. As for citation, *The Chicago Manual of Style* suggests a form for bibliography, but none for a note (1982, Chs. 16–17). Recorded speech is so unwieldy to use that analysis is commonly done from a written transcript. Links between a sound recording and written information have traditionally been lumpy, as print and sound could not be easily interspersed before the advent of the computer. In addition, the equipment and storage medium used to record sound makes access more difficult. Recorded sound requires at least a basic player/recorder and power supply. Older technologies require more exotic equipment because of the variety of technology used since sound recording was pioneered a hundred years ago.

Photographs, in comparison with sound recordings, are easy to reference but consist of discontinuous 'frames' and are not innately linked to verbal references. Backtracking, skimming and jumping from picture to picture are all easy procedures. Yet a single photograph is difficult to interpret by itself and requires a context of writing or closely related photographs to be useful in scholarly applications (Scherer 1990, p. 134). The storage medium for photographic prints, paper, is the same as that for printed text, but abstraction and reproduction are much more problematic. Text can be copied and abstracted in any number of ways at relatively little cost without losing the integrity of the text itself or without shifting to another cognitive medium. Photographs cost more to reproduce and are generally made from an original negative or print. A copy of a copy usually results in a noticeable loss of information. Slides are even more difficult to work with because they require special equipment and usually need a special environment for viewing. As with recorded sound, the storage medium inhibits distribution and this restricts their use by scholars.

Moving pictures, film and video, like recorded sound, are extremely difficult to reference, particularly in the presentation mode. Unlike sound or writing, moving pictures do not rely entirely on language to convey meaning, which means that they may be shown in very different cultures and be subject to equally different interpretations. The storage media used for moving pictures pose problems similar to those for recorded sound and still photography. Simple copying and viewing are expensive compared to printed text. Converting different film formats to video or even converting between various video formats is even more time-consuming and expensive.

Gathering data in all these different media is presently facilitated by an existing (and rapidly improving) technology of electronic recording. The problem for ethnographers, at present, is not so much how to collect information in different media, but how to process, analyze and integrate it into a generally accessible presentation format. This problem is compounded by the lack of standardisation for storage and the limitations that this lack of standardisation impose on access. Storage is already an issue when the ethnographer selects equipment to use in the field – cost must be balanced against quality. The problem is compounded after the ethnographer returns because visual and sound data must often be integrated with other visual and sound data that is only available on a different storage medium or in a different format.

The computer already offers a potential solution to this lack of integration by allowing easy reference to text, sound and video at a single location. This can be done today by close control of external machines like videodisc or videotape players. It is now possible to store cognitive media in a digital form, but the costs of doing so are still prohibitive. If current trends continue, digital storage for all the different media will be cost effective within a decade. Hypermedia computer software facilitates the forging of relationships between text, sound and picture, but it is not in itself a new genre of presentation.

## The computer, multimedia and ethnography: hypermedia and interactive multimedia

In the past, technical limitations constrained the amount of multimedia data ethnographers could gather in the field and limited the sophistication of multimedia presentations. Writing field notes by hand was and is a rather slow process. Early cameras and wax recorders were fragile and difficult to operate, limiting the amount of data that could be gathered or processed. Even thirty years ago, cameras and reel-to-reel recorders were relatively heavy and complicated. They took time to learn, were expensive to buy and use and required special care and skill. These constraints limited the quantity of the data the ethnographer could gather. As the ethnographer's tools have grown more powerful and sophisticated, the diversity, complexity, and density of the data have grown as well, creating a requirement for more powerful tools for organisation, analysis, and producing ethnographic products like monographs and audiovisuals. The trend toward complexity in field data has a parallel in the growing sophistication and increasing use of computers in ethnography. The computer is an evolving, all-purpose tool that can be used to gather, organise and analyse field data as well as aid in the production of ethnographic products. The utility of this tool is determined by its storage capacity, raw processing power and the sophistication of the programmes that control it. In the next decade, it will become powerful enough to store all cognitive media except three-dimensional artefacts on a single storage medium; portable enough to use in almost any field situation; inexpensive enough to be widely used; and capable of linking multimedia field data by means of hypermedia or interactive multimedia programmes.

New technology brings with it new terminology. The word 'multimedia', which is often used to describe a collection of media tools, has been joined by the term 'hypermedia' to describe one way to interrelate the information. Since both terms are essential to our discussion and surrounded by the confusion often engendered by new words, we will attempt to define them. In computer science, the word 'medium' refers to the physical place where data is stored, such as paper, disks or tape. Used in this sense, 'multimedia' would refer to data traditionally stored on different media. Text is usually stored on paper, pictures on any number of different media and motion pictures on film or videotape. Digital forms of motion pictures, sound, graphics and text can use the same storage media, so the computer science definitions of 'medium' and 'media' are distinct from the 'media' used in the word 'multimedia'. A more appropriate definition in the *Oxford English Dictionary* is 'An intermediate means, instrument or channel'. When used in this sense, 'multimedia' implies different intermediate instruments or cognitive systems, used to convey knowledge: text, pictures, schemes like diagrams and maps, artefacts and sound. The 'multi-' reinforces the plural 'media' and the whole word now connotes integration of the media used. Thus, 'multimedia' means the use of more than one intermediate instrument to convey knowledge – the storage medium is immaterial. Used in this sense, an illustrated book is perhaps the simplest form of multimedia. More complex forms would integrate text, full-motion video, sound, and graphics into a single 'reading'.

'Hypermedia' is a relatively recent concept derived from 'multimedia' hybridised with the term 'hypertext' and refers to a computer programme, or series of programmes, that manage multimedia. The mechanisms behind hypermedia vary and there is as yet no agreement on a definition. Nielsen (1990) provides a description of hypertext and hypermedia. He gives illustrative examples but not brief or concrete definitions. Nor is he able to distinguish hypermedia from the more general 'interactive multimedia.' For our present purposes, hypermedia simply connotes less structured types of interactive multimedia and implies more potential guides or pathways available to the user than does the term interactive multimedia.

Hypermedia software is meant to serve two different purposes. Firstly, it should allow 'authors' to build, quickly and simply, associative links between different media. Secondly, it should allow 'readers' to traverse these links quickly by moving through the associative structure. The nature of the links depends on the hypermedia programme. In many of these programmes, the distinction between 'author' and 'reader' is blurred because 'readers' are often allowed to create links of their own and even delete those in existence. In any case, the overriding concern is that information should be quickly and easily related and accessed by association. Instead of building or following a linear stream of information, one builds or follows an interconnected multidimensional structure. The structure depends on the associations made by the 'author' and the needs of the 'reader'. Just as two authors of a written work would never write the same footnotes or cross-references and two readers would never choose the same footnotes to read, or cross-references to follow, 'authors' in hypermedia will build different structures and 'readers' will select different paths through them (Howard 1988). Hypermedia, then, is a way of providing an interactive but ordered structure for multimedia. In its most general sense, hypermedia should make 'readers' feel, 'that they can move freely through the information, according to their own needs' (Nielsen 1990, p. 4). In its most restrictive sense, hypermedia imparts this freedom to both 'authors' and 'readers'.

Hypertext, the text-only predecessor of hypermedia, offers examples of the simplest links between information. The cross-references and see-also links in the *New Electronic Encyclopedia* may be viewed as a form of hypertext (for a description see Perratore 1989). An intermediate form of hypermedia is suggested by the VideoCards software, which combines images of scientific subjects on videodisc with sparse text annotation and an apparatus for building presentations based on annotations, graphics and selected images from the videodisc (Walker 1990).

For the computer to most effectively create links across media, information should be put into digital form because only then is complete integration possible. This also simplifies most aspects of production. Visual material and sound can be indexed and any desired segment retrieved almost instantly. Text and graphics can be linked to any indexed segment or frame. Any of these media may be edited or copied to another form of digital storage without information drop-out. This is especially important for sound and video recordings, which lose quality as they are copied in analog form. Precursors of such a system can be seen in digital video editors, such as those produced by AVID, which provide this digital integration but which lack a hypermedia interface and high quality visual images.

Storing visual or sound data in digital form, however, requires enormous data storage capacities. As of this writing, one minute of uncompressed PAL or NTSC broadcast quality colour video in digital form would require at least 800 to 1,000 megabytes of storage, or approximately a quarter to half again as much storage as is required for the text of the complete first edition of the *Oxford English Dictionary*, with all the required computer indexes and search programmes (we call this an *OED equivalent*). Images of roughly the quality of the future high-definition television (HDTV) standard would require four times more storage, or five to six and one-half OED equivalents (Baran 1990, p. 289). To substantially reduce these storage requirements, data compression standards are being developed for both still and full-motion video. With current technology it is possible to reduce the storage requirements for full-motion video by 160 to 1 and video stills by 25 to 1 (the difference is due to the large amounts of redundant information from frame to frame in full-motion video). Using special equipment, one hour of VCR-quality full-motion video can be squeezed onto a CD-ROM disk, one OED equivalent, that can then be played back on a specially equipped personal computer. A personal computer with the appropriate added hardware can compress and uncompress pictures with 200 lines of resolution in real time using the same amount of storage. One manufacturer hopes to be able to provide near broadcast quality compression by the end of 1992 (Loveria and Kinstler 1990; Robinson 1990, pp. 208–10). Even if this prediction is too optimistic, it is not unreasonable to expect relatively inexpensive computer-based digital systems within five years.

Hybrid integration, on the other hand, where the computer controls external equipment for most pictures and perhaps sound as well, is already an effective way to integrate text, sound and visual material. The technology has been used by several museums to catalogue artefacts or photographs. At the Tuscan Photographic Archives, for example, a researcher can use a computer connected to a special microfiche reader to see copies of archive images (Chiozzi 1990). At the Southwestern Museum in Los Angeles, some 65,000 photographs have been transferred to two videodiscs and linked with the indexes of the museum's artefact collection. More ambitious projects are underway as well. The Naga videodisc at Cambridge contains pictures of 1,200 artefacts, reproductions of some 7,000 black and white photographs, 200 maps, 150 film sequences and an unspecified number of sound recordings. In addition to providing access to this material, the controlling computer will also provide access to some 20,000 paragraphs of text. Both the text and the videodisc can be searched rapidly by means of a customised relational database (Macfarlane 1990, p. 11).

Such systems, using current technology, make it possible to go to any frame of 30 minutes of video collected on a single videodisc in about half a second and to play full-motion video sequences in any order with only a slight pause between each sequence. With a detailed index to the film and related written and graphic information on computer, it is possible to move, at will and with almost no waiting time for search servo-mechanisms, between a detailed explanation of, for example, a ritual performance, a text of the verbal utterances, a map showing spatial details of the same performance, and a video recording of the same event. The index can also be used to find similar sequences and play them either as an impromptu slide show, using representative frames from each sequence or as an *ad-hoc* assembly of full-motion. Although these multimedia systems are examples of the viability of integrating different media, they also indicate the enormous amounts of labour necessary to construct them.

An ethnographer going to the field ten or twenty years from now may take along as equipment a video camera, one or two microphones, a computer, disks or tapes for storage, a printer, paper, and maybe some lights. Using this equipment, he or she would be able to shoot and edit digital video in colour with a resolution approximating that of 16 mm film or better. The computer would be the repository for written notes, sound, schematics and video, all of which could be linked for reference and annotation. It would allow almost instant retrieval of any clip from an hour or so of video. Additional hours would have to be copied in from disks or tapes. The computer itself, when folded, would be no larger than the portable 3/4 inch video-cassette units now in use and would cost the same or less. The technical skill required to use the equipment will be quite low, but the organisational and analytical skill required to use such a mass of data effectively will be extremely high. Imagine, for example, the amount of labour involved in shooting forty hours of film or video, logging the footage, making transcripts and translations, linking it to field notes and reviewing and annotating each event and each actor. These steps involve the preparation of the data only, entirely leaving aside the processes of analysis and presentation.

Today, although the minimum equipment needed for field work is a pen or pencil and some paper, most ethnographers have used other tools to support and enhance the written perspective. The growing sophistication of the available tools imply a much larger corpus for the ethnographer to work with. Typed notes on a computer can be produced more quickly and more legibly than notes written by hand. Automatic and small format still cameras require less skill to use and are faster and less expensive to operate than those that rely on manual modes of operation. Video is less expensive, easier to use, more portable, and more flexible than film. Similarly, almost anyone can easily obtain reasonable sound from a portable cassette recorder and it is now common to collect such sound recordings along with video images on videotape. A single scholar can now bring back from the field a large quantity of 'notes' – written, visual, and sound – suitable for scholarly use. Adding a computer increases both the quantity and the sophistication of the 'notes'. More sophisticated ethnographers are using spreadsheets, databases and hypertext to gather information (Lansing, forthcoming).

The immense volume and diversity of original field data that can now be easily collected, however, often overwhelms the ability of the ethnographer to organise and edit publications from them. The necessity to transform data from one medium to another has long been a fundamental obstacle in the ethnographer's use of sound recordings. For example, twenty years ago one standard handbook in methodology advised against making extensive tape recordings:

Since the tape recorder as note taker is so far superior to the paper-and-pencil ethnographer in most instances, field workers are sometimes tempted to try to 'get everything on tape'. This strategy is ill advised, however. Transcribing materials from tapes into typewritten notes is an extremely tedious and time-consuming task at best. (Pelto 1970, p. 141)

The tedious task of digesting and organising 'notes' collected in a number of different media has become an even greater problem today. Even while fieldwork is in progress, efforts must begin to bring order out of a heterogeneous collection of data that may contain written notes, moving or still pictures in film or electronic form, sound, and graphics in the form of kinship diagrams, drawings, and maps. This recalcitrant mass must be catalogued and indexed in such a way that the appropriate snippet can be found later for the lecture, film, book, or article being prepared.

Most ethnographers organise their data to fit their current interests. An ethnographer working on religious ritual will index and arrange notes very differently from one working on ecology. On the other hand, data is cumulative, and questions asked of it change both in the original process of organisation and in subsequent projects when new questions may be under consideration. It is not unusual for one's perspective on the data to change as one finds that the data collected does not fit the conceptual framework prepared for it (Plath 1990, pp. 375–78). Or, as one's interests change, material gathered for a project on religious ritual may later be mined for information it may have on kinship, marriage practices or economic patterns. The goal, then, is to organise the data in such a way that it provides what answers it can for questions instantly while at the same time being flexible enough to provide answers to unknown future questions with a minimum of reorganisation. Although easily stated, this is a frightfully time-consuming proposition to carry out.

## Some implications of hypermedia in ethnography

Perhaps the best way to illustrate the issues of using hypermedia as a tool for ethnographic research is to consider the media used by three hypothetical ethnographers or ethnographic teams with and without hypermedia.

A typical ethnographer might return from the field with several hundred pages of field notes, several hundred slides or photographs, and perhaps a few hours of video and sound recordings. Conventionally, the ethnographer would extract from this material one or more papers, a monograph and some formal lectures, all of which might be illustrated by slides or still photographs. Most of the visual and sound data collected in the field would only be used for purposes of analysis because the original quality would probably be too low to justify the effort necessary to edit and publish it. In addition, even if the raw data was of reasonable quality, the ethnographer would likely lack the skills, equipment, and distribution channels necessary for a formal presentation. With current technology and hypermedia tools, this same ethnographer might utilise the same field data to produce an electronic monograph based on text and graphics recorded on computer or CD-ROM disks. Such a publication would incorporate many more graphics and a few more photographs than would normally be the case for a conventional print publication. It could also be structured to allow for differing levels of usage by, for example, students in an introductory course or by graduate students for advanced research projects. This could be accomplished by two linked pathways through the material or by a single pathway with branches leading off to more in-depth analyses, related information and supporting documentation. With future technology (i.e. in five to ten years) it will be relatively easy to incorporate relevant visual and sound data into such a monograph at a reasonable cost. By improving media production and editorial skills, or by teaming up with another person who has those skills, the ethnographer might find it feasible to publish monographs on CD-ROM disks for more general distribution.

A second example could be an ethnomusicologist returning from the field with several hundred pages of field notes and music transcriptions, several hundred slides or photographs, and several dozen hours of audio tapes. From this material the ethnomusicologist will probably produce papers, books, lectures (illustrated by musical recordings or slides) and, perhaps, a cassette tape or compact disc. With current technology and hypermedia tools, the same ethnomusicologist may produce a CD-ROM publication containing up to an hour of music and dense hypertext annotation. Models for such a publication already exist in the form of annotated versions of classical music, such as the one for Beethoven's Ninth Symphony published by the Voyager Company (Winter 1989). Future technology will lower the cost of production for CD-ROM publications and make the incorporation of appropriate stills or video sequences more feasible.

In our third example, a visual ethnographer returns from the field with field notes, slides or photographs, and several dozen hours of film, video and sound recordings. This ethnographer will produce one or more documentary films or videos in addition to scholarly papers and other print publications (Kendall 1988; Kendall and Lee 1991). Using current technology and hypermedia tools, however, the visual ethnographer could put a thirty-minute film or video onto videodisc which could then be coupled with a dense hypertext annotation of the contents. By integrating filmic or other media presentations through hypermedia, the ethnographer could provide instantaneous referencing, translation, theoretical or methodological contexts, and other 'hypertextual' commentaries on the presentations, or even provide simultaneous alternative 'presentations'. The 'replay' structure of such presentations could be made strict or relaxed, according to the predilections of either viewer or author, by manipulating the computer software programmes to provide more or fewer options. In the case of film, individual shots, other iconic features, or even purely time-driven parameters could be selected as reference points. Bibliographic or other contextualising information could then be displayed directly as overlay or on a consort computer. We are, of course, used to the convention of subtitles as the most familiar example of overlay. This simultaneous translation technique, implicit in the use of subtitles, can be taken a step further by including references, short commentaries, etc. by direct links on the computer screen. With a little ingenuity, film images could even become the referential source for conceptual analyses of, for example, ritual behaviour or exchange systems.

These three hypothetical examples show that hypermedia-based ethnographies will probably range continuously from text-oriented presentations analogous to monographs to full-motion video-based presentations analogous to film. The best hypermedia ethnographies will be a fluid mix of sound, image and text constructed in such a way as to take advantage of the strongest features of each. Ethnographers will struggle with such questions as confidentiality, coherence, structure, the appropriate choice of media for a topic, and the appropriate size for a presentation. Considerations of confidentiality will cause some ethnographers to alter images, perhaps by distorting an informant's face, or eliminate images from their presentations entirely.

A coherent structure of linkages between and among the different chosen media will be much more difficult to establish and maintain in hypermedia environments than in linear presentation modes. In fact, instead of having to maintain a single train of thought, the ethnographer will have to establish a structure that allows multiple points of access while still maintaining a consistent point of view. It will be even more difficult to accommodate conflicting aesthetics that have evolved in the linked media. In other words, a given segment of text or image may be accessible from two or more pathways through this structure, so transitional devices will have to be evolved to avoid cognitive disjunctures. For example, economic data related to marriage practices may vary widely: a description of items used in ritual prestation, a video segment of gifts made to the bride, a sound recording of music and the graphic designs used on clothing for the occasion. Each of these media segments may be accessed by pathways from many other different topics, ranging from discussions of sexual taboos to graphic abstractions of cross-cousin mating preferences. The transitional devices used in constructing the linkages between these different information nodes ideally should not themselves introduce barriers to understanding the presentation. Moreover, all the media segments must be constructed so that they are compatible with the potential links to other media segments.

These hypermedia technologies will have a significant impact on every phase of the ethnographic process. Obviously, hypermedia ethnography will require academic institutions and associated knowledge industries to adapt to these technologies by evolving new genres of ethnographic publication, some of which may be of a highly experimental nature. For example, future technology will obviate the need for a videodisc by digitising the video signal and recording directly on the computer. At some point, conventional text-based monographs distributed in electronic format will begin to contain such features as 'video footnotes' and at that point, if not before, new standards governing electronic monographs will have to be established.

As we can see from the above discussion, hypermedia presentation is not in itself an ethnographic genre. Rather, new ethnographic genres will develop to use hypermedia technology, ranging from presentations in a single medium, like text, to attempts to incorporate all media. Similarly, some hypermedia compilations will range from loose structures with little coherence intended primarily to encourage research and analysis, to very coherent, tightly structured presentations intended to accomplish didactic ends. An example of the former might be the archiving of an individual ethnographer's *Nachlass*, while the latter would include hypermedia textbooks or parts of formal lecture presentations.

Standards for the length and complexity of hypermedia presentations will also have to be established. The magnitude of this issue can be illustrated by considering the amount of time and effort involved in establishing several coherent interconnected paths through, let us say, 150 pages of text, 30 minutes of full-motion video, several hundred video stills, and associated graphics. A related question is who will be willing to traverse such a landscape, and how it will be used for scholarly purposes. Printed monographs and linear video presentations will, of course, continue to be published for the foreseeable future. However, we should see increased publication of books, sound recordings and videos that are also integrated into a hypermedia construct.

### References

Baran, Nick (1990), 'Putting the squeeze on graphics', *Byte* 15, 13, pp. 289–94.

*Chicago Manual of Style* (1982), University of Chicago Press, Chicago.

Chiozzi, P. (1990), 'The Tuscan Photographic Archives and the roots of anthropological photography in Florentine cultural tradition', *Visual Anthropology*, III, 2–3, pp. 175–78.

Howard, A. (1988), 'HyperMedia and the future of ethnography', *Cultural Anthropology*, 3, 3, pp. 304–15.

Jacknis, I. (1990), 'James Mooney as an ethnographic photographer', *Visual Anthropology*, III, 2–3, pp. 179–212.

Kendall, L. (1988), *The Life and Hard Times of a Korean Shaman*, University of Hawaii Press, Honolulu.

Kendall, L. and D. S. Lee (1991), *An Initiation* Kut *for a Korean Shaman*, (videotape recording), University of Hawaii Press, Honolulu.

Lansing, J. S. and J. N. Kremer (forthcoming), 'Socio-ecological analysis of Balinese water temples' in D. M. Warren (ed.), *Indigenous Knowledge Systems: The Cultural Dimension of Development*, Routledge & Kegan Paul, New York.

Loveria, Greg and Don Kinstler (1990), 'Multimedia: DVI arrives', *Byte* 15, 11, pp. 105–8.

Macfarlane, A. (1990), 'The Cambridge Experimental Videodisc Project', *Anthropology Today*, VI, 1, pp. 9–12.

Nielsen, J. (1990), *Hypertext and Hypermedia*, Academic Press, New York.

Pelto, P. J. (1970), *Anthropological Research. The Structure of Inquiry*, Harper, New York.

Perratore, Edward L. (1989), 'The new electronic encyclopedia', *PC Magazine* 8, 2, pp. 216–18.

Plath, D. W. (1990), 'Fieldnotes, filed notes, and the conferring of note', in R. Sanjek (ed.), *Fieldnotes – The Makings of Anthropology*, Cornell University Press, Ithaca, pp. 371–84.

Robinson, P. (1990), 'The four multimedia gospels', *Byte*, XV, 2, pp. 203–12.

Scherer, J. C. (1990), 'Historical photographs as anthropological documents. A retrospect', *Visual Anthropology*, III, 2–3, pp. 131–55.

Walker, Timothy (1990), In Ambron, Sueann and Kristina Hooper (eds.) 1990. *Learning with Interactive Media: Developing and Using Multimedia Tools in Education*, pp. 331–47. Redmond, WA, Microsoft Press.

Winter, R. (1989), *Ludwig van Beethoven: Symphony No. 9 CD Companion*, Voyager Company, Santa Monica.

# The potentials of videodisc in visual anthropology: some examples

In 1927 John Logie Baird recorded images on a waxed disc called 'phono vision'. The system used thirty lines at twelve and a half frames per second and was sold in Selfridge's store under the name of 'Major Radio Vision'. It was not a success.

In the 1970s the marriage of two technologies, television and lasers, gave birth to a revived attempt to store visual images on a disc, called optical disc or videodisc. Information is engraved by a laser on the steel surface, which is then coated with plastic. The 'information' consists of one visual track and two sound tracks. It is read off each separate track by a laser beam.

At first this new medium was used, as an alternative to videotape, to record films to be played through in real time. But since one could not record onto this medium, it was a limited success, although there are many such videodiscs on sale in Japan. Indeed, it is from Japan that my first example of the use of videodiscs in anthropology is taken.

After the 1974 'World Expo' in Osaka, a great deal of money was put into developing the fine National Museum of Ethnology on the Expo park site. It was decided at first to use videotape technology to create a large library of ethnographic films which the visitors to the museum could use. Two years ago, the whole system was converted to optical disc. There are thirty-six 'booths', each with two seats. A visitor can use a touch-screen and 'menu' system to select one of the 390 ethnographic films on different parts of the world. These are then selected by a 'robot' and played – usually lasting some twenty minutes or so – with sound.

The major advantage of videodisc in this setting is its durability. Since the laser does not touch the groove, one can play through the same disc, or pause it for as long as one likes on a single frame, without damaging the source. For a museum this is obviously a great benefit. A roughly similar system is used in the Science Museum in Paris.

The Japanese experiment, however, does not exploit the other major strengths of this new medium. With videodisc, there is the ability to hold very large quantities of still frames, with good resolution, and to show them for as long as is needed. A conventional videodisc will hold 54,000 images on each side, that is 108,000 frames on a disc. For the storage of slides, or black and white negatives, this is obviously very useful.

A second advantage is the direct frame address system. Each of the 54,000 tracks or images has a number. It takes the reader less than a second to go to a precise frame. There is none of the slowness of film or videotape which has to be searched through sequentially. The importance of this feature becomes apparent when we link a videodisc to a computer. The computer can use the videodisc as a large bank of visual images (and sound). With an appropriate index, the computer can take one directly to the relevant image. With an appropriate 'authoring' program, the computer can show the images in any order.

Furthermore, textual material in the form of digital data can be stored on the two 'sound' tracks, and be picked off by the computer. Again, surprisingly large quantities of such material can be stored in this way. Over 600 megabytes of information, the equivalent of about 1,000 normal books or more, can be held on each side of the videodisc. Put in the startling talk of the industry, this would mean that the text and illustrations of the whole of the Encyclopedia Britannica could be stored three times over on one disc. It is estimated that the whole of the largest library in the world, the Library of Congress, would fit into a large living room in this format.

Thus, combined with a computer, we have a medium that is very durable, retains high quality visual images, and will hold moving film, still photographs, sound and text. It can be directly accessed, and is reasonably cheap to reproduce once a master copy has been made.

What then is this medium? It is difficult to categorise or pigeon-hole. It encompasses the previous genres. You can 'read' it like a book, but it has sound and moving film. You can watch it like a film, but stop it and search it like a book. You can explore it like a gallery or museum, but are not forced to follow the tour laid out by the curators. With its depth, combined with the interactivity and involvement of the viewer, it is perhaps the perfect medium for a postmodernist, reflective, and involved age; breaking down part of the gap between 'author' and reader.

A second example of the use of videodisc technology concerns the most ambitious project to date using this new medium, the two videodiscs and associated software made by the British Broadcasting Corporation to commemorate the 900th anniversary of the making of the Domesday Book in 1086.[1] These videodiscs were made over a period of two years, at a cost of several million pounds. An editorial board (of which I was a member) oversaw the process. Their contents included the *Community Disc* and the *National Disc*.

The Community Disc contained 20,000 photographs and 200,000 screen pages of information created by local groups (schools, voluntary groups etc.) describing their local areas. One side of the National Disc consisted of sixty minutes of moving film of news events between 1980 and 1986. The other side included the following: 22,000 photographs, 'surrogate walks' around half a dozen selected landscapes and houses, forty five extended commissioned essays, 2,000 short pieces or 'ephemera' from newspapers, leaflets and other sources, and 6,000 statistical data-sets of a demographic, economic and social nature.

There were four principal methods developed to find and examine the exhibits in this electronic museum. Firstly, there was the 'gallery' concept, derived from work at the Massachusetts Institute of Technology, whereby one can select items by moving through a three-dimensional simulation of a gallery, and 'selecting' iconic representations of data-sets. Secondly, there were hierarchical indexes, both geographical hierarchies so that one could start with the top level and gradually move down to very detailed maps of a specific street or village; and also selection by subject, starting with large categories like 'Culture' or 'Economy' and then working down to a specific topic. A third method was by keyword; a single word or string of words could be typed in and the user was offered data sets in a 'probable' order of likely interest. Finally, the huge set of statistical materials could be displayed in tabular or map form using various specially written programs.

This 'Domesday' project, and others currently being made, usually have a mix of uses in mind for the new technology. Firstly there is an archival purpose, the preservation for future generations of as much high quality visual and textual material as possible. The BBC Domesday Project was explicitly laying down a 'time capsule' for the future. It is this use of optical disc technology that attracts 'rescue anthropologists' and those concerned at the loss and deterioration of old films and photographs.

A second use is in research. As Marc Bloch, the great historian, put it, 'the deeper the research . . . the more the light of the evidence must converge from sources of many kinds' (1954, p. 67). The new optical disc technology allows the user to combine films, photographs, images of artefacts, sound, books, manuscripts; and to move swiftly from one to the other, or juxtapose them. In particular, the ability to have complete control over film, to examine it frame by frame, to go immediately to a particular photograph, to hold an image from a moving sequence for as long as one likes, to vary the play-through speed, all these are valuable for research. It is also becoming possible to 'grab' an image, digitise it, enlarge part of it, and print it out.

A further use is in teaching and the dissemination of information. In schools, there are now various projects (in England, for instance, the 'Interactive Videodisc in Schools' project) to replace the rather boring CAL (Computer Aided Learning) approach with this more exciting medium. The Domesday System was intended to do this, but the cost of the player and other factors have lessened its impact. There are now signs that much cheaper players with inboard computers will make the original promise achievable in the near future.

In universities a variety of disciplines, including anthropology, will be able to combine this technology with the increasing use of computers. As in schools, the great advantage of an optical disc system over conventional films is that it can be 'inter-active'. With 'branching' and 'looping' possibilities, the student can move at his or her own pace and at an appropriate level, can ask questions and become involved. Ultimately, it may be possible to create a simulation of such real experiences as anthropological field-work.

In museums and galleries, the videodisc is already beginning to show its value, as in the Osaka Museum. But much more could be done. For instance, all the reserve collections of objects could be made 'accessible' and full information be made available about each. In the Cambridge Museum of Archaeology and Anthropology, we have recently opened a new exhibition on the Nagas of north-eastern India, which uses the videodisc as a source of an ever-expanding set of films about the background to the current exhibition.

One problem which has long perturbed anthropologists concerns the hoarding of cultural items away from the areas which they represent. The arguments for and against returning the artefacts are fairly evenly balanced, but even if the native artefacts were returned, it is very doubtful whether the increasing number of films, photographs, fieldnotes and so on could ever be 'sent back'. The new media represent a partial way out of the dilemma. Once a master copy is made, copies can easily be pressed and 'sent back', assuming that the receiving institutions have the appropriate player. This is something which a large organisation like UNESCO should be encouraged to fund.

There is no better way to learn about the potentials and difficulties of a new medium than to use it. My last brief example will thus be taken from our own work in Cambridge.[2] With Martin Gienke, Head of the Audio-Visual Aids Unit, I co-directed a project to make the first Cambridge Experimental Videodisc on the Nagas of the Assam-Burma border. It has just been completed and exemplifies on a small scale an attempt to explore, unite and compare the virtues of various media in the communication of anthropological information.

There is the book, which, with its 250 full colour plates and more than 400 black and white archival photographs and analytic text, goes as far as a book can go in combining visual and written materials. There is the museum exhibition mentioned above, occupying one of the two galleries in the newly re-furbished Andrews Gallery. This adds a third dimension to the two-dimensional pictures. Then there is the videodisc, which adds another seven thousand or so field photographs, 1,200 colour photographs of artefacts, seventy-two minutes of sound, and 150 sequences of moving film. But this still leaves all the textual data. This is held on a 20-megabyte hard disc, and includes much unpublished background material – field notes, tour diaries, and letters of those who collected the artefacts and took the photographs, as well as some of their completed monographs.

This means that one has roughly 25,000 'items' of information at one's disposal, whether photographs, songs, film sequences or paragraphs of text. How does one quickly find what one wants?

Here we have developed for our own use the Museum Cataloguing system,

MUSCAT, in association with Dr Martin Porter, its author, to create the Cambridge Database System (CDS). This allows one to do 'Boolean' (structured) searching on fields. Thus one can search for all 'items' that are related to a certain day, person, place, ethnic group, archive or medium, and to build up searches of an 'and' 'or' kind. A second form of searching is called 'free text' searching. In this, a word or words can be put in and the computer will provide a list of the 'best' matches, starting with the most likely to be an answer and then the next most likely and so on. This technique was used for the BBC Domesday Disc, but in the CDS system has the added powerful feature of 'relevance feedback and automatic query expansion' not available on Domesday, whereby an interrogator can use the system to suggest links from those answers which seem interesting to other items which he or she has not yet seen.

The projects I have described give a very preliminary idea of developments which will take on a new impetus with the rapid application of compact disc technology in the 1990s. It seems likely that this will be the most important communications and educational technological field in the next ten years. It is one where anthropological materials, because of their intrinsic interest, their complexity and their visual immediacy, can play an important part.

### Notes

This chapter was previously published in the *CVA Review*, Fall 1990. I am grateful to Asen Balikci for permission to re-publish it here.

1   I have given a detailed account of the contents, searching systems and some of the editorial decisions behind the choice of materials in relation to the Domesday Discs, in Macfarlane (1990b).
2   The project was funded by grants from the Nuffield and Leverhulme Foundations, the Economic and Social Research Council, Trinity and King's Colleges, Cambridge, and the Department of Social Anthropology in the University of Cambridge, to all of whom I am most grateful. There are more detailed descriptions of the project in Macfarlane (1990a) and Macfarlane and Gienke (1989).

### References

Bloch, M. (1954), *The Historian's Craft*, Manchester University Press, Manchester.
Macfarlane, A. (1990a), 'The Cambridge Experimental Videodisc Project', *Anthropology Today*, VI, 1, pp. 9–12.
Macfarlane, A. (1990b), 'The social construction of Britain on videodisc', *Society for Visual Anthropology Review*, VI, 2, pp. 25–41.
Macfarlane, A. and M. Gienke (1989), 'The principles used in selecting, editing and transferring materials for an archival videodisc', *Journal of Educational Television*, XV, 3, pp. 131–41.

# Index

Italics indicate film titles. When used in pagination they indicate whole chapters.